THE ADVENTURE OF THE MURDERED MOTHS OF THE

and other radio mysteries

ELLERY QUEEN
Frederic Dannay (left) and Manfred B. Lee
In Frederic Dannay's library, Larchmont, New York, 1967
(Photograph courtesy of Frederic Dannay family)

ELLERY QUEEN

THE ADVENTURE OF THE MURDERED MOTHS

OF THE

and other radio mysteries

Crippen & Landru Publishers
2005

Cover design by Deborah Miller

Crippen & Landru logo by Eric D. Greene

ISBN (10): 1-932009-15-9
ISBN (13) 978-1-932009-15-6

10 9 8 7 6 5 4 3 2

Crippen & Landru Publishers
P. O. Box 9315
Norfolk, VA 23505
USA

Email: info@crippenlandru.com
Web: www.crippenlandru.com

Table of Contents

Publisher's Preface

The year is between 1939 and 1948. The family is gathered around the dome-shaped radio to listen to *The Adventures of Ellery Queen*. Father or mother turns on the radio with a crackle and a hiss, and the announcer (Bert Parks or Ernest Chappell or another man with deep and perhaps a bit "fruity" radio voice) invites listeners to "match wits with the celebrated gentleman detective in person as he recounts the story of a crime that he alone unraveled . . . At the point where he was able to solve the mystery, he stops the play and gives you a chance to guess the criminal's name." And then the family listens to a tale of thrilling and mysterious events — a murder in a cave with only the victim's footprints, a corpse hidden in snowman, a murder and an impossible disappearance on a cross-country railroad train, a mysterious woman who vanishes in the moonlight on a country estate. And then, just as the listeners' curiosity has become almost unbearable, the announcer stops the play, explains that all the clues have been revealed, introduces guest jurors from the world of entertainment or journalism or sports or public service, and challenges them to solve the mystery. Then the story resumes, and Ellery explains whodunit, and why. At the conclusion, the actor playing Ellery thanks the studio jurors for their (almost always) wrong solutions and presents them with his latest novel and a subscription to *Ellery Queen's Mystery Magazine*.

The creators of this show which could not only scare the listener but challenge his or her intellect were two cousins, Frederic Dannay (1905-1982) and Manfred B. Lee (1905-1971), who invented "Ellery Queen" both as their joint-pseudonym and as the name of the sleuth — and to make things just a bit Kafka-esque, the character "Ellery Queen" is also a writer of detective stories, though the name of *his* sleuth is never revealed.

In a series of intricately plotted detective novels, beginning in 1929 with *The Roman Hat Mystery* and continuing through such classics as *The Greek Coffin Mystery*, *The Egyptian Cross Mystery*, *The Chinese Orange Mystery*, *The Tragedy of X* and *The Tragedy of Y* (the latter two books under a second pseudonym, Barnaby Ross), Queen created a world of bizarre clues, multiple solutions, and some of the most mind-boggling complex cases ever put to paper. Queen was the king of the Golden Age detective novel in which all the clues were placed fairly before the reader. As another Golden Age writer (and friend of the Queens), John Dickson Carr, wrote, the mystery story had become "The Grandest Game in the World." And the early Queen novels emphasized the challenge by breaking the action two-thirds of the way into the novel, announcing that the clues had all been given, and telling the reader that he or she should now be able to solve the puzzle.

By the late 1930's, Ellery Queen (the sleuth, that is) was probably the best known detective in American fiction, and his entourage — his father, Inspector Richard Queen, Sergeant Thomas Velie, Doc Prouty, and others — were almost as well-known. Manny Lee and Fred Dannay were also interested in bringing Ellery to other mediums. Not even his greatest fans, however, would find that the early Ellery Queen movies (*The Spanish Cape Mystery*, 1935, *The Mandarin Mystery*, 1937) did justice to the character — the screenplays were prepared by screenwriters who had little idea of the EQ books — but the radio series would be written by the cousins themselves. George Zachary of CBS had been looking for a detective character to feature on the radio, and he was attracted to the Ellery Queen stories. Lee and Dannay devised a show called, *Author! Author!*, in which well-known writers were challenged to explain a series of mysterious events propounded by the cousins (who were introduced as "Mr. Ellery" and "Mr. Queen"), and Zachary had them hone their skills by doing uncredited work for the radio programs *Alias Jimmy Valentine* and *The Shadow*, before *The Adventures of Ellery Queen* went on the air on June 18, 1939. It was then a hour-long drama, and in many ways it followed the pattern of the books. Ellery (a writer of detective stories) his father Richard Queen (Inspector of New York City Police) were the main characters. At the insistence of CBS, Dannay and Lee added a female interest, Ellery's secretary Nikki Porter, whose hope that her boss will take a romantic interest in her is a recurring subplot. Sergeant Velie is also present, but much more than in the books he is a comic character — he is the butt of the Inspector's jokes and anger and so often (and not always fairly) called a "lunkhead" that some listeners must have wondered why the New York police kept him on duty. It is a pleasure to report that in "The Adventure of the Lost Child," he has the opportunity to call Inspector Queen a "dumb ape." As with the Ellery Queen novels and short stories, Fred Dannay did most of the plotting of the radio shows and Manny Lee the actual writing.

The early cases in *The Adventures of Ellery Queen* featured Hugh Marlowe as Ellery and Santos Ortega as his father. The show switched to a 30-minute format in February 1940, and the cast changed frequently, with Carlton Young, Sydney Smith, Lawrence Dobkin, and Howard Culver successively playing Ellery. In 1943, it was reported that the show had a listenership of some 15 million a week. Eventually,

Frederic Dannay found that his responsibilities with *Ellery Queen's Mystery Magazine* meant that he could no longer plot new scripts for the radio program, and in June 1945 Anthony Boucher (pseudonym of William Anthony Parker White) was brought in to contribute the plots. Boucher was himself an experienced mystery writer, with a detective named Fergus O'Breen whom Boucher created as a West Coast version of Ellery Queen. Manfred Lee continued to turn the plots into fleshed-out radio scripts. The final show was broadcast in May 1948, but the story wasn't over. The cousins turned a dozen of the radio plays into the fine collection *Calendar of Crime* (1952), with Nikki appearing in each case.

In preparing the scripts for publication, we had to make some editorial decisions. In several cases, lines of dialogue were deleted or added, probably during rehearsal, to make the play fit the required timing; in such instances we kept the longer version. In one play, a character was removed before broadcast, and his lines assigned to Nikki — except in one instance when the authors (or director) forgot to make the change. We felt justified in letting Nikki have those lines as well. We also kept as much of the stage directions as possible, even including "ad libs" directing the characters to choose appropriate words of greeting, or departure, or astonishment at Ellery's observations. Letting the modern reader know when sound effects were being used — footsteps, doors opening and closing, light switches clicking on and off, wind whistling, car engines racing, railroad cars clicking and clacking — will, we hope, help to recreate the feeling of sixty years ago when the audience could *hear* the plays.

This book is published in honor of Ellery Queen's one-hundredth birthday. Both Manfred B. Lee and Frederic Dannay were born in 1905, and according to the novel *The Finishing Stroke*, so was their great creation, Ellery Queen the detective.

Acknowledgments

We are grateful to the families of Frederic Dannay and and Manfred B. Lee for permission to publish *The Adventure of the Murdered Moths and Other Radio Mysteries*. They lent us the scripts of almost 350 plays, and three E.Q. experts — Jon L. Breen, Theodore B. Hertel Jr., and Marvin Lachman — each read more than 100 scripts and recommended which might be included in this book. We owe much to Messrs. Breen, Hertel, and Lachman. The publisher made the final choices, and decided to include only plays written by Lee and Dannay (and not those which Anthony Boucher and others had collaborated on when Dannay retired from the radio show). We also did not include scripts that were later re-written as short stories.

In addition, we are grateful to Arthur Vidro who first recommended that we publish this book, then helped with the difficult task of proofreading the typeset versions to make certain that they were presented in a consistent format and that the typesetter had accurately interpreted the sometimes fuzzy lines of the original mimeographed copies.

Thank you all — and, especially, thank you especially Ellery Queen author and detective. As Anthony Boucher wrote, "Ellery Queen *is* the American detective story."

"The Adventure of the Last Man Club," was one of the earliest Ellery Queen plays, broadcast on June 15, 1939. It contains a favorite plot device of the Queens, the Tontine — in which a group of "investors" contributes to a fund, and the last surviving member receives the entire pot of money — a perfect motive to eliminate the other members one by one.

The Adventure of The Last Man Club

The Characters

Ellery Queen	The detective
Nikki Porter	His secretary
Bill Rossi	The victim
Mama Rossi	His mother
Joe Sullivan	Member of Last Man Club
Ernie Phillips	Member of Last Man Club
Lucille Cherry	Member of Last Man Club
David W. Frazer	A millionaire
Sid Paramore	Owner of the 66 Club
Inspector Richard Queen	Of the New York Police
Doc Prouty	Of the New York Police
Sergeant Thomas Velie	Of the New York Police

Cop, ambulance surgeon, hat-check girl, bartender, two thugs

Setting: New York City, 1939

(Background throughout this scene: a few street noises. Light traffic.)

Ellery: Awfully sorry I've had to work you all day, Nikki. But that serial installment had to be typed.

Nikki: Nikki Porter, Secretary-at-Large — Service with a Smile. No Extra Charge for Sundays. (*Slyly*) Your manuscript cost me a date today, Mr. Queen.

Ellery: Nikki! Why didn't you tell me? Here — instead of walking you home, I'll get you a cab. Maybe you'll still have time —

Nikki (*quickly*): Never mind. My date was a Napoleon of finance with the soul of a Princeton senior . . . Besides, I enjoy walking with you, even in this sun.

Ellery (*dryly*): I can't imagine why. You've been limping ever since we left my apartment.

Nikki: I have not! . . . All right, it's these new shoes. You notice everything, don't you?

Ellery (*chuckling*): Everything *worth* noticing.

Nikki: Don't you notice anything about . . . people except sore feet?

Ellery: You're fishing. By the way, talking of feet, Nikki — what can you deduce about that chap running across the street?

Nikki: Where?

Ellery: There — the tall, dark man who just dashed out of that little Italian restaurant.

Nikki: Oh, that one. Wait . . . I know! He's in love!

Ellery (*chuckling*): In love? How do you arrive at that?

Nikki: Well, he's sprinting across the street toward the other corner, isn't he? There's nothing on that corner but a mailbox, is there? And why should a man *run* to mail a letter if it isn't a love-letter?

Ellery (*laughing*): Nikki the logician . . . My child, you're wrong.

Nikki: You would say that! Why am I wrong?

Ellery: Because he *hasn't* any letter.

Nikki: But he *is* making for the mailbox, smarty!

Ellery: By George, he is at that . . . No, I was right. See that? He dashed up to the mailbox, took a good look at it, turned around — there, now he's running off again! Up the street!

Nikki: All right, you tell me — what's he running for?

Ellery: Not enough facts. There he goes, crossing the street again —

Nikki (*alarmed*): Ellery! That car!

Ellery (*shouting*): Look out, you fool! You'll be run over! Stop!

(*Under the last few speeches a high-powered car approaches and passes — no screech of brakes — man's hoarse yell — and thud — car speeding away.*)

Nikki (*screaming*): He's been hurt! That car — it hit him!

Ellery: And didn't even stop! Nikki — come on!

(*Short musical interlude — ambulance gong — fade into excited buzz of spectators' talk — "Get back!" "Give him air!" "Let the doc work on him!" etc.*)

Cop (*gruff*): You two saw the accident? What's *your* name?

Ellery: Ellery Queen, officer. 212-A West Eighty-seventh Street.

Cop: You, miss?

Nikki: Nikki Porter —

Cop: Nikki? How do you spell that?

Ellery: N-I-K-K-I. List my address, officer. Miss Porter is my secretary.

Cop: Say, are you the son of Inspector Queen of the Homicide Squad?

Ellery: Yes.

Cop (*change of tone*): That's different. Look, Mr. Queen, you don't have to be mixed up in this —

Ellery: But I want to be, officer. I don't like hit-and-run drivers.

Cop: Catch the license-number, Mr. Queen?

Ellery: No, but from the color of the plate, I'd say it was a New York license. Black sedan.

Nikki: The driver of that car is just a — a murderer, that's what he is!

Cop: That's about the size of it, miss. 'Scuse me, I've got to see if maybe some other witnesses didn't see . . . (*fade*)

Nikki: Ellery, is he — badly hurt?

Ellery: Here's the ambulance surgeon. How is he, doctor?

Ambulance surgeon: Not a chance. Internal injuries, hemorrhage . . . Can't even move him. He'll die any minute now. (*Groan from victim*) Here! He's regaining consciousness. Officer, if you want to talk to this man, you'd better hurry.

Cop: Yeah, yeah. Lemme through here — Listen, Mister! Who hit you? Who ran you down?

Victim (*faintly*): Tell — Joe . . .

Cop: He's out of his head.

Ellery: No, officer, he's trying to give you a message.

Cop: Tell Joe? Joe who?

Victim (*faintly*): Joe — Joe Sullivan — 66 Club —

Cop: Yeah, Joe Sullivan, 66 Club . . . Tell him what?

Victim (*faintly*): Tell — the others, too . . . Be careful . . .

Cop: The others — be careful . . . Be careful about what?

Victim (*more clearly*): Murder . . . (*Gasps*)

Ellery: Murder!

Nikki: Ellery, do you think he was really —

Cop (*excited*): Murder? You mean you were hit on purpose? Who was it? Who tried to kill you?

(*Pause*)

Ambulance surgeon: He's dead.

(*Silence. Through it, fading on, a heavily-breathing sobbing woman, as if pushing through crowd.*)

Mama Rossi: Dat's-a my Guglielmo — dat's-a my Bill . . . my Bill . . . my son . . .

Cop (*awkwardly*): Wait a minute, lady. You'd better not —

Mama Rossi (*screaming*): I'm-a Mama Rossi, from da Rossi Rest'rant. Dat's-a my son Bill! Bill! (*Heavy sobbing*)

Cop (*snarling*): Stand back there! All o' youse!

Nikki: Of all the cold-blooded, deliberate crimes I ever heard of —

Ellery (*quietly*): Joe Sullivan, 66 Club . . . I think we'll have a chat with Mr. Sullivan, Nikki — before the newspapers sink their teeth in him!

(*Music up . . . and into dance band, off, and subdued murmur.*)

Girl: Check your hat, please.

Ellery: Here you are, miss. Is Joe Sullivan around?

Girl: Joe? He'll be here any minute, sir. He comes on duty at nine o'clock to relieve the other bartender.

Ellery: Thanks.

Nikki (*whispering*): A bartender in a night-club. I'll bet he's a gangster.

Ellery: Quiet, Nikki. Here, we'll sit at the bar. (*Slaps bar*) Bartender!

Bartender: Yes, sir. What'll it be?

Ellery: What will you have, Nikki?

Nikki: Something *expensive*. Let's see now . . . Bartender, what's in those tall, thin, cut-glass bottles?

Bartender: Those are cordials, miss — finest brand in the world . . . Bouchère.

Nikki: Aren't those bottles *tricky*, Ellery? The haven't even a label!

Bartender: The name's cut into the bottom, where it don't show. That's so people can use the bottle as a decanter when the cordial's used up.

Nikki: Well, I want some! You're sure it's expensive? Cointreau, please.

Ellery: Make mine Scotch and soda.

Bartender: Yes, sir. (*Off*) Oh, Joe! Thought you'd never show up. One Scotch an' soda for the gentleman, an' the lady gets some o' that Bouchère Cointreau. I'm late for the fights.

Sullivan: Okay. (*Sound of fixing drinks.*)

Ellery (*casually*): You're Joe Sullivan, aren't you?

Sullivan: That's the handle, sir. Heavy on the ice?

Ellery: Not too much. Bill Rossi mentioned your name.

Sullivan: Yeah? You a friend of Bill's?

Ellery: In a way. Seen Bill lately?

Sullivan: Oh, Bill's in here 'most every day. Here's your drinks, sir. Hi, Ernie.

Phillips (*fading on*): 'Lo, Joe. Sid Paramore in?

Sullivan: I dunno, Ernie. I just came on. Wadda ya wanna see the boss for?

Phillips: He wants to see *me*. Double Scotch, Joe.

Sullivan: Say, how much you in hock to Sid for, anyway, Ernie?

Phillips (*gloomily*): Plenty.

Ellery: By the way, Sullivan, Bill Rossi was in an accident today.

Phillips: What's that? Bill's had an accident?

Ellery: Oh, you know Bill Rossi, too?

Sullivan: Yeah, this is Ernie Phillips. Accident? Why, I only saw Bill yest'day, it was —

Phillips: That's a tough break. What happened?

Ellery: He was struck by a hit-and-run driver, Mr. Phillips.

Phillips: Run over! Did you know about that, Joe?

Sullivan: No. Is Bill hurt bad, sir?

Ellery (*indifferently*): Couldn't be worse. He's dead. (*Falling glass*)

Sullivan (*low*): Bill Rossi's — dead?

Phillips (*thickly*): Give me that Scotch, Joe.

Ellery: Before he died, Rossi left a message for you, Sullivan.

Sullivan: For me? What did he say?

Ellery: He said, "Tell Joe to be careful —"

Sullivan (*puzzled*): Be careful?

Ellery: Yes, and he said to tell "the others" too.

Phillips: The others! (*Pause*) You're sure he said — the *others*?

Ellery: That's what he said, Mr. Phillips.

Sullivan: What else did Bill say?

Ellery: The officer taking his dying statement asked him what you and the others were to be careful about, and he said, "Murder." Then he died.

Phillips (*thickly*): Murder? (*Bang of glass*) Look, Joe — tell Sid Paramore I had to — see an art director about an ad I'm working on . . . (*Fade off*)

Ellery (*after a pause*): Now, why should your friend want to see an art director?

Sullivan: Oh, he's Ernie Phillips, the commercial artist . . . Bill said — Murder?

Ellery: Yes. What do you suppose he meant, Sullivan? Queer sort of thing to say.

Sullivan (*tightly*): Can't imagine. Maybe — maybe he was delirious . . . 'Scuse me, sir. I gotta customer . . . (*Fade off*)

Nikki (*after a pause*): So they won't talk, eh?

Ellery: I believe I know someone who will, Nikki — the dead man's mother!

(*Music up and into —*)

Mama Rossi (*stonily-dead voice*): Why you come? Can you help-a my Bill? He's-a die.

Ellery (*gently*): We don't want to intrude on your grief, Mrs. Rossi —

Mama Rossi: You wanna see Mama Rossi cry, no?

Nikki: Oh, no! That's not at all the reason —

Mama Rossi: I no cry. Cry no good . . . (*Abruptly*) You *poliziotti?*

Ellery: A policeman? Well . . . yes.

Mama Rossi: Den I tell-a you. My Bill, he's-a — how you say? — murd' . . .

Ellery: How do you know your son was murdered, Mama Rossi?

Mama Rossi: Alla time Bill say, "Mama, you wait. Just-a wait a littl'a while. I get a whole lot of mon'. Den you don' cook no more spaghett'."

Alla time he talk about da mon' he gonna get. He say da on'y way he no get da mon' is if he die . . . An' now he's-a dead. He's-a murd' so he won't get da mon'.

Ellery: I see. Just what money was your son going to collect, Mama Rossi? Did he ever tell you?

Mama Rossi: Bill say some day he get da mon' from da Club.

Ellery: The 66 Club, Mama Rossi?

Mama Rossi: Naw. Not dis-a Club. Some odder Club — Joe Sullivan, he b'long too —

Ellery (*quickly*): And a man named Ernie Phillips?

Mama Rossi: Si. He, too. An' — an' I t'ink a rich man — his-a name is . . . Frazer. Dat's-a da name, Frazer. An' a girl — Cherry. Lucille Cherry. She's-a — what you call — she's-a make pi'ture of woman's clo'es.

Nikki: She must mean the fashion designer. There's a Lucille Cherry on Madison Avenue who designs women's clothes.

Ellery: Hmm. I wonder, Nikki, if this man Frazer she mentioned can be David W. Frazer, the millionaire head of the Chemical Products Corporation?

Mama Rossi: Dat's-a da one! Ev'ry year dis-a Club have a party — in Mama Rossi's Rest'rant. Just-a once a year.

Ellery: What's the name of this Club, Mama Rossi?

Mama Rossi: Dat's-a funny name. Da Las' Man Club.

Nikki: The Last Man Club! With a *woman* in it?

Ellery: Sounds hectic. Mama Rossi, what sort of club is this? What do they do?

Mama Rossi: I do' know. Dey eat, drink, make-a speech. My Bill, too. I t'ink it's-a from da Navy. My Bill, once he useta be a sailor in da United States-a Navy.

Ellery: Really? Thank you, Mama Rossi. We shan't disturb you again unless we have to. (*Scrape of chairs*)

Mama Rossi (*venomously*): You find da one who murd' my Bill — I pay you!

Ellery (*gently*): That won't be necessary, Mama Rossi.

Mama Rossi (*mumbling*): A riv'derci . . . (*Steps walking off*)

Nikki: How now, Sir Detective?

Ellery (*grimly*): Bill Rossi run down by a mysterious car — a man's fantastic club with money behind it — and one woman-member — somewhere in the background the Navy —

Nikki: All it needs is the United States Marines!

Ellery (*briskly*): Nikki, it's a case! Look up David W. Frazer and this fashion-designer, Lucille Cherry. Have them at my apartment at ten o'clock tomorrow morning!

(*Music up . . . and into ring of doorbell.*)

Ellery: There's one of them now, Nikki!

Nikki: It must be this stuffed shirt, Frazer. You should have heard him on the phone last night . . . (*Fade off*)

(*Door opens. Quick heavy steps fade on. Door closes.*)

Frazer (*brusquely*): You Queen, the detective? I'm David W. Frazer. Now what's all this about?

Ellery: Do sit down, Mr. Frazer.

Frazer: Sorry. No time. On my way to the office. Well?

Ellery: In that case, I'll come directly to the point. You were acquainted with Bill Rossi?

Frazer: Oh, I see. Yes, I was. I hear he died in an accident yesterday. Well, we all go sooner or later. Bill and I were shipmates together in the Navy twenty years ago.

Ellery: I believe you both belonged to an organization known as the — er — Last Man Club?

Frazer: Oh, that. Adolescent nonsense. I haven't attended a meeting in ten years. Outgrown it, you know. (*Laughs shortly*)

Ellery: Exactly what, Mr. Frazer, was the purpose of this —

Frazer: Now look here, Queen, I can't go into a long rigmarole about some sentimental falderal I forgot years ago. Just what do you want? I'm a busy man.

Ellery: Before Bill Rossi died he said something about — murder.

Frazer: Murder? Fantastic!

Ellery: He also left a warning to Joe Sullivan — I presume you know him?

Frazer: Yes, but —

Ellery: — And the "others," Mr. Frazer . . . Could he have been referring to you as one of the "others"?

Frazer: Murder — warning — Poppycock! (*Fading*) Look, I can't waste time discussing a crackbrained detective story. Good day!

Nikki: But Mr. Frazer — (*Door slams*)

Ellery: Let him go, Nikki. Did you check up on him?

Nikki: Yes. He was a wild kid with oodles of money who ran away and joined the Navy during the War. After the War his father died and he inherited millions. Also, he's an art collector. Spends most of his spare time buying old masters; even writes about 'em, and — (*Doorbell*)

Ellery: Answer the door, Nikki. That must be Lucille Cherry. (*Door opens off*)

Nikki (*off*): Oh, come in, Miss Cherry. (*Door closes*) Mr. Queen's expecting you.

Ellery: How do you do? Won't you sit down?

Miss Cherry (*fading in*): Thank you, Mr. Queen. I don't know why I've come except that I'm a curious female, I suppose. Yesterday Bill Rossi died in an automobile accident, and today the great Ellery Queen asks poor me to call. May I ask why?

Nikki (*jealously*): One of your public, I see, Mr. Queen.

Ellery: Miss Cherry, Bill Rossi's mother believes her son was run down deliberately — murdered.

Miss Cherry: Why, that's — that's ridiculous, Mr. Queen!

Ellery: Ridiculous or not, Bill left a warning before he died for Joe Sullivan and the "others." I believe you're one of the "others"?

Miss Cherry: But I can't see how Bill — I mean, how can I be? Unless —

Ellery: Yes, Miss Cherry?

Miss Cherry (*slight laugh*): I was about to say — unless it has something to do with the Last Man Club, because that's the only connection that's ever existed between Bill and me — and the others.

Ellery: How are you connected with the Last Man Club, Miss Cherry? The very thought piques me.

Nikki (*low*): It would.

Miss Cherry: Well, my father, Gilbert Cherry, was a naval submarine commander during the War, Mr. Queen. He was in command of the L-5 when it went down off the coast of Southern California in 1919. Only eleven men were saved of the entire crew, and they owed their lives to father, who was the hero of the disaster. Father died in saving them.

Ellery: I see.

Miss Cherry: The eleven survivors formed a club, and because father was their hero, they elected mother and me to an honorary life membership. Mother died a few years ago, so I'm the last member of the Cherry family — and the only woman — in the Club.

Ellery: A purely commemorative organization, then.

Miss Cherry: Not quite. You see, Mr. Frazer — that's David W. Frazer, you know, the head of the Chemical Products Corporation — he was one of the crew who survived, and out of gratitude for my dad's sacrifice Mr. Frazer's father started a trust fund which he donated to the Club.

Ellery: Really!

Miss Cherry: The fund was invested, and now it must be worth a hundred and twenty thousand dollars. The idea was that twenty years after the fund was started, the money was to be divided equally among the then surviving members of the Club, and —

Ellery: One moment, please! You say twenty years after? That means the money will be divided this year!

Miss Cherry: Yes, in a month or so. (*Gasps*) Oh! I hadn't thought . . .

Ellery: Yes?

Miss Cherry: Could that be why Bill — died? I mean — only those alive a month from now can collect, not their heirs . . . No, that's absurd! I refuse to believe it!

Ellery: How many survivors are now living, Miss Cherry?

Miss Cherry (*nervously*): Myself, Joe Sullivan, and Ernest Phillips. There was Bill Rossi, but now that he's dead it's just — the three of us.

Ellery: How about Frazer? Doesn't he share with the rest of you?

Miss Cherry: Oh, no. The Frazers are wealthy, so his father excluded him, although the fund's in his possession.

Ellery: Very illuminating. It seems, Miss Cherry, that we now have a possible motive. Whichever of you dies, loses his right to his share of a hundred and twenty thousand dollars, and thereby increases the size of the others' shares. Since there are only three of you left, each of your shares is now worth forty thousand dollars. But if you should die, Miss Cherry, before the month is up, Sullivan and Phillips —

Miss Cherry: No! It just can't be. It can't!

Ellery (*firmly*): Sullivan and Phillips would collect, not forty, but sixty thousand apiece. And if one of *them* should die . . .

Miss Cherry (*nervously*): I've known these men since I was a child. They've been like fathers to me. It's a mistake, Mr. Queen — there's something wrong somewhere —

Ellery (*dryly*): Indeed there is. When does the next annual meeting of the Last Man Club take place, Miss Cherry?

Miss Cherry: In two weeks. At Mama Rossi's. We hold it there every year.

Ellery: And the hundred-and-twenty-thousand dollar melon is to be cut two weeks after that? Miss Cherry, I advise you to be very, very careful during the next month.

Miss Cherry (*angrily*): Nonsense! You're trying to scare me! (*Pause — then in a low voice*) Will that — will that be all?

Ellery: That will be all, Miss Cherry. (*Pause*) Goodbye. (*Door opens*)

Miss Cherry: Goodbye . . . (*Door closes*)

Nikki: Scared to death, for all her fancy get-up.

Ellery: They're all scared — this girl, Sullivan the bartender, Phillips the commercial artist, even Frazer the millionaire. Well, Nikki, let them have their annual get-together two weeks from now!

Nikki: What are you going to do?

Ellery: I'll be there — but they won't know it!

(*Music up . . . and into chink of dishes, clatter of a spoon.*)

Phillips: I don't know what's the matter with me tonight. Mama Rossi, another spoon!

Mama Rossi: Si, Signor Phillips. (*Slight sound of spoon set down*)

Sullivan: I'm nervous myself tonight, Ernie. I guess it's because —

Miss Cherry (*warningly*): Joe — don't. Mama Rossi.

Mama Rossi: I hear. Caus-a my Bill. Mama Rossi know.

Miss Cherry (*distress*): We really should have called it off this year, Mama Rossi.

Mama Rossi (*quietly*): Dat's-a all right, Miss Cherry.

Sullivan: I'm glad it's the last one. It — ain't so hot comin' back every year an' findin' somebody else — kicked off.

Phillips: I don't know why I came tonight.

Miss Cherry: I don't know why any of us came.

Phillips: Let's drink the old toast and get out of here!

Miss Cherry: How about drinking this year, not to my dad, as we've always done, but to Bill Rossi?

Sullivan (*effort at spirits*): That's a good idea! Mama Rossi, we've got a bottle of the old stuff left in our private stock, ain't we?

Mama Rossi: Sure. Dere's-a one bottle left in da cell'. Da last-a bot'. You drink-a to my Bill?

Phillips: Sure, Mama, sure. Go get the bottle, will you?

Mama Rossi (*eagerly*): Si, si, Mist' Phillips. (*Fade off*)

Sullivan: I don't want to hurt the old lady's feelin's, but I can't drink that toast tonight.

Miss Cherry: Joe! Why not?

Sullivan: Doctor's orders. My heart's gone on the bum.

Miss Cherry: Oh, Joe, I'm so sorry. Well, just pretend to drink for Mama Rossi's sake. This is our last meeting, and —

Mama Rossi (*fading on*): Here's-a da bot'. But dere's-a somepin wrong, Mist' Sullivan.

Sullivan: Wrong? . . . Say, this ain't our private stock! This one's green creme de menthe!

Mama Rossi: Dat's-a what I say. Dis bot' da wrong color.

Miss Cherry: Why, all our bottles were cherry liqueur.

Phillips: That's funny, Lucille. It's the same Bouchère brand in the tall cut-glass bottle . . .

Mama Rossi: Dat's-a da on'y bot' I find.

Miss Cherry: Oh, there must have been a bottle of creme de menthe mixed up with the cherry cordial. Open it, Joe, and let's drink to Bill.

Sullivan: Okay. (*Sound of ripped seal, glass decanter top being removed*)

Mama Rossi: Here's-a da glasses, Mist' Sullivan.

Sullivan: Right, Mama. (*Sound of liquid being poured*) There's one for you Ernie, one for Lucille — how about you, Mama?

Mama Rossi: I can't drink. I watch-a you drink to my Bill. You no drink, Mist' Sullivan?

Sullivan: Uh — yeah, sure, Mama. There! That's mine.

Miss Cherry: All right, everybody. Raise your glasses. Here's to Bill Rossi — (*Clink of glasses*)

Ellery (*fading on — fast*): Stop! Don't drink that liquor! (*Glasses broken, as if dashed from their hands*)

Miss Cherry: Why, Mr. Queen! Where — how —

Sullivan: It's the guy was pumpin' us two weeks ago, Ernie, at the 66.

Phillips (*furiously*): What do *you* want? Why shouldn't we drink?

Ellery: Because that creme de menthe is poisoned!

(*Music up . . . Murmur of voices*)

Inspector Queen: All right, all right, I know it. You people stay put in here for a while. I'll be right back. (*Slam of door*) Ellery, hasn't Doc Prouty got here yet? Oh, there you are, you old windbag. What's the lowdown on the bottle?

Ellery: Prouty's not finished analyzing it, dad.

Inspector: Come on, Doc, we haven't got all year.

Doc Prouty: Aw, keep your shirt on, Inspector. Don't know why you called me in on this, anyway. It's really the City Toxicologist's job. I haven't got enough work, I s'pose, digging a scalpel into every loafer bumped off in New York . . . There we are. Yep. That's it, all right. (*Chink of glass*)

Ellery (*eagerly*): What's it? What's in the bottle besides creme de menthe?

Doc Prouty: Prussic acid. Enough to kill a horse.

Ellery: Prussic acid. Well, that was a fair guess.

Inspector: Prussic acid, hey? Rossi gets his, now this wholesale attempt at poisoning . . . It comes under the head of homicide, all right!

Doc Prouty: That's your department. (*Fading*) Me, I'm going back home to finish my poker game. Night! (*Slam of door*)

Ellery: What have you found out, dad?

Inspector: Not much. It seems they started with twenty bottles of cherry cordial, all this Bouchère brand, twenty years ago — cracking open one bottle a year . . .

Ellery: Why Cherry?

Inspector: Because their hero, this Gilbert Cherry, the girl's old man, was named Cherry. That's a reason, isn't it? More like a kid's secret society. Anyway, tonight's the twentieth anniversary, so this is the last bottle.

Ellery: Kept on a special shelf in Mama Rossi's cellar?

Inspector: Yep, and apparently nobody's looked at it since last year's get-together.

Ellery: Which means that this bottle of Bouchère creme de menthe could have been dosed with prussic acid and substituted for the bottle of Bouchère cherry cordial any time during the past year. Not much to go on.

Inspector: It's screwy, the whole thing. Well, I guess I'll let 'em go. No point in holding them any longer.

Ellery: How are they taking it?

Inspector: Nervous. This Ernie Phillips is chewing his nails off, Joe Sullivan, the barkeep, acts as if he'd swallowed some prohibition gin, and the girl, Lucille Cherry, looks about ready to pass out . . . By the way, where's this Nikki wench of yours? The way she hangs around you —

Ellery: I warned her to stay away tonight. Too much imagination. She'd either have messed things up or got into trouble.

Inspector: Yeah. (*Opens door*) All right, you people, go on home!

Ellery (*grimly*): And I advise you all to — be careful.

(*Music up . . . Closing of street door*)

Sullivan (*nervous*): Well . . . good night, Ernie. Night, Lucille. I — I guess I'll sort of mosey on home. (*Quick steps fading off*)

Miss Cherry (*low voice*): Good — good night, Ernie.

Phillips (*mutter*): Maybe I'd — better see you home, Lucille. It's late —

Miss Cherry (*fast*): No. No, don't bother, Ernie. I'll take the cab. (*Cab door opens*)

Phillips: Good. (*Slam of cab door. Cab starts and drives off — then man's footsteps are heard on pavement, slow. They stop short suddenly. Phillips gives a cry of surprise.*) Hey! What — what —

Nikki (*urgently*): Mr. Phillips —

Phillips (*angrily*): Say, don't you know better than to sneak up on a man from behind? Get going, sister!

Nikki (*eagerly*): I'm Nikki Porter! Mr. Phillips, I — I followed you tonight, when you came to Mama Rossi's, and —

Phillips (*sore*): Followed me? You've got your nerve!

Nikki: Wait! You don't realize — someone else followed you, too!

Phillips (*feebly*): What's — that? Followed *me*?

Nikki: Yes, a big black sedan. I'm sure they were following you, and I wanted to warn you — Oh! (*Sound of powerful car dashing up, grinding of brakes, quick opening of car door*)

1st thug (*rough*): You — Phillips! Git in dis car!

Phillips (*fearful*): What — what — (*Sound of footsteps running off*)

2nd thug (*from car*): Grab the jane. Don't let her git away.

1st thug (*shouting, running*): Hey you! Come back here! Got you!

Nikki: Let go of me, you ape! Help! Let go! (*Sounds of struggle. Dragging sounds to car, slam of door, motor pick-up. Nikki's voice fades off*) Help! Ellery! Help!

(*Music up . . . and into inexpert peck-peck at typewriter*)

Ellery: Blast it! (*Doorbell*) Well, it's about time! Come in, Nikki! (*Door opens and shuts*) Do you know what time — (*Disappointed*) Oh, it's you, Sergeant.

Velie: Sure it's me. Who'd you think it was — Lord Fauntleroy? What's the matter? You look peeved, Mr. Queen.

Ellery: I am! My secretary hasn't shown up this morning. Just when she had some important typing to do!

Velie (*oddly*): You mean this Nikki Porter? The cute little trick who's always on the make for you?

Ellery (*annoyed*): Nonsense, Velie. You're as evil-minded as my father . . . Well, well? What's wrong? You didn't drop in here at eleven a.m. to read my horoscope!

Velie (*slowly*): The Inspector sent me up from Centre Street with a message.

Ellery: Message? What message?

Velie: Ernie Phillips's disappeared.

Ellery: Phillips of the Last Man Club? Disappeared! When?

Velie: Last night. Right after the Inspector let 'em go from this Mama Rossi's restaurant. He was snatched.

Ellery (*agitatedly*): Kidnaped! I warned them to be careful! Now what in thunder's this all about?

Velie: I don't wanna put any ideas in your famous noodle, but — did this secretary of yours sleep home last night?

Ellery (*quickly*): What do you mean?

Velie (*awkwardly*): Well, a cab driver saw what happened last night. Phillips had just left the Rossi joint. A big black sedan drove up and forced Phillips in, and drive off. Cabby didn't catch the license number.

Ellery: But what about Nikki? Talk, will you?

Velie (*still awkwardly*): Well . . . seems there was a girl with Phillips when he was picked up, and they snatched her, too, and . . . well, she was a perky little trick somethin' like this secretary of yours, wearin' a green hat with a red feather, and the Inspector sort of thought . . .

Ellery (*groaning*): Oh, the fool! The dumb, rash little fool! Of course that's Nikki . . . she has a hat like that. Nikki — in the hands of kidnappers!

Velie (*still awkwardly*): Of course, it might have been some other ditzy doll —

Ellery: No, no, it was my special ditzy doll, Sergeant, I'm sure of it. I specifically ordered her to go home last night, so of course she disobeyed and went sleuthing on her own. It's Nikki, all right. What are we to do? We've got to find her. We've got to —

Velie (*anxiously*): Say, you ain't falling for her, are you?

Ellery: Don't be a foul idiot! I — I'd feel the same about any girl in a spot like this. Well, don't just stand there gaping. Do something!

Velie (*simply*): What?

Ellery (*distractedly*): I don't know. Poor kid. Lord knows what they're doing to her — she's only a child, Velie — it's all my fault — I should have discouraged her from — (*Phone rings*) Maybe that's dad with news! (*Grabs phone*) Hello! Hello!

Nikki (*filtered — sweetly*): Is this Mr. Ellery Queen's residence?

Ellery (*shouting*): Nikki! (*Off*) Velie, it's Nikki — she sounds all right. (*On*) Nikki, are you all right? You're not hurt? Where are you? What happened? Nikki, speak to me!

Nikki (*filtered*): I will, if you'll give me a chance. Were you worried about me, Mr. Queen?

Ellery (*shouting*): Worried about you! I'm out of my mind! Where are you?

Nikki (*filtered*): Aren't you sweet — worried about *me*! Now I'm glad I was snatched. I've been snatched, did you know that?

Ellery (*with an effort*): Nikki, listen to me. Every cop in Greater New York is out searching for you and Phillips. *Will* you talk?

Nikki (*filtered*): Yes, dear. I'm at Sid Paramore's place drinking Cuba Libres and flirting with the cutest gangster, and the others are here, too —

Ellery: Others! What others?

Nikki (*filtered*): Oh, Lucille Cherry and Joe Sullivan — and of course Mr. Phillips . . . Wait. Mr. Paramore wants to speak to you.

Ellery: Sid Paramore. So he's the ruffian who —

Paramore (*filtered — annoyed*): Hello! Queen? This is Sid Paramore, of the 66 Club. Say, this little dame wearing a green hat with a red feather in it — she claims she's your secretary. Is she? Nikki something . . .

Ellery (*grimly*): That's the little darling. Well?

Paramore (*filtered*): Listen, come on down and take her off my hands, will you? She's a pain in the neck! (*Click*)

Velie: Did I hear you say Sid Paramore? Why, that guy's got the fanciest gambling layout in New York in his 66 Club, and a slick mob, and he's one tough baby.

Ellery: Not tough enough to digest Nikki, apparently.

Velie: You going down there — alone?

Ellery: Certainly! I've two things to do — spank Nikki Porter and find out Paramore's connection with Bill Rossi and the Last Man Club!

(*Music up . . . and into opening of door.*)

Thug: Whadda *you* want?

Ellery (*fading on*): Oh, get out of my way . . . Are you Sid Paramore?

Paramore: Yeah. Okay, Louie. You Queen? Here's your baby doll — and good luck to you!

Nikki (*gladly*): Hel*lo*, Mr. Queen!

Ellery: I'll attend to *you* later. (*Sharply*) Well, Paramore, I see you've got Miss Cherry, Sullivan, Phillips, *and* my secretary. Kidnaping's a little out of your line, isn't it?

Paramore (*easily*): You got me wrong, fella. Ernie, were you kidnaped?

Phillips (*nervous*): No. No, I wasn't. Sid's — a friend of mine.

Paramore: See? And Joe Sullivan tends bar for me, and Miss Cherry came here under her own steam just a little while ago.

Ellery: Get to the point.

Paramore: Sure. Ernie Phillips is my tie-up with this business. Ernie, tell Queen where Sid Paramore figures.

Phillips: I — I dropped a lot of money to Sid Paramore in the 66 Club, Queen. A whole lot. And I'm broke. So in payment of my gambling debts I've signed over to Sid my share of the Last Man Club fund. Did it three months ago.

Miss Cherry: Oh, Ernie — what a foolish thing to do!

Phillips: I had to, Lucille. I — couldn't pay off otherwise. But my share will now come to about forty thousand, and —

Ellery: How much do you owe Paramore, Phillips?

Phillips (*slowly*): Fifty — thousand.

Paramore: Yeah, Ernie's in hock to me for fifty grand. So even after the fund's split up and I collect Ernie's share, he'll still owe me ten grand — hey, Ernie?

Phillips: Sure. Sure, Sid. I — I'll get the rest of it some way.

Paramore (*slyly*): Sure you will. (*Hard*) Queen, I got a stake in this Last Man Club — understand? If Ernie's knocked over before the pay-off next month, I lose my dough, because only the ones living at the time of the pay-off collect.

Ellery: I still don't grasp the reason for this little tea-party.

Paramore: This guy Phillips is my baby — get it? I'm giving him protection! One of these palookas killed Bill Rossi and tried to poison the others last night, so I'm declaring myself in, to protect my investment . . . see? I'm warning all of you!

Sullivan: Sid, you — you don't think I got anything to do with it —

Paramore: I'm just warning you, Joe.

Miss Cherry: Are you insinuating that I'm a murderess, Mr. Paramore?

Paramore: I ain't insinuating nothing, Miss Cherry. I'm telling you. Anybody tries to kill Phillips in the next two weeks before the kitty pays off won't live long. Now beat it.

Nikki (*admiringly*): Isn't he grand, Ellery? Just like Edward G. Robinson in the movies!

Paramore (*howling*): And take this babe with you before I strangle her with my bare hands!

Ellery: Mr. Paramore, my condolences. Nikki — you . . . come . . . with . . . me!

(*Music up . . . and into chink of dishes.*)

Nikki (*mouth full*): You're some hero, you are. Lets a girl be insulted by a thug — the great Ellery Queen!

Ellery: Quiet, nuisance — I'm trying to think.

Nikki (*mouth still full*): And what's worse — to *agree* with him. Where would you be if I hadn't followed up Phillips and got myself snatched and called you up . . . Mama Rossi! More spaghetti, please.

Mama Rossi: Si, Signorina.

Nikki: And then dragging me here to Mama Rossi's . . . Well, all right, I'll pay for my own lunch, you tightwad. Can I help it, if I'm hungry?

Ellery (*musing*): There's a gasket missing somewhere. Just one little gasket . . .

Nikki: You're not even listening to me!

Ellery: What? Oh. Certainly I'm not. Nikki, where is it?

Nikki: Where is what?

Ellery: The missing gasket. The last link. The straw that broke the camel's back. It's lying about somewhere, but darned if I can spot it.

Nikki: If you're trying to figure out who poisoned that bottle, why don't you start with Bill Rossi's murder?

Ellery: Nothing in that. Dad's checked over everybody. No one has an alibi for the time of Rossi's death, the black sedan hasn't been identified, and anyone might have run him over.

Nikki: Yes, but how could the murderer be sure Bill Rossi would cross the street at just the right time to be run over?

Ellery (*groaning*): Nikki . . . He could merely have been lying in wait, and when Rossi ran out he seized his opportunity!

Nikki: Well, I don't think so. *I* think Bill Rossi was *lured* to his death, *lured* out of this restaurant —

Ellery: By Mata Hari, I suppose?

Mama Rossi (*fading on*): Here's-a spaghett'.

Nikki: Ask Mama Rossi! She ought to know —

Mama Rossi: You find out who kill my son?

Nikki: Mama Rossi, the day your son Bill was . . . had his accident —

Mama Rossi (*doggedly*): No accident. He's-a murd'.

Nikki: Did Bill get a message — a letter, a note, a telephone call or something — just before he ran out into the street?

Mama Rossi: Naw. He got no lett', no call.

Nikki (*low*): Well, you don't have to *leer* so hatefully! (*Aloud*) But Mama

Rossi, if he got no message, why did your son run out into the street? He seemed in an awful hurry.

Mama Rossi: *I* send Bill out.

Nikki: *You?*

Mama Rossi: Si, account of da fire.

Ellery: What's that? On account of the *fire?* What fire?

Mama Rossi: We have littl'a fire in kitchen —

Ellery (*rising excitement*): Fire in your kitchen? *Fire?* How did it start?

Mama Rossi: Don' know. Just-a start, like by himself.

Ellery (*excited*): Yes, yes, and what happened?

Mama Rossi: I send-a Bill to call-a da fire engine an' den we put out da littl'a fire, Luigi an' me — (*bitterly*) but my son, he's-a run over by da car, he's-a die. If not for da fire, Bill still live . . . 'Scus'a please. I gotta go to da kitch'. (*Sound of retreating footsteps*)

Ellery (*low*): Well, what do you know about that! Nikki, I take it all back. You're a jewel. You're wonderful. You asked just the right question —

Nikki: What did I do now?

Ellery: Can't be. Can't. And yet — it *is*. It's *true*. The little gasket. That precious missing link . . .

Nikki (*tense*): Ellery! You've learned something! You've found something!

Ellery: Something? I've found everything!

Nikki: But how *could* you? All she said was that a fire started —

Ellery: Blessed fire!

Nikki: What do you mean?

Ellery: It's solved the whole case! (*Music up*)

Challenge to the Listener

[The show then moved to the "Jury Period" in which guest armchair detectives presented their solutions. Ellery normally introduced the jury with words such as the following from "The Adventure of the Last Man Club":]

Ellery: At this point, ladies and gentlemen, I was able to reach a conclusion, based on the facts of the case up to now . . . Let's hear what our armchair detectives have to say. Will their conclusion match mine, I wonder?

(*Music up*)

Inspector: All right, I get all these people down here at headquarters, and they're yapping their heads off, and I don't blame 'em a bit! What's it all about, Ellery?

Ellery: I feel conversational.

Nikki: He goes on that way for hours, Inspector. I'm ready to *scream*!

Inspector: I lost my voice years ago, young woman. So you feel conversational. Now what?

Ellery: Let 'em cool their heels in there for a while, and I'll show you a simply wonderful thing. First — motive. Are we agreed on motive?

Inspector: Sure. Whoever poisoned that bottle of Bouchère creme de menthe did it to kill his fellow club-members and collect the whole fund of a hundred and twenty grand for himself.

Nikki: But we know that. What's *new* on the Rialto?

Ellery: Simply this: Why didn't the poisoner pour prussic acid into a bottle of cherry liqueur, since these people had always drunk their toasts in cherry liqueur at their get-togethers? *Why did he poison a bottle of creme de menthe?*

Nikki: You know, that *is* queer.

Inspector: It's been worrying me, too.

Ellery: Don't you see what it means? All the Bouchère bottles, as we know, have no obvious identification marks. The maker's name and so on is etched into the glass bottom, where it isn't easily seen. The only superficial means of identifying the contents of those bottles is their . . . color! The color of the cordials seen through the cut glass!

Nikki: Come, come. How could he have made a mistake in color? Cherry cordial is red, and this creme de menthe was green.

Ellery: How could he make a mistake in color, Nikki? Simply if he couldn't *tell* red from green! *If he was color-blind.*

Nikki: Color-blind!

Inspector: That's it! That explains it! This bird is color-blind — has red-green blindness!

Ellery: Just a moment, dad. Where are you going?

Inspector: Going? Why, to test these people for red-green color-blindness! It's a cinch one of them suffers from it, and when we find out which one, we'll have the guy who killed Bill Rossi and tried to poison the others!

Ellery: Oh, but that's so unnecessary. I already know.

Inspector (*impatiently*): Go on — how can you know which of 'em is color-blind? We've got to test 'em, I tell you! (*Pause*) And by George — I know how!

(*Music up . . . and into —*)

Velie (*puffing*): Here's the ten bottles of sissy-water, Inspector. You throwin' a party?

Inspector (*puffing*): That's fine, Velie, fine. Here, set 'em on my desk. (*Sound of bottles being set down*) In a straight row. That's it. Now we've got eight bottles of cherry soda and two of lime. Eight reds and two greens!

Velie: But why'd you have me take the labels off?

Inspector: So they can't read the flavor, you dope! Now they'll have to tell me which ones the limes are just from the *green color* —

Velie: I guess I'm not hittin' on all twelve.

Ellery: Madness runs in our family, Sergeant.

Inspector (*gleefully*): Now, Velie, we'll have our friends in here one at a time. Sid Paramore first.

Velie: You're the keeper. (*Door opens*) Hey, Paramore! Come 'ere!

Nikki: Inspector, something tells me you're riding to a fall.

Paramore (*fading on*): How long you gonna keep me here, anyway? I've got rights! I pay taxes! I'm an American citizen —

Inspector: Sure you are, Paramore. Close that door, Velie. (*Door closes*) Now, Paramore, just one question and you can go — maybe.

Paramore: Wait a whole hour for one question? What goes on? I've got a business waiting!

Inspector: See these ten bottles of soda?

Paramore (*suspiciously*): Yeah?

Inspector: Pick out the bottles of lime.

Paramore (*blankly*): Huh?

Inspector: I said pick out the green ones!

Paramore: What is this, a gag?

Inspector (*genially*): Yeah, we're playing games. (*Hard*) Play!

Paramore (*dubiously*): There's two green ones — this third bottle and the — four, five, six — and the seventh.

Inspector (*after pause*): Let him go, Sergeant.

Paramore (*fading off*): A crazy cop. Picking out soda bottles — *soda* . . . (*Door closes*)

Ellery (*lazily*): I could have told you Paramore isn't color-blind. When he spoke to me on the phone this morning he identified Nikki by saying she was wearing a *green* hat with a *red* feather. That let him out.

Inspector: All right, so he's out. Velie, get this Ernie Phillips in here!

Velie (*as door opens*): Phillips!

Phillips (*fading on — nervous*): Yes? You want me? Here I am . . .

Inspector: See these bottles, Phillips? I want you to tell me which are the red-colored ones.

Phillips: The red ones? It's easier to tell you which are the green ones. The third and seventh. Why?

Inspector: Nothing. I just wanted to know. That's all!

Velie: This way out, Phillips. (*Door opens and closes*)

Ellery: You should have known Phillips isn't color-blind, dad. He's a commercial artist. A color-blind man couldn't possibly work with paints.

Inspector: Get Sullivan, the bartender! (*Muttering*) I'll switch 'em. Maybe they overheard. Put the green ones in the fifth and sixth positions.

Ellery: You know, dad, Sullivan must be . . .

Inspector: Oh, Sullivan. Come in. Pick out the green bottles!

Sullivan: What for?

Inspector: Pick 'em out!

Sullivan: Okay. These here — these two.

Inspector: Velie, get the girl — this . . . Lucille Cherry!

Velie (*as door opens*): Miss Cherry . . .

Miss Cherry (*fading on*): Inspector, I must protest against . . .

Inspector: I'll listen to complaints later. First tell me which one of those bottles has green soda in it.

Miss Cherry: I beg your pardon?

Inspector: You heard me. Pick out the green one.

Miss Cherry: This is just silly. There are two green ones. The others are red.

Inspector: Smart, aren't you? Which *are* the green ones?

Miss Cherry: Why these — the fifth and sixth bottles.

Inspector (*softly*): Thank you. That will be all, Miss Cherry. You too, Sullivan. Show 'em out, Sergeant.

Velie (*bored*): This way.

Miss Cherry (*fading off*): I don't know how they permit a man in his position to drink on duty . . .

Sullivan: Must be pooped to the ears. (*Door closes*)

Ellery (*slyly*): All totally unnecessary, dad, as I warned you. If you'd consulted me, I'd have told you. I eliminated Sullivan because, when Mama Rossi fetched the bottle that night at the get-together, Sullivan remarked: "This one's green creme de menthe" before he opened the bottle and was able to smell it. He certainly wouldn't be able to distinguish green then, if he'd failed to do so in substituting green for red in the first place.

Nikki: And what about Miss Cherry? I suppose you eliminated her because you liked the color of her eyes —

Ellery: No, darling, because she's a fashion-designer. No color-blind woman could work creatively with colored fabrics. Anyhow, I'm more partial to the color of your eyes, Nikki.

Nikki: Are you really?

Inspector: All right, all right, you two! Sullivan and Miss Cherry are out. (*Pause, then excitedly*) And that gives us our man. I don't know why yet, but he's elected.

Nikki: Who, Inspector?

Inspector (*grimly*): This big shot, Frazer — David W. Frazer. He's the only one left, so he must be our man. Of course, he doesn't share in the fund . . . I've got it! The fund's in his possession. He's probably up against it financially and nobody knows it, and he's swiped the hundred and twenty thousand. So he's had to kill everybody off, or try to, because if no survivors are left by next month there'd be no one to collect and so nobody'd find out the money was gone . . . Velie, get Frazer! (*Door opens*)

Nikki: Frazer? It doesn't seem possible.

Ellery: Dad, before you call Frazer in, there's something I'd like to point out.

Inspector: Now, Ellery . . . I know what I'm doing . . . (*Off*) Frazer! Come in here!

Frazer (*fading in*): Inspector, I demand an explanation and an apology! I don't mind cooperating with the police, but as I've told your son I've had nothing to do with this childish Club for years, and what do you mean keeping me here like a common —

Inspector (*quietly*): Frazer, I arrest you for the murder of Bill Rossi and the attempted poisoning of Lucille Cherry, Joseph Sullivan, and Ernest Phillips.

Frazer (*absolutely flabbergasted*): What?

Inspector: It's my duty to warn you that anything you say —

Ellery (*lazily*): Dad. I suggest, before you clap Mr. Frazer in the brig, you give him your favorite eyesight test.

Frazer (*spluttering*): Arrest — me — for murder — *Me*!

Inspector: Okay, we may as well sew it up. See those bottles, Frazer?

Frazer (*bewildered*): What? Bottles?

Inspector: Pick out the four green ones. (*Snaps fingers*) Quick!

Frazer: Four green ones? (*Sternly*) See here, Inspector —

Inspector (*enjoying himself*): Stalling, Frazer?

Frazer (*indignantly*): I'm doing no such thing! This is utter lunacy! I demand to be permitted to call my attorney at once!

Inspector (*softly*): In a minute, Frazer. But first pick out the four green bottles.

Frazer (*spluttering*): Why — why — there are only *two* green ones. The fifth and sixth bottles. The others are all red. What is this — a joke? (*Silence, then in a terrible voice*) Well, sir?

Inspector (*feebly*): Yes, yes, a joke, Mr. Frazer. It — it gets kind of dull down here at Headquarters. (*Tries to laugh*) But you're a sport. Dave Frazer can take a joke — everybody knows that. Hey, Mr. Frazer?

Frazer (*snaps*): You're a feeble-minded idiot! Good night! (*Slams door*)

Ellery (*plaintively*): If only you'd listened to me, dad —

Inspector (*furiously*): It's all your fault, Ellery!

Ellery (*continuing*): — I could have told you Frazer isn't color-blind.

He's a famous art-collector, so expert he writes articles on the subject. No fancier of paintings could be color-blind.

Inspector: But it's impossible! Wait — wait. Could it be — yes, I've got it. It's the old Italian woman.

Nikki (*gasping*): Mama Rossi? Killed her own son? Inspector!

Inspector: No! Somebody else did him in, but she's the one who poisoned that bottle. She thought one of these people, murdered her son, and she went nuts and decided to wipe 'em all out —

Nikki (*giggling*): Oh, Inspector.

Ellery (*chuckling*): No, dad. Not Mama Rossi. Because, if she'd poisoned that creme de menthe, would she have said, on fetching the bottle from the cellar that night, "Dere's-a somepin wrong"? She was the first to call attention to the bottle, the one thing she wouldn't have done had she been the poisoner!

Nikki: But Ellery, I don't understand how — I mean, there's no one left. No one!

Inspector: Ah, I'm sick of the whole loony business. No one left is right. *Nobody* poisoned that cordial. That's the answer. I dreamed the whole blasted thing!

Ellery (*briskly*): If you'll permit me, I'll tell you who did poison that bottle of creme de menthe.

Inspector: Listen, only six people alive had motive to do it — even theoretical motive. And they've all been eliminated.

Ellery: Perfectly true.

Inspector: Then what are you talking about?

Ellery: Question — why do you insist that the poisoner is *alive?*

Nikki (*after a pause*): Ellery! You can't mean — Oh, my!

Ellery: As a matter of fact, the poisoner is dead. He's been dead and buried for over two weeks . . . *Bill Rossi.*

Inspector (*gasping*): Rossi! *Rossi?*

Velie: Listen, I *gotta* butt in. Rossi? You're sick in the head, Mr. Queen. Why, Rossi was murdered!

Ellery: Who says so? *I* never said so. He was simply the chance victim of a hit-and-run driver. Everybody *assumed* Rossi was murdered because Mama Rossi thought so, and because before he died he warned Joe Sullivan and the others to be careful — and when he was asked "be careful about what?" he gasped, "Murder . . ." and died. What he meant was that he'd prepared that poisoned bottle months before, knowing it would be used on the night of the get-together, and now that he was dying and no longer could collect the fund for himself, he wanted to ease his conscience and warn his intended victims that they'd be poisoned if they drank their annual toast two weeks later. But he expired before he could explain. Certainly it was Rossi.

Nikki: But — but —

Ellery: He probably stole the bottle of creme de menthe from the 66 Club. We know the 66 Club has the Bouchère brand because Nikki ordered a drink of it there, and Joe Sullivan himself told me that Bill Rossi came in to the 66 Club almost every day. But being color-blind and the bottle having no label, Rossi mistook the green cordial for the red, and never knew the difference.

Inspector: Rossi . . . Whew! That's one on the button. But how can you be sure he was color-blind? You'll never prove it by digging him up.

Ellery: I didn't know until a few hours ago, when Nikki and I learned something from Mama Rossi. The day Bill was killed, we happened to notice him run out of the restaurant and make for a mailbox on the opposite corner. He ran right up to the mailbox, stopped, took a good look at it, and then ran off in another direction.

Inspector: What's that got to do with color-blindness?

Ellery: I didn't know myself until Mama Rossi told me that she had sent him out to turn in an alarm because there was a fire in the kitchen. In other words, *Rossi was looking for a fire-alarm box* when we saw him running. Yet the first thing he did was make for a *mailbox*. It was broad daylight. How could he have mistaken a mailbox for a fire-alarm box? From a distance, seen from the rear, you could easily mistake one for the other if not for their difference in color. All mailboxes are green; all fire-alarm boxes are red. So I knew Bill Rossi couldn't tell red from green, I knew he was color-blind, I knew he'd poisoned that bottle — and I knew he was the criminal we've been searching for for two weeks.

Velie: Well, I'll be a monkey's second cousin!

Inspector (*weakly*): Magic. Plain magic.

Ellery (*chuckling*): No, dad, logic. Plain logic. Coming, Nikki?

Nikki (*worshipfully*): Oh, Mr. Queen . . .

Ellery (*seriously*): What, Nikki?

Nikki: May I have your autograph?

(*Music up*)

Ellery Queen loved impossible crimes, in which a person is murdered in a locked and guarded room with no way for the murderer to enter or leave; or, as in this instance, jewels vanish from an enclosed space. In "Napoleon's Razor," broadcast on July 9, 1939, Queen expertly distinguishes his characters for a radio audience by their accents — the African-American porter, the southwestern sheriff, the professor from France.

The Adventure of Napoleon's Razor

The Characters

Ellery Queen	The detective
Nikki Porter	His secretary
George Latham	A salesman
Smith, Jones, and Brown	Wise guys
Lili Dodd	A movie star
Mr. and Mrs. Henry Stiles	Honeymooners
Marcel Cossart Xanthippe Dubois	Of the *République de France*
Sheriff	Of Amarillo, Texas
Senator Howard McNulty	Of the Missouri legislature
Inspector Richard Queen	Of the New York Police
Sergeant Thomas Velie	Of the New York Police
Cab driver, conductor, porter	

Setting: Railroad train from California to New York, 1939

(*Roar of taxi speeding through city streets*)

Ellery (*urgently*): How much farther to the Santa Fe station, driver?

Cab driver: Few blocks. That the Super-Chief you're catchin'?

Ellery: Yes! Think we'll make it?

Cab driver: I dunno, brother. I'll do my best. (*Speed up motor*)

Nikki: Go on, Ellery Queen — say it. If we miss that train East it's my fault.

Ellery (*chuckling*): The good old conscience. Bothering you, Nikki?

Nikki: Well . . . (*Defensively*) When you took me along on this trip to Los Angeles, I expected to have *some* time to shop at Magnin's and meet Garbo and Gable and people . . . but no! You rush me into Hollywood, work me like — like one of Bing Crosby's fillies, and rush me right out again!

34

Ellery: Very attractive, that pout. Very.

Nikki: Naturally I was out rubber-necking when I should have been packing my bags. After all, I'm *human* —

Ellery (*laughs*): Cheer up, Nikki. Some day we'll do the State of California up brown. But now that I've completed that deal with Paramount, I've got to hurry back to New York . . .

(*Screech of brakes*)

Cab driver: Santa Fe station, bud! (*Open cab door*)

Ellery (*excited*): Here, driver. No, keep the change. Porter! These bags. Nikki — shake those fetching legs of yours!

Nikki (*morosely*): I'm coming, I'm coming.

Porter: Yassuh. Makin' Numbah Two, suh? (*Bags being dumped on walk*)

Ellery: We're booked on the Super-Chief to Chicago — (*Cab driver off*)

Porter: Ah'm afraid you won't make the Super-Chief no mo' today, suh. She's done been an' went.

Ellery (*groaning*): Missed it!

Nikki (*contrite*): Oh, Ellery! What'll we do now?

Ellery: Next Super-Chief's on Friday . . . three whole days away. Porter, what's the earliest extra-fare train East?

Porter: Chief, suh — eleven-thutty tomorruh mo'nin'. El Capitan's two houhs latuh'n that, suh.

Ellery: Means staying overnight here. Isn't there another train out of this station tonight?

Porter: Yassuh, but it's jest an o'dinary train, suh —

Nikki: We're ordinary folks. When does it leave, Porter?

Porter: Two minutes, Ma'am. Eight-fifteen p.m.

Ellery: We'll take it! Grab these bags, Porter! (*Begins to run*)

Porter: Yassuh! Yassuh!

Ellery: Nikki, hurry! Here — let me take your arm! You're such a *tiny* bundle of trouble —

Conductor (*off*): 'Boooooard!

Nikki (*panting*): California, here I go — darn it!

(*Music up railroad theme. Into soft background of very fast click of rails, faint locomotive whistle from front of train . Rest of script takes place in the rear car.*)

Conductor: May I see your tickets, sir?

Ellery: Oh, Conductor. I'm the man who missed the Super-Chief. Here's all the evidence. Yards of it.

Conductor: Oh, yes. Mr. Queen. And that lady — your wife —

Ellery: No, no, she's not my wife. My secretary.

Conductor: Oh! Yes, sir. We can fix this up all right, Mr. Queen. I can give you a couple of compartments —

Ellery: Rather fancy this rear car, myself. Less crowded. And with the bar and lounge back here in the same car, and the observation platform outside there, it's tailor-made for a lazy man. Can you accommodate Miss Porter and me in this car?

Conductor: Yes, sir, though we've no compartments here. Drawing room's taken, too. Two sections, Mr. Queen?

Ellery (*chuckling*): I've learned not to argue with conductors about sections. All right, Conductor — two sections.

Conductor: Yes, sir. (*Fade off*) I'll have the porter make them right up.

Latham (*fading on*): 'Scuse me. Mind if I sit down here, brother?

Ellery: Not at all.

Latham: Name's Latham — George Latham, theatrical joolry. Gets kinda monotonous on these long rides, don't it, Mr. — Mr. —

Ellery: Queen.

Latham: Make this jump often? I'm out here all 'a' time. Just pulled off a wow of a deal in L.A. — to supply M-G-M with all their imitation costoom joolry —

Ellery: How nice for you. (*Murmur of three men fading on*)

Latham: Yes, *sir* . . . Ah! Evenin', gents! (*Murmur fades off*) Well, I like that. See the stuck-up galoots just passed?

Ellery: That trio of large, silent individuals?

Latham: Yeah. Call 'emselves Smith, Jones, an' Brown. Wise guys. Wouldn't even give you the — the time o' day! (*Laughs*) Reminds me . . . Ten-fifty. Won't pull into Barstow till forty minutes past midnight. Guess I'll hit the hay. Be seein' ya, brother! (*Fade off*)

Ellery (*low*): Not if I see you first, Latham old boy! (*Rear door opens letting in burst of clack-rail noise, shuts and noises subdue again*) Ah, there you are, Nikki. How's the California night-air on that observation platform?

Miss Dodd (*passing*): Good night, my dear.

Nikki (*effusively*): *Good* night, Miss Dodd! (*Low*) Ellery, do you know who *that* is? I just met her outside!

Ellery: Hmm. Good-looking, in a stupendous sort of way. Who is she?

Nikki: A real, live *movie* star! Lili (*Pronounce "leelee"*) Dodd! She's travelling all alone, Ellery — *incognito*. She *confided* in me — (*Ellery laughs*) What are you laughing at?

Ellery (*still laughing*): At your deliciously ovine innocence.

Nikki (*suspiciously*): Now what have I done?

Ellery: A movie star's travelling incognito, yet ten minutes after she meets a perfect stranger she gives away her identity. Nikki, Nikki, won't you ever learn?

Nikki: Learn *what?*

Ellery: To see through people! Lili Dodd's on the skids in Hollywood. She's almost broke. Would she travel on a no-extra-fare train if she weren't? She *wants* her identity known. Her public's practically forgotten her.

Nikki: The poor thing.

Ellery: You'd better start feeling sorry for your boss, little one. I don't sleep well on trains. Porter, have you made up our sections?

Porter: Yes, *suh*. Seven an' eight, suh.

Ellery: Right. (Night, Nikki — see you in Arizona!)

(*Music up . . . into louder rail sounds as if on platform outside*)

Nikki: The last sentence? It's — "He listened at Ormsby's door and thought he heard a despairing cry."

Ellery: Let's leave Ormsby despairing, Nikki. I don't feel like dictating now. Where are we?

Nikki: Well, we left Ash Fork at ten-fifty-five Mountain Time this morning, and we haven't reached Williams yet, so I imagine we're still somewhere in Arizona.

Ellery: Get to Williams about noon, don't we? By George, Nikki, I'm almost tempted to make the side trip from Williams up to the Grand Canyon!

Nikki: Oh, could we? (*Disappointed*) But I suppose you won't.

Ellery: Can't, Nikki. You know, you're exceptionally pretty when your eyes light up?

Nikki (*brightening*): So you've noticed that! Tell me some more —

Stiles (*fading on*): I couldn't help overhearing you mention the Canyon, sir. Worth going out of your way to see.

Mrs. Stiles: Henry and I were there before we were married — Oh, dear! I've let it out, Henry!

Stiles (*shyly*): It's nothing to be ashamed of, sweets. My name's Stiles, sir — Henry Stiles, Hardware Supplies, 'Frisco. This is my wife. We're on our honeymoon, you know. Going right through to the New York World's Fair.

Ellery: How do you do. Miss Porter. My name is Queen.

Nikki: Honeymooners! Isn't that *sweet?*

Mrs. Stiles (*softly*): You two must be engaged. I was saying to my husband that you were the *nicest*-looking couple . . .

Ellery (*hastily*): So kind of you, Mrs. Stiles, but —

Nikki: Do we *really* look engaged, Mrs. Stiles? (*Open and close of platform door*) Did you hear that, Mr. Queen? Let that be a *lesson* to you!

Dubois (*fading on*): Ah, *cherchez la femme!* Monsieur Queen?

Ellery (*relieved at interruption*): Yes? Yes?

Dubois (*gaily*): I search the train entire for you. I do not find you anywhere. I say: "Dubois, *cherchez la femme*." *Et voilà*, I find you! Permit me to introduce myself: Marcel Cossart Xanthippe Dubois, of the *République de France*.

Ellery: Charmed. Monsieur Dubois, Miss Porter, my secretary —

Mrs. Stiles (*embarrassed*): Oh! Your *secretary*? And I thought —

Ellery: — and Mr. and Mrs. Stiles. (*Ad lib greetings*) I'm afraid there's no room to sit down out here, Monsieur Dubois —

Dubois: *Non, non, cela ne fait rien!* Are you by chance Monsieur Ellery Queen, *l'agent amateur*?

Ellery: Guilty as charged, Monsieur.

Dubois: Then I am right! I hear the name, I say: "Dubois, this is good fortune of the most marvelous!" Monsieur Queen, I have for you to solve — a mystery!

Stiles: *Ellery* Queen! Honey, you've heard of Ellery Queen —

Nikki (*giggling*): Your past's caught up with you again, Mr. Queen.

Ellery (*uncomfortably*): Really . . . I merely dabble in detection . . .

Dubois: You are too modest, Monsieur! In my native France you are much admired. Next to Hercule Poirot, *le petit Belge*, you are my favorite detective —

Ellery: So kind of you. What is this mystery, Monsieur Dubois?

Dubois: It is a small one — of the most trivial. But it might relieve the boredom, exercise the brain cells, *n'est-ce pas*?

Mrs. Stiles: This is *thrilling*! Do tell Mr. Queen about it, Mr. Dubois.

Nikki: Oh, yes. Please do!

Ellery (*feebly*): Nikki . . .

Dubois (*briskly*): Permit me. I am a great student of the life of Napoleon. I am the *professeur* of French history — I have just finished a large critique of the Napoleonic wars, in fact — and am on sabbatical leave from *le* Sorbonne — a vacation, *comme on dit*, seeing your so magnificent country . . .

Nikki: But your mystery, Monsieur Dubois!

Dubois: *Mais oui. Le mystère. C'est diabolique, ça!* I collect relics of the Emperor Napoleon as — how do you say — the hobby. Recently in Paris I purchased the veritable razor of Napoleon.

Ellery: Napoleon's razor? How amusing.

Dubois: *Une drôlerie, n'est-ce pas?* It is supposed to have been a gift to Napoleon from the Empress Josephine,* to celebrate Napoleon's victory at Austerlitz in 1815.

---

* Publisher's note: The statement that Napoleon was still married to Josephine in 1815 (they were divorced six years earlier) is not a clue but a rare error on EQ's part.

Ellery: Really? Go on, Monsieur.

Dubois: *Alors*, this morning I am shaving in the men's washroom in this car with the razor of Napoleon when —

Stiles: You *shave* with the thing? (*Laughs*) Pardon me, but for some reason that strikes me funny . . .

Dubois: It is a joke, *non*? I forget to explain that upon purchasing the razor I discover it to be — you have the word — a fff . . .

Nikki: Fakeroo, Monsieur Dubois?

Dubois: Fakeroo, Ma'mselle? What is that? *Non*, the fff — phony! Dubois has purchased the phony. So I replace the rusty old blade with a modern straight blade and I shave with it!

Ellery: But your mystery, Monsieur Dubois?

Dubois: It arrives quickly, Monsieur Queen. I forget to bring with me to the washroom the talc powder. No one is present. I leave the razor on the bowl. I go for the talc in my berth. I return to the washroom. Zzzzt! The razor of Napoleon it has vanished — stolen! *Un mystère magnifique, hein?*

Nikki: Somebody got a pig in a poke.

Ellery: You say, Monsieur, that you replaced the old blade with a new one. How about the handle?

Dubois: Handle? Ah, you mean where you hold it. That is a thick ivory piece — oh, most clumsy, six inches long, a half-inch thick and wide. Inset in the ivory, in brilliants, are the words in French: "To Napoleon, from Josephine."

Ellery: Hmmm. Razor's not genuine, eh? It's worthless?

Dubois: Of a value deplorable, Monsieur. As an imitation, perhaps a few francs. Yet someone steals it. Why?

Nikki: Probably the thief read the inscription and *thought* the thing had value.

Dubois (*disappointed*): Ah! I do not think of that. That might be.

Ellery (*slowly*): Nevertheless, Monsieur Dubois, your little mystery has its points. (*Laughs*) We'll look into it, eh, Nikki?

(*Music up . . . into slowing click of rails . . . train brakes . . . jerk to stop . . . puff of engine at standstill . . . up with hiss of water from tap in metal bowl*)

Ellery (*splashing*): Ahhh . . . Feels good after all that alkali today. Stiles, may I have one of those towels from the rack?

Stiles: Certainly, Mr. Queen.

Ellery: Thank you . . . We've stopped. Where are we now?

Dubois: It is eleven and thirty-five, consequently we must be in Vaughn. That is New Mexico, is it not? Ah, this tremendous country of yours, gentlemen! The glorious desert, those purple tints of sky, those so strange hills protruding from the plain like prehistoric mounds —

Stiles: Buttes, we call 'em, Mr. Dubois. Pretty nifty, aren't they?

Latham (*fading on*): Hi, gents! Who'll have li'l drink out my private stock? 'Fore poundin' the pilla? Huh?

Ellery (*dryly*): I see *you're* all prepared for Morpheus, Latham — dressing gown, alligator slippers, *and* a bottle of rye.

Smith (*curtly*): Excuse me, brother . . .

Latham: Shay, who ya shovin'? Oh, it's Mis'er Smith. Mis'er Smith an' Mis'er Jones an' Mis'er Brown. Hi, fellas! Have a snort?

Brown (*shortly*): No, thanks. 'Night. (*Ad lib "Good Nights"*)

Latham (*hotly*): Wiseacres! Think 'cause they have a drawin' room — Who they think they are, anyways? Hi, M'soor! Wet yer whistle?

Dubois (*hastily*): Non, non, merci. I go to seek *le barbier* — the barber. To cut the hair on the train! It is gay, an adventure, *hein? Bonne nuit, messieurs!*

Latham: How 'bout you, Shtiles? Snifter?

Stiles (*haslity*): No, thanks. Wait, Mr. Dubois. I'll go with you. Wife's waiting for me —

Ellery: Good night, Latham. Pleasant dreams.

Latham (*fading off*): Whassa matter you guys? Nob'dy gonna have a drink? 'En I'll drink all by m'lonely . . .

Dubois: He is the gay one, *non*? Monsieur Queen, have you yet solved the mystery of my razor of Napoleon?

Ellery: Not yet, Dubois . . . (*Fade off all*)

Conductor (*faint — off*): 'Boooooard!

(*Jerk of train starting — whistle — slow pick-up of rail sounds . . . off Latham sings drunkenly "How dry I am" . . . Music up and into rapid rail clicks, etc. — faint snores*)

Nikki (*guardedly*): Ellery. (*Pause*) *Ellery*. Wake up.

Ellery (*out of sleep*): Uh — what — (*Off, as if behind curtain*) Who's it? Whassa matter?

Nikki: It's Nikki, Ellery. Poke your head out of your berth. (*Sleeper curtain pulled aside*)

Ellery (*yawning*): Nikki? What's the trouble?

Nikki: No trouble, silly. I just thought you'd like to see a simply breath-taking sight —

Ellery (*still sleepy*): Huh? What time's it?

Nikki: Almost six o'clock; we'll be in Amarillo soon. Get up, lazybones — I want to show you the sun!

Ellery (*groaning*): Nikki Porter, did you disturb my uneasy slumbers for a mere Texas sunrise? Go back to bed.

Nikki: Oh, you . . . ! Haven't you any romance in your soul? The sky's been all melted golds and dripping reds for an *hour* —

Ellery (*yawning*): Yes, yes, very poetic, no doubt. Go to sleep.

Dubois (*off — sleepy*): *Qu'y a-t-il?* Ah, Ma'mselle Porter. *Pardonnez-moi.* I hear voices, I look to see —

Ellery: There, you see? You woke up Monsieur Dubois!

Nikki: I'm terribly sorry, Monsieur Dubois —

Dubois: *Non, non,* I do not sleep well anyway. I am the creature of misfortune, *mes amis.* Last night I go to seek the barber, alas! and he has closed for the night. I return to this car and go to my berth and what do I find? Monsieur Latham he is getting into *my* berth!

Nikki: Latham? That awful salesman person?

Ellery: Latham had a skinful when we left him alone in the men's washroom last night, Nikki.

Dubois: *Oui,* to an intoxicated man one lower berth is very like another, *hein?* Mine is Number Five, his is Number Six — they are directly across the aisle from each other.

Nikki (*slowly*): That — Latham man is in — Lower *Five?*

Dubois: *Oui,* Ma'mselle, there. I say: "*Diable,* Monsieur, you are about to occupy my berth!" But he climbs in and immediately begins to snore, so what is poor Dubois to do? As you see, I am in Number Six — I sleep in *his* berth!

Ellery (*yawning*): Everything seems to happen to you, Dubois. Mind? Believe I'll snatch a few more fugitive winks —

Nikki (*tensely*): Ellery. There's — something — wrong.

Dubois: Wrong? *Mais certainement, Ma'mselle!* The pig he is in my —

Ellery (*alertly*): What's wrong, Nikki?

Nikki: L-l-look . . . The curtain over Lower Five. Those . . . curtain buttons. They're on the floor. (*Pause*) They've been slashed off to — to open the curtains!

Ellery (*pause*): Nikki. Go back to your berth.

Nikki: But, Ellery —

Ellery: Please don't argue, Nikki. Do as I say.

Nikki (*small voice*): All . . . right, Ellery. (*Fade off*)

Dubois (*agitated, low*): You send Ma'mselle away, Monsieur Queen. What is it that is the matter?

Ellery (*grimly*): Not only are the curtain buttons slashed off, Dubois, but, unless I'm mistaken, that stain on the carpet directly below the curtain is blood . . . Latham. *Latham?*

Dubois (*whisper*): *Mère de dieu!* Blood?

Ellery (*urgently*): Latham . . . ! (*Pause*) Here goes, Dubois. (*Sound of curtain sliding. Pause. Then slowly*) Your mystery's solved, Dubois. I've found Napoleon's razor.

Dubois (*whisper*): *Le rasoir*, Monsieur? In . . . *my* berth?
Ellery (*grimly*): Yes! Buried in George Latham's back!

(*Music up . . . no sound of train . . . into babble of voices*)

Mrs. Stiles (*sobbing*): B-but we *can't* stay here in Amarillo —
Stiles: Don't cry, sweets. Please. It won't be long —
Miss Dodd: I *must* get to Kansas City! My fiancé is meeting me there!
Dubois: *Incroyable*. Murder. My own razor. *Monsieur le shérif* —
Sheriff (*Texan drawl*): Sorry, folks, but this bawlin' won't do you no good.
   Git in that lounge an' stay there. (*Babble fading off*) Well, Mr. Queen,
   this is a fine howdy, ain't it?
Ellery: What did the coroner say about the time of death, Sheriff?
Sheriff: He figgers Latham died 'tween three-thirty an' a quarter of five
   durin' the night.
Ellery: Time-table, Nikki.
Nikki (*subdued*): Here it is, Ellery.
Ellery: Three-thirty . . . We were pulling into Clovis, New Mexico about
   that time — that's where we changed to Central Standard time . . .
Sheriff: An' somewhere 'tween Clovis an' the next stop — Hereford,
   Texas — is about where we figger this man was murdered.
Nikki: But in which State, Sheriff? Can't the coroner tell whether it — it
   happened in New Mexico or Texas?
Ellery: Apparently not. Nice point.
Sheriff: Nice *mess*. Yeah, Tommy?
Texas voice: Wire for you, Sheriff, from 'Frisco.
Sheriff: Must be from the 'Frisco police. (*Rips open telegram — pause*) Say,
   know who this bird Latham really was?
Ellery: He said he was a travelling salesman, in costume jewelry.
Sheriff: Not on your life he wasn't! This wire says he's Georgie Latham,
   a jewel thief!
Nikki: *Jewel* thief?
Sheriff: Yes, ma'am. What's more, 'Frisco police claim he's got his last
   haul right on him. Rustled three flat emeralds worth fifty thousand
   pesos in Noo Yawk couple o' weeks ago, and moseyed out to 'Frisco
   to sell 'em. But the hombre he tried to sell 'em to got leery, wouldn't
   buy, went to the police, an' Latham hit the back-trail from 'Frisco to
   Noo Yawk pronto.
Ellery: Could he have disposed of the emeralds in San Francisco after
   this man turned him down and went to the police?
Sheriff: No, this here wire says he couldn't 'a' had the time. 'Sides,
   Latham's always been a lone coyote. Say, he's still got them there
   emeralds on him, if that's the case!

Ellery: Did you run across them in searching his belongings?

Sheriff: Well, now, no, I didn't . . . You s'pose he was knifed for the emeralds, Mr. Queen?

Ellery (*grimly*): It seems obvious, Sheriff.

Nikki: Well, one thing's sure. Whoever killed Latham and stole those emeralds is still on this train!

Ellery: Conductor!

Conductor: Yes, sir?

Ellery: You say you sat in the lounge back here all night, from midnight until the murder was discovered this morning. Did anyone come into the lounge during the night?

Conductor: No, sir. I'd swear to that. I didn't even leave the car at Clovis or Hereford. Just waved my lantern from the observation platform.

Ellery: Porter!

Porter: Y-yes, suh? It ain't my fault, suh. I didn't —

Ellery: You claim you remained at the head of the car all night, near the door and the men's washroom. Didn't leave that spot once. And no one passed by you, either in or out?

Porter: That's the troof, suh. Didn't shet mah eyes all the livelong night. Got the rheumatiz bad in mah back —

Ellery: There you are, Sheriff. No stranger could have got into this rear car during the night or, if he'd been hidden here, could have made an escape — the porter was at one end and the conductor at the other all night, and both were wide awake. What's more, everyone supposed to be in this car is still here: those three men, Smith, Jones, and Brown — Mr. and Mrs. Stiles, Professor Dubois, Miss Lili Dodd, and ourselves.

Nikki: Then the emeralds are still here!

Sheriff: Ought to be a wall-eyed cinch to find 'em, then. These folks ain't set foot outa this car since, neither! Mr. Queen, I'm gonna find me them stones!

(*Music up . . . no railroad Sounds*)

Operator (*filtered*): Ready, Amarillo? Here's your New York party.

Ellery: Hello! Hello! Dad?

Inspector (*filtered*): Ellery? What's this about Gabby Latham bumped off on your train? I've been getting calls from California, New Mexico, Texas —

Ellery: We're in a situation, dad. Can't determine in which State Latham was murdered. There's a jurisdictional squabble going on here over who has the authority to investigate the case, and besides we can't locate those emeralds even though we're certain they're still on the car —

Inspector (*filtered*): I know, I've been getting reports. You're under guard on a siding in Amarillo, aren't you?

Ellery: Yes, just our one car. Sealed tight. The rest of the train's been sent ahead on schedule.

Inspector (*filtered*): Well, I'll tell you what. I think I can blarney the local officers down there into waiving jurisdiction and shipping that car on to New York. Latham's wanted here for grand larceny, so in a way it's New York's case.

Ellery: Swell! I'll airmail the murder weapon to you at once — it's a razor. See if you can find any prints on it —

Inspector (*filtered*): Ellery, I'm relying on you to see that not one of those people even steps out on the observation platform on the trip to New York!

Ellery: Right. And I'll try to have your murderer for you before we pull into Grand Central.

Inspector (*filtered*): Oh, you will! Well, I'm meeting that train in Chicago!

(*Music up . . . into fast click of rails subdued*)

Miss Dodd: I've never been so humiliated in my life. When the papers get hold of this — Lili Dodd mixed up in a *murder* — the Hays office — my contracts —

Mrs. Stiles (*weepily*): I *knew* we should have stayed on the Coast, Henry. All this trouble — it's spoiled everything —

Stiles: There, there, honey, don't cry.

Nikki: Don't feel badly, Mrs. Stiles. We've only lost twenty-four hours. Here it is Friday, and we'll be in Topeka in less than two hours . . .

Dubois: *Oui*, and from there it is near to Kansas City, and tomorrow morning — Chicago, Madame Stiles! Ah, you smile. That is good. Porter, cognac for everyone!

Porter (*dully*): Cohnyak, suh? Yes, suh. Comin' up. (*Fade off*)

Ellery (*fade on — irritably*): Well, Sheriff, they're not on Latham's body.

Nikki (*low*): Ellery Queen, you mean to say you actually went out into that baggage car and — and searched the *coffin*?

Ellery: What? Yes. Can't understand it. Thing's not *possible*.

Sheriff: Told you it wasn't there, Mr. Queen. Well, I'm durn glad I'm jest along for the scenery!

Nikki: But, Ellery, those emeralds *must* be in this car.

Ellery: I know they must. And yet they're not. I was over Latham's berth, Lower Six, with a fine comb. Everything's there as we found it after the crime — his dressing gown, his alligator slippers, his luggage, even two hundred dollars in cash — nothing touched, apparently. And in Dubois's berth, where Latham died, there's no trace of them, either.

Sheriff: Railroad won't cotton to what we done to their car. Practically tore the upholst'ry to bits.

Ellery (*feverishly*): Searched people, clothes, luggage, shaving brushes, toothpaste tubes, powder boxes, porter's pantry, washrooms, observation platform, lanterns, bar — I've even looked into the bottles of liquor — I've even climbed up to the roof of the car — I've examined every blessed thing big enough to contain three emeralds. It's maddening. They *must* be here.

Nikki: Whoa, don't look at me, Mr. Queen. *I* haven't got 'em — I've looked!

Ellery: For that matter, Nikki, I've searched myself, too. (*Raises voice*) Miss Dodd, you're positive you heard nothing during the night?

Miss Dodd (*sullenly*): I didn't hear anything, I told you.

Ellery: You, Mr. and Mrs. Stiles? (*Pause*) You, Dubois? (*Pause*) How about you three gentlemen?

Smith (*a little amused*): Not guilty, friend.

Jones (*peevishly*): This is one rap you won't pin on *me* —

Brown (*gently*): Quiet, Jones. Look, Queen, we're three peaceful citizens occupying a drawing room —

Sheriff: Mighty cute gophers, if y'ask *me*. Travellin' men, you say?

Smith: You might call us that. Hey, Brown?

Brown: Ask Jonesy.

Jones (*sullenly*): I'm not talkin'.

Ellery: Smith, Jones, and Brown. Three very original names, gentlemen. I suppose, reading from left to right, your first names are Tom, Dick, and Harry?

Smith: Why, now that's a funny thing. I *am* Tom Smith.

Brown: And I'm Harry Brown. And our pal's Dick Jones — hey, Dick?

Jones (*same*): I'm not talkin'.

Ellery: You men seem very close friends. How is it you're always together — never out of one another's sight?

Smith (*amused*): Tell him, Brown.

Brown: We just like each other, Queen.

Smith: We can't bear to be separated.

Ellery (*nettled*): I'm beginning to understand why Latham disliked you. Before I'm through with you, I'll know who you are!

Jones (*growling*): Aw, go peddle yer fish somewheres else, copper.

Ellery (*angrily*): Why, you low-browed specimen of Pithecanthropus —

Nikki: Ellery! Please!

Sheriff: Take it easy, son. These mavericks won't get away with nothin'.

Ellery: It's not that. If I don't find out who killed Latham and where those emeralds are before we reach Chicago, I'll never hear the end of it from dad!

(*Music up . . . train slowing down . . . jerks to stop . . . faint shouts from outside as if in big station*)

Conductor (*nervously*): Nine-ten on the dot. She made up that twelve minutes comin' in here to Kansas City. Can't I even go out on the platform, Sheriff? We've got a fifty-minute stopover here.

Sheriff: Sorry, Conductor. Nobody means you, too. I'll go see what that herd out there's bawlin' about. (*Fade off*)

Nikki (*sighing*): I can't say I'm feeling chipper, Mr. Queen. With no cooking facilities in this car, and those cold meals the porter's making up . . . what a trip! (*Dishes clink*) More of this tinned salmon?

Ellery (*gloomily*): I'm not hungry, Nikki.

Nikki: But you've got to *eat*. Oh, Monsieur Dubois. Maybe you've some influence with your hero. He won't eat a thing.

Dubois (*nervously*): Me, I do not have hunger, either. Monsieur Queen, I have been exercising the brain cells.

Ellery: I trust more successfully than I, Dubois.

Dubois: I say: "Dubois, there is something wrong. Think!" And I think. And — zzzt! I remember! Monsieur, my life is in danger!

Ellery: Oh, so *you* saw that, too?

Nikki: Ellery! What do you mean? Monsieur *Dubois's* life?

Ellery (*wearily*): Well, the killer, using the Napoleon razor stolen from Dubois, slashed the buttons off Lower Five, reached inside in the dark, and stabbed the occupant of the berth in the back as he slept.

Dubois (*whisper*): Précisement, Ma'mselle! You see? It was *my* berth that was attacked! Consequently it was *I* who was intended to be murdered!

Nikki (*horrified*): You mean Latham was killed because he stumbled into the wrong berth? But that's — horrible!

Dubois (*soberly*): I owe to him my life, Ma'mselle.

Nikki: But if that's so — I don't see — the emeralds —

Ellery: That's what's bothering me. The emeralds, blast them!

Dubois (*nervously*): Monsieur Queen, you will not let them — I mean, the murderer he is still present. Perhaps he will try again —

Ellery: I'm keeping my eye on you. And so is the Sheriff, Dubois.

Dubois: *Ah, bien des remerciments, Monsieur!*

Nikki: But why did the murderer steal Monsieur Dubois's razor before the crime, Ellery?

Ellery: To procure a weapon which couldn't possibly be traced back to himself. Sit down here, Dubois; don't wander off.

Dubois: *Oui, oui.* This baffles me. I have no enemies. I do not know anyone in this car. Never have I seen them. And yet they try to kill me!

Nikki: Didn't the razor have any fingerprints, Ellery?

Ellery: I doubt it, but I'm having it checked in New York.

Dubois: Ah, that razor! I shall keep it as a memento of this horrible affair. I may have it back, Monsieur Queen?

Ellery: When the New York police are through with it. (*Commotion and argument ad lib from outside car*) Seems to be some fuss out there in the station.

Nikki: Now what? I suppose we may as well go and see . . . (*Fade off*) (*Ad lib from other characters* — "What is it?" "What's the matter now?" "What's happening out there?" etc. *Running steps through car. Pounding on car door*)

Ellery (*calling*): Unlock this door, Sheriff! (*Door unlocked, opens*) What's the trouble out here?

Sheriff (*fading on*): Keep back, you people! . . . All right, Senator, go on in. I'm not goin' to fight a State Legislature about a thing like this.

Senator (*coldly*): It's about time! Let me through, please.

(*Closing and locking of door — tumult cut off*)

Sheriff: This is Senator McNulty of the Missoura Legislature, Mr. Queen. He insisted on gettin' on —

Miss Dodd (*fading on*): Howard! At last! (*Sobbing*) Oh, I'm so glad you've come, Howard. I'm so glad —

Senator: Lili . . . don't cry, dear . . .

Miss Dodd (*same*): I've been through the most terrible experience! A . . . a murder, and these awful brutes keeping me sealed in this car like a — like a film in a can —

Senator (*awful voice*): Sheriff, have you been abusing Miss Dodd? If you have —

Sheriff (*hastily*): Now look here, Senator, law's law —

Ellery: One moment, please. Sheriff, why did you permit this man to board our car?

Sheriff: But he's a Senator, Mr. Queen —

Senator (*pompous*): I'm Senator Howard McNulty of the Missoura Legislature!

Ellery: I don't care who you are. You've no business on this car. It's officially sealed by joint order of the Sheriffs of Deaf Smith, Randall, and Potter Counties, Texas, and by the New York Police Department.

Miss Dodd: Howard! Are you going to stand there and let yourself be insulted by a — by a *detective-story* writer?

Senator: Out of my way, young man. Lili, get your things. Porter! Miss Dodd's luggage.

Ellery: Porter! Stop. Where do you think you're going, Senator?

Senator: See here, young man! Miss Dodd is a great public personality. I might say that I, too . . . (*Coughs — then fiercely*) She is my fiancée, do you understand? She's booked to Kansas City, this *is* Kansas City, and I'm taking her off this train!

Ellery: Oh, no, you're not. Miss Dodd doesn't step out of this car until we reach New York.

Senator: Sheriff, open that door! We'll see about this! Kidnapping, plain kidnapping! I'll call the Kansas City police! I'll —

Ellery: You'll do nothing of the sort. Now that you chose to enter this sealed car, Senator, you're going to stay in it. That door won't be opened again until we reach Chicago, and then it will be opened only to admit the police!

(*Music up . . . and into sounds of car being hitched onto a train in trainyards*)

Nikki: Oooh. My tummy. This going back and forward and back — it's making me feel sick. (*Creaking, lurching stops*)

Ellery: All over, Nikki . . . Oh, there you are, dad.

Inspector (*fading on*): Whew. What a day. Well, we're all set, Ellery. We're hitched onto the Wolverine and we'll be in Grand Central eight-twenty tomorrow morning.

Nikki: Tomorrow's Sunday. It's a swell way to come into New York — (*Lurch, train starts*) Here we go!

Inspector: Ten minutes to one on the dot. Well, son, this thing's got you stymied, eh?

Nikki: Stymied, licked, and hog-tied, Inspector Queen. He's been acting like a wounded grizzly . . . Perk up, Ellery!

Ellery (*muttering*): It's those confounded emeralds. Where are they?

Inspector: Don't get it myself. Funny set-up, all right.

Nikki: Do you know how desperate he's been, Inspector? He asked me to sort of scout around and see if those two women — Mrs. Stiles and Miss Dodd — haven't got *wooden legs*! (*Giggles — inspector laughs*)

Inspector: You're sure you searched everything, Ellery?

Ellery: A hundred times . . . Wait! I'm a fool! The Senator!

Nikki: Senator McNulty? But he couldn't possibly have them, Ellery — he didn't get on the train till Kansas City!

Ellery: Oh yes, he could. They could have been slipped to him or onto his person by the one who had them . . . Senator McNulty!

Senator (*stiffly*): What do you want now, you maniac?

Ellery: Sorry, Senator, but we'll have to search you.

Miss Dodd: Oh! Howard, are you going to stand for *that*?

Senator: Certainly I'm not, dear! Inspector Queen, I demand —

Inspector (*mildly*): Better let him do it, Senator. It's just a formality. You know — a formality? Go ahead, son.

Ellery: Raise your arms, please . . .

Senator (*through his teeth*): Last straw! I'm waiting until we reach New York, gentlemen. Then we'll see if this high-handed —

Ellery: Pockets, please. Turn 'em out. Dad, you tackle his coat. (*Mrs. Stiles giggles*)

Senator (*terrible voice*): Woman — are you — laughing at — *me?*

Dubois (*whisper*): But Madame Stiles — *Monsieur le sénateur* he is angry — please —

Stiles (*low*): Josephine! For the love of Mike, stop that! Want to get us into more trouble?

Senator (*snarling*): Are you satisfied? Stolen emeralds on *me*, eh? This will cost you plenty, believe me!

Inspector (*disregarding him*): Not in his coat, Ellery. You find 'em?

Ellery: No . . . No!

(*Music up . . . and into soft click of rails*)

Inspector (*softly*): Ellery?

Nikki (*startled*): Oh!

Inspector: It's only me, Nikki. What are *you* doing up at six a.m.?

Nikki: Putting ice-packs on your son's fevered brow, Inspector.

Ellery (*muffled*): Proving every woman's part angel and part bulldog. Nikki, I tell you I'm all right! Treat me as if I were a child. It's just those emeralds.

Nikki (*soothing*): There, there — try to go to sleep —

Inspector: If I may interrupt this touching scene long enough to get a word in edgewise — I want a powwow.

Ellery (*alertly*): What's up, dad?

Inspector: Been thinking all night. We'll be in Poughkeepsie in half an hour and we've got to work fast . . . Wait a minute. (*Pause — off*) Dubois? Dubois, wake up! (*Curtains being pulled*)

Dubois (*awakening*): Ungh — ah — (*Scared*) Qu'y a-t-il? Qu'y a-t-il?

Inspector: Keep your voice down. Dubois, know what you are? You're a murderer!

Dubois (*gasping*): I? A murderer? *Monsieur l'inspecteur*, you jest —

Inspector (*chuckling*): In a way. Come closer, kids — we don't want anyone overhearing this.

Ellery: What's this about Dubois's being a murderer?

Inspector (*grimly*): I'm going to put on an act. Or rather, Dubois is!

Ellery (*sharply*): An act? What do you mean?

Inspector: Latham was carved for those emeralds. They're still in this car somewhere. When we pull into Grand Central this morning whoever's got 'em will expect a thorough search. Result: He may abandon the emeralds, leave 'em wherever he's hidden 'em in this car, to save his hide.

Nikki: If he has half a brain, he *will* leave them behind.

Dubois (*nervously*): *Mais* Monsieur, you call *me* the murderer —

Inspector: Only chance to nab this bird, the way I dope it, is to get him to *try and walk off this train with the emeralds on him.*

Nikki: But he'd never do that, Inspector! He'd have to be a fool —

Inspector: *He'd do it if he saw us arrest somebody for the crime!* Suppose we fake an arrest, say in Harmon, one hour out of Grand Central. Our man sees his chance. It's a cinch, he'll think, that there'll be no search after that. So when we pull into New York he walks off this car with the emeralds —

Nikki: And then you search everybody! Inspector, that's *marvelous.*

Dubois (*agitated*): You want *I* should be arrested? But why me?

Inspector: 'Cause they'll fall for you as a possible criminal, Dubois. I'll pretend to have received a cable from the Paris police saying you're *not* a French history professor, that you're wanted in France as a notorious jewel-thief. It'll look good, Dubois! What do you say?

Dubois: I do not like it. To be arrested! *Non, non* —

Nikki: Be a sport, Monsieur Dubois. Think of the glory when the true story comes out — you'll be a hero in France —

Dubois (*uncertainly*): You think so, Ma'mselle? Monsieur Queen, what do you advise? Do you too believe —

Ellery: It would be — ah — Napoleonic of you, Monsieur Dubois.

Dubois: Ah, yes, yes. A rôle worthy of Bonaparte! Dubois agrees. *Monsieur l'inspecteur*, I am at your service!

Inspector: That's swell. Come into the lounge, Dubois — we'll have to plan this thing so there won't be the slightest hitch . . . (*Fade off*)

Dubois (*fade off*): Oui . . . oui . . .

Nikki: A couple of hours, this awful case will be solved, and then we'll *all* be able to get some rest.

Ellery (*groaning*): Rest . . . (*Pause — softly*) *Wait* a second . . .

Nikki: What's the matter now?

Ellery: Wait! Wait! Don't talk! (*Pause*) (*Ellery laughs immoderately*)

Nikki (*scared*): Ellery! Don't you feel well? Here — I'll get more ice for your head —

Ellery: Ice! Rest! Don't be silly, Nikki! *I've just solved it!*

Nikki (*unbelieving*): You mean — you know where the emeralds are?

Ellery: Of course! Two plus two. X equals Y. They *must* be there! I've been a punch-drunk palooka. It's the only thing we haven't searched!

Nikki: But *everything's* been searched . . . Ellery Queen! If you know where the emeralds are, you must know who stole them — you must know who stabbed George Latham!

Ellery (*absently*): Oh, that? Of course. I knew that in Amarillo, Texas. (*Music up*)

Challenge to the Listener

Ellery then announced that all the clues have been given and challenged the listeners to solve the mystery.

(*Music up . . . no click of rails . . . call of "booooard!" faintly off . . . train starts — now an electric engine at Harmon . . . picks up speed*)

Miss Dodd: Howard, if you let these beasts get away with this —
Senator: Don't you fret, Lili. They'll pay through the nose!
Mrs. Stiles (*nervously*): There goes Harmon. Henry, do you suppose they'll put us in jail when we reach New York?
Stiles (*miserably*): Don't know, sweets. This is one heck of a honeymoon. If we'd taken that trip through Mexico —
Smith: You'd have missed all the fun.
Mrs. Stiles: You call this fun, Mr. Smith? I like your idea of fun!
Brown: Fun? (*Chuckles*) It's a regular circus!
Dubois: Me, I do not think so, Monsieur Brown. And you, Jones?
Jones (*sullenly*): I ain't talkin'.
Dubois: You Americans. Inexplicable. In my beloved France —
Inspector (*grimly — fading on*): Marcel Cossart Xanthippe Dubois!
Dubois: *Oui, Monsieur l'inspecteur?*
Inspector (*same*): I just received a cable in Harmon you'll be interested in, Dubois!
Dubois (*nervously — acting*): C-cable, Monsieur? What has that to do with Dubois?
Inspector: Don't you know? It's from the French *Sûreté* in Paris!
Dubois (*stuttering*): *Le — le — le Sûreté?*
Inspector: Let me read it to you, my friend. It says: "Replying your inquiry regarding Dubois stop Marcel Cossart Xanthippe Dubois masquerades as Sorbonne professor of French history stop Dubois is notorious French jewel thief —" Ellery! Sheriff! Grab him!
(*Gasps and ad lib cries of astonishment from all as scuffle ensues, climaxed by click of manacles*)
Sheriff (*panting*): There y'are, all nice an' roped, M'syour. (*Growl and struggle from Dubois*) Be good, you ornery maverick!
Mrs. Stiles (*gasping*): It was Mr. Dubois? I can't *believe* it!
Miss Dodd (*excitedly*): You know, I suspected that Frenchman *all* along!
Stiles: Jewel thief! Can you tie that!
Inspector (*sternly*): Dubois, I arrest you for the murder of George Latham.
Dubois (*snarling*): Fool! Pig! I do not murder him!
Inspector: Sure, you're just Little Red Riding Hood. What'd you do with those emeralds you stabbed Latham for, Dubois?

Dubois (*same*): I know nothing of emeralds!

Inspector: Brazening it out, eh? Well, whether we find those emeralds or not, Dubois, the main thing is we've got the goods on you. You'll fry for this! Ladies and gentlemen, I'm sorry for all the inconvenience you've been put to, but it's all over now. We're through with you, and I want to thank you —

Senator: Never mind your thanks! I'm not through with *you*.

Inspector (*humbly*): Sorry, Senator McNulty. I've got to do my duty. (*Roughly*) Come along, Dubois. Got to take special care of *you* till we pull into Grand Central . . . (*Fade — then on, low*) Thanks, Dubois!

Dubois (*chuckling*): How do I perform, Inspector? Good?

Inspector (*chuckling*): Good? Say, it was perfect! Now remember, Dubois, you're supposed to be a caught killer, so keep acting as if . . . (*Fade off*)

(*Music up . . . and into train in underground Grand Central . . . slowly, as if pulling in . . . bustle and conversation*)

Mrs. Stiles: We're in the tunnel, Henry! Oh dear, that valise — it's coming open —

Stiles (*urgent*): I'll close it, darling . . . Porter — these bags!

Porter: Yes, suh, yes, suh. Brush you off, suh . . . (*Fade*)

Miss Dodd (*irritably*): There are probably a *million* reporters waiting in Grand Central, Howard. Please don't let them annoy me. I'm so *upset* I could scream . . .

Senator: Now don't you worry, sweetheart. Leave everything to me . . . (*Fade off*)

Smith (*curtly*): Okay, Jonesy. We're in.

Brown: He won't talk.

Jones (*sullenly*): What have I got to talk about? (*Fade*)

Inspector (*low*): Keep up the act, Dubois. You're doing fine. Just a couple of minutes more —

Dubois (*nervously*): I shall be delighted when this is over . . .

Conductor (*fading on*): Grand Central, last stop. Grand Central . . . (*Train slowing, slowing amid ad lib babble of passengers. Grinds to stop*)

Stiles: We're in, honey!

Mrs. Stiles: Thank goodness!

Miss Dodd: Well, why doesn't somebody unlock this car?

Senator: Unlock this door! Porter! Conductor! Inspector!

Inspector (*mildly*): Sure, sure, Senator. (*Unlock door — admit noises*) 'Lo, Velie. How many men you got?

Velie (*fading on*): A ver-it-able army. (*Raises voice*) Okay, boys! You got your orders! (*Men piling into car — cries from passengers — "What's this, now?" "Keep your hands off me, you!" "Why, they're searching us *again*!" etc.*)

Velie (*shouting*): One man to a passenger! Search everything — clothes, bags, toilet articles — the whole works!
Inspector (*same*): You policewomen — make a thorough body search of the ladies! Take 'em into the women's washroom!

(*Continue ad lib protests and cries . . . then fade out and pause . . . no music — just a pause to indicate lapse of time . . . then up into hubbub again*)

Inspector (*eagerly*): Well, Sergeant — hand 'em over!
Velie: Hand what over?
Inspector: The emeralds, you nitwit! Who's got 'em?
Velie: Nobody.
Inspector: What! Say, do I have to make these searches myself? One of these people *must* have 'em!
Velie: Listen, Inspector, we stripped these guys down to their strawberry birthmarks. We poked in their gullets like they were horses. We took their baggage apart — I tell you we didn't overlook a thing!
Sheriff: How about the conductor and the porter?
Inspector: I took care of them myself, Sheriff . . . (*Morosely*) Well, we're pooped. Trick didn't work, hang it.
Ellery (*mildly*): I suggest you let them go, dad.
Inspector: What else can I do? Got their names and addresses, Velie?
Velie: That's about all I *did* get.
Inspector: Let 'em go.
Velie (*loudly*): All right, folks — scrambo! Flint . . . ! Pass 'em out that door one at a time — make sure nobody slips 'em anything as they leave . . . (*Bustle of departure amid further hubbub and protests, quickly fading and ending with slam of car door*)
Inspector: Well, that's that. Our man got cold feet, or saw through the trick, and refused to bite. He's left the emeralds behind. Okay, Dubois, you can go. Thanks for playing ball.
Dubois: Playing at ball? Ah, you mean . . . I am desolated, *Monsieur l'inspecteur* . . .
Ellery: Just a moment. Sergeant, did you bring along Napoleon's razor, as I asked you to when I called from Harmon?
Velie: Yep.
Inspector: Don't get it. Don't get it at all. The one who had those emeralds is our killer —
Ellery: Then I suggest you arrest Sergeant Velie for the crime.
Velie: Huh?
Inspector: What's this? What's this?
Ellery: Well, you said the one who had the emeralds is your man. And Velie has the emeralds.

Velie: *Me?* (*Laughs uncertainly*) You're kiddin', of course.

Ellery: Not at all. They're right in your hand.

Nikki: In his hand? The only thing he's holding is that razor!

Ellery (*laughs*): Sorry, Velie. I'm entitled to play around a bit. I've had a hard time . . . Dad, you'll find those three stolen emeralds hidden inside the handle of Napoleon's razor.

Inspector: In the *razor?* Velie, gimme that thingmabob! (*Pause*)

Nikki (*clapping her hands*): It's true, it's true! Oh darling, you're wonderful! (*Low*) Ump! Sorry, Inspector.

Inspector (*gladly*): Sorry for what? Say, the handle's hollow — that little piece comes out —

Velie: Whadda ya know about that?

Dubois: *Incroyable!* Within my razor — ah, that is clever, clever, Monsieur Queen.

Ellery: Extremely. Dad, will you make your little speech again to Monsieur Dubois? But this time be serious about it.

Inspector: Huh?

Ellery: Arrest Dubois for the murder of George Latham and the theft of these emeralds!

(*Music up . . . and into purr of cab*)

Nikki: No, don't *touch* me. You're a wizard. A — a Houdini. I still can't *believe* it. The Inspector faked a cable from France saying Dubois *wasn't* a French history professor, that he was a jewel-thief . . . and it turns out to be true! Ellery, how did you know?

Ellery: *That* was simple. There were two clues that pointed to Dubois. One was his statement that the stolen razor had been Josephine's gift to Napoleon to celebrate Napoleon's victory at Austerlitz in the year 1815.

Nikki: What's the matter with that?

Ellery: Eighteen-fifteen was the date of Waterloo. The battle of Austerlitz was fought in Eighteen-five. An incredible error for a French history professor who claimed to have written a critical work on the Napoleonic Wars!

Nikki: I see. So you figured he was an impostor then and there.

Ellery: Obviously. Then there was the curious matter of Latham's dressing gown and alligator slippers. You recall I said that in examining Latham's berth after the murder, I found all his belongings there? — including his gown and *slippers*? But if Dubois's story of what happened the night before was true — that he found Latham climbing into Dubois's own berth — then Latham's gown and slippers should have been found in *Dubois's* berth, not in Latham's.

Nikki: So you knew Dubois had lied.

Ellery: Yes. I knew then that Latham *didn't* get into the wrong berth at first, that he'd gone to his own berth, taken off his robe and slippers, and then was *lured* out of his berth into Dubois's, where he was ultimately stabbed. Lured by whom? It could only have been by Dubois himself, who lied about the whole thing.

Nikki: So that's why you said you knew who killed Latham as far back as Amarillo, Texas!

Ellery: Yes. But while these points indicated Dubois, they didn't constitute proof. The best possible proof was to find the emeralds. Everything had been searched. Then what had Dubois done with them? Suddenly I recalled that one object *hadn't* been searched — the *only* thing that hadn't, Nikki — and that was the murder weapon itself! I had airmailed it to New York from Amarillo. Logically, it must have been the hiding-place of the emeralds. The handle was six inches long, and a half-inch thick and wide.

Nikki: Imagine concealing loot in the weapon itself! That was a stroke of genius. But what I don't understand is how Dubois expected to regain possession of the emeralds, since the razor was in the hands of the authorities.

Ellery: That was the most brilliant part of his crime. Don't you remember how at Kansas City Dubois asked me if he could have his razor back when the police were through with it?

Nikki: The nerve of the little guy!

Ellery (*sigh*): There's only one other thing that really bothered me.

Nikki: Don't *I* bother you, Mr. Queen? Never mind. What was it?

Ellery: Those three fellows travelling together — Smith, Jones, and Brown. I couldn't fit them in. They still worry me. (*Nikki giggles*) What are you giggling about?

Nikki: The Inspector knows them. He told me all about them. You're a great detective, you are!

Ellery (*nettled*): Dad knows 'em? Who are they?

Nikki: Jones is a crook who's been using the mails to defraud, and he was being brought into New York from California by Smith and Brown . . . who are, darling — surprise! — *two G-men*!

Ellery: G-men? (*Pause*)

(*Then Ellery begins to laugh, the laugh grows, Nikki begins to laugh too, and they are both laughing uproariously as*)

(*Music up*)

Those who have read Frederic Dannay's autobiographical novel, The Golden Summer *(by "Daniel Nathan"), know how important childhood was to the Queens. Here, in a program broadcast on July 30, 1939, we see the world through the eyes of a rebellious boy.*

The Adventure of the Bad Boy

The Characters

Bobby Hayes	The bad boy
Sarah Brink	His aunt
Florence Hayes	His mother
Dr. Melton	Washington Square medico
Mr. Gordini	Magician
Herr Webber	Violin teacher
Ellery Queen	The detective
Nikki Porter	His secretary
Inspector Queen	Of the New York Police
Sergeant Velie	Of the New York Police
Doc Prouty	Of the New York Police
Flint	Of the New York Police

Setting: New York City, 1939

(*Interior — canary singing — off and on — as if from adjoining kitchen background sounds of cooking and meal preparations — on mike occasional rustle of a newspaper*)

Sarah (*off — suspicious*): Bobby? (*Pause*) Bobby!

Bobby (*on mike — peevishly*): Yeah?

Sarah (*same*): Bobby Brink, is that a way to talk to Aunt Sarah? Can't you say: "Yes, Auntie, what is it?"

Bobby (*indifferently*): Yes, Auntie. (*Rebelling*) But my name's *not* Bobby Brink!

Sarah (*same — grimly*): It is in *this* house.

Bobby: It is *not*! It's Bobby *Hayes*!

Sarah (*fading on*): How *dare* you take that tone with me, young man!

Bobby (*belligerently*): It is so Hayes! That's my father's name. That's mummy's name. So it's gotta be my name, too!

56

Sarah: Children don't understand such things.

Bobby (*doggedly*): I know my own name, I guess.

Sarah: Your father's a bad man. He ran away and left you and your mother alone —

Bobby: He did not! Mummy says he's dead.

Sarah (*grimly*): You'd be better off if he were, and so would your mother. At least you'd have his insurance —

Bobby: Inshur'nce? What's that, Aunt Sarah?

Sarah: Never mind. (*Winningly*) Bobby, don't you feel . . . a little grateful to your Aunt Sarah? When Auntie takes her sister into her home, and her sister's little boy, and gives them a nice place to sleep, and good food to eat, and money to spend, don't you think the little boy ought to . . . love his Auntie?

Bobby: Aw, I don't get so much money to spend.

Sarah (*sharp change of tone*): You're a wicked, ungrateful boy! What have you been doing in here so quiet while I've been making supper in the kitchen? You've been up to some mischief, I'll bet!

Bobby: I'm not doing nothin'. I'm just readin' the paper.

Sarah (*sniff*): Reading the paper! Chasing the cat, most likely.

Bobby: I was not! I was readin' the radio page!

Sarah: Oh. (*Pause, then slyly*) You miss all those nice radio programs since your mother's radio . . . got broken, don't you, Bobby?

Bobby: Gee, I wish we could have it fixed, Aunt Sarah. I gotta ask the kids in the Park what's been happenin' to Buck Rogers, an' the Lone Ranger.

Sarah (*slyly*): How'd you like Aunt Sarah to buy you a *new* radio, Bobby? Just for *you*?

Bobby (*gladly*): Gee! Would you, Aunt Sarah? Gee!

Sarah (*same*): I might, if you'd give me a great big kiss once in a while . . . (*Door opening and closing off*) (*Sharp tone*) Is that you, Florence?

Florence (*fading on — weary*): Yes, Sarah . . . Bobby. Darling.

Bobby (*joyfully*): Mummy! (*His running steps — kisses*)

Florence: My, what a hug! What did you do today, darling?

Sarah (*sharply*): He was a bad boy, as usual. Always getting into trouble . . . I declare I don't see why you —

Bobby: Aaaah, you're always snitchin'! I played with the boys in Washington Square Park, an' a cop chased us when we tried to swim in the fountain —

Florence: Bobby, you didn't! You might have been drowned —

Sarah: And that isn't all —

Bobby: Go on, go on, snitch some more! I threw a rock — it was just a little bit of a rock, mummy — it couldn't 'a' hurt no one — an' it just *happened* to break a window . . .

Florence (*helplessly*): Bobby Hayes, you're a bad boy. And I *don't* like you to talk to your Aunt Sarah that way, Bobby —

Sarah (*sharply*): If you'd stay home instead of gallivanting around all day, Florence, you'd be able to keep an eye on your child. *I* can't do everything —

Florence (*low — fading off a little*): I wasn't gallivanting, Sarah. I was looking for a job. (*Sound of tap water off, splashing as if washing face and hands*)

Sarah (*voice raised*): You and your jobs! Your duty is to your child. And you know perfectly well you don't have to work, as long as you live with me —

Florence (*off — muffled*): Bobby, hand me the towel, dear, please. (*Oddly*) Yes, I — know, Sarah.

Sarah: Coming home at all hours! Supper's ruined. (*Fading off*) The stew! It's burning! (*Sounds of moving pots and pans off*) Just in time! Another few seconds —

Bobby (*fading on*): Stew? I don't want your ol' stew, Aunt Sarah. I don't like ol' stew.

Sarah (*off*): I'm not giving *you* stew, Bobby. How would you like a nice raspberry-jelly omelet?

Bobby: Boy! I *love* jelly omelets! (*Rattle of bird-cage*)

Sarah (*fading on*): As soon as I set these two plates of stew down, Bobby, I'll fix your omelet. (*Sets down dishes on table*) Florence, for pity's sake, hurry, will you! Bobby! Stop playing with the canary's cage!

Florence (*fading on*): Bobby, didn't you hear what Aunt Sarah said? Stop it, Bobby!

Bobby: Yes, Ma'am. (*Sound of scraping chair*) May I have prune juice, Aunt Sarah? I 'specially like prune juice —

Sarah (*shrewishly*): You'll get a good licking, that's what you'll get, Bobby Brink! See what you've done? You've left the canary's cage-door open!

Florence: Oh, Bobby . . . There goes the canary. Sarah, catch him!

Sarah (*same*): Of all the spoiled, mischievous children . . . (*Cries and sounds of chasing canary around room — from Sarah and Florence only — not the boy — cat meowing excitedly*)

Florence: I've got him! Oh dear, he's flown up on the chandelier!

Sarah: Come down here, drat you!

Florence: Sarah, shut the dining-room door — he'll fly out!

Sarah (*shutting door*): Close the window, Florence!

Florence: Look out — the cat!

Sarah: Darby — stop that, you bad cat!

Florence: There! *Now* — Sarah!

Sarah (*panting*): Got you! (*Sounds of chase stop — shut door of canary's cage*) (*Fiercely*) Now that *that's* over, Bobby Brink, suppose you tell me why you opened the canary's cage? And why you've been sitting there at the supper table and haven't so much as lifted a finger to help catch him!

Bobby (*low*): I don't care. I was just playin' with the ol' bird. He flew past me, the dirty ol' bird.

Florence (*distressed*): What's come over you, Bobby Hayes? You've always been so kind to Aunt Sarah's pets. But now you chase Darby, and torment the canary, and go fishing in the goldfish bowl here — you seem to take a delight in torturing the poor things!

Bobby: Awww, I didn't hurt none of 'em.

Sarah (*sharply*): The trouble is, Florence, that you don't discipline him properly. If he were mine —

Florence (*quietly*): But he isn't, Sarah. Bobby, we'll talk about this after supper.

Bobby (*low*): Yes, Ma'am.

Sarah (*sharply*): Eat your stew, Florence. (*Scraping chair*) And I'm eating mine, too, right this minute, before it gets icy.

Florence: But Sarah — Bobby's omelet . . . Here, Bobby, I'll make your omelet for you . . .

Sarah (*same*): You'll do nothing of the kind! I've told you a thousand times I won't have you or anyone else messing in my kitchen. Bobby'll wait for his supper, since he's spoiled ours.

Florence: But you can heat the stew, Sarah —

Sarah (*same*): Our gas bills are high enough as it is. (*Sounds of eating in silence, during which strains of a violin playing a very mournful tune, like "Hebrew Melody" or "Ave Maria," are heard faintly, as if coming from an apartment below. No piano accompaniment. Playing should be competent. Violent dropping of fork on dish*) There's that awful music again! Everytime we sit down to eat, he starts playing. I swear that man does it on purpose, just to annoy me!

Bobby: That's only Mr. Webber downstairs, Aunt Sarah. He *likes* to play that song —

Florence (*gently*): Bobby. Please.

Sarah (*viciously*): I'll fix *him*. I'll give him a dispossess!

(*Music up, following theme of the mournful tune that the violin has been playing, of course with full orchestra . . . then into sound of dishes again, with orchestra dropping out and single violin still playing solo*)

Florence (*low*): The stew was delicious tonight, Sarah. Bobby, you may leave the table.

Bobby: But please, mummy, why can't I have a piece of apple pie? I'm awful hungry for a piece of apple pie.

Sarah: I've already told you, Bobby. If your mother won't punish you, I will!

Bobby: But that's *mean*! You know how I love apple pie, Aunt Sarah!

Florence (*choked*): Don't say things like that, Bobby. I told you to leave the table.

Bobby (*calmly*): Yes, Ma'am. (*Brightening*) May I go downstairs and see Mr. Gordini? I promised to.

Sarah: No, you may not! Florence, I've told you I won't have Bobby spending all his time with that worthless, greasy actor!

Florence (*spoon against cup sharply*): Sarah, I'm Bobby's mother and I'll bring him up as I think best. Mr. Gordini is very nice. Bobby, you may visit Mr. Gordini for a half-hour. Then come upstairs to bed.

Sarah (*shrilly*): Bobby Brink, I forbid it! Florence, as long as you stay with me, in my house, living on my money, you'll do as *I* say!

Florence (*bursting into tears*): I can't stand this any more! Always throwing up to me how dependent I am on your charity — dictating my life just because I've no other place to live. I'll leave, I'll take Bobby, I'd rather starve —

Sarah (*viciously*): Don't be a fool! If you'd listened to me, you wouldn't have been deserted by a rapscallion husband and left penniless to support a child! I was good enough to take you in, and I'm good enough to dictate what I think is best for both of you . . . Stop that silly crying, Florence.

Bobby (*near tears himself*): Please, mummy, please. I'm sorry. I don't wanna see Mr. Gordini. Really I don't.

Florence (*trying to control herself*): I — I'm all right, Bobby. Go downstairs now. Please, Bobby —

Sarah: Bobby Brink, you're staying here! If you dare . . . *Oh!* (*Sharp gasp of pain*) I . . . feel . . . funny . . . (*Thud of falling body*)

Bobby (*scared*): Mummy! Aunt Sarah — she fell down! She —

Florence (*scared*): Sarah! Sarah, what's the matter?

Sarah (*gasping*): My throat — my stomach — they're on fire — I can't breathe —

Florence (*screaming*): Bobby! Run downstairs for Dr. Melton! Hurry!

(*Music up . . . and into rattle of typewriter*)

Ellery (*dictating*): ". . . and into the umbrageous interior of the tomb . . ." No, make that "the shadow-crowded interior," Nikki. Let's see, now . . .

Nikki: "Shadow . . . crowded . . . interior . . . of . . . the . . . tomb." (*Typewriter stops*) Oooh, what a pleasant thought. How do you manage to sleep nights, Mr. Queen?

Ellery: As a matter of fact, badly. But not for the reason you think. I've had something on my mind for several days.

Nikki (*eagerly*): Is it female, does it weigh a hundred and ten pounds, and are its initials N. P.?

Ellery (*sarcastically*): No, Miss Porter. It's that call I got the other day from Dr. Melton — that Washington Square medico. What time is it?

Nikki: Noon.

Ellery: He should have been here an hour ago with this Brink woman. Curious case, Nikki. Apparently an attempted poisoning.

Nikki (*darkly*): A . . . lot of people I know need — well, maybe not poisoning, exactly, but . . . at least a jab in the arm.

Ellery: Hmmm. Well, the house seems to be an old brownstone facing Washington Square Park — one of those three-story ex-mansions of Victorian vintage converted into a four-family apartment house. This Sarah Brink, who owns the place, occupies the entire top floor, Dr. Melton lives on the ground floor, and the second floor's occupied by two tenants —

Nikki: How interesting. (*Sighs*)

Ellery (*continuing*): — an old German violin-teacher and an actor of some sort . . . (*Doorbell rings*) Here comes my case now!

Nikki (*fading off*): And there goes your shadow-crowded tomb! We won't be crawling back into *that* until this case is solved if I know *you*, Ellery Queen . . . (*Open door off*) Come in, please. (*Ad lib murmurs — close door*)

Dr. Melton (*fading on*): Mr. Queen? This is Miss Sarah Brink, the patient I 'phoned you about the other day.

Ellery: Please sit down. My secretary, Miss Porter. Miss Brink, Dr. Melton. (*Ad lib exchange of greetings*)

Dr. Melton: There . . . easy, now, Miss Brink. You see, Mr. Queen, she's still pretty shaky, although it's four days since —

Sarah (*weakly*): The accident. The accident. I told you, Dr. Melton, it was some sort of accident. I don't know why I've let you bring me up here. A detective —

Dr. Melton: It couldn't have been an accident, Miss Brink.

Ellery: What do you suspect, Dr. Melton?

Dr. Melton: I don't suspect — I know. Miss Brink was poisoned.

Ellery (*crisply*): I suppose you can establish that as a fact?

Dr. Melton (*same*): Absolutely. In the first place, a few moments after she fell writhing on her dining-room floor, she showed every symptom of poisoning . . .

Ellery: What *were* the symptoms?

Dr. Melton: Attack about ten minutes after eating on an empty stomach — burning pain in throat and stomach — uncontrollable vomiting — intense thirst — collapse, cyanosed skin, difficult respiration, cramps in the calves of the legs . . . all symptoms, Mr. Queen, of *arsenical* poisoning!

Nikki: How perfectly awful!

Ellery: Arsenic, eh . . . You checked the stew, of course, Dr. Melton?

Dr. Melton: Yes, I had the remains of Miss Brink's portion analysed — and it was heavily dosed with arsenic.

Ellery (*abruptly*): Miss Brink, who are your heirs?

Sarah (*low*): My sister Florence — and her ten-year-old boy. They're my only living relatives.

Ellery: Are you well-to-do?

Sarah: I . . . own my own house and have a . . . few thousand dollars.

Ellery: Servants, please?

Sarah: I do my own housework and cooking. Can't afford servants.

Ellery: I see. Dr. Melton, didn't you tell me that Mrs. Florence Hayes, Miss Brink's sister, ate the same stew that night and showed no ill effects?

Dr. Melton (*dryly*): That's what I said. None at all.

Ellery: Obviously, then, only the stew on your plate, Miss Brink, was loaded with arsenic. Was Mrs. Hayes in your kitchen at any time during the preparation or cooking of the stew?

Sarah: No. Florence was out of the house all day. She didn't get back until a few minutes before I fetched the two plates of stew from the kitchen and set them on the dining-room table.

Ellery: Was your *nephew* in the kitchen while you were cooking?

Sarah: Bobby? Not at any time.

Ellery: After you set the plates down on the dining-room table, did your sister have an opportunity to poison your stew?

Sarah (*whisper*): Florence . . . poison me? No, no. Just as I set the plates down, Bobby let the canary escape, and Florence and I began to chase it —

Ellery (*sharply*): Really! And what was your nephew doing while you and your sister were chasing the bird?

Sarah (*confused*): Bobby? Why . . . he was seated at the table . . .

Ellery (*significantly*): Alone. Alone . . . and unobserved.

Sarah (*pause*): Oh!

Nikki: That's . . . that's horrible.

Ellery: I'm only examining the situation logically.

Sarah (*hysterically*): Dr. Melton, take me home!

Dr. Melton: But Miss Brink, you can't let this drop —

Sarah (*same*): I don't want another word said about the entire matter!

Ellery: You may have no choice, Miss Brink. This is attempted murder —

Sarah (*same*): I — I don't care! If you interfere, Mr. Queen, I'll — I'll deny everything! And don't think you're going to send me a bill — I won't pay it! Good day! (*Fade off and open door*)

Dr. Melton (*awkwardly*): I'm terribly sorry about this, Mr. Queen. I didn't realize myself how things stood . . . I think you ought to know, though, that she's not telling the truth about her financial status. She owns half a dozen houses in Greenwich Village. Everybody in the neighborhood knows she's a wealthy woman.

Ellery: I suspected as much. Well, Doctor, it doesn't seem as if there's much we can do. Good-day.

Dr. Melton: I'm sorry. I'll have to hurry her back home. She's still pretty weak, you know — it was a narrow escape — (*Fade off, close door*)

Nikki: Ellery Queen, that's *hideous*! A ten-year-old boy!

Ellery (*thoughtfully*): Queer, too, Nikki. Apparently the child released the canary just to lure his mother and aunt away from the table — deliberately distracted their attention —

Nikki: But if that boy poisoned his aunt's stew — no matter what sort of old crone she is — he must be a . . . fiend, or a psychopathic case! Something ought to be done about it. That woman's in danger — another poisoning attempt might work —

Ellery: Hellish situation . . . Nikki, what kind of stew did Miss Brink say it was she cooked that night?

Nikki: What kind of stew? I don't believe she did say.

Ellery: Very careless of me. I should have asked her. (*Sighs*) Well, that's that. If she insists on digging her own grave, it's her funeral!

(*Music up . . . and into tuning in on baseball broadcast*)

Nikki: Ellery Queen, either dictate your novel to me, or sit and hold my hand — but *don't* make me listen to a Saturday afternoon baseball broadcast!

Ellery (*guiltily*): I just wanted to hear how the Giants are making out . . . (*Phone rings*) Answer that, will you, Nikki?

Nikki (*picking up phone*): Hello?

Inspector (*filtered*): Nikki? Put Ellery on the 'phone.

Nikki: It's for you, John McGraw. Inspector Queen.

Ellery: Dad? (*Into phone*) Yes, dad.

Inspector (*filtered*): Oh, Ellery. El, you'd never forgive me if I didn't let you in on this.

Ellery: Let me in on what?

Inspector (*same*): The cockeyed-est case *I* ever saw. If you can get down here in fifteen minutes, I'll try and hold 'em.

Ellery: You'll try and hold whom?

Inspector (*same*): The witnesses to the crime. Dozens of 'em.

Ellery: Dozens of witnesses? What is this, dad — a gag?

Inspector (*same*): Fact, if you don't hurry, there'll probably be hundreds of 'em. (*Chuckles*) These witnesses are funny that way. Thirteen-B Washington Square North, and make it snappy, Ellery! (*Hang up*)

Nikki: A new case, Mr. Queen? I'd find it more exciting than listening to a baseball game.

Ellery: Witnesses — dozens — hundreds — if dad were a drinking man . . . Thirteen-B Washington Square North . . . Nikki!

Nikki: What's the matter?

Ellery: That's the address of the woman who came to see us last week — Sarah Brink — Dr. Melton's poison case! Come on!

(*Music up . . . into cab braking to stop at curb . . . street noises . . . far-off cries of children at play . . . open cab door*)

Ellery (*excited*): Hop it, Nikki! You're slow as molasses!

Nikki: Why don't you carry me? You did, once, in Los Angeles.

Driver (*off*): You forgot yer change, Mister.

Ellery: Never mind. Keep it!

Driver (*fading off*): Say, t'anks. (*Drive off. They run up stone steps. Thunderous knocking with door knocker*)

Velie (*open door — fade on*): Ah-ha! Mr. Queen and Miss Porter to the res-cue! Right this way, Master-Mind — the old man's waitin' for you. (*Close door . . . up inside steps as they talk*)

Ellery (*quickly*): What's the lay, Sergeant? What's happened?

Velie (*coyly*): I got my orders, Mr. Queen — no talkee.

Nikki: Is it a surprise? That's father love for you!

Velie (*chuckling*): Surprise? I'll say it's a surprise. (*Laughs*)

Ellery (*irritably*): Mystery, nothing but mystery! I write 'em, I solve 'em, but I don't *like* 'em. Velie, I'll strangle you!

Velie: Strangle your old man. Here we are. Top floor.

Inspector (*fading on*): Ah, the son and heir. Wait'll you see this, Ellery. Wait'll you see it!

Ellery (*grimly*): I'm waiting.

Nikki: If you don't hurry, Inspector, there won't be anything left of your son's teeth — he's been grinding them so. And they're *such* beautiful teeth . . .

Ellery (*impatiently*): Never mind the blarney, Nikki —

Nikki: But it's not blarney! I think they're simply *lovely* . . .

Velie: May I have the next dance, handsome?

Ellery (*howling*): What *is* this? A conspiracy to drive me mad?

Inspector (*chuckling*): All right, all right. This way. (*Steps*) This is the upper hall. Doors off here all lead to various rooms of the Brink apartment. Here we are. (*Steps stop*) Velie, Flint, Piggott, Hagstrom — you boys all ready? (*Ad lib gloomy agreement*)

Velie: Nice work for a grown man. Chasing —

Flint: Say, Inspector, we got to go through all *that* again?

Velie: Isn't once enough, for the love o' Pete?

Ellery: *I'm* not mad. They are. All of them.

Nikki (*soothing*): Now, now, Mr. Queen, calm yourself. Let your daddy have his little joke.

Inspector (*grimly*): Joke? Some joke! Okay, boys — take your positions just outside this door. (*Grumbling, movements*) Now Ellery, this is exactly what we found when we got here and opened this door . . . *Open it, Velie!*

Velie: Remember, boys, it's all for dear old Siwash. Two — fourteen — eighty-nine — hep! (*Opens door. Instantly a rush of tiny scampering feet — of rabbits — ad lib bedlam breaks loose as four detectives try to catch the bunnies — "Catch 'em, Hagstrom!" "There's one got away!" "Where?" "That one!" "Come here, you little devil!" "Into this bag!" etc.*)

Nikki (*gasping*): Rabbits . . . *Rabbits!*

Ellery: Rabbits! Now I *know* I've gone mad!

Inspector: Yes, rabbits — dozens of 'em. Spent a half-hour chasing through the house trying to recapture the pesky little things. And they all came out of this room — Sarah Brink's bedroom.

Ellery: The spinster's bedroom, eh? Let's have a look. (*Pause. Abruptly*) No, Nikki. Stay in the hall.

Nikki: But why? You always treat me as if I were made of candy — (*Gasps. Then sickishly*) Oh . . . *Ellery.*

Inspector (*grimly*): Yes, and that's what *we* saw when the rabbits scooted past us . . . Sarah Brink lying on her bed . . . dead. *Murdered.* (*Suddenly same violin tune as before begins to play, off and unaccompanied. Fade and . . .*)

(*Music up . . . and into same faint playing of violin*)

Ellery: From the appearance of these bedclothes, dad, there might have been a struggle.

Inspector: What do you think, Doc?

Prouty (*a trifle off*): Sure there was a struggle — with old man Death. You'd struggle, too, if you'd died of what *she* died of.

Ellery: What was that, you dissector of cadavers?

Prouty (*same*): Hold your horses. Old Doc Prouty makes sure.

Inspector: Seems they lunched on rabbit stew this afternoon, and right after lunch the old girl came in here and lay down for a nap.

Prouty: Had some vittles in her tummy, I'll bet, before she tackled the stew at lunch. Otherwise she'd have passed out at the table. Well, gentlemen, it's arsenical poisoning. Sunken features, cyanosed skin, irritation of eyelids and skin eruptions —

Ellery: Any doubt about it, Dr. Prouty?

Prouty: Doubt, my boy, is the god of science. But in this case I'd swear it

was arsenious oxide — white arsenic. We'll do an autopsy to make
sure, though — Reinsch's test will do the trick. She'd have been luckier
if she'd been born a rabbit — arsenic won't kill 'em; they're immune ..
. Okay, call the wagon. I've got a date with my dentist.

Velie: Wagon's on its way, Doc.

Prouty: Here's your removal order. Say, this is a nice time for a fiddle to
be playing! Who's plinking that violin — Nero?

Velie: Some fiddle maestro lives downstairs. Name of Webber.

Ellery (off): What's this?

Inspector: What's what?

Ellery: This shiny black top-hat on Sarah Brink's night-table. (*Fading
on*) Miss Brink wasn't a male impersonator, was she? (*Chuckles*)
Gentlemen, let me show you a trick with this hat. Observe I have
nothing up my sleeve — I insert my right hand in the hat — I say:
Hocus-pocus, abracadabra, open sesame, Till Eulenspiegel — and
out comes — a bunny! (*Rabbit bleats*)

Velie (*admiringly*): He did it, too!

Ellery (*laughing*): No, Sergeant, merely one little bunny who was too
scared to run when you opened the door; it took refuge in this silk
topper. Top-hat and rabbits — the murder must have been committed
by a professional magician!

Velie (*reproachfully*): Mr. Queen, you threw me. You threw me!

Inspector (*chuckling*): Ha, what did I tell you, Velie? Fork over that buck.
I told you he'd say that!

Velie (*mumbling*): Here's your buck. I bet it's a frame.

Ellery: But I wasn't serious, dad.

Inspector: You'd better be. She was poisoned by a magician, all right.
I've got him in the living-room under arrest!

Ellery: You mean there's actually a magician mixed up in this?

Inspector: Yep. Lives downstairs across the hall from Webber, the violin-
teacher. Vaudeville magician. Calls himself Gordini the Great.

Ellery: Magician . . . (*Abruptly*) I want to see him, dad!

(*Music up . . . and into door opening*)

Inspector: Has he been acting up, Flint?

Flint: Naw. Gentle as a rabbit. Haw!

Gordini (*tightly*): You're making a mistake, Inspector. I didn't poison
Sarah Brink.

Inspector: Yeah, yeah, you're just the victim of a foul plot, Gordini.

Ellery: Mr. Gordini, my name is Queen and I'm interested in Sarah
Brink's death. I'm told you were home — in your apartment today —
about noon, when she was poisoned.

Gordini: Yes, I'm — temporarily at liberty, Mr. Queen.

Ellery: I'm told, too, that the fire-escape from your first-floor apartment passes the Brink kitchen on its way to the roof, and that therefore you could have been just outside the Brink kitchen window while the two plates of rabbit stew — which Miss Brink and Mrs. Hayes ate for lunch today — stood on the serving-cabinet near the fire-escape window.

Gordini: Yes, but the kitchen window has a panel of iron grillwork which can be opened only from inside — all the rear windows in this house have. How could I get past those bars?

Inspector: I'll tell you how, Gordini. With this thingamajig.

Gordini (*quickly*): Where did you get my lazy-tongs, Inspector?

Velie: Lazy-tongs? What's that?

Inspector: That's what friend Gordini here used to get at that plate of stew, Sergeant. It's like a pair of scissors that opens up and shoots out on a series of crisscrossing slats — see —

Velie (*alarm*): Hey, watch that thing! You missed my schnozzola by a half-inch!

Inspector: Yes, and at a distance of eight feet, Velie. Get the idea? This is part of Gordini's magic equipment — it comes from his stuff downstairs. Gordini, you stood on the fire-escape outside that kitchen window and dropped arsenic into Sarah Brink's plate of stew from the end of the tongs!

Gordini (*hoarsely*): I didn't. I didn't, I tell you!

Inspector: And the top-hat — it has pockets inside, a regular magician's hat. You admit it's yours?

Gordini: Yes, but —

Inspector: How did it get into the Brink woman's bedroom?

Gordini (*pause*): (*Sullen*) You tell me.

Ellery: Dad —

Inspector: Just a minute, Ellery. I've had you checked up this afternoon, Gordini. Your real handle's Gordon — John Gordon. You were a chemist before you became a stage magician. Then you'd know all about arsenic, wouldn't you?

Gordini (*bitterly*): I see I'm to be convicted on coincidences.

Inspector: It's no coincidence that you've been having quarrels with the dead woman, Gordini! The whole neighborhood knows about it. The old lady wanted you to lay off her sister and that boy Bobby!

Ellery: That's all pretty circumstantial, dad.

Inspector (*dryly*): Is it? Well, chew on this, then. I've got a witness who lives in a MacDougal Alley house opposite the back windows here. My witness says she saw you, Gordini, standing on the fire-escape outside Sarah Brink's kitchen window at just about the time that rabbit stew must have been poisoned! What d'ye say to that?

Gordini (*miserably*): I admit that, Inspector. I — I was there. But I was — well, snooping. That's no great crime, is it?

Inspector (*grimly*): If that's the best you can do, Gordini —

Ellery: Dad, I've spoken to Florence Hayes' boy, Bobby, and he told me *he* put Gordini's top-hat in Sarah Brink's bedroom — he'd been playing with it there this morning — and that the rabbits were Sarah Brink's — she sometimes fed them in her room . . . *Mr. Gordini, you know who poisoned Sarah Brink, don't you?*

Gordini (*pause*): (*Low*) Yes.

Ellery (*quickly*): Who was it?

Gordini (*passionately*): I . . . can't tell you! (*Pause — low*) I mean . . . I *won't*.

(*Music up . . . and into sobbing by Florence*)

Florence (*sobbing — muffled*): I knew . . . something horrible . . . would happen in this house. I knew it. I knew it.

Bobby (*trying not to cry*): Don't cry, mummy. Mummy, don't.

Nikki (*undertone — with revulsion*): Go away, you — you . . . *boy!*

Florence: No! No, please, Miss Porter. Bobby — darling —

Bobby (*bursting into tears*): Oh, mummy! (*They both cry*)

Nikki: Please, Mrs. Hayes. You'll make yourself ill. You've got to control yourself —

Florence (*with an effort*): Yes. Yes. Bobby dear — it's all right — don't be frightened — Aunt Sarah's just . . . just gone away on a long trip . . . (*Knock on door*) Oh! Who's that?

Nikki: Don't be scared. (*Calling*) Come in!

Ellery (*open door — fade on*): Ah, I'm glad you're with Mrs. Hayes, Nikki. (*Bobby stops sniffling*)

Florence: She's been — a perfect angel, Mr. Queen.

Bobby: Are you a *real* d'tective?

Ellery: Sometimes I wonder, Bobby. (*Abruptly*) Mrs. Hayes, did your sister Sarah always keep pets — canary, cat, goldfish?

Florence: Yes, Mr. Queen. Recently she bought the — rabbits, too.

Ellery: Did she always keep those rabbits in her bedroom?

Florence: No, most of the time she kept them in the backyard.

Bobby (*excitedly*): In a reg'lar rabbit-hutch! You oughta see it!

Ellery: Who fed them, Mrs. Hayes?

Florence: Sarah. She wouldn't let anyone else take care of them — (*Stops*)

Nikki: What's the matter, Mrs. Hayes?

Florence (*low*): I just remembered. Sarah had an argument with Mr. — Webber last week. She caught him feeding the rabbits in the backyard . . . (*Faint sound of violin playing as before*)

Bobby: Boy, did she tell that ol' Mr. Webber!

Ellery: Webber . . . That must be Webber playing the violin now. Excuse me a moment. (*Steps, open door, call*) Sergeant Velie!

Velie (*off*): Yeah, Mr. Queen?

Ellery (*off*): Have this man Webber brought up here!

Velie (*off*): Anything to stop him playin' that fiddle! (*Close door*)

Ellery (*fading on*): Have rabbit stew often, did you, Mrs. Hayes?

Florence: At least once a week. Sarah and I are — were very fond of it. She killed her own rabbits — they were multiplying so rapidly we had to do *something* —

Bobby: Not me. I don't like that ol' stew. I like jelly om'lets, an' apple pie, an' choc'late marshmallows —

Ellery: You've felt no ill effects from the stew you ate at luncheon today, Mrs. Hayes?

Florence (*low*): No.

Ellery: Just after the stew was brought into the dining-room today did anything unusual happen?

Florence (*puzzled*): Unusual, Mr. Queen?

Ellery: Yes, like the escape of the canary last week.

Florence: Oh. (*Pause*) You mustn't think Bobby's a bad boy — he's just playful, like most boys his age —

Ellery (*gravely*): Then something did happen?

Bobby: You c'n tell him, mummy. *I* ain't scared. I pushed over the fishbowl! (*Defiantly*)

Nikki (*low*): Ellery . . . please . . .

Ellery: Sorry, Nikki. (*Pause*) And while your mother and aunt were rescuing the goldfish, Bobby, what were *you* doing?

Bobby: Sittin' at the table. Aunt Sarah was yellin' at me — she said just for that I couldn't have dessert. I'm *glad* she went on a trip. Ol' . . . ol' . . . *yeller!*

Florence (*shocked — half-crying*): Bobby! Oh, Bobby dear, you mustn't talk that way about — (*Door opens, murmur fading on*)

Velie (*fading on*): Here's Webber, *and* Doc Melton, *and* me and the Inspector. Regular kaffee-klatsch.

Inspector: What's going on here, Ellery?

Ellery: Oh, I've been having a bit of a chat with Mrs. Hayes. By the way, Herr Webber. You're the violinist we've been hearing all afternoon?

Webber (*thick German accent*): Ja. Frau Hayes, I am terrible sorry your *schwester* — Fraulein Brink — I hear what happens —

Florence (*sobbing again*): Yes, you are! My poor sister lying — dead up here and — you playing music downstairs! Haven't you any feelings?

Webber (*distressed*): Ach, Frau Hayes, *aber das ist* . . . how you say . . . sad moosic. I haff sad feelings, I play sad moosic.

Ellery: Why do you feel sad, Herr Webber?

Webber (*bitterly*): What I am, mein Herr, and where from I come — it is all sad. Everything. Everyone. We are men of sadness.

Ellery: Oh . . . Herr Webber, I understand you fed Miss Brink's rabbits last week.

Webber: Ja. Ja. Mit ledduce.

Ellery: And Miss Brink scolded you?

Webber: I sid in the backyard t'inking uff Köln, und Stuttgart und Zwickau. I play my violin. I lay it on the bench und feed the rabbits. Miss Brink, she comes out, she takes my violin — ach, she is like a crazy woman — she breaks it in liddle pieces. Dot iss my goodt violin — the odder, the one I play on now — it iss not so goodt —

Florence (*distressed*): Sarah had a vile temper. I'm sorry, Mr. Webber. I didn't know — about that.

Webber: Ach, *natürlich*, I vant she should pay for my violin. I am a poor refugee. But she says no. She says I should moof. *Alzo* . . . I moof. *Morgen.* Tomorrow. Herr Doktor Melton, he is moofing also —

Inspector (*sharply*): Is that right, Dr. Melton?

Melton: As soon as I find new quarters in the neighborhood.

Ellery: But why are *you* moving, Dr. Melton?

Melton: All my patients are from the Village — they're poor people and they don't pay very well. I've been — behind in my rent. The other day Miss Brink said she wouldn't wait any longer . . . that I'd have to get out.

Florence: Wait! Dr. Melton, I — I didn't know that, either. I . . . I suppose I own this house . . . now. Please don't move. You've been here so many years —

Dr. Melton (*low*): That's awfully decent of you, Mrs. Hayes.

Florence: And you, too, Mr. Webber. Stay here. I'll — as soon as I . . . I can, I'll pay for your broken violin . . .

Webber: *Ach! Dänke schoën, gnädige Frau! Dänke schoën!*

(*Music up . . . and into silence*)

Inspector (*explosively*): Blast it! (*Meowing of cat*)

Ellery: What's the trouble, dad? You almost kicked the cat that time.

Nikki: Poor pussy! Here, puss — don't let the nasty-tempered old man hurt your feelings . . . Inspector, you ought to be ashamed of yourself!

Inspector: Cats! Rabbits! Goldfish! Canaries! Regular zoo! And stop looking at me that way, Nikki! I *didn't* kick that confounded cat. I didn't know he was there.

Nikki: Hear that, puss? He's apologizing. But then we knew he wouldn't do a mean thing like that, didn't we? (*Meow, purrs*)

Inspector: What's the answer to this blasted riddle, Ellery, if Gordini didn't poison that stew?

Ellery: I've a notion — the vaguest notion —

Nikki: The great man has a notion, puss . . . imagine that! Do you suppose it will ever grow up to be a big strong idea?
(*Door kicked open*)

Velie (*fading on — howling*): Somebody swiped my gun!

Inspector: *What!*

Velie (*embarrassed, half in tears*): I tell ya it's — magic! Somebody steals *my* gun — right outa my pocket! (*Nikki, Ellery laugh*)

Inspector: Velie, I'm surprised at you. How'd you ever let a thing like that happen?

Velie (*miserably*): I dunno. I can't believe it yet. All I know is I had it, an' then it's gone. *My* gun. I'll never hear the end o' this downtown!

Nikki (*laughing very hard*): Oh . . . my . . . that's the funniest thing I've ever heard in my whole life!

Velie (*sourly*): Well, wipe the tears off your pretty pan — they're cuttin' cow-tracks in your make-up.

Nikki (*same*): Oh, Sergeant . . . (*Snaps open handbag*) Where's my handkerchief? (*Stops laughing*) That's funny. (*Pause*) I'd swear I had it in my bag. I *know* I had it.

Ellery (*sharply*): Something missing, Nikki? Your handkerchief?

Nikki: No. My vanity-case. Ellery, it's *gone*.

Velie: Her vanity's gone. (*Laughs*) Fawncy that, now! (*Laughs*)

Inspector (*peevishly*): What the deuce . . . What's going on here? Anybody else have something stolen?

Ellery (*slowly*): My fountain-pen. Right out of my vest pocket.

Velie (*laughs*): His fountain-pen, he says. (*Laughs harder*)

Inspector (*laughing too*): That calls for a pinch of snuff! (*Laugh cut off abruptly*) Hey! My snuffbox is gone!

Velie (*almost helpless*): His snuffbox . . . His . . . (*Howls with glee*)

Inspector (*roaring*): Sergeant Velie, search this house! Swipe my snuffbox, will they? Search the house, Velie!

Velie (*attempt at gravity*): Yes, yer Worship . . . (*Laughs*) Oh, Flint. Know what just happened?

Inspector (*hastily*): Never mind! What is it, Flint?

Flint (*fading on*): Doc Prouty just phoned from the Morgue, Inspector. He says the old dame died of arsenic poison, all right. Somethin' about submucous hemorrhages showin' up in the post-mortem —

Inspector: So she died of arsenic. We *knew* that!

Flint: Got a report from the City Toxicologist's office, too. Know that white stuff — looked like flour — we scraped up from the floor of the rabbit-hutch in the backyard?

Ellery (*sharply*): What? You found a white powder in Sarah Brink's rabbit-hutch?

Inspector: Sure. Before you got here this afternoon. Well, Flint?

Flint: Well, the Toxicologist says it's arsenic, too.

Ellery: Arsenic in the rabbit-hutch! Why didn't someone *tell* me!

Inspector: Why didn't you ask? Okay, Flint. Velie, go ahead and —

Flint: Oh, say, Velie. What'd you want to leave your gun layin' around for? With a kid in the house, too!

Velie: My gun? Where? Where is it?

Flint: On a table downstairs in the hall. Your gun, and the Inspector's snuffbox, and a fountain-pen and a vanity-case . . . I says it's screwy. I says it must be Bank Night —

Nikki: My vanity — downstairs in the hall? But I didn't leave it there!

Inspector (*thoughtfully*): Hold it, Velie. Someone swipes something from each one of us — leaves 'em on a table downstairs —

Velie: You know what I think? I think we've fallen into a nest of *gonophs*!

Ellery (*thoughtfully*): A thief who returns his loot . . .

Inspector (*exasperated*): But if he didn't want the stuff, why in time'd he steal it in the first place?

Ellery (*suddenly*): By George! That's it!

All: That's what?

Ellery: The secret of the whole case!

(*Music up . . . violin theme . . . and into solo violin off*)

Nikki (*low*): But *why* are you snooping about in Bobby Hayes' bedroom, Ellery?

Ellery (*same*): Because, my child —

Nikki: Yes, gran'pa!

Ellery: Sorry. You *are* grown up, aren't you, Nikki? What's this? (*Opens closet door*)

Nikki: So *that's* why you don't pay any more attention to me than if I were a — a brat in pigtails! Yes, I *am* grown-up, Mr. Sherlock Holmes Queen. And what's more, I'll *prove* it to you. I've been wasting too much of my time on you, you — you selfish oaf. I'll go out nights — I'll find myself a nice, kind, understanding man . . . (*Exasperated*) Ellery Queen, don't go hiding in closets! Come out of that closet and listen to me!

Ellery (*muffled but excited*): Nikki Porter, come *into* this closet and listen to *me*!

Nikki (*quickly — into closet*): Ellery! You've found something!

Ellery (*on mike now*): Yes, and if my flashlight isn't playing tricks on my eyes — it's a sliding panel.

Nikki: A sliding *panel*! (*Laughs*) Why, that's — that's mediaeval!

Ellery: No, simply ten-year-old boy. Bobby's sawn through the back wall of this closet. Let's see what's behind this door he's made . . . (*Slides wood*)

Nikki: A passageway! Ellery, it's a . . . (*Giggles*) a secret passage!

Ellery: And unless I'm mistaken, that's a flight of wooden stairs . . . going up . . . Nikki, come on! (*Fade off. Steps hollow*)

Nikki (*scared*): Ellery! Wait for me! It's so dark . . . (*Climbs stairs. Violin still playing, but a little louder now. Whispers*) Isn't that violin music of Webber's — louder, Ellery?

Ellery: Yes. This passage must act as a gigantic amplifier.

Nikki (*whisper*): I wonder where these stairs go. It's so — eerie.

Ellery: Obviously lead to an attic of some sort . . . (*Opens creaky door*) There you are, Nikki. An attic, as predicted.

Nikki: Oooh! (*Laughs nervously*) I — I thought that was a bat. But it was just a cobweb. I wonder how these stairs happen to be here.

Ellery: It's an old house. The stairs to the attic were probably boarded up during some past renovation. Bobby's rediscovered them . . . What's that? (*Creaking steps going off*)

Nikki (*panic*): Ellery! Don't leave me in the dark!

Ellery (*off*): Oh, come, Nikki, I thought you were boasting a moment ago of how grown-up you are. Look at this sign.

Nikki (*fading on*): Sign? What does it say?

Ellery: It says: Robert Hayes, Magician — in the crude printed capitals of a boy of ten, Nikki. And this box here . . . (*Pause. Opens box*)

Nikki: What *is* that mess in there?

Ellery: Wand, magic handkerchiefs, cards, trick coins, handcuffs, ropes, collapsible knife . . . the usual magician's truck. Ah!

Nikki: Now what are you ah-ing about? Oh, that little packet. What's that — magic paper?

Ellery (*gravely*): No, Nikki. It's a subtler and more deadly magic.

Nikki: Ellery! You don't mean —

Ellery (*same*): But I do, Nikki. It's white powder. Arsenic.

Nikki: Arsenic! (*Pause*) Oh, I can't believe it. It's too — revolting, Ellery!

Ellery (*thoughtfully*): I wonder why Gordini didn't tell the truth. He knew all the time.

Nikki (*sick*): But Ellery . . . a boy. A boy of ten!

Ellery (*abruptly*): Let's go downstairs, Nikki, and get it over with!

(*Music up . . . and into jury spot*)

Challenge to the Listener

After giving the studio jury a chance to give solution(s) to the mystery, Ellery returned to the story.

(Music up . . . and into background of murmurs from cast)

Inspector *(low, irritated)*: But how *can* you know, Ellery? I've seen everything you've seen — I've got all the facts you've got — and they don't add up to anything.

Ellery: Oh, but they do, dad. You're just a bad mathematician.

Inspector *(reluctantly)*: Unless this kid — this Bobby —

Velie: Say, you don't think *he* . . . *(uncomfortably)* Nuts. I'm in the wrong business, I guess.

Nikki *(distressed)*: Please, Ellery — do it quickly, and . . . painlessly. That poor woman . . .

Inspector *(harshly)*: All right, all right, let's go. We'll all be bawling in a minute. *(Raises voice)* Attention, please! *(Murmurs stop. Curtly)* Okay, Ellery. *(Silence)*

Florence *(scared by it)*: Bobby. Bobby, come here to mother.

Bobby: Why's everybody so quiet, mummy? What they gonna do now?

Florence *(same)*: Bobby. Go to mummy's room. Go, Bobby!

Bobby: But I wanna see it, mummy! I never seen how a real d'tective gets his man. I wanna see —

Florence *(half-hysterical)*: Bobby, go, I tell you!

Ellery *(gravely)*: I think, Mrs. Hayes, it would be better if Bobby remained here.

Florence *(whisper)*: If Bobby . . . remained? But —

Gordini *(harshly)*: Why don't you let the boy go, Queen? This is no place for a kid of ten. His mother's right!

Ellery *(gently)*: Then suppose you tell us, Mr. Gordini, who poisoned Sarah Brink. Tell us, and I'll send Bobby away.

Gordini *(explosively)*: No! *(Despair)* No.

Bobby: I don't wanna go 'way!

Ellery *(gently)*: *Why* won't you tell us, Mr. Gordini?

Gordini *(despair)*: Because — I've no proof! You wouldn't believe me.

Ellery *(gently)*: I see. *(Pause. Abruptly)* Gordini, you and Bobby are great friends, aren't you?

Bobby *(proudly)*: Sure, me and Mr. Gordini are pals.

Florence *(half-crying)*: Bobby, be quiet!

Ellery: And Bobby's at the age when he's most susceptible to the fascinations of secret passages, sliding panels, and — magic, Gordini. Eh? You've been teaching Bobby magic, haven't you?

Bobby: Yes, *sir!* Y'oughta see all the tricks Mr. Gordini showed —

Gordini (*despair*): Bobby — don't say anything —

Ellery (*gently*): And when Mr. Gordini showed you all these wonderful magic tricks, Bobby, what did he tell you?

Bobby: Oh, he tol' me I hadda practice — all the time. That's the on'y way I'd *ever* grow up to be a great m'gician.

Ellery (*same*): And when you took Sergeant Velie's revolver, and my fountain-pen, and Inspector Queen's snuffbox, and Miss Porter's vanity-case . . . when you took them from us right under our noses, Bobby — you *were* practicing, weren't you? Practicing to make your hands quicker than other people's eyes? (*General gasp of astonishment*)

Florence (*shocked*): Bobby — you . . . *stole* things? Mr. Queen, he couldn't have — he's only a child — he didn't know what he was doing —

Bobby: I did, too, mummy. On'y I wasn't *stealing* 'em. I left 'em right on the ol' table in the downstairs hall, didn't I? I just wanted to see if I *could*. That's not stealin' . . . (*Getting scared*) Mummy, I *didn't* steal! Don't cry, mummy —

Inspector (*mutter*): Come on, Ellery. Get it over with, will you?

Ellery (*gravely*): And you took that packet of white powder, too, didn't you, Bobby? And hid it in your attic hideout?

Florence: White *powder?* (*Sharply*) Bobby! Don't answer!

Bobby: But why not, mummy? Sure I took it. Mr. Gordini tol' me to look for pack'ges of white powder, like flour, an' to take 'em an' give 'em to him soon's as I got the chance to. But that one in the attic — I . . . I didn't get the chance. I was *gonna* give it to Mr. Gordini, but —

Gordini (*low*): Bobby. Don't say any more. Don't!

Inspector: Why not, Gordini? What *is* this? Are you going to talk —

Ellery (*sharply*): One moment, dad. Bobby, what else did Mr. Gordini tell you to do?

Bobby (*hesitating*): He tol' me . . . Nothin'. Nothin'.

Ellery (*more gently*): You can tell me, Bobby. You see, I *know*.

Bobby (*surprised*): You do? Yeah, sure, you're a d'tective. D'tectives gotta know everything. (*Sadly*) But I promised not to tell. So I can't, you see.

Ellery: Mr. Gordini told you there was something you had to do to *save your mother's life*. Was that it, Bobby?

Bobby: Gee! How'd you know that, sir? Gosh!

Florence: To . . . save . . . *my* life?

Ellery: And you had to do that thing every time your mother and your Aunt Sarah had rabbit stew, didn't you, Bobby?

Bobby: Gee, that's right. It was somethin' fierce. I hadda watch all the time. I hadda save my mother's life. I dunno why but that's what Mr. Gordini tol' me.

Gordini (*groaning*): Bobby . . .

Ellery: And when you couldn't do this thing without your mother and aunt seeing you, Bobby, you were a very clever little boy and decided to *distract their attention*. So a week ago you deliberately let the canary out of its cage. And this afternoon you deliberately upset the fishbowl . . .

Inspector: But why, Ellery? For the love of Mike, *why*?

Ellery (*curtly*): Because, dad, while his mother and aunt were chasing that canary last week, while they were saving the goldfish today, *Bobby switched his mother's and his aunt's plates of rabbit stew!*

Nikki: What!

Ellery (*same*): And so, when they returned to the table, Sarah Brink ate the stew intended for her sister Florence . . . Instead of Florence being poisoned, it was Sarah Brink who was poisoned! (*Gravely*) . . . and who, today, died.

Inspector (*incredulous*): You mean that Sarah Brink — Sarah *Brink* . . .

Ellery (*incisively*): I mean that the poisoner in this case is, and was from the beginning, *Sarah Brink*. She was trying to poison her sister Florence. But through Bobby's watchfulness and intervention, instigated by Gordini, Sarah Brink succeeded only in poisoning herself!

(*Music up . . . and into soft dance band background, murmurs*)

Ellery (*sighs*): Dim lights, soft music, happy people, food that's reasonably free from arsenic . . . Let's dance, Nikki!

Nikki: Ellery Queen, you're the meanest man! You always ask me to do things I want to do when I — I don't want to do them. I mean . . . *how* in the world did you ever figure out that Bobby switched those two plates of stew to save his mother's life? I won't sleep until I know!

Ellery: Lord, I couldn't have *that* on my conscience. Although you should have seen through it yourself, Nikki.

Nikki: Go on — rub it in. I'm a simpleton . . . But *tell* me!

Ellery (*laughing*): Well, Nikki, it was the rabbits — the rabbits told me the whole yarn. Doc Prouty said today that *rabbits are immune to arsenic*. Immune to arsenic, Nikki! So if you fed rabbits on lettuce which had been dosed with the poison, it wouldn't hurt them a bit. But what about their flesh? Naturally their flesh would become impregnated with the arsenic. Then if you made a rabbit stew of the flesh of the arsenic-fed animals, you'd be arsenically poisoned. Isn't that simple?

Nikki: But how did you *know* the rabbits were being fed arsenic?

Ellery: Because Flint reported that arsenic had been found in the rabbit-hutch in Sarah Brink's backyard. That proved the animals were being fed the poison *while they were still alive* . . . that the poison was in the flesh of the rabbits *before* they were killed and cooked!

Nikki: But how did that lead you to Sarah Brink's guilt?

Ellery: That was the easiest part of all. Knowing arsenic to have been present in the rabbits even before the stew was cooked and knowing that only *one* portion of the stew was poisoned — remember that twice Florence Hayes ate and was unaffected — I asked myself: Who could have controlled the preparation of the stew, *so* rigidly, that one portion of stew was cooked with poisoned rabbit and the other with *unpoisoned* rabbit? The answer could only have been: One person, and one person alone — the *cook.*

Nikki (*seeing it*): And Sarah Brink was her own cook!

Ellery: Exactly, Nikki. She herself testified to that. She was her own cook, she permitted no one in her kitchen — so it had to be Sarah who had controlled the poisoned and unpoisoned portions. Next question: Was Sarah Brink trying to poison herself? Obviously absurd. Then was she trying to poison Bobby? No, he detested rabbit stew — wouldn't eat it, and apparently Sarah made not the slightest effort to force him to eat it. So she could only have been trying to poison the only other person in the family — who was very fond of rabbit stew — her sister Florence.

Nikki (*excitedly*): I see, I see. Sarah's plan could only have gone wrong if someone switched the two plates. And Bobby was the only one who could have switched them on both occasions. So that's how you knew!

Ellery: Yes. Of course I realized a child of ten couldn't be aware of the significance of what he was doing. So he must have been directed. Who could have been his director? Obviously Gordini — Bobby's magic-teacher, his tin god.

Nikki: How did Gordini know what was going on? How did he *know* Sarah was trying to poison her sister Florence?

Ellery: He told dad about that a few minutes ago. He saw Sarah feeding one of the rabbits in the backyard with a carrot sprinkled with a white powder. He investigated, found some grains of the powder on the hutch floor, as dad's men did over a week later, and analyzed the powder. Being a former chemist, he found it was arsenic, knew rabbits are immune to arsenic, and realized that Sarah was trying to poison her sister. But he had no real proof, and he saw a way to prevent the murder. Under the cloak of teaching Bobby how to become a magician — admirable psychology to use on a boy of ten! — he impressed on Bobby the necessity of always switching his mother's and aunt's plates of rabbit stew. Gordini rather grimly chose to act as Sarah Brink's judge and executioner, using Bobby as his innocent instrument. His plan was simply to make Sarah Brink, a would-be poisoner, poison herself instead.

Nikki: And Sarah — *why* did she want to poison her sister? Mrs. Hayes has nothing . . .

Ellery: Oh, no, Nikki, Mrs. Hayes very definitely has *something*. Mrs. Hayes has a son — a son who was Sarah Brink's nephew, and Sarah Brink was a spinster who resented her sister's youth and motherhood, and wanted her sister's child for herself. We'll never be sure, since the woman's dead, but I'm convinced it was a psychopathic case — a case of frustrated mother love.

Nikki *(thoughtfully)*: Frustrated mother love . . . *(Abruptly)* Ellery, let's dance!

Ellery *(laughing)*: With pleasure, Funny-Face . . . Hold on! What connection is there between frustrated mother love and your asking me to dance?

Nikki *(grimly)*: Mr. Queen, you'd probably be surprised!

(Dance music up)

Detective-story writers of the 1930's were known for favorite plot-devices — John Dickson Carr for the locked room, Agatha Christie for the least-likely suspect, Dorothy L. Sayers for strange murder-methods, Freeman Wills Crofts for seemingly unbreakable alibis, and Ellery Queen for the dying message — in which the victim leaves a cryptic message identifying his or her killer. In "The Adventure of the March of Death," broadcast on October 15, 1939, Queen presents the listener with a "filthy with dough" old man about to change his will, and a dying message which seems to implicate all of his children.

The Adventure of the March of Death

The Characters

Ellery Queen	The detective
Sergeant Velie	Of the New York Police
Inspector Queen	Of the New York Police
Samuel March	Filthy with dough
Jasper Bates	His secretary
Lt. Patrick March	March's son
Robert March	March's son
Edwina Fay	Robert's wife
Roberta March	March's daughter
Marquis of Grange	Roberta's husband
Mr. Fitzroy	March's attorney

Army colonel, orderly, Philippine, Argentinian, Peruvian, Monte Carlo, Puerto Rican, French, Algerian, and Egyptian telephone operators, doctor

Setting: New York City, 1939

(*Interior running auto, through Fifth Avenue traffic . . . Sergeant Velie (driving) sings lustily ad lib . . .*)

Ellery (*grumpily*): Cheerful little soul aren't you, Sergeant?
Velie: Merry sunshine — that's me. 'Course you (*Whistles tune*)
Ellery (*dangerously*): Yes? What about *me*?
Velie (*hastily*): Nothin', Mr. Queen, not a thing. (*Whistles tune*) (*Casual*) Hear from Nikki Porter yet?
Ellery (*shouting*): No!

Velie: Look, I didn't — (*Toot horn . . . squeal of brakes. Velie yelling out*) You
tired o' livin', jaywalker? (*Mumbles to himself as motor becomes louder*)
Ellery (*softly*): What made you ask if I'd heard from Nikki Porter *yet* —
Sergeant?
Velie: Huh? Why, nothin'. I just asked.
Ellery (*steely*): How did *you* know I hadn't heard from her?
Velie: Why . . . uh . . . I know she went on a vacation, and . . . uh . . . I just
imagined . . .
Ellery (*same*): You *have* no imagination! Dad told you!
Velie (*feebly*): Well, maybe the Inspector did sorta mention —
Ellery (*deceptive softness*): You know what, Sergeant? You and my father
are a couple of gossipy old biddies.
Velie: But, Mr. Queen, all I said —
Ellery (*raving*): I know what you said! And I'm sick of it! That's all I've
been hearing since Nikki went away — Nikki this, Nikki that. Suppose
she *hasn't* written to me? That's her privilege, isn't it?
Velie (*hastily*): Absolutely, Mr. Queen.
Ellery: *I* don't own her!
Velie (*same*): You sure don't, Mr. Queen.
Ellery: She's just a secretary, a typist, an — an employee of mine!
Velie: That's the truth, Mr. Queen.
Ellery (*subsiding*): Well, then, there you are . . .
Velie (*sighing*): I didn't think we'd make it. (*Quickly*) How much further
up Fift' Avenoo is this place you're goin' to, Mr. Queen?
Ellery (*with a start*): Hnnh? Oh, a few blocks north of here.
Velie (*trying to re-establish entente cordiale*): Samuel March's house, did ye
say?
Ellery: Did I? I suppose I did.
Velie (*trying flattery*): You sure get around, Mr. Queen. Visitin' mer-can-
tile princes! Guys lou — filthy with dough! What sorta bug is this
Sam March? My wife's always runnin' up charge accounts in his
department store.
Ellery (*indifferently*): Never saw the man in my life.
Velie: Oh, a case, huh? I thought you wasn't takin' cases days.
Ellery (*another burst of temper*): Why not? Why shouldn't I take a case?
Just because Nikki went off on a vacation, you and dad think — I
won't have you bringing Nikki into the conversation again, Velie!
Velie (*feebly*): Who — me? (*Hastily*) Well, here we are. (*Car drawing to
curb*) I *think* this is it. There's the number. But it looks like the Mu-
zeem of Natural History! (*Pulls emergency brake, motor running*)
Ellery (*glumly*): It's the Museum of Samuel March. (*Opens car door . . .
steps out*) Uh, Sergeant.
Velie (*off a little*): Yeah, Mr. Queen?

Ellery (*embarrassed*): Uh . . . thanks for the lift.

Velie: 'sall right, 'sall right. Happy hunting! (*Releases brake*)

Ellery (*same*): Uh . . . Sergeant . . .

Velie (*off a little*): Yeah, Mr. Queen?

Ellery (*very quickly*): Sorry Ilostmytempergoodnight! (*Slams car door. Footsteps fading quickly on pavement*)

Velie (*softly on mike*): A case, huh? Man, oh man, have *you* got a case!

(*Music up and into . . .*)

Bates (*fading on . . . oldish man*): Mr. Ellery Queen?

Ellery: Yes. Mr. March?

Bates: Oh, no. I'm Jasper Bates. Sorry to have kept you waiting, Mr. Queen. If you'll come with me?

Ellery: Thank you. (*Steps across polished floor*)

Bates (*over steps*): You see, Mr. March isn't feeling well —

Ellery (*absently*): Nothing serious, I trust.

Bates: No, no. Just a slight cold. (*Steps stop*) Up this staircase, Mr. Queen. (*No step sounds*)

Ellery: Are you a member of the March family, Mr. Bates?

Bates (*laughing*): Heavens, no! I'm a sort of secretary, companion, watchdog — an all round what-have-you. This way, please. (*Steps again on floor*)

Ellery: What's the nature of the case, Mr. Bates?

Bates: I'm afraid Mr. March will have to tell you himself, sir. Here we are. (*Discreet raps on wooden door*)

March (*sharp old voice . . . muffled*): Come in, Bates, come in! Is that fellow Queen with you? (*Door opens*)

Bates: This is Mr. Ellery Queen, Mr. March.

Ellery: How do you do, sir.

March (*grunts*): Bates, shut the door. (*Door closes*) Sit down, Queen. No, Bates, don't go. Nurse, get out of here!

Nurse (*hastily fading*): Yes, Mr. March . . .

Ellery: Sorry to see you in bed, Mr. March. I hope nothing —

March: How can you be sorry I'm in bed? You don't know me from Adam. That's the kind of useless talk that wastes time!

Ellery (*astonished*): But I merely — (*Stops, laughs*) Mr. March, you're perfectly right. What did you want to see me about?

March (*brusquely*): What d'ye know about me?

Ellery: Only that you own the largest department store in New York . . .

March (*grunts*): Queen, I've got three children.

Ellery: Yes?

March: Take my word for it . . . you couldn't find three more self-centered, ungrateful, and completely useless individuals than my elder son Patrick and my twins Robert and Roberta!

Ellery: I'm sorry to hear that, Mr. March.

March: Now you're wasting time again. What do I care whether you're sorry! Keep still and let me talk!

Bates (*low*): That's just his way, Mr. Queen. He's really not —

March: Stop mumbling, Bates! Queen, I want you to find my three children!

Ellery (*astounded*): *Find* them! Do you mean you don't know where your own children are?

March (*shouting*): Would I ask you to find 'em if I did? (*Calmer*) Haven't seen 'em for years. They cleared out. Deserted me! After what I did for them! Well, never mind. The point is: Can you find them for me?

Ellery: My dear sir, I don't think —

March: Don't "dear sir" me! I asked you a simple question. Can you find them!

Ellery: Of course I can. But —

March: All right, then. My older son, Patrick, is in the United States Army, or was, last time I heard of him —

Bates: He can be traced through Washington, Mr. Queen —

March (*quiet menace*): Bates.

Bates (*mumble*): Sorry sir.

March: Now. The twins.

Ellery: But Mr. March —

March: Don't interrupt. Robert married a concert pianist, a woman called Edwina Fay. Robert's always travelling with her on her eternal concert tours, so he can be practically anywhere. Roberta, his twin sister, is on the loose, too . . . world doesn't seem big enough for *my* children . . . (*Fit of coughing*)

Bates (*alarmed*): Mr. March, let me call the nurse —

March (*stop coughing*): Bates, you're annoying me! Where was I? Oh, yes, Roberta. On the loose. Roberta married a title — some English loafer or other — what's his name, Bates?

Bates: The Marquis of Grange, Mr. March.

March: Yes, yes, something like that. They're probably in Biarritz or the Swiss Alps or some other expensive place, spending the money I settled on Roberta when I was temporarily out of my mind.

Bates (*hastily*): Mr. March doesn't mean —

March: Queen knows what I don't mean! All right, Queen, there's your data. Go to work. Bates, show Queen out.

Ellery: I'm afraid there's a slight misunderstanding, Mr. March.

March: Eh? Misunderstanding?

Ellery: I never said I would take your case. In fact, I shan't. It's not in my line. What you need is an ordinary run-of-the-mill detective agency. (*Pause*)

March: You won't take it, you say?

Ellery: Sorry.

March: Good night. Bates, find another detective.

Bates: Yes, Mr. March. This way, Mr. Queen . . .

Ellery: Thank you. (*Door opens*) Oh, one question, Mr. March —

March (*off a little*): Eh? What d'ye want?

Ellery: Indulge my curiosity. How is it, after years of separation, you suddenly want to locate your three children?

March (*pause . . . then grimly*): I'm having a new will drawn up.

Ellery: Strictly speaking, that doesn't answer my question. (*Softly*) Or perhaps it does. (*Louder*) Then you haven't changed your will yet?

March: No. (*Pause*) (*Laugh*) That would spoil the . . . ceremony.

Ellery: I see . . . (*Suddenly*) Mr. March. I've changed my mind. I'll accept this assignment.

March (*grunts*): You will. Well, it's up to you. All right, Bates, give him a ratainer. Whatever he asks. I warn you, Queen, even if you locate them, they may not come. And you don't get paid the full fee unless they come home!

Ellery (*quietly*): I think they'll come, Mr. March. You see, I'll tell them you're — dying.

March: Dying? (*Chuckles*) Just the thing — just the thing. Brilliant idea. (*Sudden yell*) Well, what are you waiting for? Get busy and find those — three — vermin!

(*Music up . . . "Communications" theme . . . then down under*)

New York Operator (*light filter*): New York calling Lieutenant Patrick March, Washington, D.C.

Washington Operator (*light filter*): Washington, D.C. We cannot locate Lieutenant Patrick March.

New York Operator (*same*): New York calling Lieutenant Patrick March, United States Army Post, Manilla, Philippine Island.

Philippine Operator (*heavy filtration*): Manilla, Philippine Island. We cannot locate Lieutenant Patrick March.

New York Operator (*light filter*): New York calling Lieutenant Patrick March, United States Army Post, San Juan, Puerto Rico.

Puerto Rico Operator (*heavy filtration*): San Juan, Puerto Rico. Lieutenant Patrick March is not at United States Army Post.

New York Operator: New York calling Lieutenant Patrick March, United State Army Post, Panama City.

Panama Operator (*heavy filtration*): Panama City, Lieutenant Patrick March. Just a minute. Here's your party.

(*Music up . . . with suggestion of military theme of U.S. army and fade into opening of door (off) with soldierly steps fading on*)

Orderly: Lieutenant Patrick March to see the Colonel, sir.

Colonel: Oh, yes, Corporal. Send the Lieutenant in. (*Steps fading, murmur off . . . Lieutenant's steps on*)

Patrick (*formally*): Lieutenant March reporting to the Colonel —

Colonel (*cordially*): At ease, Lieutenant. Sit down, sit down.

Patrick: Thank you, sir. (*Crackle of document*)

Colonel: March, I find you've applied for an extended leave and stated the reason as "personal."

Patrick: Yes, Colonel.

Colonel: Well, now, Lieutenant, you know how we're fixed down here at the Canal. With world conditions the way they are . . . Especially important to be fully staffed. Why do you want leave at just this time?

Patrick: I've received a communication from a man signing himself Queen . . . private detective, I gather — who's been trying to locate me for my father for some time, Colonel . . .

Colonel (*astonished*): You mean your father doesn't know where you're stationed, Lieutenant March?

Patrick (*embarrassed*): That's right, Colonel. We're not on — very good terms. Matter of fact, I haven't seen the gov'nor for five years. I suppose I haven't been a very good son.

Colonel (*coldly*): I should think not. Well?

Patrick: This man Queen says my father is dying.

Colonel (*coldly*): I see. Sorry.

Patrick (*low*): Thank you, Colonel. I can cut the time down if I fly. Say, to Havana or New Orleans, and catch a New York plane from there . . . My father wants to see me, Colonel. If the Colonel could possibly —

Colonel (*formally*): Leave granted. I'll send this through at once. That's all, Lieutenant.

Patrick: I don't know how to thank you, Colonel . . .

Colonel (*coldly*): Dismissed, Lieutenant . . .

(*Music up . . . "Communications" theme . . . then down under*)

New York Operator (*light filter*): New York calling Robert March, Hotel International, Rio de Janeiro.

Rio de Janeiro Operator (*heavy filtration*): (*Spanish accent*) Rio de Janiero. We cannot locate Robert March.

New York Operator (*light filter*): New York calling Robert March, Hotel Ambassador, Lima, Peru.

Lima Operator (*heavy filtration*): (*Spanish accent*) Lima, Robert March cannot be reached at the Hotel Ambassador.

New York Operator (*light filter*): New York calling Robert March at the Hotel Coronado, Buenos Aires.

Buenos Aires Operator (*heavy filtration*): (*Spanish accent*) Here is Mr. March.

(*Music up . . . and fade into concert rendition of piano playing Beethovan's Sonata in A-Flat . . . the wind-up . . . repeated applause as of large audience . . . shouts of "Brava" . . . into backstage murmurs and babble of enthusiastic approbation . . .*)

Argentinian (*enthusiastically*): Ah, Señora Fay — magnifico — brilliante! Hear the applause . . . I may keess the Señora's hands — these inspired, impassioned hands?

Edwina (*happily*): Such extravagance, Señor Miranda! But you're very kind. Your countrymen . . . all of you.

Argentinian: Never has Buenos Aires heard such music of the piano! The Beethoven Sonata in A-Flat . . . such sweep, such emotion, such sadness . . .

Edwina: Thank you, Señor Miranda. It's been a great honor to perform in your beautiful city. Where's my husband? Oh, there you are, darling! Aren't you going to congratulate me? Listen to them out there! (*Still applause off*)

Robert (*fading on . . . harassed*): Edwina . . . I must talk to you at once . . . alone.

Edwina (*alarmed*): Robert! What's happened? You're so pale! Robert, you're not ill —

Robert: No, no. Let's go to your dressing-room, Edwina —

Argentinian (*off*): But Señora — they are shouting for you —

Edwina (*distressed*): Señor Miranda — so sorry — please explain to them — something's happened — (*Open door. Close. Shut out sounds*) Robert! Darling! Tell me what's happened.

Robert (*slowly . . . strained*): I've just received a cable from — some detective named Queen. Father's — dying.

Edwina: Oh, Robert. (*Softly*) You poor dear.

Robert (*shouting*): Poor dear! That's not what you really mean! You've heckled me for years about my attitude towards father. Go on — say it! It's my fault!

Edwina: Robert, I've *heckled* you? Oh, darling . . . you're upset. Of course, we must go to New York at once.

Robert: We? Don't be idiotic . . . Edwina. You can't cut your concert tour short . . .

Edwina (*firmly*): Oh, yes, I can. No arguments. Robert, we'll pack and leave immediately.

(*Music up . . . "Communications" theme . . . then down under*)

New York Operator (*light filter*): New York calling Roberta March Grange, Hotel Le Ville, Monte Carlo.

Monte Carlo Operator (*heavy filtration*): (*French accent*) Monte Carlo. We cannot reach Roberta March Grange.

New York Operator (*light filter*): New York calling 187 Biarritz, 187 Biarritz.

Biarritz Operator (*heavy filtration*): (*French accent*) 187 Biarritz. There is no answer.

New York Operator: New York calling Roberta March Grange, Grand Hotel, Algiers.

Algiers Operator (*heavy filtration*): (*Thick French accent*) Algiers. Your party cannot be located.

New York Operator (*light filter*): Will you try under the name of Roberta March.

Algiers Operator (*heavy filteration*): (*Thick French accent*) Try Cairo, Egypt.

(*Music up . . . into Egyptian dancing-girl native music . . . with background of babble in polyglot tongues as is in native cafe . . .*)

Marquis (*drawl*): Amazin'. Simply amazin'.

Roberta (*bored*): What's amazin', My Lord Marquis?

Marquis: The way these females wiggle. Inhuman! Look at that handsome wench, Roberta! Marvelous . . .

Roberta (*indifferently*): Seems to me you're doing enough "Looking" for both of us. Vivian, I'm bored. Cairo's no place for a civilized woman.

Marquis: Dashed good place for a civilized man. (*Sharp*) Well! What do *you* want?

Native (*fading on*): 'Scuse. Please. Got 'Merican cable for Marchioness of Grange. Send me here — this place —

Marquis (*sharp*): Let's have it! (*thrown coins on table*) Here — bakshish.

Native (*fading — battle*): My Lord Marquis — Madam —

Marquis: Dirty beggar. Faugh. (*Bored*) Here you are, M'dear. Trust it's the usual from your father's solicitors. I'm stony.

Roberta (*over tearing open of envelope*): What do you do with my father's money — eat it? (*Unfolds cable*) (*Slowly*) It's from someone named Ellery Queen, from New York.

Marquis: Bother. (*Music stops. Up on noise*) Hi, that was — stirrin', by George! (*Applauds enthusiastically*)

Roberta (*faintly*): Vivian.

Marquis (*still clapping*): Yes, m'dear? . . . Brava! Brava!

Roberta (*same*): It's — about father. He's dying.

Marquis (*stops applauding*): (*Blankly*) Dyin'? 'Str'ord'n'ry! I always thought Americans live to ninety . . . (*Applauds*) More! Dance more, you there — girl! Bakshish! (*Throws coins on floor*)

Roberta (*whisper*): Father . . . dying . . . (*Wildly*) Vivian, we must go to New York at once!

Marquis: Eh? Oh. Yes, yes, m'dear. Of course. (*Music starts again — up on noise. He applauds*) Wiggle, you girl!

Roberta (*furious*): Vivian! You — rabbit! Did you hear what I said? Take me back to the hotel! Suppose father should die before I return! I'd never forgive myself! (*Almost screaming*) Vivian! Did you hear what I said?

Marquis (*coldly*): Lower your voice, you — shopgirl.

Roberta (*outraged*): Vivian!

Marquis (*cynically*): Play-actress. Your father means as bloody little to you as he does to me. I know what you're afraid of — you're afraid he'll change his will and you'll get there too late to prevent it.

Roberta: Monster!

Marquis (*lazily*): Oh, I quite agree something should be done, Roberta. Can't have the source of all good things dry up, eh? (*Sharp*) You there — you native! My car! We're leavin' at once!

(*Music up . . . perhaps the Sonata theme, or theme of the Eroica Symphony . . . and into general murmur (angry) . . .*)

Robert (*furious*): Of all the low tricks! Getting me up from Buenos Aires! Cancelling Edwina's tour —

Edwina (*soothing*): It's all right, Robert. Please, dear. Don't make a scene. Your father —

Patrick: Father never looked better in his life. I don't know how I'll explain this to the Colonel —

Roberta (*hysterically*): You and your ridiculous Army, Patrick! But look at *me*! Vivian and I came half across the world.

Marquis: Rum country, this. Don't wonder people die young.

Roberta: It's all that man's fault! You there — Queen, or whatever your ridiculous name is! How *dare* you cable —

Ellery (*lightly*): Your father was a party to the deception, Marchioness.

Fitzroy (*coldly*): Don't involve Mr. Queen, please. In this matter he's acted as an agent of your father.

Robert (*furious*): Keep out of this, Fitzroy! Your fine Irish hand's probably behind whatever father's up to!

Fitzroy (*patiently*): I'm merely your father's attorney, Mr. Robert.

Edwina: Please, Robert. Don't upset yourself —

Bates (*fading on — nervous*): Mr. March is coming down. He'll be here directly. Now if you'll all please —

Roberta (*shrilly*): And Bates! You're the one! You've always had some sort of sinister influence over him —

Ellery (*dryly*): From what I've seen of your father, Marchioness, Mr. Bates would have to use hypnosis to do that.

Patrick: Cut it out, Roberta. Here's father. (*Silence*)

March (*fading on*): Ah, my loving children. (*Pause — brisk*) Well, if you'll all sit down, we'll have our little family conference. Fitzroy, you have everything ready?

Fitzroy: Yes, Mr. March. (*Three children break into ad lib queries*)

March (*coldly*): Be still! (*They stop*) I didn't have you three brought here to listen to your snarling. Queen, good job. Get your check from Bates.

Ellery: Thank you, Mr. March. May I remain?

March: Eh? (*Chuckles*) Why not? It may amuse you. (*Curt*) Now listen to me, you three. I'll take you one at a time. Patrick!

Patrick (*quietly*): Yes, father?

March: Patrick, you're my greatest disappointment. As my oldest child I expected you — trained you — to step into the March store and carry on my work. Instead of that, you joined the Army to become a common adventurer.

Patrick (*quietly*): We went all through that, father. I'm proud of my profession.

March: Don't argue with me! Robert!

Robert (*sullenly*): I don't want your sanctimonious lectures. Why did you bring us here — to preach a sermon?

Edwina (*distressed*): Robert! Darling — please . . .

March (*evenly*): When Patrick deserted me, Robert, I looked to *you* to carry on my work. But the department store business wasn't good enough for you — oh, no. You had to have a profession, a degree after your name.

Robert: I wanted to be an architect! What's wrong with that?

March: I gave in, didn't I, Robert? I sent you to the best architectural schools, to Athens, to Rome. When you got your master's degree, I set you up in business. And what did you do?

Robert (*sullenly*): I did my best.

March: You gave up, like the jellyfish you are! And since then you haven't done a lick of honest work! And when I cut you off, to make a man of you, you showed yourself for the spineless worm you are by marrying a woman to support you! You're a gigolo, Robert, a parasite — and you like it.

Edwina (*eagerly*): Mr. March, please. That isn't true. Robert's of great help to me. He helps manage me — arranges my tours — you don't know how hard he's worked, Mr. March — you don't really understand Robert —

March (*ironically*): Oh, I understand him, Edwina. Mind you I've got nothing against *you*. In fact, I admire you. You're doing something in the world. But you're a fool just the same — a fool to have married a man who lets you support him!

Robert (*shouting*): I won't stay here and have my wife insulted —

March: I'm not insulting your wife, my son, I'm insulting *you*. And now — Roberta. My dear, dear daughter. Surely you could have made me happy after your brothers proved such miserable disappointments? But what did *you* do? Married a title — a broken-down, moth-eaten, rusty old title!

Roberta (*gasping*): Father! How dare you talk about the Marquis of Grange in this — this *common* way?

Marquis (*hastily*): It's all right, m'dear — there's a good deal in what your worthy father says . . .

March (*sarcastically*): Thank you, My Lord Marquis. But that won't pay your passage back to England. Roberta, you haven't written me for years except to whine for more money, so that you can gad about the fanciest pest-holes of Europe — spending my money, parading your title, showing off this cynical, worthless he-duchess of yours . . . You fool. (*Angry ad libs from children*)

Bates: Mr. March, you're exciting yourself. Don't you think —

March: Shut up, Bates! (*Quiet*) Well, children, you've had your chance and you've thrown it away. I've given you every advantage. Now I'm through giving. I'm *taking*. I'm going to hurt you in the only spot where you feel pain. I'm cutting all of you off without a penny. (*Pause — tensely*) Yes, that's what I called you here to tell you. That neither while I live, nor after I die will any of you get a single cent of my money! (*Another pause*) By tomorrow I'll have signed a new will, and you'll be through. Through!

Roberta (*crying*): But father — everything? Your business —

March: I'm leaving the store to my employees. They've worked hard to build it up, and they deserve to share in it.

Patrick (*low voice*): Not that it makes any difference now, father . . . but what are you doing with your personal fortune?

March: After all necessary taxes and deductions there will be about three million dollars left. It goes to my only friend and companion of twenty years — Jasper Bates.

Bates (*gasping*): Mr. March! I didn't know — You can't —

Patrick (*quietly*): Nice going, Bates. You must have been voted "Most Likely to Succeed" in your Senior year.

Roberta (*screaming*): It's a — a plot, a conspiracy! We'll have *nothing!* Vivian, do something — Patrick! Robert!

Robert (*passionately*): Father, you're insane! You're *mad!*

Patrick (*gruffly*): Stop that kind of talk, Robert.

March (*softly*): Don't worry, Robert, I've thought of that, too. You won't break *my* will on the grounds of insanity. I've taken steps to insure *that*. Eh, Fitzroy?

Fitzroy (*coldly*): There isn't a chance that the new will can be attacked on any grounds whatsoever. (*Roberta sobbing*)

March (*coldly*): Now get out, the three of you. I never want to see or hear from you again.

Roberta (*wildly*): Father! Father, you *can't* —

Robert (*hoarsely*): This is a nightmare. Father, you . . .

Edwina (*gently*): Come, Robert.

Patrick (*short laugh*): I suppose it's no more than we deserve. (*Roberta still sobbing*) Well, father — goodbye. (*Abruptly*) Come on, you two! Let's clear out of here! (*They all fade off in characteristic ad libs*)

Fitzroy (*after silence, broken only by rustle of papers*): Here's the new will, Mr. March. Will you sign it now?

March (*strangled, feeble voice*): No, Fitzroy . . . not now . . . I don't feel so . . . I'll do it this afternoon, Fitzroy.

Fitzroy: You'll arrange for witnesses yourself, too?

March (*same*): Yes, yes, I'll put it in the mail for you late afternoon. You'll get it first thing in the morning. Now go. Please. All of you . . .

Bates (*low*): Mr. March, I can't tell you how —

March (*snarling*): Bates, I said go! (*Laughs without humor*) Well, Queen, did it amuse you? Funny, eh?

Ellery (*grimly*): I don't find it so, Mr. March. Good morning!

(*Music up . . . and into some short musical bridge . . .*)

Ellery: Anyway, that's what happened there this morning, dad.

Inspector (*rustle of newspaper*): What am *I* supposed to do — bust out crying? The troubles of the rich!

Ellery: Just the same . . . I'm worried, dad. I've been worried about this situation from the very beginning. That's why I decided to take the case after all.

Inspector: Oh, rats! If it isn't Nikki it's something else. What's worrying you, Ellery?

Ellery: It's — a dangerous set-up, dad. Old man March couldn't have asked for it more plainly if he'd sent out engraved invitations!

Inspector: What are you talking about? Invitation to what?

Ellery (*quietly*): Murder. (*Pause*) Murder . . .

Inspector: Oh, you're balmy. Nikki's leaving *has* done things to you. You need a vacation yourself. (*Newspaper rustle again*)

Ellery: Dad . . .

Inspector: Well?

Ellery: Send Velie up to watch the March house, will you?

Inspector: Send Velie . . . What in time for?

Ellery: Go on, dad. Tell Velie to keep his eyes open — to hang around there at least until old man March signs that new will late this afternoon —

Inspector: Ellery, you're getting to be a psychopathic case.

Ellery (*eagerly*): Then you'll do it?

Inspector (*laughing — puts down paper*): I suppose I've got to humor you. (*Picks up phone, dials once*) Operator. Get me Police Headquarters.

(*Music up . . . same bridge as before — and into ringing of phone. Remove receiver . . .*)

Ellery (*wearily*): Yes?

Inspector (*filtered throughout scene*): Ellery, where the Sam Hill you been all afternoon? I've been ringing the apartment for hours!

Ellery (*wearily*): I just got in, dad. I was over at the Library doing some research on poisons. What's up?

Inspector: What's up! Didn't you see the afternoon papers?

Ellery (*slowly*): No. Dad, you don't mean — (*Sharp*) Dad!

Inspector (*grimly*): Old Samuel March's invitation's been accepted!

Ellery (*groaning*): He's been *murdered*? Oh, lord, I knew something like this would happen! Where was Velie? Didn't you send Velie up there to watch him —

Inspector: Velie was there, but March kicked him out and he had to hang around outside. Matter of fact, it was Velie who finally found the body.

Ellery: How was he murdered? Dad, talk!

Inspector: Velie found him in his study, seated at his desk, stabbed to death. With his own paper-knife. We've just finished the preliminary investigation —

Ellery: Why wasn't I home, blast it! Where's the body?

Inspector: Been removed. Want to look the place over?

Ellery: Of course! Are you calling from the March house?

Inspector: Yes. Everybody's gone by now. I stayed behind to call you.

Ellery: Any clues?

Inspector: Just one, but it's a honey. Know what March did before he passed out? *He wrote down his murderer's name!*

Ellery: He *what?* But good heavens —! Then of course you don't need me. Who is it, dad? Whose name did he write?

Inspector: That's just it. We don't know.

Ellery (*groaning*): This seems to be my bad day. He wrote the murderer's name, but you don't *know* it?

Inspector: We do know it. I mean — Cripe! Point is, Ellery, it's so simple I don't understand it.

Ellery: Let's take this slowly, dad. March wrote down a name. What name? Spell it out for me.

Inspector: M-A-R-C-H. March.

Ellery: March! You mean he left his *own* name as a clue? Dad, I'll be right over!

Inspector: Well, make it snappy. I've got to — (*Stops abruptly as smack of something on head. Inspector groans. Thud of body on floor — all heard over phone*)

Ellery (*jiggling hook*): Dad! What's the matter? Dad! (*Clearly audible sound of other receiver being replaced on hook*) Dad! (*Jiggles frantically*) Operator! Operator!

Operator (*filtered*): You've been disconnected, sir —

Ellery (*shouting*): Don't sit there gabbing! Get me Police Headquarters! Emergency!

Operator (*swiftly — filtered*): Yes, sir! (*Clicks, etc.*)

Officer (*filtered*): Police Headquarters . . .

Ellery: This is Ellery Queen — Inspector Richard Queen's son! Send out a radio alarm! Get Sergeant Velie! Send anybody! The Samuel March house, Fifth Avenue —

Officer (*swiftly — filtered*): Yes, Mr. Queen. What's the trouble?

Ellery (*shouting*): Don't ask questions, hang it! For all I know my father's been murdered!

(*Music up . . . sirens motif . . . and into murmurs*)

Ellery (*anxiously*): Are you all right now, dad? You're sure you're all right?

Inspector (*irritably*): Oh, stop babying me, Ellery . . . Oooooh.

Velie (*heartily*): Say, you couldn't give *that* dome concussion! (*Anxiously*) But maybe you'd better go home, Inspector —

Inspector (*through his teeth*): If ever I get my hands on that . . . (*Trails off into muttered imprecations*)

Ellery (*low*): What do you think, Doctor?

Doctor (*same*): Just a nasty crack on the back of the head, Mr. Queen. Behind the ear. He'll be perfectly all right.

Ellery (*same*): You're sure there's no danger of concussion?

Doctor: Not the slightest.

Inspector: I'm okay *now*. Thanks, Doc . . . Ellery! Come here!

Ellery: Take it easy now, dad. Don't get excited —

Inspector: I'll excite somebody. Lucky for that so-and-so I didn't see him. Sneaked up on me while I was talking to you on the phone and, wham! Next thing I knew these radio-car men and Velie were cooing over me.

Ellery (*musing*): So this is the room where March was murdered . . . I wonder who assaulted you, dad.

Inspector (*sourly*): Who? March's killer, of course.

Ellery: How do you know that?

Inspector: Because after he knocked me out he *destroyed* the clue March left!

Ellery (*sighing*): I'd better start from the beginning. Velie, what was the situation when you first found the body?

Velie: The old guy was dead. I found him sittin' in that chair there at his desk, his head restin' on the desk like he'd fell asleep. The paper-knife was in his hand — tight. There was a deep, bloody stab wound in his chest, right over the heart.

Inspector: Doc Prouty said he didn't die right away, though it's a cinch his killer *thought* he was dead.

Velie: I musta scared the killer away; he musta heard me prowlin' around, and took it on the lam.

Inspector: Anyway, March wasn't quite dead. He knew who'd stabbed him, of course. So he wanted to leave a clue — to write out the killer's name . . .

Velie: Wasn't no pen or pencil handy, and he was too far gone to poke around in a drawer —

Inspector (*grimly*): Anyway, what that old bird did was — well, superhuman, Ellery. He pulled the knife out of his chest and used it to write with!

Ellery: Good lord!

Velie: Yep, scratched the name "March" into the top of the desk with the point of the letter-knife.

Ellery (*excited*): And then died! And now the killer's come back and, with a knife of his own, *obliterated the name* the dying man wrote! That's — extraordinary.

Velie: *I* calls it nuts. Look at the veneer on the top o' this desk! All scraped off where March scratched the word in!

Ellery: But what good did it do March's murderer to scrape off the word March had written? He must have known the police had already seen it . . . It's really staggering.

Inspector: That isn't all. After scraping off the name "March," this killer searched the desk and room . . . look at the mess this room is in! It wasn't that way when we originally found the body.

Ellery: Searched . . . Of course! He was looking for the new will — probably hadn't had opportunity at the time of the murder because the Sergeant here scared him away. Did he find the will?

Inspector: No, sirree. We found it when we originally examined the body.

Velie: An' I took it down to Headquarters with me when I left the Inspector here. So *he* goes and gets slugged!

Ellery: Had Samuel March signed that new will of his?

Inspector (*grimly*): He had not.

Ellery: The quixotic fool! Then March's estate will be administered under his *old* will?

Inspector: That's the ticket. March's lawyer Fitzroy says the estate under the old will is divided equally among the three children. There are no other heirs. Not even Bates.

Velie (*chuckling*): Tough on li'l Jasper, ain't it? Somebody done him outa three million bucks!

Ellery: Dad, pretend you *didn't* find the unsigned new will. Pretend you don't know what happened to it, or whether March signed it or not.

Inspector (*thoughtfully*): Good hunch. Might force somebody's hand —

Ellery: Yes. (*Pause*) "March." "March." Dying man leaves the name "March" as a clue . . . but the name "March" can apply to any of his three children . . . Patrick *March*, Robert *March*, Roberta *March* . . .

Velie: Sure is a lulu of a clue. Looks like he purposely made it tough.

Ellery (*distracted*): Nonsense, Sergeant. That happens only in detective stories . . .

Velie (*dryly*): You oughta know.

Ellery (*unheeding*): There was a reason, a *reason* . . .

Inspector: Well, it's death on rats the old man meant *one* of his three cubs — the clue "March" tells us that. Besides, only the three children benefit by his death —

Ellery: It's a three-horned dilemma, all right . . . unless . . .

Inspector (*after pause*): Unless what, Ellery?

Ellery: Unless the clue of the scratched word refers not to the *name* March but — to some *other* meaning of "march."

Velie: Say. Could be . . . could be.

Inspector: What other meaning? Ellery, you've thought of something.

Ellery (*wryly*): I've thought of some utterly *fantastic* things, that's true . . . have you had a talk with the three surviving Marches yet, dad?

Inspector: No, I'm saving that up for tonight.

Ellery: Then that's when I'll tell you.

(*Music up . . . into general subdued talk . . . Roberta weeping*)

Inspector (*harshly*): These alibis aren't worth the breath I'm wastin' on 'em. Could have been any one of you.

Patrick (*curtly*): Isn't that putting it a bit strong, Inspector.

Robert (*hotly*): Do you realize, man, what you're saying.

Roberta (*sobbing*): And father not — not cold.

Edwina (*quietly*): Roberta, try to control yourself.

Marquis (*eagerly*): Any one know if the old chap signed that new will of his?

Ellery: If you good folk disdain the thought that this was the work of a patricide, how do you explain your father's scratching the name "March" on his desk, just before he died.

Velie: Yeah. How d'ye explain that, you — para-sites.

Robert (*astonished*): You don't take any stock in *that*.

Ellery (*mildly*): Don't I, Mr. Robert March?

Roberta (*wildly*): A dying man — delirious — father *wouldn't*.

Ellery: Father did, Miss Roberta March — or beg pardon . . . Marchioness.

Patrick: How can anyone tell what was going on in poor father's brain? He certainly couldn't have meant one of *us* — he might have meant, not the *name* March, but the *word* March.

Ellery (*softly*): Very astute of you, Lieutenant.

Roberta: Vivian. What does this — this creature mean?

Marquis (*helplessly*): Haven't the remotest notion, m'dear.

Ellery: Then may I enlighten you, My Lord Marquis? Take your wife and her twin-brother, for example. I've discovered that their birth occurred during the *month* of March.

Marquis: Really. 'Str'ord'n'ry!

Robert: Of all the fat-headed jumps in the dark.

Roberta (*weeping again*): Vivian, did you hear what he said?

Ellery: And — oh, yes, Mrs. March. Or I should say, Miss Edwina Fay, since that's the professional name you use —

Edwina (*startled*): I, Mr. Queen? You mean *I* —

Robert: Now he's dragging Edwina into it. The man's insane.

Ellery: I merely wished to point out that your wife, Mr. March, is a famous pianist, and that she is particularly famous for her interpretation of Beethoven's Sonata in A-Flat and the Eroica Symphony . . .

Edwina (*bewildered*): I suppose that's so, Mr. Queen — but what —

Ellery (*softly*): Aren't those two pieces of music, Miss Fay, Beethoven's celebrated funeral *marches*?

Edwina (*laughing*): Ohhh . . . that's funny . . . that's really — funny.

Inspector (*low*): Ellery, come here, will you? Maybe we'd better —

Patrick (*angrily*): Now look here, Queen, enough's enough. Did you call us together to demonstrate what an idiot you are? I'm almost inclined to agree with Robert.

Ellery (*mildly*): Indeed, Lieutenant?

Velie (*excited*): Hey. It coulda been the Lootenant the old dope meant. He's in the Army, ain't he? There's plenty of "March-march-march" in the Army, ain't there?

Inspector (*angrily*): Velie, keep out of this. Ellery, for Pete's sake.

Ellery: And of course, the wife of a Marquis is a Marchioness, isn't that so? Not pronounced the same way, but it begins with the letters m-a-r-c-h.

Roberta: I'm going — simply mad. (*Begins to howl*)

Marquis (*uneasily*): Cut it, m'dear. We don't grasp these things. Not like Scotland Yard at all. P'r'aps —

(*Break out into noisy ad libs all . . . protests . . . "Military March" . . . "Funeral March" . . . "Month of March" . . . "Marchioness" . . . "of all the silly, ridiculous," etc*)

Inspector (*low . . . on mike, over ad libs*): Ellery, you *have* lost your mind. You don't *believe* any of this tripe?

Ellery (*same*): I don't know *what* to believe, dad. But I do know this — the dying man left that clue, and he meant one of these people — and if we could figure out the real meaning of that clue, we'd know *which* one.

(*Music up . . . and into Velie snoring off . . . tick of a clock . . . deep silence except for these sounds . . .*)

Inspector (*angry . . . almost a soliloquy*): Why'd I ever become a cop . . .? Spend the best years of my life like this, at a desk at Headquarters, between a snoring whale and a deaf-mute.

Ellery (*glumly . . . sighing*): Keep your shirt on, dad.

Inspector: Don't tell me you talk. Well, well. (*Same as before*) Nothing. Nothing. No prints in that study — or rather a *million* prints . . . of everybody, so what. The knife? Ah, d'ye suppose he'd slip up on *that*? No, sirree. No prints on the knife but old man March's. Cute, cute . . . I'll get that so-and-so who walloped me on the skull if it's the last thing I do. Velie, Velie. Stop that snoring, you wall-eyed cross between an ape and a brain pickled in formaldehyde. (*Roaring*) Velie.

Velie (*waking up with a snort*): Ohhhhhhhhhhhhhhhhhhh! Oh, (*Yawns*) (*Breaks off yawn . . . excited*) Say. I just remembered.

Both (*instantly . . . breathlessly*): Yes. Yes? What?

Velie (*importantly*): I was just havein' a dream when you woke me up, Inspector . . . I was dreamin' . . .

Inspector (*disgusted*): Aaaaahhh . . .

Velie: Yeah, but get this. I drempt about a kinda-semi-precious stone — a greenish or reddish or brownish kinda stone.

Ellery (*slowly*): You wouldn't mean a jasper, Sergeant?

Velie: Yes, sir, that's it. Saw it plain as day. An' in my dream I says to myself, "Tom," I says, "now that's a funny thing," I says, "Ain't a jasper a kinda birthstone?" I says to myself. In my dream of course. So then I wake up —

Inspector (*snarling*): That was my hard luck. Go back to sleep. Snore. Anything. But stop drooling at the kisser.

Velie (*muttering*): Try to be a help — take a lot o' guff — and for what? I shoulda joined the Navy, like Marie said —

Ellery (*indifferently*): I think jasper was a birthstone only in the ancient system, Sergeant . . . Dad.

Inspector (*barking*): Well?

Ellery: Did your men take a photograph of the desk-top — I mean before the criminal returned to knock you out and scrape off the word "March."

Inspector: Sure we mugged it. Routine. Why?

Ellery: No special reason. Except, of course, that our man doesn't know we have a photograph of the clue. That might possibly make a difference . . . let me see that photo, dad . . . You know I never did see the word as it actually appeared scratched into the top of the desk. (*Click*)

Inspector: Howie, fetch that photo of Sam March's desk-top, will you?

Voice (*filtered*): Yes, Inspector. (*Click . . . inter-office communicator*)

Ellery: How'd you take the photo, dad? Does the word show up clearly?

Inspector: Oh, sure. We used the same system as in shooting fingerprints. Cover the desk with that white chemical powder, blow, and the powder blows off everywhere except from the scratches. In the photo the word shows up white . . . (*Door opens off*)

Same Voice (*fading on*): Here's the photo, Inspector Queen.

Inspector: Right, Howie. There y'are, Ellery. (*Door closes off*)

Velie (*sarcasm*): It says, "March," see it? I went to school . . . I can read. Didn't you believe me?

Ellery: Hmmm. Spells "March" all right . . . capital M, capital A, small r — oh . . . (*Gasping*) Oh, Lord.

Inspector (*alarmed*): Ellery. What's the matter?

Velie (*same*): Say, he looks sick.

Ellery: I am sick. Of all the . . . why didn't you tell me? (*Laughs hilariously*) Lord, if this isn't the funniest thing —

Velie (*nettled*): What's 'a' matter with him?

Inspector (*sharply*): Ellery. Don't tell me you've —

Ellery: Yes, dad. I've got it. (*Gasps from both*) I know whom the old man accused of the crime.

Velie (*dazed*): From just one squint at the photo . . . I'm a dog. I'm an ab-so-loot dog. I oughta go back to a beat.

Ellery: Wait, wait . . . (*Pause*) Yes, that'll do it. Dad, I not only know who killed March, but how to nab him red-handed.

Inspector (*strangled*): All right. How. (*Yelling*) *How?*

Ellery (*quickly*): I want a certain person to find out something — this very night.

Inspector: Find out what? What, Ellery?

Ellery: That you've discovered new evidence — evidence proving that old man March SIGNED his new will.

Velie: But he didn't, Mr. Queen — I got the will right here in the office — he *didn't* sign it.

Ellery: *We* know he didn't, Sergeant, but the murderer doesn't. I want him to think it *was* signed, putting that new will in force the instant it gets into the hands of Fitzroy, the March lawyer.

Inspector (*briskly*): I'm in. What's the yarn, Ellery?

Ellery: Simply say that the old man signed the new will before the murder, had it properly witnessed, and then *mailed* it to Fitzroy. Since the murder occurred only this afternoon, the murderer will believe that now, this very night, that letter with the will in it is in the post-office . . . and that tomorrow morning, in the first mail it will be delivered to Fitzroy. Do you understand?

Inspector (*rapidly*): Got you. But we'll have to work fast — it's getting late. Who is this guy, Ellery? Who I'm supposed to tell this cock- and bull story to?

Ellery: Lean over, dad. I don't trust even the walls of your office —

Velie (*hurriedly*): Hey, wait . . . Lemme get in on this, Mr. Queen. (*Knocks over a chair*) Ouch. Okay, okay.

Inspector (*eagerly*): What's the name, Ellery? Who is it?

Ellery (*low*): The name is —

(*Music up . . . and into jury spot*)

Challenge to the Listener

Ellery (*chuckling*): Well, I almost gave it away that time, didn't I? I really did know *who* killed old Mr. March . . . I can see our armchair detectives are bubbling over with solutions.

(*Downtown early morning street noises . . .*)

Inspector (*guardedly*): Any sign of him, Velie?

Velie (*same — fading on*): Nope, Inspector.

Ellery: Dad, you're sure this is the branch post-office through which the mail to Fitzroy's office has to pass?

Inspector: Sure I'm sure.

Velie: Letter-carriers ain't left yet on their first delivery, I hope. It'd be a shame if —

Inspector: They don't leave for a few minutes yet. (*Thoughtfully*) Wonder if this is going to work.

Ellery: You managed to inform our friend, didn't you, dad, that the new will cutting out the three March children was signed, witnessed, and mailed by the old man just before he was murdered?

Inspector: Sure. Think I did it without arousing any suspicion. But I don't know — I don't know —

Ellery (*confidently*): He'll bite, dad. He must. It's his only chance. He's thinking that if he can intercept and destroy the letter containing March's new will before Fitzroy receives it, the estate remains in the family, and —

Velie: Yeah, but to hold up a letter-carrier, Mr. Queen. That'll bring the Feds in on it . . .

Ellery (*dryly*): A man who's taken a human life, Sergeant, will scarcely balk at committing a crime against the United States government — (*Murmur and footsteps off mike . . . fading out*)

Inspector (*sharp — low*): Cut it out! Here they come!

Ellery: Who?

Inspector: The letter-carriers!

Velie: There they go with their mail bags.

Inspector: Get back out of sight, you behemoth! And keep your eyes open . . .

Ellery: Give our postman a head-start, dad, then we'll trail him . . .

Velie: Which one of 'em *is* he?

Inspector: Tall red-headed one . . . OK . . . (*Steps on pavement*) Keep close to the buildings.

Ellery: You're sure the red-headed postman is the one who delivers the mail to Fitzroy's office-building, dad?

Inspector (*chuckling*): I ought to be sure — he's a detective from a Brooklyn precinct. I couldn't let the regular postman run the risk, and I couldn't use one of my squad because most of 'em were at the March house and our "friend" might have spotted 'em. (*Pause*)

Velie (*nervous*): Any sign of him yet? I'm all goose-pimples.

(The next scene should be played as fast as possible)

Ellery: Dad! (*Steps stop*) Someone just slipped out of that doorway, behind our phony postman. Look!

Inspector (*shouting*): *He slugged my man!* (*Running steps on mike*)

Ellery (*over steps*): Blast it! *He's grabbed the mail-bag!*

Inspector (*shouting*): Hey you! Stop, or I'll shoot!

Velie: I'll get him, Inspector. (*Two shots fired into the air. Car off moving closer*)

Ellery: He's running across the street — don't let him get away!

Inspector: Hey, look out — that car!

(*Screech of brakes — thud — cry of man and scream of woman bystander off mike immediately followed by crowd murmurs which fade on*)

Ellery: Good Lord, he's been hit!

Inspector (*as crowd fades on — steps come to a stop*): Get back there, you people . . .

Velie (*grimly*): Get 'em up! Don't even wiggle your ears, you! This gat talks a tough language! — you! D'ye hear me?

Ellery: Put away your revolver, Sergeant . . . he's dead.

(*Music up . . . and into . . .*)

Velie (*comfortably*): Say-a-ay, I feel swell. Ya know? Nothin' to worry about till the next homicide . . . what's th' matter, Mr. Queen? Don't you feel good?

Ellery (*glumly*): Oh, I'm all right, Sergeant. A bit low.

Inspector (*dryly*): You sure look low.

Velie (*heartily*): You sure do . . . uh . . . that wouldn't be, now, brandy you're drinkin', would it, Mr. Queen?

Ellery: What? Oh, yes, Sergeant. Brandy.

Velie (*disappointed*): Brandy, huh?

Inspector: Help yourself, Velie. Ellery's off in the mountains somewhere.

Velie: Thanks, Inspector. Don't mind if I do. (*Chink of glass . . . pour liquid*)

Ellery (*angry*): Dad, are you going to start that business . . .

Velie (*hastily*): Happy days! (*Pause*) Whooo! That's good. Say, Mr. Queen, how'd you figure this out, anyway? . . . Say, this is pretty good stuff, this brandy. Pretty good stuff.

Ellery (*laughing suddenly*): Have another, Sergeant. (*Same business of glass and pouring*) Sorry I'm such poor company.

Inspector: You'd be better company if you gave out a little. I had reporters on my neck all day. And what could I tell 'em? Only what you told *me*. And you didn't tell me anything except who it was!

Velie (*same business again*): Yes sir, this is swell brandy . . .

Inspector: Look, Velie, I don't mind your drinking my brandy, but take a drink, not a bath. You've got a wife waiting for you at home!

Velie (*belligerently*): Who said that? Who said that? Now you made me sad, Inspector. Down the ee-soph-agus! (*Drinks*)

Ellery (*absently*): Whole thing, of course, lay in the correct interpretation of the clue Samuel March scratched into his desk-top before he died . . . the word "march" . . .

Velie (*mellow now*): Ain't that the truth? (*Begins to sing "La Marseillaise"*) "March on, march o-o-on . . ."

Inspector: Pipe down, Velie. I want to hear this.

Velie: All right. *All* right. March . . . so it was the word March. Yes sir, the word march . . .

Ellery: I saw at once that the murderer fell into one of two all-inclusive categories. Either he was one of Samuel March's *family*, or he wasn't.

Inspector: Where did that get you?

Ellery: Well, could he have been *outside* the March family? No. Because if the dying man had wanted to leave the name of a *non*-member of his family as a clue, he certainly wouldn't have chosen the word "March," which is his own family name.

Velie: How true . . . how true . . . (*Hiccups*)

Ellery: The dying man would simply have scratched the name of the outsider into his desk. Such a name would have been perfectly clear and the first thing the dying man would have thought of — if an outsider had stabbed him.

Inspector (*thoughtfully*): That's so, when you put it that way. So old man March meant to accuse one of his own family.

Ellery: Yes, and since his family consisted of three children, he meant that one of *them* had stabbed him.

Velie: The in-grati-tood of it all.

Inspector: But how did you know which one of the three he meant?

Ellery: Well, look at it this way, dad. If the dying man intended to leave the *name* of one of his children, would he have written only the *last* name, the family name? In fact, would he have written the family name *at all*? Of course not. Ordinarily, he would have written down the *first* name.

Inspector: But he *didn't* write down a first name!

Ellery: True, he didn't. Therefore he *couldn't*.

Velie (*chanting*): He couldn't, couldn't, couldn't, couldn't . . .

Inspector: Quiet, you rum-pot. What d'ye mean he *couldn't* write down the first name, Ellery? Why not?

Ellery: Because he obviously realized the first name would not have been clear — that it would have been *mis*leading!

Velie (*singing*): (*Taking cue from "mis" of "misleading"*) "Ahhhh, sweet Myster-ee of life-a an' love-a I fou-ou-oun' you . . ."

Inspector: *Will* you stop that braying? Gimme that bottle! (*Velie stops*)

Velie (*dreamily*): Yessssss . . . m'lord . . .

Ellery: You see what I mean, dad. For instance, I said to myself: Could Lieutenant March — that is, Patrick — have been the one his father meant to indicate? But if it *had* been Patrick, why didn't his father write down the name Patrick, or Pat?

Inspector: But I still don't get it, Ellery. How'd you know which of the twins he meant to signify by that?

Ellery: I saw immediately that the answer to the whole riddle lay in the capitalization of the second letter of the word — the fact that the letter *A* had been capitalized. Why should the dying man have capitalized that A? The second letter of the word? In fact, why did he capitalize the first *and* second letters, and then write the third, fourth, and fifth letters in small, or lower-case, form? The only reason could be that it wasn't a *name* he had written at all! A capital letter, a capital letter, and three small letters could only have represented — an *abbreviation*! (*Velie snores*)

Inspector: Abbreviation! But what? . . . Capital M, Capital A, small r-c-h . . .

Ellery (*incisively*): Capital M for *Master*, Capital A, small r-c-h for . . . *Architecture*! Master of Architecture! And old man March himself had said, when he disinherited his three children, that his son Robert had a master's degree in architecture! Therefore I knew he had meant Robert, and that Robert had stabbed his father to death . . . (*Phone rings*) I wonder what that is. No, I'll take it, dad . . .

Inspector: Beats me. Beats me . . . (*Picks up phone*)

Ellery: Yes? (*Don't hear voice on other end*) Yes, yes, go ahead!

Inspector: Who is it, Ellery?

Ellery: Telegraph office — they've got a wire for me . . . Yes, read it to me, please! (*Pause*) Yes . . . yes . . . (*Yells*) *Hurrah!* (*Bangs receiver*)

Velie (*awakening from sleep*): Hunnnnnh — what . . . What happened?

Ellery (*gleefully*): What *happened*? Oh, nothing much. Nothing much! That was a wire from Nikki, dad! Nikki's coming home! Sergeant, fill 'em up — drinks on the house!

(*Music up*)

Another impossible crime — and an especially tantalizing one in which a psychic researcher is strangled in a haunted cave with only his own footprints leading to the entrance. E.Q. asked the Director to add "judicious and clever use of 'ghost-sound' effects and music." Originally broadcast on October 22, 1939.

The Adventure of the Haunted Cave

The Characters

Ellery Queen	The detective
Nikki Porter	His secretary
Inspector Queen	Of the New York Police
Sergeant Velie	Of the New York Police
Professor Collins	Of Tecumseh Lodge
Susan Collins	Of Tecumseh Lodge
Colin Montague	Who believes in ghosts
Laura Montague	His daughter
Alexander Lewis	Who doesn't believe in ghosts
Gabriel Dunn	A woodsman
Finch	The Collins' houseman

Setting: The Adirondacks, 1939

(*Impatient pacing to and fro . . . door opens off*)

Inspector (*yawning*): (*Fade on*) Morning, Ellery. Up early, huh?
Ellery (*over pacing*): (*Irritable*) I haven't even been to bed, dad.
Inspector (*incredulously*): Haven't been to bed! What's the matter?
Ellery (*stop pacing*): It's Nikki, bl . . . ess her!
Inspector (*dryly*): Oh.
Ellery (*raving*): Sends me a wire last week. She'll be in in six days. Says she'll call me when she gets home. I wait all night. No word. Nothing. I 'phoned and 'phoned. No answer. Called all night. Called this morning. Dad, she hasn't come back from the Adirondacks! I can't understand it.
Inspector (*dryly*): I can. She decided to extend her vacation. You're quite a detective, my son.
Ellery: But Nikki wouldn't do that to me! Not without notifying me. I don't mind her staying on —
Inspector: Not much.

103

Ellery: Mountains probably have done her a world of good. But just the same — (*Two phone rings . . . long distance*)

Inspector: I'll take it.

Ellery (*fading*): Oh no, you won't! That's a long-distance signal! (*Snatches phone. On mike*) Hello! Hello?

Operator (*filtered*): One moment, please. Go ahead, Kenoka. (*Clicks*)

Nikki (*filtered throughout*): Ellery?

Ellery (*shouting with joy and relief*): *Nikki!* Nikki . . .

Nikki: Ooops! My *ear*, Mr. Queen. But you do sound glad to hear my voice.

Ellery: Glad! I'm delirious!

Nikki: Really? How've you been without your secretary?

Ellery: Terrible! Nikki, are you still at Tecumseh Lodge?

Nikki: No, Ellery. I met some awfully nice people — a Professor and Mrs. Collins — Sue is a darling —

Ellery (*glumly*): Oh. I see.

Nikki: — and they took a shine to me, I guess, because they've invited me to be their guest for a few days at their log-cabin up here in the Adirondacks . . . Log-cabin! It's more like a château!

Inspector (*fading on into 'phone*): Hello, Nikki!

Nikki: *Hello*, Inspector! . . . So you see, darlin', I'm sort of between the devil and the deep blue sea. I'd love to stay, and yet — well, you *are* my boss —

Ellery (*nobly*): Nonsense, Nikki. Stay as long as you like.

Inspector (*off*): Liar.

Nikki: That's awfully sweet of you, Ellery! I'm 'specially anxious to stay because — well, you'll laugh at this —

Ellery (*glumly*): I'm practically convulsed already.

Nikki: Ellery — there's a ghost up here!

Ellery: A — *what*? (*Laughs*) Wait, Nikki, I want to tell that to dad . . . Dad, Nikki's playing around with a ghost!

Inspector (*off*): No wonder you're laughing. Last week you suspected it might be a football player.

Nikki: Ellery Queen, I *heard* you guffawing! It's no laughing matter. This ghost goes about strangling people. Lives in a sort of cave near Professor Collins' log-cabin.

Ellery (*chuckling*): How cosy!

Nikki: Skeptic! But Colin Montague and Alexander Lewis — *they're* both up here waiting to *test* that ghost —

Ellery: Montague? Lewis? (*Damply*) You mean there are — men up there?

Nikki (*airily*): Men? I should say! And *what* men, darlin'. I'm having a simply glorious time. Glorious!

Ellery (*abruptly*): Nikki, when are you leaving?

Nikki (*astonished*): On Wednesday, I think —
Ellery: I'm driving up for you — today.
Nikki (*same*): But Ellery, I thought you said —
Ellery: I don't mean — Of course, you stay until Wednesday. But I . . . well, I can use a few days' vacation, and I'll stay at Tecumseh Lodge, and then I'll drive you back to New York —
Nikki: You're *such* a lamb!
Ellery: Never mind the cracks. How do I get there?
Nikki: Inquire at Tecumseh Lodge. For the Collins cabin —
Operator: Your five minutes are up, Madam.
Nikki: *Already?* Ellery, goodbye! (*Click*)
Ellery: 'Bye, Nikki. (*Hangs up. Mutters*) Montague . . . Lewis . . .
Inspector: Say, I think I'll drive up with you, Ellery.
Ellery (*absently*): What, dad? Oh, of course. Glad to have you.
Inspector: A ghost, eh? (*Chuckles*) I'll get Velie to go along, too. I've always wanted to see what would happen if Velie and a ghost met face to face!

(*Music up . . . and into car motor climbing mountain. Bad road.*)

Ellery (*impatient*): Where the deuce *is* the Collins place, anyway? We've been climbing steadily since we left Tecumseh Lodge.
Inspector: This is the only road up here. If you can call it a road.
Ellery: We must be close to the top of the mountain.
Velie (*enjoying himself*): Yes, sir, an' the way I feel, I'd just as soon fly right off the top into the circum-am-bi-ent ether! (*They laugh*) What trees! What a sky! What air! (*Inhales deeply*) Smell that air. Go on — smell it!
Inspector (*chuckling*): Just a natural-born drunk.
Ellery (*same*): Why, Sergeant, you're a poet!
Velie (*hurt*): Trouble is, you guys ain't got no soul. Now me, when I get out in God's country, I feel like — what's-'is-name? — Pan. Yes, sir. Pan! Wanna jump an' sing — (*Suddenly*) Say, ain't that Nikki Porter walkin' up there ahead — with that middle-aged couple?
Inspector: It *is* Nikki, by thunder! (*Up on motor-sounds*) Hey, son, you *will* fly off the mountain! (*Quick brakes. Stop*)
Nikki (*off*): Ellery! (*Opens car door quickly — jumps out on road*)
Ellery: Nikki! Come here, you! (*Other car door opening*)
Nikki (*squeezed, embarrassed*): Ellery, you're — Ellery, stop! I can't breathe! Oooh, my ribs.
Ellery (*happily*): Well, I'm glad to see you. Nikki, you're looking wonderful! Dad, isn't she?
Inspector (*chuckling*): Pretty as a picture. 'Lo, Nikki.

Nikki: Hello, Inspector! And Sergeant *Velie*. This is a lovely surprise!

Velie: Yeah, the Inspector an' me kinda felt like we wanted to see a tree.

Nikki (*laughing*): You'll see plenty up here! Professor and Mrs. Collins, I want you to meet Inspector Queen, Mr. Queen, and Sergeant Velie. (*Ad lib greetings*)

Sue: Nikki's told us *so* much about you three —

Collins: Yes, we feel as if we've known you a long time.

Ellery: Thank you, Professor Collins. Lovely country up here. Is your cabin much farther on?

Collins: Just a few hundred yards. We're practically at the top of this mountain, you know.

Sue: Of course you'll stop with us, Mr. Queen — you and your father and Sergeant Velie. (*They protest ad lib*)

Ellery: Couldn't think of putting you out, Mrs. Collins —

Sue: Nonsense, Mr. Queen! We've loads of room —

Collins: No arguments, now. You'll be our guests.

Nikki (*laughing*): It's no use, Ellery. You'll find Sue and the Professor are irresistible. That's how they shanghaied *me*.

Sue: Why, right now we have Alex Lewis staying with us, and Colin Montague and his daughter Laura —

Ellery: Montague has a *daughter*? (*Laughs*) And I thought —

Nikki (*demurely*): Yes, Mr. Queen? You thought?

Collins (*chuckling*): Oh, I see. No, no competition, Mr. Queen. Montague's over fifty, and Alex Lewis is a dried-up little fellow —

Sue: With no more oomph than an Egyptian mummy.

Nikki: Sue! That's unkind. Mr. Lewis is a *darling* little man.

Inspector (*dryly*): Ellery, looks as if you've had your drive up here for nothing.

Ellery (*embarrassed*): Nonsense! That yarn about the ghost is what really brought me up here —

Nikki: *Thank* you, Mr. Queen.

Ellery: Nikki! I mean — Look, let's all get into my car and drive the rest of the way.

Inspector (*as they get into car*): Nice of you to ask us to stay, Professor Collins. To tell the truth, I'm sort of fascinated by that ghost-story myself. (*Close car doors*)

Collins (*laughing*): It's quite a story, Inspector . . .

Velie: Bring on your ghost — I'm r'arin' to go! (*Drive off*)

(*Music up and into general conversation as if on open veranda of lodge . . . chink of glasses off . . .*)

Inspector: Thanks, Mrs. Collins. I think I will.

Sue: Finch, pour another cocktail for Sergeant Velie, too.

Finch (*off*): Yes, Madam. (*Business of cocktails*) Here you are, sir.

Velie (*luxuriously*): Finch, you're a swell guy! Boy, this is the life. Ain't it? (*General laughter*)

Montague (*Prouty type*): Where's my daughter Laura?

Sue: Out taking a walk, Mr. Montague, to watch the sun go down. She went with Mr. Queen and Nikki.

Inspector (*chuckling*): There's something about a mountain — love and ghosts —

Lewis: Montague, I'm afraid the Queens don't have much respect for psychic phenomena.

Montague: And not only the Queens, Lewis. Take Collins here —

Collins (*hastily*): Leave me out of this, you two. It's bad enough I've turned my lodge into a laboratory for your psychic researches. Psychic claptrap!

Sue: Here come Laura and Nikki and Mr. Queen. (*Ad libs fading on, with crunchy steps. Then porch steps*)

Nikki (*fading on*): Laura, I'm simply *tingling*!

Ellery (*same*): Marvelous up here. Simply marvelous. Hullo, there! (*Ad lib greetings from all*)

Laura (*fading on*): Mr. Queen's just *drunk* on this mountain air — like Emily Dickinson's bee —

Inspector: Like *who*?

Velie: Me, too, Miss Montague! Now ain't that a funny thing?

Sue (*dryly*): You're not immune yourself, Laura. Although I do wish you wouldn't carry romanticism to the point of exploring the Haunted Cave.

Montague (*chuckling*): Laura reads poetry there.

Nikki: Laura! Can't you pick a more cheerful spot?

Laura: Isn't it *gruesome*, Nikki? But the place fascinates me.

Nikki: *I* wouldn't go near that cave alone for a million dollars.

Ellery (*chuckling*): I wanted Nikki to show me the cave, but she begged off —

Inspector: Nikki, you don't *believe* that stuff?

Velie: Women are funny that way. Ghosts! Nuts, *I* say.

Laura: Don't talk that way, Sergeant Velie. I'm not afraid, but — there *are* ghosts, you know.

Velie (*astonished*): Say! You ain't serious, Miss Montague.

Montague: She's her father's daughter, Sergeant. Our family's always had a healthy respect for the supernatural.

Ellery: Yes, you're an expert in psychic research, aren't you, Mr. Montague?

Montague (*modestly*): Well, now, I'd hardly say an *expert* —

Lewis: Nor would I. Montague, you're a gullible idiot. The way you were taken in by the ectoplasmic mumbo-jumbo in Seattle —

Montague (*hotly*): I suppose you wouldn't have been fooled, too, Lewis!

Lewis (*snorts*): I? Don't be funny, Montague! Why, you remember, down in Nashville that time, how I exposed that gang of fake mediums. But you were all ready to —

Montague: Lewis, you're a fool!

Collins (*chuckling*): Gentlemen, gentlemen. (*They subside into mutters*) That's the way it's been with these two, Mr. Queen, for twenty years. Bitter enemies. Yet they'd cut the throat of anyone else who attacked the other one's reputation.

Sue: You know, Mr. Montague has probably the largest and most valuable library on psychic phenomena in the world —

Lewis: Lucky dog! He's got books I'd give my right arm for!

Ellery: And you two gentlemen are up here to investigate the ghostly nature of the so-called Haunted Cave?

Montague: That's right, Mr. Queen. We're going to conduct a scientific experiment.

Collins: Scientific! Don't make me laugh, Montague. There's science in my test-tubes at the University, but this witch-doctor stuff —

Lewis: All you bug-ologists are the same, Professor Collins! Skeptics! Darned fools, *I* say!

Ellery: What's the nature of these psychic phenomena?

Nikki: I told you, Ellery — somebody strangled somebody in the cave many years ago, and — (*A rising moan in distance. Half-human, half-ghostly, as might be made by wind*)

Inspector (*sharply*): What's that?

Velie: Sounded like a — like a wolf.

Nikki: Do they have wolves in the Adirondacks?

Velie (*mutter*): They better have.

Montague (*excited*): Quiet! Listen! (*Moan again. Pause*)

Lewis (*same*): That's the moan, Montague! The ghost-sound!

Nikki (*faintly*): Isn't it — weird?

Laura: Gives me the creeps . . . Ooh, it's wonderful!

Sue: I don't find it so, Laura! (*Pause. Moan*)

Velie: Say, who's *doin'* that? Monkey-business!

Montague (*excited*): Oh, no Sergeant. We've checked *that*. The sounds actually seem to come from the empty cave . . .

Collins: Pshaw! Pure natural phenomen caused by wind and some peculiar rock formation. (*Snorts*) Ghosts! I — (*Stops. Moan again*)

Inspector: It sure sounds . . . funny. Doesn't it.

Ellery (*sharply*): I'm going over to have a look at that cave!

(*Music up . . . develop ghost theme around moaning sound . . . and into crunch of footsteps as if on trail in woods . . .*)

Inspector (*chuckling*): I never saw anyone duck faster than those three women. Mmmm. Smell these pines!

Velie (*muttering*): Ghosts, huh. Lemme get my mitts on that ghost an' I'll wring his ghostly neck!

Ellery: Must we cross this strip of woods to get to the cave, Professor Collins?

Collins: Yes. It's between my cabin and the cave. No way of going round it — sheer cliff to either side. Runs right to the top of the mountain, you see, then there's a clearing, and the cave is beyond the clearing.

Lewis: At the very crest of the mountain overlooking the lake.

Ellery: Oh! The same lake that's behind the Professor's cabin, I take it, Mr. Lewis.

Montague (*intently*): The moans seem to have stopped, Lewis.

Lewis (*fretfully*): They always seem to, just when we —

Inspector: Isn't someone coming? (*Footsteps fading on*)

Collins: Must be old Gabriel Dunn. Gigantic old woodsman who lives in a shack down the mountainside a bit . . . Yes, it is. Hi, Gabe!

Gabe (*fading on — bass voice*): Howdy, Professor. You hear them moans from the Haunted Cave, too?

Collins: We certainly did. Meet some friends of mine, Gabe — (*Ad lib greetings. Resume walking*)

Gabe: Strangler's gittin' purty rambunctious lately.

Velie: *You* believe in this hogwash, too, Daniel Boone?

Gabe (*quietly*): Man gits to believin' a lot o' things livin' up here alone in the mountains, Mister.

Ellery: What *is* this legend of the Strangler and the cave?

Lewis: Tell him, Montague.

Montague: Some mountaineer is supposed to have lured wayfarers into the cave and strangled them for their money.

Lewis: A hundred years or more ago, Mr. Queen.

Ellery: What did he do with the bodies of his victims?

Lewis: Threw 'em into the lake. There's a natural opening in one wall of the cave — like a window. Overlooks the lake from a height of about fifty feet.

Gabe: Yes, sir, an' ever since, them folks he murdered keep moanin', like you heard.

Inspector (*groaning*): Of all the succotash!

Velie: Baloney! Tripe! Gar-bidge!

Montague: Of course the man was finally caught and hanged.

Collins (*chuckling*): And the good people around here claim that every time you hear a moan, it's the ghost of the Strangler murdering one of his ghostly victims all over again.

Gabe: Here we are. (*Steps stop*)

Velie: Is that the entrance to the cave — just across the clearin'?

Inspector: Why, it's got a wooden door!

Ellery: Let's go closer. How's that, Professor? (*No steps*)

Collins: Gabe knows more about it than I do.

Gabe: Some city feller few years back put the door in. Charged admission to folks to see the Haunted Cave.

Velie: His name musta been P. T. Barnum!

Gabe (*chuckling*): He didn't last long. One night he was in here alone an' the moans started. He lit out like a buck-deer an' he ain't been seen since.

Ellery: Let's have a look at this remarkable cave. (*Open heavy door, creaking. Voices echo a little from here until they leave cave*) Hmmm. Can't see much in this gloom. (*Steps on rocky floor*)

Montague: Sold rock, Mr. Queen — floor, walls, roof. That roof is really the inside of the very crest of the mountain. And there's the window in the wall.

Ellery (*off a little*): Yes, I see. Looks right out over the lake, almost at the top of a sheer cliff . . .

Inspector: You gentlemen say you're going to conduct an experiment? What kind of experiment? Mr. Lewis?

Lewis: We plan to spend an entire twenty-four hours in here, Inspector Queen. From six tomorrow morning until six a.m. the following day.

Montague: We'll take blankets, oil lamps, food, water, and a sound-recording apparatus. We want to be in this cave when the moaning begins.

Collins (*laughing*): Very scientific, you see.

Lewis: Go ahead — laugh, you Philistine!

Velie (*drawl*): S'pose you meet up with this ghost — don't you think you better pack a rod? Just in case?

Gabe (*quietly*): If whatever's makin' those sounds could be shot, Mister, he'd 'a' been a dead ghost long ago. I wasn't born in the woods yest'day.

Montague: As a matter of fact, we're taking every precaution against the possibility that the sounds are made by a human agency. You see, if it doesn't rain tonight, although it looks as if it will, we'll soak down that loose earth of the clearing just outside the cave, get it good and soft — so that anyone approaching the cave will have to walk across mud and leave footprints.

Lewis: And the clearing is the only possible approach to the cave, as you saw.

Ellery: You two gentlemen aren't ghosts. To get into the cave you'll both leave footprints in the clearing.

Lewis: Oh, we'll go barefoot to identify our own prints.

Montague: Of course, no one but us is to cross the clearing. That's understood. And it's to be a secret —

Collins (*gravely*): Hear that, Gabe? Don't say a word about this to anyone. (*Chuckles*)

Gabe: 'Pears to me like ye're aimin' to trifle with trouble, you two gentlemen.

Lewis (*snaps*): It won't be *we* who get into trouble. Let's go back. Montague, you have that new lock? (*Steps out of cave. Clank of large lock*)

Montague: Yes. (*Closes door, clicks lock shut*) And the key stays in my pocket. Well, gentlemen, that's all until tomorrow morning at six. If you want to see us off, you'll have to be up early.

Inspector (*grimly*): And, believe me, I want to!

Velie (*chuckling*): Me, too!

Ellery (*same*): And your humble servant!

(*Music up . . . and through music get heavy rain effect as if throughout night and into dawn, birds, etc. . . crunching steps of two in woods . . .*)

Ellery: Nikki, we ought to do this more often.

Nikki: You mean get up to see two middle-aged men make darned fools of themselves at six in the morning?

Ellery: *No*, Nikki. I mean get up to walk in the woods.

Nikki: *Mr.* Queen! You *are* a child of Nature, aren't you?

Ellery (*chuckling*): Chiefly of ill nature, I'm afraid. You don't know how — well, impossible to live with I've been during the past couple of weeks, Nikki. Ask dad — *he* knows.

Nikki: I've asked dad — and he gave me an earful. (*Softly*) You really missed me?

Ellery: Terribly.

Nikki (*melting*): Oh, Ellery . . .

Ellery (*hastily*): Of course, it's natural. Man gets used to having a certain woman around —

Nikki (*coldly*): Isn't it the truth? Like a pair of old shoes.

Ellery (*contritely*): Nikki, I didn't mean —

Nikki: Oh, didn't you! Are the others following us?

Ellery: Nikki, I've offended you. I don't want you to —

Nikki: Yes, there they are. All except Mr. Montague. Where on earth do you suppose he is?

Ellery: Oh, what difference does it make? He's probably waiting for us at the entrance to the cave. Nikki —

Nikki (*firmly*): No, Mr. Queen. I won't discuss us with you any further. (*Laughs*) Oh, Ellery, don't look so drippy. I'm just ragging you.

Ellery (*brightening*): You are? (*Briskly*) Well! Fine morning. Simply colossal.

We'll see the two experimenters into their cave, then we'll have breakfast, a plunge in the lake —

Nikki: Brrr! Not *me*, thank you . . . Oh, there's that old woodsman Professor Collins mentioned last night — what's his name?

Ellery: Gabriel Dunn. 'Lo, Gabe! Up early to see the fun? (*Steps stop. One man's steps fading on*)

Gabe (*fading on*): I just been over to the clearin' . . . front of the cave. Somebody's in that cave! (*Many steps fading on, murmurs*)

Lewis (*fading on, irritable*): Can't understand where Montague is. Unless he got up early to —

Collins: Morning, Gabe. Did I hear you say somebody was in the cave? (*Ad lib exclamations*)

Gabe: Wa-all, come over to the edge o' the clearin' an' see for yerselves. (*Steps again of all*)

Sue: Isn't Mr. Montague there?

Laura: It can't be daddy, Mrs. Collins. He wouldn't —

Inspector: What's wrong, Ellery?

Ellery: I don't know. Gabe says someone's in the cave.

Nikki: Oh, it's probably Mr. Montague.

Velie: But he said he an' Lewis would go in together —

Gabe (*a little off*): See what I mean? (*Steps stop. Pause*)

Ellery (*slowly*): Footprints of a small man's bare feet —

Nikki: And they go straight across the clearing to the door of the cave —

Inspector: Just one set of prints — in-going . . .

Lewis (*bitterly*): He's tricked me! The — pretzel! A human pretzel, that's what that man is! His word of honor — we'd do it together — and *now* see what he's done!

Laura: How dare you talk about my father that way, Mr. Lewis!

Collins: But Laura, it does seem as if your father got up earlier this morning and went into the cave by himself, cutting poor Lewis out —

Lewis (*furious*): Those are his footprints, aren't they? They couldn't be anyone else's, they're so small — the . . . the weasel! The snake!

Laura: Mr. Lewis, you're a dreadful man!

Sue (*laughing*): Oh, come, Mr. Lewis. It's probably a joke. (*Calling*) Mr. Montague! (*Outdoor echo*)

Lewis: I'm going in there and give him a piece of my —

Ellery: It's a shame to spoil the perfect surface of this mud, Mr. Lewis. The rain during the night smoothed the clearing out like an iron.

Inspector: Not a mark on it but the prints of Montague's bare feet. Montague! (*Outdoor echo*)

Lewis: Lugged this duffle all the way through the woods . . . I'm through! Let him do it alone. A man capable of such a slimy low trick . . .

Ellery (*calling*): Montague! (*Echo*) Montague! (*Echo. Pause*)

Nikki: That's funny, Ellery. He must be in there. And the door's a little open . . .

Inspector (*yelling*): Montague! (*Echo. Pause. Ad lib murmurs*)

Ellery (*sharply*): Wait! (*Murmurs stop*) There's something devilishly wrong in there —

Laura: Wrong with — daddy? Mr. Queen, you're joking!

Nikki (*quickly*): It's probably nothing, Laura. Look, dear — how about walking back to the cabin with me —

Laura: No, Nikki! . . . Daddy! (*Echo. Almost hysterical*) Daddy! (*Echo*)

Inspector (*low*): This looks bad, Nikki. Keep an eye on her.

Nikki (*same*): Of course, Inspector. (*Fade a little*) Laura dear, you're being stubborn. Why not . . .

Ellery (*sharp*): I'm crossing the clearing alone. I'll detour in a half-circle to keep out of the way of Montague's footprints and if you have to follow me, follow my trail across the mud. Understand? (*Low-voiced agreement among men*) Keep the women back, please.

Inspector (*low*): Make it snappy, Ellery.

Velie (*same*): And if you find anything, Mr. Queen —

Ellery (*fading*): I know, Sergeant. (*Sucking footsteps in mud fading off. Pause. Halfway creak of heavy door off. Pause. Then Ellery speaks as if across clearing — tense*) Dad. Velie. Come here. (*Ad libs*)

Collins (*calling*): What's the matter in there, Mr. Queen?

Laura (*screaming*): Something's happened to my father!

Nikki: Laura, for heaven's sake — Laura —

Ellery (*sharply — off*): Get those women away from here! Nikki — Professor Collins — take them back to the cabin — at once! (*Murmurs*) Do as I say!

Inspector: Come on, Velie. Let's see this thing.

Velie: I'm comin', but my dogs ain't exactly yelpin' with joy. (*Sucking footsteps in mud. Murmurs fade off. Slight creak of door*)

Ellery (*on mike — grim*): There's your Mr. Montague — on the cave floor. (*Sucked-in breaths of Inspector, Velie*)

Inspector: Dead! With his supplies all around him!

Velie (*wildly*): Looka his — neck . . . He's been . . . strangled. Strangled, Mr. Queen!

Ellery (*grimly*): Yes, Sergeant. And as far as I can see, the only one who could have strangled him is — the ghost of the Haunted Cave!

(*Music up, ghost-theme, and into low ad libs by Ellery, Inspector, Velie — still in cave*)

Velie (*muttering*): It ain't possible. It's a gyp. It's —

Inspector: Stop that jabbering, you ape, and help me turn him over. (*Straining of two men*)

Velie (*panting*): A — ghost! I'm laughing. (*Laughs feebly*) (*Then savagely*) I
   don't believe in ghosts!
Inspector: Looks as if we'll have to believe in *this* one.
Ellery (*troubled*): I don't understand it. There's something horribly wrong
   here . . .
Inspector: Those marks of strangulation are — queer, Ellery.
Ellery: Yes. Yes, they are, dad.
Inspector: The main welts are on the throat — at the *front* of the neck,
   and the thumb-prints of the strangler are at the *back* of the neck, with
   the thumbs pointing upwards . . .
Ellery (*disturbed*): Yes . . . yes . . . I've seen it, dad.
Velie (*relieved*): I got it! Ghosts . . . nuts, *I* say! Know what happened?
   This guy Montague choked *himself!*
Inspector: Rats, Velie. First place, it's next to impossible to strangle
   yourself with your own hands — your grip would relax automatically
   the second you began to go unconscious . . .
Ellery: And even if you could strangle yourself, Sergeant, you'd naturally
   place your thumbs on your windpipe in *front* of the neck, not at the
   back. No, Montague didn't choks himself . . . (*Creaking door off*)
Inspector (*sharply*): Who's that?
Collins (*fading on — hoarse*): It's Collins, Inspector, with old Gabe. Lord,
   poor Montague. It's — I —
Ellery: You didn't mess up Montague's footprints out there?
Collins: No. They *are* the prints of his bare feet?
Inspector: No doubt about it. We measured.
Velie: Hey, you. Daniel Boone. You notify the Sheriff?
Gabe: Professor Collins 'phoned him from the house. You fellers are
   sort of detectives, huh?
Inspector (*dryly*): Sort of, Gabe.
Gabe: Wa-all, I backtracked on the trail through them woods an' I seen
   somethin'. Ain't no sign to read 'cause it's a narrer trail an' the whole
   bunch o' ye trampled it over at six o'clock this mornin'.
Ellery (*sharply*): What have you found, Gabe?
Gabe: No footprints, 'cause of the tramplin', but right at the edge o' the
   woods, where ye enter the trail after leavin' Professor Collins' cabin —
   it's jest a few yards from the cabin — there's a lot o' loose stones on
   the trail, an' they're slipp'ry from the rain last night.
Inspector (*impatiently*): Well? Well?
Gabe: Wa-all, 'longside those slipp'ry stones there's a couple o' small
   juniper bushes. They been crushed flat. I figger as how this feller
   Montague slipped on them stones an' fell off the trail on top o' them
   junipers on his way to the cave this mornin'.
Collins: It wasn't any of the others, because I've asked.

Velie (*sarcastically*): That's a help, that is.

Gabe (*quietly*): I'm jest a-tellin' ye.

Collins (*hoarsely*): What are we going to do? Poor Laura — in hysterics. Nikki Porter frantically trying to console her — my wife physically ill from shock — and Lewis hasn't said a single word since this — happened. He's — scared. Pale as a — as a —

Inspector (*harshly*): Why don't you say it? Pale as a ghost!

Ellery: It's a — disconcerting problem, Professor Collins. You see, it does look as if only a ghost could have murdered poor Montague.

Collins (*amazed*): What do you mean, Mr. Queen?

Inspector (*harshly*): What my son means, Professor, is that when you examine the possibilities, they don't make sense! How did Montague's strangler get in and out of the cave? There was no one here but Montague when Ellery came in, and Montague was dead.

Velie: Dead a full hour, I'd say.

Ellery: You see, Professor, Montague entered the cave alone — only the tracks of his bare feet are on the mud of the clearing. Then how did his murderer get in? Murderer had to cross the muddy clearing — it's the only way to get into the cave.

Collins: But . . . but that's not possible!

Velie: Don't be a pla-ja-rist, Professor. I said it first.

Collins: Someone *must* have got in!

Ellery (*dryly*): How, Professor? The only other opening into the cave is this natural window in the side wall overlooking the lake — and that window is fifty feet above the lake, almost at the top of a sheer cliff.

Velie: Dra-cula himself couldn't climb it!

Collins: The roof of the cave — let a rope down —

Inspector: Then how'd the killer get up there? Only way to climb to the top of the cave outside is from this clearing. *But* — no prints.

Velie: Besides, we been up there. It's covered with dirt an' no foot's ever stepped on it . . . No human foot, that is . . . Say, now *I'm* doin' it!

Collins (*wildly*): The other side of the cave — no, that's impossible. It's a sheer precipice for hundreds of feet . . . A grappling-iron at the end of a line!

Ellery: You mean thrown up from the lake, Professor?

Collins: Yes! Somebody stood in a boat on the lake and threw up a grappling-iron, caught the window —

Ellery: No, Professor Collins. A grappling-iron would have left unmistakable scratch-marks on the edge of the rocky opening. And there *aren't* any scratch-marks.

Collins (*wildly*): But Mr. Queen — you're . . . you can't believe this! It's manifestly impossible for anyone to have gone in or out, you say —

Ellery: The facts say it, Professor — the facts.

Collins: Then how do you explain it?

Ellery: Until we *can* explain it — we'll have to assume that poor Montague was strangled by a ghost!

(*Music up . . . and into distant roll of thunder . . . front door opens . . . steps of two on porch . . .*)

Ellery (*tense*): Let's sit down on the porch here, Nikki. That madhouse in there's getting on my nerves.

Nikki (*shakily*): Everything seems so — eerie tonight. (*Sits down*) In the darkness here — no stars, no moon — it's — easy to believe in ghosts, Ellery.

Ellery (*angrily*): There *must* be an answer to this riddle!

Nikki: That Sheriff hasn't been much help. If you ask me, he's shaking. And Inspector Queen — whom's he been telephoning so secretly all day?

Ellery: He won't say. But he's as baffled as I am — and just as angry.

Nikki (*fretfully*): If we could only get past those *footprints*, Ellery —

Ellery: What do you mean, Nikki?

Nikki: Well, it's the lack of the murderer's footprints that makes this crime look like — like the work of a ghost. Couldn't the strangler have walked across that muddy clearing and *not* left prints — somehow?

Ellery (*dryly*): Well — how? I examined the terrain very carefully. No prints were made and then smoothed over. No boards were set down to walk on, and then removed. Only two things with weight crossed that clearing, Nikki — Montague's two bare feet.

Nikki: Ellery! Suppose the murderer stepped *into Montague's footprints!*

Ellery (*softly*): Very good, Nikki. Except that he didn't.

Nikki: How can you know that?

Ellery: If the murderer has *smaller* feet than Montague's, he might have stepped into Montague's prints. But the murderer can't have smaller feet, because Montague had the smallest feet of anyone here, even among the women — they're incredibly tiny for a man. Besides, smaller prints would show *in* Montague's prints. So that's out.

Nikki: Then suppose he had feet exactly the same size!

Ellery: I just told you Montague's feet were the smallest here; I've measured everybody. But even if that were possible — try stepping so exactly into another set of footmarks that you won't overlap anywhere. It can't be done, Nikki. (*Thunder*)

Nikki: Then he has *larger* feet!

Ellery: Obviously. But since he has, he certainly didn't cross the muddy clearing by stepping into Montague's tracks, Nikki. He'd have obliterated them.

Nikki (*desperately*): Then maybe *Montague* stepped on the *murderer's* tracks — while going into the cave!

Ellery: How could that be if Montague had the smallest feet, Nikki? The murderer's tracks would show up around the edges of Montague's. No, Nikki, the strangler apparently *didn't cross that clearing!* (*More thunder, closer*) It's — remarkable.

Nikki: But Ellery, it . . . (*Pause*) It gives me the shivers. He didn't cross the clearing — yet he couldn't get to the cave by any other route . . . Ellery, I *don't* believe in ghosts! I don't!

Ellery (*muttering*): I know just how you feel, Nikki, because — (*Both catch breaths. Ghostly moaning rises again. Again. And again*)

Nikki (*whispering*): Ellery — that awful — *moan* again!

Ellery: Steady, Nikki, steady . . . (*Moan again, loud clap of thunder, instantly a heavy downpour of rain*)

Nikki (*whispering*): Ellery, I'm — afraid . . . (*Moan again*)

(*Ghost music up . . . and into steady downpour off . . . interior murmurs . . . Laura crying.*)

Nikki (*brokenly*): Laura — you've cried your eyes out — all night —

Laura (*whispering*): They took daddy away — last night — and now it's another day — and I'll never see him again . . . Oh, Nikki! (*Cries softly as Nikki croons over her. Ad libs of all trying to console her. Open door off. Close*)

Velie (*sharp*): Hold it, the lot o' you. (*Ad libs stop*)

Inspector (*curt*): Velie, set that behemoth's back of yours against the door and — watch.

Velie (*grimly*): I'm awful good at that. (*Yells*) Get me? (*Mutters*) Ghosts, huh . . . I'll ghost somebody!

Nikki: Inspector, what's happened? You look — grim.

Ellery (*quietly*): Something up your sleeve, dad?

Inspector: You bet your sweet life! I've worked twenty-four hours by 'phone filling up this sleeve of mine — and believe me, it's full!

Collins (*quietly*): If you have something — significant to tell us, Inspector —

Lewis (*shrilly*): Stop being so all-fired mysterious!

Inspector (*softly*): All right, Mr. Lewis. You seem to be anxious — I'll start with you. You and Montague have been enemies for twenty years —

Lewis: En —! You're crazy, man! We've been friendly enemies, that's true. But — Are you accusing *me* of having murdered Colin Montague?

Inspector (*same*): It's wonderful how friendly enemies can turn into unfriendly ones, Mr. Lewis. Besides — Montague owned something you want — badly.

Lewis (*astonished*): Eh? But Montague was a poor man — (*Angrily*) This is childish! I won't even discuss it! (*Mutters*) Owned something . . .

Inspector (*same*): Montague has a *library* you've always hankered after, Lewis. It's supposed to be the largest, most valuable library on psychic research in the world . . .

Ellery: But dad, even if Montague died, how could Lewis —

Inspector (*grimly*): I had a man look up Montague's will. In that will he leaves his library to his "friendly enemy Alexander Lewis"! (*Ad libs*)

Collins: But Inspector, that's so absurd — to kill a man for possession of some books. Simply unthinkable.

Inspector: You think so, Professor Collins? Then suppose I tackle *you*.

Collins (*gasping*): *Me?*

Sue (*shocked*): Dearest, the man's insane —

Inspector: You keep out of this, Mrs. Collins. Yes, Professor, you. Montague borrowed a great deal of money from you — didn't he? (*Pause*) Didn't he!

Collins (*quietly*): Oh. I see. Yes, Inspector, he did.

Laura (*slowly*): I didn't know that. I didn't know —

Nikki: Laura, why don't you go and lie down?

Ellery (*warningly*): Nikki.

Inspector (*sharply*): Professor, Montague wasn't able to repay those loans. So you and he made a deal. Montague took out an insurance policy on his life to the amount of twenty-one thousand, five hundred dollars — the exact amount of his debt to you!

Laura (*gasping*): You — you killed my father?

Ellery: Dad! You mean Montague made Professor Collins his beneficiary?

Inspector: Yep! Now that Montague's dead Collins collects the insurance and the debt's paid . . . And you're a little strapped these days, aren't you, Professor?

Sue (*crying*): Darling, deny it — don't let them think — you couldn't kill anyone — did you . . .

Collins (*quietly*): Sue dearest, I didn't kill Colin Montague. Does that satisfy you?

Sue: Oh, darling, yes . . . yes, it does. (*Furious*) Inspector Queen, how *dare* you suggest my husband . . .

Inspector (*softly*): But how about you, Mrs. Collins? (*Pause*) (*Sharply*) Yes, you! Does your husband know that you and Colin Montague *were once man and wife?* That you ran away from Montague, leaving your baby with him, and then married Collins? (*Gasps. Pause*)

Sue (*faintly*): So it's out — it's out —

Collins (*dazed*): You mean you and Montague, Sue, were —

Inspector (*triumphantly*): So you *didn't* know, Collins!

Laura (*whispering*): Mrs. Collins is my — *mother?* (*Faintly*) I — don't . . . feel . . . (*Thud of body, as if fainting*)

Nikki: She's fainted! Laura! Laura darling!

Collins (*furious*): Even if that's true, Inspector — to bring this out — now — it's criminal idiocy!

Sue (*wildly*): I didn't want Laura, anybody, to know. Laura! Dearest! Oh, Laura . . . (*Sobs*) (*Pandemonium*)

Lewis: Please, please. All this shouting —

Collins: Inspector, I ought to — to throttle you —

Velie (*shouting*): Pipe down with that kind o' talk, you — you Professor!

Inspector (*shouting*): I'm checking that "divorce" you were supposed to've got from Montague, Mrs. Collins!

Sue (*gasping*): What do you *mean*?

Collins: Are you suggesting —?

Inspector: I mean how do I know she ever *was* divorced, that's what I mean! I'll bet you when this thing's cleared up we'll find Montague came up here to blackmail you, Mrs. Collins — threatening to expose you as a bigamist —

Nikki: Ellery, make them stop! Please . . .

Ellery (*sharply*): Dad! Dad, for heaven's sake, we shan't get anywhere brawling . . . (*Frantic knocking on door prolonged. Ad libs stop. Pause*)

Nikki (*whispering*): Who's . . . that?

Inspector (*strangled*): Velie. Open that door. (*Open door. Up on rain*)

Collins (*thickly*): It's Gabriel Dunn. What do you want, Gabe? We're too busy to —

Gabe (*grimly*): Ye're not too busy to hear this! Your houseman — that Finch — I jest found him in the Haunted Cave . . . strangled to death! (*Ghostly moan from distance*)

(*Music up . . . and into heavy rain outdoors . . . feet blundering through woods . . . panting . . .*)

Ellery (*panting*): Finch . . . Why, we've hardly seen the man. The Collins houseman, butler, chauffeur . . . Strangled — in the cave —

Gabe (*same*): It's the Strangler, I tell ye! I said 'twa'n't healthy to go pokin' aroun' —

Velie (*same*): Shut up, you — you Hunchback o' Notre Dame.

Inspector (*same*): Anyone says "ghost" to me again, I sock! Quiet, the pack of you!

Ellery (*same*): Here's the clearing — rain's washed out all footprints, blast it — (*Splashes through mud*)

Inspector (*yelling*): Lemme in this blankety-blank cave! (*Creaking door. Off on rain a bit. Pause*)

Velie (*uneasily*): Nobody — nobody here except —

Inspector: Except a corpse! Well, Velie, there's your mountains for you. Drunk on air, are you? Poetry, my foot!

Ellery (*thoughtfully*): Strangled . . .

Inspector: But the orthodox way this time. Thumb prints in *front* of neck. Dead as a mackerel.

Velie: Been dead about ten hours, I'd say — strangled around one o'clock in the morning.

Ellery (*off a little*): Ah! (*Slowly*) See what *I* found. (*Sharp*) Gabe, was this here when you discovered Finch's body a few minutes ago?

Gabe: Yes, sir. Right on the floor where ye jest picked it up. I ain't teched it.

Velie: What is it, Mr. Queen? Say, it's all broke!

Inspector (*roughly*): Let's see that, Ellery.

Ellery (*absently*): Here you are, dad.

Velie: It's a camera — a busted camera!

Inspector: Smashed to bits. On purpose. Stepped on, jumped on. Film gone . . . (*Splashing fading on*)

Collins (*fading on breathless*): I followed as fast as I . . . (*Pause. Faintly*) Finch. It *is* Finch. Poor Finch. Is he — he looks so —

Velie (*growling*): I thought I told you to stay put in that log-cabin of yours, Professor Collins!

Inspector (*softly*): It's all right, Sergeant. Professor Collins, do you recognize this camera from its remains?

Collins: What? Camera? . . . Oh, yes. That's Finch's . . . Poor little Finch. Incredible. He hardly ever spoke. I knew nothing about him. A good servant. To meet death like this — alone — in a cave —

Gabe (*heavily*): It's the Strangler, Professor. That pesky ol' ghost — he's a holy terror.

Inspector (*low*): Ellery, Velie. Come aside here. Collins — Gabe! Wait for us outside! (*Ad libs fading*)

Ellery (*absently*): Yes, dad?

Velie (*eagerly*): What's up, Inspector?

Inspector (*softly*): This is Finch's camera. And Finch's camera is a sure cure for ghosts.

Ellery: Cure for ghosts? Oh, of course.

Velie: Of course what? I don't get it, Inspector.

Inspector: Finch must have witnessed the murder of Montague yesterday morning! Probably got up early to see Montague and Lewis off on their experiment, took his camera, followed Montague when Montague beat it alone to steal a march on Lewis, snapped a picture of the killing . . .

Velie: And was all set to blackmail the killer!

Inspector: Yes, *sir*. Probably made an appointment with the killer in the cave for last night, was fool enough to take the camera along — and got choked to death for his pains, the dope. Killer smashed the camera and beat it . . .

Velie: Yeah, but who was it? Who *was* it?

Inspector: I don't know — yet. But one thing I do know . . . it *wasn't* a ghost!

Ellery (*softly*): No, dad, it wasn't a ghost. Ghosts aren't interested in destroying evidence against them. Only human killers are interested in *that*. Montague and Finch were strangled by a living person.

Velie (*snorting*): Even I could make a deduction like that, Mr. Queen!

Inspector (*muttering*): Question is — who? Who strangled Montague in this cave? It could be any one of 'em —

Ellery (*softly*): I can answer your question, dad.

Velie: You can *what*?

Ellery: I reconstructed the whole amazing thing as we ran to the cave here through the woods. Saw it all!

Inspector: You know who choked Montague? But —

Ellery: Yes, dad! And if you'll get everyone together at the edge of the clearing there, I'll show you *how* it was done, too!

(*Music up . . . and into jury spot*)

Challenge to the Listener

We do not have a script for Ellery's introduction of the jury for this case, but we hope readers of 2005 will find the solution a challenge.

(No rain now . . . many feet crackling through woods . . . background of usual woods sounds . . . ad libs)

Nikki (*guardedly*): But Ellery, just what is it you're going to *do*?

Ellery: Re-enact the modus operandi of the original crime, Nikki — the strangulation of Colin Montague.

Nikki: You should have been a theatrical producer! What's the idea?

Ellery: Seeing's believing, Nikki. The brain may be quicker than the eye, but it doesn't carry as much conviction . . . Here's the clearing. (*Their steps stop. Steps in background fading on*)

Nikki: Well, you've got a perfect stage for your production, Mr. Queen. Now that the rain's stopped, the mud in front of the cave's as clean and smooth as Milady's pan . . .

Inspector (*fading on*): All right, you people! We stop here.

Velie (*same*): And don't step on that mud! (*Steps on. They stop*)

Lewis (*angrily*): Theatrical exhibitionism!

Gabe: With this feller Finch dead, it don't strike me —

Laura (*hysterically*): Why doesn't somebody do something constructive?

Sue: Laura dearest — come to mother —

Laura (*same*): Don't "mother" me! After all these years, do you expect me to fall into your arms? I'll never forgive you — never!

Nikki: Don't say that, Laura —

Sue (*sobbing*): It's my punishment . . . (*Laura cries, too*)

Nikki: You two are acting like babies — both of you!

Collins: Sue — Laura . . . Lord, what a mess!

Ellery: Please. (*Silence*) I've asked you all to gather here at the edge of the clearing in front of the — uh — Haunted Cave because the time's come to explode this nonsense about a ghost and get back to earth.

Laura (*hysterical*): My *father's* back to earth!

Ellery (*gently*): You don't want your father's murderer to get away with this, do you, Miss Montague?

Laura (*passionately*): No! I don't care — who gets hurt! I want to scream, and tear, and kill —

Inspector (*sharply*): Stop that childish talk. There's been all the killing around here there's going to be!

Velie: How d'ye know, Inspector? If Finch could get it —

Ellery: The murder of Finch last night, Velie, was an inevitable result of the murder of Montague, as I've already explained. Obviously committed by the same person. Consequently, if we can fix the identity of Montague's murderer, we'll have solved both crimes.

Velie (*dryly*): Sorta wholesale . . . Excuse *me*, Mr. Queen.

Ellery: The crux of Montague's murder was — how was it done? This morning we have identical conditions as existed then — it has rained, the rain has stopped, and the mud of the clearing before the cave is smooth and unmarked. In other words, what you see now is what Montague saw when he set foot in this clearing — to cross it, enter the cave, and there meet his death at the hands of a very clever criminal. (*Laura crying in background*) Sorry, Miss Montague. But this is necessary.

Nikki (*off*): Laura — lean on me. There, darling . . .

Ellery: Montague was strangled by no ghost, ladies and gentlemen. The strangler's hands were human hands — they left human fingermarks on Montague's throat and neck. Please forgive the fancy — but if the strangler had human hands, he also had human feet, and human feet leave prints in mud.

Collins: Isn't it possible Montague was strangled in the woods back there, and then staggered across the clearing into the cave to die?

Ellery: No, Professor Collins. Don't you recall that the trail left by Montague's bare feet across this mud was *perfectly straight*?

Nikki (*off*): I think I even remarked about that when I first saw the footprints, Ellery!

Ellery: You did, Nikki. And a dying man doesn't walk in a straight line.

No, when Montague crossed this clearing and entered the cave, he was perfectly well, and unaware of his impending doom. In other words, the murder was committed in the cave, and for the murderer to have strangled Montague in the cave he had to *get* there. So we must assume that the murderer *did* cross this clearing, because — as we've noted before — it's the only possible way to reach the cave. The question therefore is: How did the murderer cross this mud and still not leave footprints? I'll show you. Sergeant Velie!

Velie (*startled*): Huh?

Ellery: Sergeant, I want you to act the part of Colin Montague.

Velie: Do I gotta be a stiff, Mr. Queen? Have a heart.

Inspector: Stop groaning, Velie. Do as Ellery says.

Velie (*muttering*): That's all he ever wants me to do — be a stiff. "Sergeant, be the stiff," he says. Even in the mountains I gotta be a stiff . . .

Ellery: And I — I'm your murderer, Sergeant. (*Murmur*) This is the morning of the crime — about five a.m. Sergeant, you rose a full hour earlier than the time you were supposed to start the experiment with Lewis' assistance —

Velie: *I* did? Oh, you mean Montague.

Lewis: Montague tricked me! If that man weren't dead —

Ellery: But he is, Mr. Lewis . . . At any rate, Montague wasn't alone. (*Ad libs*) That's right. His murderer was with him. Now Montague and his companion entered the woods, crossed them, and came to this spot — the edge of the clearing before the cave. Come with me into the woods a little way, Sergeant, and we'll demonstrate what it was poor Finch snapped with his camera — the evidence for which he was murdered last night. We'll show them — (*Begin to fade*) just how Montague and his murderer appeared when they crossed the mud of the clearing.

Velie (*fading*): Okay. If I gotta, I gotta . . . (*Others ad lib for a few seconds*)

Ellery (*off*): Yes, that's what I mean, Sergeant!

Velie (*off — astonished*): Well, I'll be my uncle's monkey!

Ellery (*off*): Come, come, Sergeant. (*Sounds of Velie panting*) All right, now — walk out from behind this bush and cross that mud! (*Crunch steps of one fading on. Sudden gasps of astonishment from all*)

Nikki: Inspector! Sergeant Velie — he's *carrying* Ellery on his *back*!

Inspector: A piggy-back, as I live and breathe!

Collins (*excited*): Of course, there they go across the mud — only one set of footprints — Sergeant Velie's . . .

Ellery (*off*): That's enough, Sergeant. Let me down!

Velie (*panting*): With a-lac-rity! You ain't no goose feather! (*Sound of being set down in mud. Mud steps fading on*)

Sue: So that's how it was done!

Ellery (*fading on*): Yes, Mrs. Collins, that's how it was done. Montague simply carried his murderer across the mud on his back. And into the cave! How did I know that? For one thing, because that's the only way Montague's murderer *could* have crossed this clearing without leaving footprints.

Inspector: I see it now! The other thing was the position of the strangler's thumbs on Montague's neck . . . Drat it!

Ellery: Exactly, dad. The thumbs were pointing upwards on the *back* of Montague's neck. That could only be if the murderer at the time of his crime was *behind* Montague. So it confirmed my other deduction.

Nikki: But Ellery, how on earth did he make Montague carry him? What excuse —

Ellery: Important question, Nikki. Naturally, it occurred to me at once. Grown men don't play piggy-back at five o'clock of an Adirondack morning. One person carrying another suggests — that the person carried *had* to be carried.

Collins: *Had* to be carried, Mr. Queen?

Ellery: An injury, Professor! And that was confirmed by a significant fact. Your friend Gabe here had stated that he'd found a place on the trail in the woods yonder where someone had slipped on loose stones and fallen into some juniper bushes. Gabe said it was Montague, because he thought Montague was alone. But since we know Montague *carried* someone, isn't it evident that it wasn't Montague who fell, but his *companion*?

Inspector: Sure! It was a prat-fall! This companion of Montague's faked a tumble, pretended to twist his ankle or something, said he couldn't walk — and Montague carried him all the way through the woods to the cave!

Ellery: Yes, dad. And the reason for all that was to leave only one set of footprints — Montague's — in the mud — to make us believe the murder had been the work of — well, the convenient ghost of the Haunted Cave.

Nikki: That's why strangulation was used! To foster the old wives' tale! Didn't the ghost-story say the ghost of the cave had choked his victims?

Sue: But Mr. Queen, you've accounted for this — this horrible person's getting *into* the cave —

Gabe: Yep, but how'd he git *out*? Fly?

Ellery (*chuckling*): Why, yes, Gabe — in a way. He flew through the air with the greatest of ease — downwards. You see, he escaped from the cave in the only way possible without leaving prints, now that his victim was dead — through that natural window in there!

Velie (*groaning*): Sure, sure. Why didn't *I* think o' that?

Ellery: I don't know, Sergeant. It was perfectly obvious. For while no one could have got *into* the cave through that opening in the cave wall, because it's fifty feet above the lake, someone could have got *out* simply by *diving* out — into the lake! You can't dive up, but you can dive down. (*Pause. Up on birds, etc.*)

Nikki (*low*): But Ellery — who was this . . . person? (*Pause*)

Collins (*eagerly*): Yes, Mr. Queen. You said you — knew.

Ellery (*gravely*): I do know, Professor Collins. Where was this little "accident" of the murderer's staged — I mean the place where he fell and pretended to twist his ankle?

Gabe: I told ye that myself. Right at the edge o' the woods as ye enter the trail leavin' the Professor's cabin.

Ellery: Yes, Gabe, that's what you said. In fact, you said it was "only a few yards" from the Professor's place.

Inspector: But Ellery — I don't get it.

Ellery: Don't you see, dad? Montague's companion apparently injures himself a few yards from the Professor's cabin — *and yet Montague carries him all the way through the woods to the cave!* Why? Why did Montague carry his companion to the *cave?* Why didn't he rather carry his companion back from the scene of the accident over the few yards to the cabin? Wouldn't Montague have done that if, say, his companion had been Professor Collins, or Mrs. Collins, or his own daughter, or *anyone* except a single person? (*Murmur*) (*Sharp*) There was only one reason why Montague didn't carry his companion back to the cabin, but carried him instead to the cave. And that was — because he and his companion were *bound* for the cave — because his companion was supposed to *share* the cave with him for the next twenty-four hours! (*Gasps. Quick*) Yes! Montague's companion — the man who got his victim up an hour earlier than scheduled on some trumped-up last-minute change of plan — who wanted to kill Montague because he hated him and because Montague had willed his valuable and unique psychic library to him, worth fame and fortune to their owner — (*Scuffle*) *Catch him, Velie!*

Inspector: No, you don't!

Velie: Got you!

Nikki (*shrieking*): It's Mr. Lewis! Mr. *Lewis!*

(*Music up*)

In "The Adventure of the Lost Child," broadcast on November 26, 1939, Ellery Queen combined formal detection with mounting suspense and grim terror in one of the most powerful stories in E.Q.'s radio career.

The Adventure of the Lost Child

The Characters

Harvey Morrell	Owner of *Hessian Chronicle*
Elsie Morrell	His wife
Alice Morrell	Their daughter
Arthur Livingston	A politician
Bill Flynn	Managing Editor
Miss Dorley	Morrell's secretary
Grischa Dorubny	An inventor
Silky Barrett	A gangster
Ellery Queen	The detective
Nikki Porter	His secretary
Inspector Queen	Of the New York Police
Sergeant Velie	Of the New York Police
Newspapermen	

Setting: Hessian, New York, 1939

(*Roaring of presses up . . . then down and out under . . . ringing of telephones on three tones up . . . then down under*)

Voice 1 (*fading in*): Good morning — Hessian Chronicle . . .

Voice 2: Good morning — Hessian Chronicle — Mr. Morrell? One moment, please —

Voice 3: Good morning, Hessian Chronicle — Sorry, Mr. Morrell is in conference . . .

Voice 4 (*fading out*): Good morning . . . Hessian Chronicle . . . (*Telephones out*)

(*Click of teletype and clatter of typewriters up . . . then down under murmer of conversation*)

Voice 1 (*fading in*): City desk. What? Speak up.

Voice 2 (*slightly off*): Boy. Copy.

Voice 1: I can't get to Morrell, I tell you.

Voice 3: Hey, Johnny, what happened to that page three layout?
Voice 4 (*off*): Copy.
Voice 1: OK. Kill the story. Morrell wants the whole front page for the Livingston spread.
Voice 3 (*fading out*): Morrell's sure ripping the hide off the Livingston gang, ain't he?
  (*Teletype and typewriters out. Presses come up full then down under ring of telephone . . . lift receiver*)
Foreman: Press room.
Morrell (*on filter*): Hold up the presses.
Foreman: What?
Morrell (*on filter*): I said stop the presses.
Foreman: Who in blazes are you?
Morrell (*filter*): Harvey Morrell.
Foreman: Oh, excuse me, Mr. Morrell. Yes, sir. Hey, boys, stop 'em.
  (*One big gong . . . presses come to a slow stop under following*)
Foreman: How long for, Mr. Morrell?
Morrell (*halfway*): Five minutes.
Foreman (*halfway*): That's about all we can wait if we're gonna make the street . . .
  (*Presses out*)
Morrell (*on*): There's a new front page coming down. As soon as you get it, shoot it in.
Foreman (*on filter*): OK, Mr. Morrell . . . I'll do that.
Morrell: Then you can speed 'em up for all they're worth. And don't stop for anything.
Foreman (*filter*): Yes, sir.
Morrell (*bang, receiver*): (*Phone rings . . . picks up phone*) Harvey Morrell speaking . . . (*Pause*) . . . Thanks, Commissioner, but it won't do you the least good. I'm in this fight for the duration . . . (*Bangs receiver*) The nerve of that boot-licker . . . (*Door opens . . . typewriters heard in background*) Oh, hello, Bill . . . (*Closes*) . . . (*Phone rings again*) Hang, this phone.
Flynn: Go ahead, Mr. Morrell . . . I'll wait . . . (*Picks up phone*)
Morrell: I'll cut this short, Bill . . . (*Into phone*) . . . Harvey Morrell . . . No. Absolutely not . . . (*Pause*) Well, I don't care what you heard in the capital. You stick to your chores, Judge, and I'll stick to mine . . . Yes, goodbye. (*Jiggles hook*) Operator . . . I'm in conference for the next ten minutes . . . (*Bangs receiver*) All right, Bill Flynn, what are you grinning about?
Flynn (*chuckling over rustle of newspaper*): Here's the proof of the new front page, Mr. Morrell . . . (*More rustle*) Like the banner?
Morrell (*chuckling*): Swell, Bill . . . this is fine . . . that's the ticket . . . keep

hammering that exposure story. Don't let up on Livingston till the polls open next week . . .

Flynn: Right . . . Uh . . . Mr. Morrell?

Morrell: Yes, Bill . . .

Flynn (*slowly*): You know I'm no shrinking violet . . . I love a scrap — 'specially when I'm scrapping for something I happen to believe in . . .

Morrell (*laughing*): Come on Bill, get it off your chest.

Flynn (*soberly*): I've been your managing editor ever since you bought out the Hessian Chronicle . . . and I've never shown the white feather yet, have I, Mr. Morrell?

Morrell (*slowly*): You're trying to tell me to watch my step, Bill.

Flynn: I'm trying to tell you you've never been up against a man like Arthur Livingston before, Mr. Morrell.

Morrell: Arthur Livingston's never been up against a man like Harvey Morrell before . . . or a newspaper like the Morrell-managed Chronicle.

Flynn: Just the same, Livingston's dangerous. He's a bushmaster. I tell you, Mr. Morrell, there's something funny about the way he's taking our campaign against him. He's too quiet . . .

Morrell (*contemptuously*): He's scared stiff . . . we've got Livingston licked, Bill, and he knows it.

Flynn (*dryly*): If you think that, you're making the biggest mistake of your publishing career. I was born and brought up in this town, Mr. Morrell, and you're practically a newcomer. I've watched Arthur Livingston ever since he broke in as a ward-heeler for the old Mack machine. There isn't a dirty trick he wouldn't pull . . . that he *hasn't* pulled. And that goes for the book, Mr. Morrell . . . (*Peculiar emphasis*) . . . the book . . .

Morrell (*after pause, quietly*): Murder, Bill?

Flynn (*grimly*): And worse.

Morrell (*puzzled*): Worse? (*Pause*) What d'ye mean, Bill?

Flynn: I wasn't going to mention this, but you may as well know what you're up against. There's a rumor going around Hessian that I know . . . I can't prove it, but I *know* . . . was deliberately started by Livingston . . . it concerns you and your family . . .

Morrell: My family . . . (*quietly*) . . . My wife? My daughter?

Flynn: It's nasty talk, Mr. Morrell . . . talk about . . . well . . .

Morrell (*quietly*): Thanks for tipping me off, Bill. So that's the kind of snake Livingston is, eh? Attack my family life, try to smear Elsie, little Alice . . . (*Curtly*) On your way out tell my secretary to send Livingston in . . .

Flynn (*surprised*): Livingston? He's *here* . . . to see *you*? (*Whistles*)

Morrell: I've had him cooling off outside for an hour. (*Grimly*) Tell Miss Dorley to send that skunk in, Bill — and get that front page down to the presss room pronto . . .

(*Music up . . . short . . . into opening of door*)

Secretary (*off*): Here's Mr. Livingston, Mr. Morrell . . . (*Door closes*)

Livingston (*soft bass voice . . . fading on*): Decided to see me after all, eh, Morrell?

Morrell (*coldly*): Well?

Livingston: Morrell, the Hessian Chronicle is beginning to annoy me.

Morrell (*dryly*): That was the general idea, Livingston.

Livingston: I shan't waste your time or mine with the usual offers of ah — political preferment, guaranteed advertising contracts . . . you're what is known as . . . (*Sneers*) . . . an honest man; I know the type . . .

Morrell (*curtly*): What d'ye want, Livingston? I'm busy.

Livingston: But you're also a man of good sense, Morrell. So I've come to give you some friendly advice.

Morrell: Yes?

Livingston: Call off this press campaign of yours against me, or . . . (*Pause*)

Morrell: Or what, Livingston?

Livingston (*softly*): Or you'll regret it as long as you live . . . (*Cheerful*) There. That's what I came to say, Morrell, and now that I've said it — no hard feelings, I hope?

Morrell (*deliberately, without heat*): Livingston, let me tell you something. You're the worst type of political termite, a crook, a pork-barrel gangster. You and your organization have squeezed millions out of the people of this State. You're a stench in the nostrils of every citizen interested in decent government. Somebody had to do something, Livingston — and I elected myself to the smelly job. Livingston, I'm going to keep you from being elected Senator if it takes every penny I've got, and there isn't a threat you can make, or imply, which will stop me. Is that clear?

Livingston (*softly*): I don't think you quite realize what you're up against, Sir Galahad. But I think you will — I think you will . . . before you're very much older, Morrell!

Morrell: You're through, Livingston. And you can thank me and the Chronicle for booting you into obscurity!

Livingston: You'll sing a different tune before . . . the day is over. (*Beginning to fade*) Good day, Mr. Morrell . . .

Morrell: Just a moment! If you can spare another minute of your valuable time . . . (*Click of inter-office communicator*)

Secretary (*filtered*): Yes, Mr. Morrell?

Morrell: Come in and bring your book. (*Click again*) I think you'll want to hear this, Livingston. (*Door open off, close*) Oh, Miss Dorley. Take a memorandum. "Reminder to Mr. Morrell — For Election Night."

Secretary: Yes, Mr. Morrell.

Morrell: "In re Livingston-inspired rumor concerning Morrell family life — Remind Mr. Morrell night polls close —" that's when you'll be a political has-been, Livingston — where was I, Miss Dorley?

Secretary: "Remind Mr. Morrell night polls close —"

Morrell: "— to go down to Livingston campaign headquarters and thrash Arthur Livingston to within an inch of his life."

Secretary: Yes, Mr. Morrell.

Morrell: On second thought, change "inch" to "half-inch," Miss Dorley. Good day, Mr. Livingston.

Livingston (*softly*): Good day . . . *sucker!* (*Door opens, closes*)

Secretary (*giggling*): Oh, Mr. Morrell, that was wonderful!

Morrell (*grimly*): But I meant it, Miss Dorley.

Secretary: Oh! I beg your pardon, Mr. Morrell . . . By the way, there's an angry, excited little foreign man outside — waiting to see you — a Russian, I think —

Morrell (*groaning*): Grischa Dorubny? For the lord's sake!

Secretary: Yes, sir. Some name like that. Shall I send him away?

Morrell (*wearily*): No, send him in, Miss Dorley. May as well get it over with. He's been phoning me for days.

Secretary: Yes, sir. (*Opens door. Off*) Will you come in, please, Mr. Dor — Mr. Dorubny?

Dorubny (*off — excited — don't make accent comic*): I come in! I come in — fast! (*Fading on*) Ha — Morrell! I call — I try see you —

Morrell (*wearily*): That's all, Miss Dorley.

Secretary: Yes, sir. (*Closes door*)

Morrell: Now. What's the trouble, Dorubny?

Dorubny: Trouble! *You* ask what is trouble! Is it so you refuse offer of five hundred thousand dollar for patent rights to my invention?

Morrell (*patiently*): Yes, Dorubny.

Dorubny (*panting*): How do you dare! To refuse half million without consulting me — the inventor! How do you dare!

Morrell: Now look, Dorubny, I've been very patient with you, because you're a screwball and I happen to like screwballs. But enough's enough. We've gone all through this a dozen times. I control the rights to your invention, and you know it.

Dorubny: But it is my invention! You steal from Grischa Dorubny blood — blood of his life —

Morrell: Please . . . I supported you for eight years, didn't I? Financed your experiments when nobody else would even talk to you. It's cost me fifty thousand dollars — more.

Dorubny (*dramatically*): Me, it cost eight year of my life!

Morrell: I gambled. If you failed, I took a cold loss. If you succeeded — Well, you made a bargain. Stick to it!

Dorubny: You rob me, Morrell! You cheat poor Dorubny!

Morrell (*getting mad*): See here, Dorubny, you signed that agreement of your own free will — you were glad enough to get my money then! That agreement's in my attorney's safe, understand? It won't do you the least good to come raving to me now.

Dorubny: You take everything! I get nothing!

Morrell: The usual Slavic exaggeration. I take seventy-five percent, Dorubny, by agreement, and you take the remaining twenty-five. You call that nothing?

Dorubny: But you — you take from me right to sell invention!

Morrell: You legally assigned to me the right to negotiate, Dorubny. Thank heaven I thought of putting *that* in the contract! (*Mildly*) Now go on home, Dorubny. Stop worrying. I'll make a rich man of you — soon as I get a deal I like.

Dorubny (*frenzy*): I was fool! You think you cheat me! Morrell, I make you pay for this! I get revenge —

Morrell (*suddenly very angry*): Are *you* threatening me, too? By heaven, I'm sick and tired of threats! Get out!

Dorubny: You will see — you will see — I make you suffer —

Morrell (*same*): If you think our agreement won't stand up in court, Dorubny, sue me!

Dorubny (*shouting*): Liar! Thief! *Amerikansky maschenik!*

Morrell (*same*): Get out, Dorubny — before I kick you out!

Dorubny (*fading*): I get out — I get out — but you see — you wait — (*Open door. Trail off excited Russian lingo. Phone ring on mike. Close door off*)

Morrell: Whew! (*Picks up phone*) Yes?

Elsie (*filtered*): Harvey?

Morrell: Elsie! How are you, dear. How's Alice?

Elsie (*filtered*): That's what I'm calling about, Harvey. Dearest, I'm . . . worried. I wouldn't have called — I know how busy you are — but . . .

Morrell (*alertly*): Elsie! What's wrong? Don't tell me Alice is sick! I *thought* she had the sniffles this morning —

Elsie (*filtered*): That was your imagination, Harvey. It's not that . . . Harvey, Alice isn't home from school yet!

Morrell (*slowly*): Not home from — school?

Elsie (*filtered*): She should have been home half an hour ago.

Morrell: Oh. (*Pause; then elaborate lightness*) Oh, Alice probably stopped in at some kid's house to play, Elsie . . .

Elsie (*filtered*): But Harvey, she's never done that before! Harvey, I'm — scared.

Morrell (*quickly*): Now don't get panicky, Elsie. It's probably nothing at all. (*As if to himself slowly*) Nothing . . . at . . . all . . .

Elsie (*filtered*): I know, Harvey, but — you'll come right home?

Morrell (*forced laugh*): Of course, Elsie. All this fuss about a child's being a half-hour late . . . However, 'phone the school if it'll make you feel any better.

Elsie (*filtered*): Yes, Harvey. Harvey . . . hurry home —

Morrell (*lightly*): All right, Elsie. *All* right. I'll leave right away. 'Bye. (*Click of phone. Pause. Then in dull heavy whisper*) Oh Lord. (*Click of communicator. Harsh*) Miss Dorley! Order my car — at once!

(*Music up . . . and into Elsie weeping softly . . .*)

Nikki (*sympathy*): I know just how you feel, Mrs. Morrell, but you must get a grip on yourself. Mustn't she, Ellery?

Ellery: She certainly must. Mrs. Morrell, little Alice's absence probably has the simplest explanation —

Elsie (*crying*): Where's Harvey? Why doesn't he come *home*?

Nikki: Do stop crying, Mrs. Morrell. You'll be ill.

Elsie (*trying to stop*): I . . . I suppose I am being silly, Miss Porter. But — oh, it's been such a day! I'm all alone in the house here. All three of my servants walked out on me the other day, and I simply haven't been able to find *anyone*. If you two hadn't dropped in just now, I don't know *what* . . . (*Doorbell rings insistently off*) There's Harvey! (*Fading*) Please — excuse me — I must . . .

Nikki (*quick — low*): Ellery! What do you think?

Ellery (*same*): Hard to say, Nikki. It might be . . . bad.

Nikki (*same*): It's — terrifying. An eight-year-old child. I —

Ellery (*same*): Careful! Here they come. Don't let them see we think anything's wrong . . .

Elsie (*fading on*): — and oh, Harvey, I've been going crazy!

Morrell (*same — tries to pass it off lightly for wife's sake*): Now, Elsie. Anyone would imagine a child had never been late from school before . . . Hullo! I didn't know you had company, Elsie . . . Wait! Wait a minute, now . . . Nikki Porter, by George!

Nikki (*laughing*): Hello, Harvey.

Morrell: Nikki Porter . . . Why, I hardly recognized you, Nikki. Last time I saw you — let's see, now — back in Kansas City —

Nikki: The Morrells were old friends of my family, Ellery. Mr. Morrell — Mr. Ellery Queen. (*Ad lib greetings — short*)

Ellery: Nikki and I were driving back from Boston, Mr. Morrell — we'd been on a case up there — and of course Nikki insisted on stopping in Hessian to see you —

Morrell (*absently*): Yes, yes, delighted to have you both . . . Elsie, about Alice. I mean — you haven't found a *trace* of her?

Elsie (*crying again*): Oh, Harvey . . . I even spoke to Alice's teacher! Alice wasn't in school *all day*! And none of her little friends have seen her, either. I've called everywhere . . .

Morrell (*dazed*): Wasn't — in school — all day —

Nikki (*low*): Ellery — maybe we can help. If it's — really bad . . .

Ellery (*quietly*): If there's anything we can do, Mr. Morrell . . . I've had some experience in — well, of course, we needn't jump at conclusions —

Morrell (*hardly hearing*): Yes . . . thank you . . . gone . . . all day. (*Pause*) I've got to think. *Think* . . . Elsie! Didn't you take Alice to school this morning, as you always do?

Elsie (*sobbing*): Yes. I drove her to the school corner, and she got out — she always insists on walking the rest of the way herself. She waved goodbye and . . . and then I drove off to do some shopping in Lower Village and . . . Oh, Harvey — she skipped away so — so — (*Sobs*)

Nikki (*low*): It's past four, Ellery. That means the little girl's been missing more than *seven hours* . . .

Ellery (*low*): I know, Nikki, I know. It does look — serious.

Morrell (*feverishly*): Wait! It's possible that . . . Elsie! Did you look in the play-room in the back yard?

Elsie (*dazed*): Play-room? Back yard . . . Why . . . no, Harvey. I didn't think she'd — Do you think — do you really think —

Morrell: She may have come home and gone directly to the back yard! She may be out there right this minute —

Nikki (*forced*): Of course! She probably fell asleep, or something —

Elsie (*wildly*): I'm going out to look!

Morrell (*forcefully*): Elsie! Stop!

Elsie (*dazed*): But Harvey . . .

Morrell: Mr. Queen and I will — go, Elsie. Queen?

Ellery (*quietly*): Of course, Morrell. Nikki . . .

Nikki (*quickly*): Mrs. Morrell, you and I — we'll stay right here, in the house. Alice might come marching in —

Elsie (*faintly*): But — I — Alice — you think —

Ellery (*low*): Come along, Morrell! Quickly. (*Nikki ad lib fading as steps on wood of two men on*)

Morrell: Down this hall, Queen — we'll cut through the kitchen — Oh Lord!

Ellery: This door? (*Opens door*) Morrell, you've got to get hold of yourself. (*Closes door — steps on linoleum floor*)

Morrell (*panting*): Get hold of myself . . . Yes. Yes.

Ellery: Your wife's in pretty bad shape. *You* can't fold up. (*Opens back door*) Out here, eh? (*Down three wooden steps*)

Morrell (*outdoors*): Yes. (*Calling*) Alice! (*Pause*) *Alice*!

Ellery: Is that Alice's play-house — that little shack there, beside the garage?

Morrell (*running steps on turf*): Yes. *Alice!*

Ellery: Alice! Are you in there? (*Stop steps. Open creaky door*)

Morrell (*despair*): Empty! She's not here! I knew she wouldn't be. I knew it . . . She hasn't even *been* here! Oh, Lord — Alice —

Ellery (*off a little*): Morrell! There's a . . . note pinned up on the back of this play-room door!

Morrell (*faintly*): A . . . note? A . . . no —

Ellery (*off a little*): Pencil, crude block letters, on a sheet of paper torn from a child's writing tablet — let's see, now —

Morrell (*whisper*): A note. A note.

Ellery (*fading on — grave*): Morrell. It's — bad news.

Morrell (*sudden agonized outburst*): Queen, for the love of mercy! Don't just stand there feeling sorry for me! *What does that note say?*

Ellery (*very grave but clear*): I'm frightfully sorry, Morrell. Your little girl's been . . . kidnapped.

(*Music up . . . and into gasping of Elsie . . .*)

Nikki (*compassionately*): Sip some more water, Mrs. Morrell — Elsie . . .

Morrell (*anguished*): Is she all right? Elsie, are you all right?

Ellery: She's fine now, Morrell. Naturally, the shock —

Elsie (*feebly*): Alice . . . Alice . . . (*Begins to cry*) Oh, my darling!

Morrell (*hoarsely*): Elsie —! Oh, I'm losing my *mind*. What are we going to *do*? Elsie! Dearest!

Nikki (*sniffling*): Let her alone, H-Harvey. Let her c-cry.

Morrell: Queen, read me that — that kidnap note again. Read it again. It seems like a nightmare. Read it, Queen!

Ellery (*pityingly*): Of course, Morrell. Easy, now. It says: "We have your girl. She's safe and she'll stay safe as long as you obey orders —"

Elsie (*weeping*): Safe . . . Oh, God, I hope so. I hope so . . .

Ellery: "Don't notify the police. Don't tip off the Feds. Your house is being watched. Your telephone is tapped. We can hear every word you say on it, so don't 'phone anybody. Don't answer the 'phone when it rings. Don't answer the doorbell. Nobody is to leave the house. If you make the slightest move to notify anybody outside your house we will kill your girl."

Elsie (*weeping*): She'll be — They'll — heaven knows what they're doing to her! She must be hungry — frightened — Alice . . . (*Breaks down*)

Nikki (*half in tears*): Elsie — darling — Alice will be all right. The note says she's safe, doesn't it? Come on, brace up . . .

Morrell (*strangled voice*): They won't get away with this! I'll — I'll . . .

Elsie (*screaming*): Harvey, no! Harvey, do what they say! Harvey, please . . .
(*Sobs*) . . . oh, please . . . I want Alice back . . . (*Sobs*)

Morrell (*groaning*): My sweet kid — that sweet little kid —

Ellery: There's more to the note. It goes on to say: "At noon tomorrow
the girl's mother — nobody else — is to *pick up the phone*. It won't
ring, but *pick it up just the same*. Our tapper will be connected so we'll
be able to talk to the mother. Remember — noon tomorrow, pick
'phone, girl's mother. We will give you instructions for paying the
ransom. Follow orders and you get your child back. Don't — and she
dies." (*Pause*) That's all. No signature — nothing.

Elsie (*whisper*): Noon tomorrow — a whole night — a whole morning . . .
I'll go — mad. Oh, God. (*Cries again*)

Nikki (*low*): Ellery, can't we do *anything*?

Ellery (*same, gently*): We're powerless, Nikki. In a case like this — it's up
to the father and mother. No one else has a right to interfere.

Morrell (*raving, crying mad*): Hanging — electrocution — quartering —
too good for them! Take an innocent child — practically a baby —
eight years old — brutalize her — terrorize her — (*Whisper*) . . . what
a *foul* way to get back at *me* . . .

Elsie: Harvey! You're not going to — to —

Morrell (*wildly*): Fight? Yes, I am, Elsie! I'm going to call their bluff —
notify the authorities — I read somewhere about what to do in cases
like this — notify the Federal Bureau of Investigation in Washington —
they know how to handle these things —

Elsie (*panic*): Harvey — no! (*Breathless determination*) *No!*

Morrell: But Elsie, we can't knuckle under to these — these savages!
We've got to fight back! It's our duty to!

Elsie: But what about Alice? Oh, Harvey, I . . . I know it's wrong. I know it!
But what's duty to me if Alice is . . . is . . . We've *got* to do what these —
animals say! Anything! Anything, Harvey! (*Begins to sob again*)

Morrell (*brokenly*): Elsie . . . how do you think I feel? My own child . . . Do
you think I want Alice to — to — (*Chokes*)

Elsie: I don't care if it costs every dollar we have — if we have to sell the
house, the car —

Morrell: Do you think I'm thinking of the *money*?

Elsie: Oh, Harvey, I know you're not. But — please do it my way. Harvey,
please . . . (*Crying*)

Nikki (*crying herself*): Oh, Elsie . . . this is the most terrible . . . Ellery, do
something!

Morrell (*dully*): You said you've had experience in cases like this,
Queen . . . I don't know where to turn! Help us — please —

Ellery (*slowly*): Morrell, much as I should like to . . . I can't decide for
you. It's too personal a problem. It's your child's life that's at stake.

You've got to make the decision, take the responsibility for the decision. Of course, whatever you decide — it goes without saying that Nikki and I will help in every possible way.

Morrell: Nikki — what do *you* think?

Nikki (*through tears*): There can't be any question about it, can there?

Morrell (*heavily*): No. When you get right down to it . . . (*Pause*) No, there can't. (*Tenderly*) Elsie darling — whatever you say — come here to me, Elsie —

Elsie: Oh, Harvey! (*Sobbing becomes muffled as if against chest*)

Morrell (*soothing*): There, now — everything's going to be all right . . .

Ellery (*slowly*): You've decided, Morrell? You'll obey the instructions of the kidnapers?

Morrell (*simply*): Yes, Queen.

Ellery: Then we'll play the game for all it's worth —

Elsie: "We," Mr. Queen? But you — you and Nikki don't have to —

Ellery (*gravely*): We're in this, too, Mrs. Morrell, because we're in the house, and the note specifically says "Nobody is to leave the house." Since the house is being watched, Nikki and I must have been seen coming in. So we can't leave.

Nikki: We don't want to leave!

Ellery: So we're in a state of siege. (*Phone rings. Insistently, repeated. No dialogue*)

Elsie (*hysterically*): (*Over ringing*) Harvey! Don't touch that phone! They wrote not to answer the — phone! (*Ringing still*)

Morrell (*fading on*): I won't, Elsie. I won't. (*Pause. Phone stops ringing*)

Nikki: Prisoners — we're prisoners! Marooned — blockaded —

Ellery (*heavily*): Yes, cut off from the outside world. But we've got to see it through. Mustn't take the slightest chance. Mustn't give the kidnapers the least excuse to . . . (*Stops*)

Elsie: Say it! To kill my girl! (*Pause. Phone starts ringing again*) Oh, Alice . . . Alice darling . . . (*Phone keeps ringing*)

(*Music up through ringing phone — motif of phone and doorbell ringing — give madness feeling — and into doorbell off . . .*)

Nikki (*hoarse — almost hysterical*): If those bells don't stop ringing soon, Ellery, I'll — scream! All afternoon, evening . . . Oh, *stop!*

Ellery (*gently*): Come on, Nikki, pull yourself together. You won't help the Morrells by having hysterics. (*Bell stops*) There, it's stopped. No, don't touch the window shades, Nikki!

Nikki: I'm sorry, Ellery. It's just — this waiting, *waiting* . . .

Ellery (*dully*): Where's Harvey Morrell gone to?

Nikki: He's upstairs trying to get Elsie to take a sleeping powder . . .

This is like living in a — a house of the dead! Telephone a foot away — the living world all around us — and we have to sit here and stare at each other. It's maddening!

Ellery: I know, Nikki . . . How do you think *I* feel? Here I am, chained to this chair — can't make a move for fear it would cost that little girl her life —

Nikki (*again hysteria*): You can think, can't you? You're so good at that, Mr. Queen! Well, go on — think your way out of this!

Ellery (*gently*): Nikki . . . (*She begins to cry softly*) I *am* thinking, Nikki. But for once thinking does no good. I've never in my life been so literally — and to such little purpose — an armchair detective . . . I'm not so sure it wouldn't have been wiser to call in the Federal men.

Nikki (*crying*): Poor Elsie — she's cried her eyes out — those lovely blue eyes — so red now — so full of dumb pain —

Ellery: Nikki, stop it! Here's Morrell — (*Nikki stopping, sniffling*)

Morrell (*fading on very strained*): Queen . . . I can't stand it. There must be something we can do between now and tomorrow noon!

Nikki: Sit down, Harvey — you're wearing yourself out —

Ellery: If we could only get outside help without tipping off the kidnaper!

Morrell (*bitterly*): It's a big "if." With the phone tapped, the house watched . . .

Ellery: If we only could, though! There's *someone* we could trust —

Nikki: Ellery! The Inspector!

Morrell (*dully*): Inspector? Inspector who?

Ellery: My father, Morrell — Inspector of police in New York. If I could only reach dad undercover! But how? *How?* Can't phone, can't send a wire, can't risk sending one of us out of the house — (*Morrell begins a slow, hysterical laugh*)

Nikki (*alarmed*): Harvey, stop! Ellery, he's hysterical —

Ellery: Come on, old man — stop that!

Morrell (*choking*): Oh Lord, I've lost my mind. Sitting here like a fool all day . . . It never occurred to me. Not once. (*Excited*) (*Low voice*) Queen, there is a way! (*Nikki ad lib exclamation*)

Ellery: Morrell! What way? Talk, man!

Morrell: Come with me! (*Chairs scraped back. Quick steps*) Upstairs. My study. Here — this way —

Nikki: Don't make any noise. Elsie needs the sleep . . . Oh, Harvey, if there only is!

Morrell: *There's a private wire in my study!*

Ellery (*quick*): Private wire? To where? Your newspaper office?

Morrell: Yes! It's a direct line to my managing editor's desk — Bill Flynn! Down this hall here . . . My end and his are both under lock and key. Flynn's the only one with a key to his private phone . . . In here! (*Open door. close*) Fact, Bill Flynn's the only one except Elsie and me who even knows this private line exists. (*Unlocks drawer*)

Nikki: Wait! You're sure the kidnapers can't — overhear, Harvey?

Morrell: Of course I'm sure! It's a private wire, I tell you! (*Picks up phone*)

Ellery: Morrell, wait a moment. Can you trust Flynn?

Morrell: Like my right arm.

Nikki: Harvey . . . I'm afraid . . .

Morrell (*savagely*): I tell you there's no danger of a leak! Do you think I'd risk my own child's life if there was? (*Click. Another click*) Bill! Flynn!

Flynn (*filtered throughout*): Mr. Morrell! Thank heaven. What happened? What's the matter? I've been trying to locate you all day. Even using the private wire — but no answer —

Morrell: Bill! I can't stop to explain. Don't ask questions! Listen to me — carefully!

Flynn (*quietly*): I'm listening, Mr. Morrell. Shoot.

Morrell: Call up Inspector Queen of the New York Police. Get him down to your office as soon as possible. Understand?

Ellery: Tell Flynn to mention my name, Morrell.

Morrell: Bill, tell Inspector Queen this is an emergency call, and it comes from his son, Ellery. Got that?

Flynn: Son, Ellery . . . Yes, Mr. Morrell. Anything else?

Morrell: He's not to tell a soul about this call. When he comes, ask him to call his son on this private line — from your office, behind locked doors, Bill.

Ellery: Morrell, hand me that phone a moment.

Nikki: Ellery, be careful. Oh, be careful.

Ellery: Flynn. This is Ellery Queen. If my father wants to take Sergeant Velie along, it's all right, but no one else. And they're to come into Hessian incognito — understand? Under false names. Now get busy, Flynn.

Flynn (*grimly*): You bet, Mr. Queen. (*click*)

(*Music up . . . and into fade-in of telephone conversation . . .*)

Inspector (*filtered throughout*): I get you, I get you, son. Pretty grim set-up.

Ellery: So now it's up to you, dad. You understand how we're fixed?

Inspector: Only too well. Flynn's here with me, and so's Velie. It's a closed corporation, don't worry about that. You're sure there's no leak on this private wire?

Ellery: Morrell says no. Dad — we're prisoners here — so you and Velie will have to be our eyes and ears and arms and legs. And everything you do has to be done on the sly. Nobody's to find out who you are or what you're in Hessian for!

Inspector: Don't worry about that, Ellery. But accomplishing anything —

that's going to be tough. Give me a description of the child.

Ellery: There's a photograph of Alice on Morrell's desk in his private office, he tells me.

Inspector: Flynn's shown it to me already. How about the details that don't show up on the photo?

Ellery: Height and weight average for her age — she's eight. Brown hair, brown eyes, and at the time she was kidnaped she wore a brown plaid dress with a Scotch coat and tam to match. She has a strawberry birthmark on her right arm, just above the elbow. Got it?

Inspector: Yep. Well, we'll check Arthur Livingston, the politician you told me about, and Grischa Dorubny, this nutty Russian inventor that's sore at Morrell —

Ellery: Yes, they're your best leads. Keep me posted, dad — every detail you pick up! All I can do is sit in this house, confound it — keep up these people's morale — until Elsie Morrell picks up that other phone tomorrow at noon to talk to the kidnaper!

(*Music up . . . and into mild background murmur as of hotel lobby . . . rustle of newspaper on mike . . .*)

Velie (*fading on excited*): Guess who I just spotted right here in the Hessian House lobby, Inspector —

Inspector (*quick low*): Keep your voice down, Velie, and *don't* call me Inspector, you ape! Who'd you just see?

Velie (*guarded but triumphant*): Silky . . . Barrett!

Inspector: Silky Barrett! The Chicago gangster?

Velie: Yep! See him over there, sittin' all alone watchin' that pin-ball game? The tall drink o' water with the flop-ears and that scar on his lip? I reco'nized him right off.

Inspector: Mmm. Silky Barrett, all right. Used to be one of Big Emma's hoods. Now what would a big-town torpedo be doing in a place like Hessian, I wonder?

Velie (*meaningly*): Where there's just been a snatch . . . Yeah, you wonder!

Inspector (*slowly*): Velie, we're going to talk to Mr. Silky Barrett.

Velie: But Inspector — I mean, Dick, he'd get suspicious!

Inspector: Not if we work it right. Look. We're registered here under phony names. Barrett's never seen either of us. So you know what we're going to be, Tom Velie? Gangsters! (*chuckles*)

Velie (*thoughtfully*): Say, we might get away with it, at that . . .

Inspector: We will, if you don't get ambitious. Come on! (*Steps*) Be nervous, Tom. Follow my lead — play up to me. I'll swing this on Dorubny, the inventor. You watch . . . It'll fool him!

Velie (*muttering*): I hope so for that kid's sake! (*Steps stop*)

Inspector: Here he is. (*Speaking from side of mouth, acting gangsterish*) Psst! Barrett!

Barrett (*startled*): Huh? Say —

Inspector (*guarded*): Hey, Silky . . . No, don't look up. We don' wanna be spotted. (*Loudly*) Got a match, brother?

Barrett (*softly*): Hey, what is this, you two?

Velie (*loud*): Give us a light, will ya, buddy? (*Low*) Come on, come on, Silky . . . act up! This is gotta look accidental, the house dick's lampin' us.

Barrett: Oh . . . I get ya. (*Loud*) Sure. Here y'are, fella! (*Strikes match*) (*Low*) Who are you two guys, anyways?

Inspector (*loud*): T'anks, friend. Say, Tom, what d'ye say we sit down here by this gent, huh? Gets kinda lonesome in these jerktown hotels! (*Laughs loudly and elaborately*)

Velie (*same*): Yeah, Dick, sure does. Move over, will ya, pal?

Inspector (*low*): Good! Now look, Silky, you don't know us two, see. But we reco'nized you right off the bat. Silky Barrett, I says. An' Tom here, he says: "Say, what's a big-time hood like Silky doin' in this one-horse town?"

Velie: So Dick here, *he* says: "We might ask ourselves the same question, Tom!" (*Inspector, Velie laugh knowingly*)

Barrett (*suspicious*): Wait a minute, wait a minute, you muggs. Who are ya? What d'ye want?

Inspector (*low*): I'm Dick Scalopino, an' this is my pal Tommy the Torp. We're from the Coast, see? In the East on — business.

Barrett (*suspicious*): How'd ya know me?

Velie: How'd ya know me, he says. (*Guffaws*) How'd ya know me — Silky Barrett! (*Laughs as if Barrett has cracked a joke*)

Inspector: Pipe down, Tom! We don't want nobody spottin' us before we pull off that Dorubny job —

Velie (*menacing*): Now ya went an' spilled it! *Ya dumb ape.* That's what I get for workin' with an old geezer.

Barrett (*alertly*): Do — *what* job? You guys in Hessian to pull a job? What kinda job d'ye say?

Velie (*menacing*): Dick, we don't cut in nobody, see?

Inspector (*low*): Wait a second, Tom. Don't get tough. I guess Silky here knows a thing or two. Maybe we could kind of make a deal — we need a right guy — a front man — for this job —

Velie: I don't like it! I t'ought there was on'y gonna be the two of us, wid all that dough we c'n pick off! Now you wanna cut in Barrett — I don't like it!

Inspector: Aw, Silky'd earn his cut, Tom. You know that. Besides, there's plenty for a dozen splits. What d'ye say, Tom?

Velie (*sullen*): I dunno. I don't like it.

Barrett (*falling for bait*): Hey, look, muggs, if you really got somethin' hot . . . Well, I'm in this burg on a little business deal o'my own, see . . . but that ain't no reason why three wise guys can't hook up an' . . .

Inspector: Now you're talkin', Silky.

Barrett: But this ain't no place to talk business. I'll meetcha in that hamburger joint down the street in five minutes.

Inspector: O.K. We'll be there.

Barrett (*fading*): Goodbye, gents. It was a pleasure.

Velie: So long! (*Low*) How'm I doin' — Dick?

Inspector: Fine . . . fine . . . (*Suddenly angry*) But you didn't *have* to call me an old geezer.

Velie: Aw, Inspector.

(*Music up short . . . into telephone conversation*)

Ellery: Silky Barrett, eh? Sounds promising, dad. What happened after he fell for the bait?

Inspector (*filtered throughout*): Nothing much. We're pretty sure he's in Hessian to do a dirty job for Livingston, but he's cagy.

Ellery: Mmm. You say Velie's with Barrett now?

Inspector: Yes . . . (*Chuckling*) and doing a swell job of getting that rat's confidence by pretending to resent him! By the way, I managed to see Livingston. Through a ruse. But I didn't get a bite. He's one smart customer, Ellery.

Ellery: So I understand. Have you seen the Russian, Dorubny?

Inspector: I've been watching him. So far — nothing.

Ellery (*sighing*): Well, keep at it, dad. Maybe something will turn up. Meanwhile, Nikki and I are having our hands full keeping the Morrells from climbing the walls.

Inspector: I'd just like to get my hands on the dirty dogs who pull stunts like this . . . (*Crisply*) I'll buzz you tomorrow on this private wire, Ellery — a half-hour past the noon call scheduled by the kidnapers!

Ellery: Right, dad. (*Grimly*) If we can keep sane until then!

(*Music up . . . into house clock striking twelve o'clock*)

Elsie (*whisper — counting with strokes*): Two, three, four . . .

Morrell (*hoarsely*): Elsie — for heaven's sake — don't crack now. You've got to pick up that phone in a few seconds —

Nikki (*tense*): Elsie — everything depends on you, now . . .

Ellery (*sharply*): Stroke of noon! Mrs. Morrell, pick up the phone!

Elsie (*whispering*): Yes, Mr. Queen . . . (*Picks up phone. Pause. Fearful*)

H-hello. (*Pause*) Yes — this is . . . Mrs . . . Morrell . . . (*Pause*) (*Crying
out*) But my girl! Is she safe? Is she there? Let me speak to Alice —
please! Please! (*Pause. Dully*) All right. I won't . . . I mean — Oh,
please! (*Long pause. Frightened*) Yes . . . Yes . . . Yes, I understand.
(*Pause*) Yes . . . (*Pause*) Yes . . . (*Pause*) I see. (*Pause*) Yes, we'll do just —
just what you say. But please — my little girl — don't hurt her — don't
. . . (*Stops. Whisper*) He — hung — up. (*Replaces receiver. Begins to cry*)
Morrell (*frantic*): Elsie! What did they say? How is Alice? Is she — did
you — Elsie, for heaven's sake, talk!
Nikki: Don't shout at her, Harvey! Elsie, darling —
Ellery (*sharply*): Pull yourself together, Mrs. Morrell. Tell me — was it a
man or a woman you just spoke to?
Elsie (*crying*): A man . . . a man . . .
Morrell: Who was it? Did you recognize the voice?
Elsie (*stopping — dazed*): I don't know. I thought once . . . But then . . .
Harvey, I don't know. It sounded — funny . . .
Nikki: A disguised voice! (*Disappointed*) Darn it!
Morrell: What did he tell you, Elsie?
Ellery: Tell us everything he said — everything, Mrs. Morrell!
Elsie (*dully*): He asked if I was Mrs. Morrell. He said Alice . . . Alice was
unharmed.
Morrell (*hushed*): Thank Heaven!
Elsie: He . . . wouldn't let me speak to her. Then he began to — give me
instructions. Harvey, you're to go to the bank, now, right away. Just
you. Alone.
Morrell (*hoarsely*): Yes? Yes, Elsie?
Elsie: You're to get a hundred thousand dollars in . . . small bills — fives,
tens, twenties . . . give no reason to the bank . . . unmarked bills, he
said, or they'll — they'll — (*Piteously*) Harvey, you've got to do what
he said!
Nikki: Of course Harvey will, Elsie. Of course he will.
Morrell (*hoarsely*): And then what, Elsie?
Elsie: Then you're to . . . come right back here to the house with the money
and . . . you're not to talk to anyone on the way — you'll be watched,
he said — and you're to wait here until midnight, and then . . .
Ellery: Yes, Mrs. Morrell? What is your husband to do at midnight?
Elsie: Harvey's to put the money in a suitcase and — drive out alone on
the Old North Road to the Three Oaks Memorial, leave the car there,
and walk the rest of the way to that empty old house — the Macauley
house, he said — on Route 62. They'll be waiting there — they'll
have Alice there —
Morrell (*rapidly*): Macauley house — it's been abandoned for years —
an old ruin in the middle of nowhere — not far from the Three Oaks

Memorial . . . Well, I've got to go. Got to go to the bank. Right now. (*Fading*) Got to go to the bank . . .

Elsie (*anguished cry*): Harvey! Oh, Harvey, be careful! Do just what he said!

Ellery (*gently*): Your husband will be careful, Mrs. Morrell. (*Low*) Nikki, keep an eye on her. She's about ready to fold up. I'm going upstairs to wait for Dad's call on the private wire!

(*Music up . . . short . . . into fade-in of telephone conversation*)

Inspector (*filtered throughout*): Well, then, all we can do is wait for tonight, Ellery. Too bad she didn't recognize that voice!

Ellery (*gloomily*): Whoever's behind this has thought of everything.

Inspector: By the way, we got a bad break. Velie — blast his soul! — let Silky Barrett get away from him.

Ellery (*appalled*): Dad, no! If Barrett's suspicious —

Inspector: I don't think so — at least not about the snatch. I don't know what to think. But Barrett gave Velie the slip just the same. Velie's out now hunting for him.

Ellery: Bad . . . bad!

Inspector: What are we going to do about tonight? I've half a mind to call in the F.B.I., surround the Macauley house, and have it out with 'em!

Ellery (*groaning*): We can't, dad. They'd kill the child.

Inspector (*distraught*): I suppose they would, the skunks. Ellery, if you hadn't tied my hands with that promise — I swear I'd go to the government men. This is too big a job for two men. It's not right, Ellery —

Ellery: I know, dad. But the Morrells made the decision, and after all, it's their child. Look. (*Quickly*) I have a plan. I'm going with Morrell tonight!

Inspector: You are? But Morrell would give it away — in his state of mind, he'd never be able to act up —

Ellery: Morrell won't know. He has a rumble-seat in his car. I'm going to play sick, go to my room, and then slip out and hide in the rumble-seat compartment before Morrell leaves — he won't know the difference. Nikki will keep Mrs. Morrell from knowing, too. Then when Morrell gets to that Three Oaks Memorial and leaves the car to walk to the Macauley house, I'll get out of the car and wait. You be there, too, dad!

Inspector: All right, son. Velie and I will be hiding near the Memorial somewhere. But be careful with that fake-sickness stunt!

Ellery: I will, dad. See you at midnight!

(*Music up . . . and into*)

Elsie (*very nervous*): What time is it now, Nikki? Do you think Harvey's got to the Memorial yet? Oh, I hope nothing goes wrong! If only Mr. Queen hadn't taken ill! He'd know what to do! I feel so much confidence in him —

Nikki: Now, Elsie, you're working yourself up to a nervous breakdown. It's too bad about Ellery, but I've put him to bed upstairs, and besides, what can go wrong? In a little while Harvey will be handing over the suitcase full of money at the Macauley house — they'll give Alice to him — and —

Elsie (*wildly*): He'll get there too late! I told him to start a few minutes earlier! Suppose he gets a flat, or something! They won't wait. They'll think — they'll —

Nikki: But, darling — he won't. You're just — upset. Come here, Elsie — sit down beside me —

Elsie (*more wildly*): The kidnapers won't keep their word! They'll kill Alice — they'll kill her! (*Pause*) (*Whisper*) Nikki, *I've got to go there. Now. Now*, do you hear?

Nikki (*alarmed*): Elsie — no! You'll spoil everything — Elsie, you're out of your mind —

Elsie (*almost screaming*): I've got to! They'll listen to me! They won't kill a child if . . . I'm going!

Nikki (*frantic — scared*): Elsie — you can't! Just a little longer — trust Harvey — trust Ellery —

Elsie (*screaming, fading*): I can't stand it, Nikki! I'm taking Mr. Queen's car . . . I'm going! I'm —

Nikki (*screaming*): Elsie! Come back here! Els — (*Door slams off. Music in low. To herself, frantic whisper*) Oh, my. Oh, *my*. Now what am I going to do? What am I going to *do*! (*Fading — crying*) Elsie! Oh, Elsie — come back — come back —

(*Music up . . . and into crickets, etc., in country at night . . .*)

Velie (*stridently*): Crickets! Blamed if it don't sound like sandpaper! Who made crickets, anyway? This is drivin' me nuts!

Ellery (*low*): Don't let it get you, Sergeant. All we can do is wait here in Morrell's car at the Memorial — We've got to give him a chance to get clear with his little girl.

Inspector (*fretfully*): But, Ellery, Morrell's been gone a half hour! Something's gone wrong, I tell you!

Velie: Yeah, an' I'll bet a Peruvian cookie that car that whizzed by here about twen'y minutes ago was *your* car, Mr. Queen. I tell you somethin' went cockeyed!

Ellery (*muttering*): It did look like my car, but . . . Blast it, just *sitting* here!

I've never felt so helpless in my life! (*Racing automobile motor fading on rapidly from distance*)

Inspector (*sharply*): Wait — there's a car coming — (*Car louder*)

Velie: But it's comin' from town — (*Car just off mike. Brakes*)

Ellery: It's Nikki! (*Ad libs. Car door open off, running steps fading in*) Nikki, for heaven's sake! What are you doing here?

Inspector (*rapidly*): And where's Mrs. Morrell, Nikki?

Nikki (*fading on — panting — crying*): Oh, Ellery, Inspector . . . Elsie cracked wide open — couldn't stand the suspense — ran out of the house — jumped into your car, Ellery, to drive to the Macauley house — she thought something went wrong —

Ellery (*groaning*): So it *was* my car that raced past here!

Velie: I told you, Mr. Queen!

Nikki (*panting*): I was frantic. I didn't know what to do. I tried to get Mr. Flynn on the private wire, but there was no answer. Finally, I hired a car in a public garage —

Ellery: Mrs. Morrell will spoil everything! Into the car! (*Running steps . . . get into car . . . close door . . . race off — very fast*)

Inspector: But it's too late to stop her. Step on that gas pedal, Velie!

Velie (*tensely*): I'm givin' her all she's got, Inspector.

Ellery: It's not far — a big Victorian house, Morrell said — only house for acres around —

Nikki: Faster, Sergeant! Oh, can't you go faster?

Velie: I got my foot down on the floor now, Miss Porter. (*Through his teeth*) *Give*, you — paralyzed — jalopy!

Inspector (*shouting*): There's the house! There it is, Velie!

Ellery (*same*): Velie, drive right up that dirt driveway to the front door! We've got to take all kinds of chances now! (*Screech of brakes on curve*)

Nikki: Ellery, there's your car in front of the house — the one Elsie drove up in! It's still here — she's still here! (*Confusion of opening doors, jumping out*)

Inspector: Quiet! (*Pause . . . crickets*) No lights. House is dark. Got your flash, Velie? Here — Ellery, take this one —

Ellery: Nikki, stay here. Stay here!

Nikki (*panting*): No. I won't. Elsie needs me. I won't, Ellery! (*Running steps of all on wooden porch*)

Inspector: Come on — don't waste time gabbing! (*More running steps*)

Velie (*off*): Front door's wide open — Wupp! (*Sound of falling body*)

Ellery: Velie! What happened?

Velie (*off a little*): Darn this . . . whatever it is. I just — fell over somethin' — right here inside the door —

Inspector (*sharply*): Ellery, flash that light on! (*Button . . . Pause . . . Nikki screams piercingly* —) Velie, search the house! And watch yourself!

Velie (*fading*): Gotta find that kid — Mrs. Morrell —

Ellery (*slowly*): Nikki . . . stop that.

Nikki (*sobbing*): Oh, Ellery . . .

Ellery: Harvey Morrell . . . Harvey Morrell, lying here with his head crushed in . . . Dad, we're too late. Too late!

Nikki (*sobbing*): Dead. Harvey's dead . . . Ellery. Where's Elsie? Where's the little girl? Oh, Ellery . . .

Inspector: He's dead, all right. Killed with this — Nikki, go outside. Get into the car. (*Sharp*) Go on! (*Nikki's crying fades off*) Killed with this hammer, Ellery. Struck a hard blow on the back of the head — attacked from behind —

Ellery (*off*): Yes, and here are Morrell's eyeglasses on the floor, dad. (*Fading on*) Smashed to bits. Must have fallen off as he fell dead.

Inspector: Morrell always wear these dark glasses?

Ellery: Yes. Weak eyes . . . Couldn't stand bright lights, he told me . . . (*Pause*) He told me. And now — he's dead.

Inspector (*suddenly calling furiously*): Velie! Velie, haven't you found those two yet?

Velie (*far off — above*): Not yet, Inspector! Place seems empty —

Ellery (*somberly*): Look into Morrell's staring blue eyes, dad. Did you ever see such naked agony?

Inspector: Poor guy . . . body's still warm. He was murdered only a short time ago . . .

Velie (*far off — above*): I found 'em! Here they are!

Ellery: Dad! Come on! (*Pounding up wooden stairs*)

Inspector (*shouting*): Velie! Where are you? Where are they?

Velie (*a little off*): In here — this room — watch my flash — (*More quick steps . . . stop . . . on mike. Grimly*) Here they are.
(*Elsie in a half-insane hysterical laugh, bubbling, continuous, inhuman: "Alice . . . Alice . . . Alice . . ."*)

Ellery (*sick*): With the child in her arms — tightly —

Velie (*through teeth*): And the kid's . . . dead. Stiff.

Inspector (*gently*): Mrs. Morrell. (*Elsie pays no attention. Sharp*) Mrs. Morrell, stop that yowling! (*She begins to whimper*) She's out of her head, poor thing. Velie, take the dead kid away from her. Get Mrs. Morrell to the Hessian Hospital — you and Nikki Porter — Nikki needs a doctor herself —

Velie (*muttering*): Right, Inspector. (*Gently*) Mrs. Morrell — give me — your — little girl — come on now — let me have your — little girl. Be nice now, please —

Ellery: I'll take the child's body, Sergeant. (*Gently*) There. Now get Mrs. Morrell out of here.

Velie (*gentle*): Come on, Mrs. Morrell — I guess I'll have to carry her. Up you go . . . (*Velie's gentle ad lib and Elsie's insane laughter fading into . . .*)

(*Music up . . . and into sounds of searching . . .*)

Ellery: Find anything over there, dad?

Inspector (*off a little*): Not a thing. Let's tackle that big parlor.

Ellery: Right. (*Steps*) Whenever I think of that child . . . murdered . . . ugh!

Inspector (*over steps*): Dead thirty-six hours at least, Ellery. A day and a half! That means the child was killed right after they kidnaped her . . . Ellery, I've seen a lot of crime in my day, but this is the rawest yet. We've got to get the rats who did this. (*Steps stop*) Here we are. I'll tackle the fireplace. (*Poking sounds*)

Ellery: Alice was never meant to be returned alive . . . no wonder poor Morrell's eyes bulge that way! He came here ready to pay the ransom — and found his child already dead. He must have just come from upstairs, on his way back to tell us — when the kidnaper, lying in wait for him, struck from behind . . .

Inspector (*over poking . . . off*): And not a blamed clue inside or outside the house. Only our two cars — no other tire tracks around the house — I've looked my eyes out. (*Sound of suitcase tumbling into fireplace from chimney orifice*) Ellery!

Ellery (*excited*): Dad! What's that?

Inspector (*on*): This suitcase — I just poked it out — it was stuck up the chimney a way . . . (*Strains*) It's heavy.

Ellery: It's the bag Harvey Morrell took with him tonight, containing the ransom money! (*Opens suitcase*)

Inspector: Yep . . . say, the money's still in here!

Ellery (*intently*): So it is.

Inspector: I guess after killing Morrell, the kidnaper heard Mrs. Morrell coming in your car and got scared and thought it might be the police. Looks like a one-man job after all. He couldn't make his getaway lugging this heavy suitcase full of a hundred grand in small bills, so he hid it, intending to come back later for it.

Ellery (*absently*): Yes — later —

Inspector (*grimly*): So all we've got to do now is salt this suitcase back in the chimney, lie low and watch. We'll nab this skunk when he comes back for his blood-money!

Ellery (*low*): Dad, we shan't have to wait that long.

Inspector: Huh? Ellery, what's this, now! Don't tell me you've —

Ellery (*crisply*): What an idiot I've been! Sitting in that house for two whole days, thinking, thinking — and being as stupid and blind as — well, as Harvey Morrell is right this minute!

Inspector (*choking*): You mean . . . say it. Go on, say it! You know the kidnaper? How can you! You *know*, Ellery?

Ellery: Yes, dad — the kidnaper-murderer! It *was* a one-man job — *and I know who it was!*

(*Music up . . . and into Jury spot*)

Challenge to the Listener

After the horror of the murders, Ellery rather cheerfully turned to the jury panel — "Yes, ladies and gentlemen, I knew who the kidnaper was right at that point — How about you?"

(*Music goes into news-calling montage backing the following:*)

Voice 1 (*fading in*): Get your morning Chronicle . . . Read all about the double murder.

Voice 2 (*on*): Harvey Morrell slain in kidnapping . . . read all about it.

Voice 3: Newspaper publisher and daughter killed last night.

Voice 1: Murderer of two in lonely house sought by police . . . (*fading out*) Get your Hessian Chronicle . . .

Voice (*fading on*): No information has yet been received about the fiendish slayer who kidnapped little Alice Morrell and killed her, and then murdered her father, Harvey Morrell, publisher of the Hessian Chronicle late last night. Police promise results within twenty-four hours . . . Here's a bulletin issued from (*Ambulance gong fades up as voice fades out*) Hessian Hospital where Mrs. Morrell's condition is described as serious . . .

(*Ambulance bell up then down and out under*)

Voice 1 (*filtered: fading in*): Hessian Hospital . . . No, we cannot give out any information about Mrs. Harvey Morrell . . .

Voice 2 (*filtered*): Hessian Hospital . . . No, you cannot speak to Mrs. Morrell.

Voice 3 (*filtered*): Hessian Hospital. (*fading*) Inspector Queen? . . . Just a minute.

(*In ante-room to Mrs. Morrell's room*)

Voices (*fading in*): Aw, come on, Sergeant, give us a break . . . Yeah, let us have a peep at Mrs. Morrell, will you? . . . Who do you think you are, anyway — you can't keep this thing a secret, you know . . . Just let me ask her one question . . .

(*Against these Velie's voice getting them out — they fade — slam door on . . .*)

Velie: Whew! This is gettin' to be too much for me. Where's the Inspector, Mr. Queen?

Ellery: In Mrs. Morrell's room with the doctors and nurses, Sergeant. He's trying to get a statement from her.

Nikki (*exhausted*): I feel so . . . tired.

Ellery (*gently*): Sit down here, Nikki.

Nikki (*same*): Poor Elsie. *Poor* Elsie . . .

Velie (*muttering*): The way she was holdin' that dead kid in her arms — and laughin' her head off . . . (*shudders*) I'll remember that laugh of hers till the day I die.

Nikki (*same*): That frightful creature — whoever he was — there's no punishment bad enough . . . To kill a little eight-year-old girl — in cold blood — you'd have to be inhuman, a monster . . . insane!

Ellery (*gently*): Yes, Nikki. Relax, now — rest —

Velie: Sit around here an' wait, wait . . . Why don't we *do* somethin'! I swear to you — if I ever get my paws on that baby-killer . . .

Ellery: That's no way for an officer to talk, Sergeant.

Velie (*muttering*): When I think of it, I kind of see red. Who is it, Mr. Queen? The Inspector told me you said you know. Why are we waitin'? Why don't we *blast*?

Nikki (*A little more vigorously*): Ellery! You know?

Ellery (*gently*): I know. And while we're waiting here for dad to talk to Mrs. Morrell, I may as well tell you what I know, and how I know it . . . Put yourself in the position of the kidnaper —

Velie (*growling*): Not me, thanks.

Nikki (*shuddering*): Think like a — a mad dog?

Ellery: Look. We know the kidnaper was in that empty house tonight, because Morrell was *murdered* there tonight. But if the kidnaper came *to* that house, he must have had some predetermined idea of how he was going to get *away* from the house after he'd transacted his business.

Velie: Well, sure. Even a dope woulda planned his getaway. And this playful guy ain't no dope, whatever else he is!

Ellery: Exactly, Sergeant. But *how*?

Velie (*blankly*): How?

Ellery: Yes, how! How did the kidnaper plan to escape from that house tonight after he collected the ransom money?

Nikki (*dully*): He could have walked — run —

Ellery: He planned to *walk* or *run* away carrying that heavy suitcase, Nikki? A hundred thousand dollars in small bills — remember the kidnaper himself ordered Morrell to bring it in small bills — is a heavy load. No, Nikki, a person planning a crime as thorough as this would take at least ordinary precautions to insure his safe getaway with the ransom.

Velie: Sure! What's the problem, Mr. Queen? Sure he would. He'd come in a car and leave in a car.

Ellery: Ah! Very true, Sergeant. But he *didn't. He had no car.*

Nikki (*faintly*): My head's spinning round and round . . . Had no car, Ellery?

Ellery: *Had no car.* How do we know? For two reasons. One: dad told me just before we found the suitcase full of money tonight that there wasn't a clue inside or outside the house — in fact, he specifically said: "*Only our two cars.* No other tire tracks around the house." So I say: there was no third car for the kidnaper to make his getaway in.

Velie: But what's the other reason, Mr. Queen?

Ellery: Well, Sergeant, if the kidnaper had a car to make his escape in, *would he have hidden the suitcase* containing the ransom-money *in the house?*

Velie (*muttering*): So he had no car — didn't plan a getaway by car — wouldn't have walked, of course — (*crying out*) For cryin' out loud, what kind of a kidnaper don't plan a getaway by car an' even leaves the ransom behind?

Ellery (*quietly*): Well put, Sergeant! What kind of kidnaper? Obviously, a kidnaper who *didn't intend to leave* the house!

Nikki (*dazed*): Didn't — intend . . . to leave . . . the house . . .

Ellery: Yes, Nikki, didn't *intend* to leave the house — because it wasn't *necessary* to leave the house!

Velie (*bewildered*): But . . . who was still there when we drove up? Morrell — Mrs. Morrell — the little girl — and that's all. You must be wrong, Mr. Queen. You gotta be.

Nikki (*slowly*): And Harvey — Alice — *they* were dead . . . (*Strained whisper*) *Ellery, what are you trying to say?* (*Pause. Rising voice in fear*) Ellery! What are you trying to *tell* us!

Ellery: Take it easy, Nikki. Please. I know it's a shock —

Nikki (*almost hysterical*): But Ellery — you're wrong. You're wrong! You'll never convince me! I won't believe it! I won't. (*Starts to cry*) I won't . . .

Ellery (*urgent*): Sergeant, fetch some water. Please.

Velie (*dazed*): I kinda — feel — funny myself. (*Fading*) Yeah . . . water . . .

Ellery (*gently*): Nikki, pull yourself together. Nikki, dear — it's true. It's true no matter how you look at it. Who gains by the death of the two actual victims, Morrell *and* his daughter? Only one person, Nikki — only one *possible* person . . .

Nikki (*sobbing*): No . . . no . . . I won't believe it. I'd just as soon believe that — that —

Velie (*fading on*): Here's the water, Mr. Queen . . . Holy smoke!

Ellery: Here, Nikki — drink this —

Nikki (*faintly*): Wait, Ellery. You mean — you really mean — that the whole thing — the kidnap note — the telephone conversation at noon — the . . . murder of Harvey — the . . . murder of Alice — the whole thing — was done by . . .

Ellery (*gently*): Yes, Nikki. The whole thing. From beginning to end. (*Nikki utters a weak cry, which dies off*)

Velie (*alarmed*): Watch out! She's gonna faint — there she goes!

Ellery (*distracted*): Nikki! I'm a beast to have told you so brutally — I tried to soften the blow — Nikki — (*Door opens off — closes*)

Inspector (*fading on*): Well, she's cracked wide open. Got the whole incredible story — (*alarmed*) What's the matter with Nikki?

Velie: Keeled over in a faint when Mr. Queen told her. I . . . feel kinda sick to my stomach myself. She really broke, huh?

Inspector (*wondering*): I can't believe it myself. But I heard her confession with my own ears. The whole job — the whole job! — was done by *Elsie Morrell!*

(*Music up . . . into door opening, closing . . .*)

Inspector (*calling*): Ellery? How's Nikki?

Velie (*same*): She all right now, Mr. Queen?

Ellery (*fading on — tired*): Well, I took her home to her own apartment, got a doctor and a nurse for her . . . She'll be all right. They've given her something to put her to sleep . . . I'm — rather done in — myself.

Inspector: Sit down, son. It's been a tough couple of days for all of us.

Ellery (*as if sitting down*): Ahhhh. This chair feels good. (*Pause*) This *room* feels good. Even the air smells clean. (*Pause*)

Velie (*suddenly*): I'll tell you one thing. If I was Morrell I'd *wanna* be dead. Married to a maniac —

Inspector (*gloomily*): Of course, the woman's insane. A frightening sort of insanity. Made up of cunning, desperation, and a total lack of any moral sense. To do a thing like that! Plan a crime like that — remove her husband, her child — in the most brutal manner — just so she'd get complete control of her husband's fortune — be rid of all responsibility —

Velie: And what a cover-up! You got to hand it to her, the — animal! The sufferin'-mother gag — get everybody's sympathy all along the line —

Inspector: The stage lost a great actress when she decided to try her hand at murder.

Ellery (*wearily*): Yes, the subtlety of her crime was that she was in a unique psychological position. Naturally we'd think only of her "loss," not her gain.

Inspector: She was cute about it — cute. She admitted she didn't drop the child off at the school corner. She took Alice right out to the abandoned Macauley house, killed her there . . . She ran away from Nikki so that she could meet her husband at the house and murder him. She figured she'd even get away with that, as the distracted wife and mother. She insisted on a large ransom to make the kidnaping look legitimate — but she didn't think we'd search the house and find the money. She expected to get rid of the suitcase and money later.

Velie: How'd she work that phone call — the tapped-wire business? Who'd she talk to, Mr. Queen? Who gave her the instructions she told you about?

Ellery: There weren't any, Sergeant. The whole thing was a pure illusion. She *pretended* she was talking to someone! Of course the wire hadn't been tapped at all, and nobody was watching the house at any time. Don't forget, Elsie Morrell was the *only* source of our information concerning that telephone call and the supposed instructions — she'd been clever enough in writing the ransom note to insist that *only* the mother should touch that phone.

Velie (*disturbed*): All right, I get all that. Knowin' it was Mrs. Morrell, it all fitted in. But — even now, I don't believe it. I can't. Insane or not — to kill your own child —

Ellery (*quietly*): Oh, the woman's insane, Sergeant, but not quite as much as you and dad think, or in quite the same way. There's an explanation of this crime that will open your eyes, both of you — and, I think, restore your faith in — well, motherhood.

Inspector (*abruptly*): What d'ye mean, Ellery? Something we *still* don't know? I don't get you at all!

Ellery: Remember, dad, when I talked to you over Morrell's private wire — our first conversation after Flynn got you down from New York?

Inspector: Well?

Ellery: Remember you asked me for a description of little Alice? What color eyes did I tell you Alice had?

Inspector: Brown.

Ellery: Yes, brown. And of course I knew the color of Elsie Morrell's eyes, too. Even if I hadn't noticed, Nikki called it to my attention when she said at one point that Elsie had "cried her eyes out — those lovely *blue* eyes" . . .

Velie: All right, so the kid had brown eyes and the mother has blue eyes. So what, Mr. Queen?

Ellery: And when we looked at Harvey Morrell, lying dead on the floor of that empty house, his shattered eyeglasses off — dad, what color eyes did I remark he had?

Inspector: Blue. Ellery, you've pulled a lot of things out of your hat in the past, and I've got so I can anticipate most of 'em. But whatever it is you're pulling this time — I can't even see its shadow.

Velie (*gloomily*): Ditto for Tom Velie.

Ellery (*wearily*): Well, the father and mother both had blue eyes — and the child brown. Mind you, I didn't know the father had blue eyes until after he was murdered — he always wore dark glasses. So I didn't suspect the truth until it was too late — until after both Morrell and his child had been killed.

Inspector: What truth, for pete's sake?

Ellery: Sergeant, would you mind reaching over to that bookshelf and getting down that book — the fifth one from the end — on the second shelf —

Velie (*off*): This one, Mr. Queen?

Ellery: That's right, Sergeant. (*Pause*) Thanks. Well, this book is called *Legal Medicine and Toxicology*, and it's written by a trio of well-known authorities — Morgan, Vance, Milton Helpern, and Thomas Gonzales.

Inspector: Dr. Gonzales? You mean the present Chief Medical Examiner of New York City?

Velie: Say, I know Doc Gonzales!

Ellery: Well, let me read you just one sentence from this book. (*Riffle pages*) It's around here somewhere . . . (*Stop*) Yes! Page three-fourteen. (*Slowly*) Quote: "*Two blue-eyed persons would not produce children with brown eyes* but only children with blue eyes." (*Gently*) End quote.

Inspector (*startled*): You mean —

Ellery (*sharply*): When I deduced that Elsie Morrell must have been the kidnaper-murderer, I too recoiled from the notion that a mother could have killed her own child. So I said to myself: Is it possible she *wasn't* the mother? Then I gathered the threads of this difference in color of eyes, based on medical fact, and I saw confirmation. I saw that Elsie Morrell was *not* Alice's true mother — that Elsie must be Morrell's *second* wife, and Alice the child of Morrell's first marriage by another woman — that Elsie was Alice's *stepmother* — (*Pause*) Her *stepmother*!

Velie (*awed*): The kid's *stepmother*! . . .

Inspector: That's different, Ellery. (*Softly*) That's different. It's as grim and terrifying a business as we've ever been involved in.

Ellery: Yes, dad, I know . . . I for one won't forget the Morrell kidnapping case as long as I live.

(*Music up . . . and into end spot.*)

Manfred B. Lee and Frederic Dannay loved books — that "lovely old book-smell" as "The Adventure of the Black Secret" puts it. It was therefore to be expected that Ellery would solve a mystery — indeed, three mysteries — in a bookstore, and doing so he not only explains a dying message but competes with a rival detective, Mike Callahan, who appeared in several of the early E.Q. radio mysteries. "The Adventure of the Black Secret" was broadcast on December 10, 1939.

The Adventure of the Black Secret

The Characters

Inspector Queen	Of the New York Police
Sergeant Velie	Of the New York Police
Mike Callahan	Investigator for the World-Wide Insurance Company
Ellery Queen	Amateur investigator
Nikki Porter	His secretary
Edmund Black	Owner of the C.D. Black Company
Abner Watson	His partner
Mr. Burbage	Bookkeeper
Casper Rydell	Employee of the Black Company
Miss Flanders	Employee of the Black Company
Police officer, customer, bearded man	

Setting: New York City, 1939

(*All in scene laughing as we fade in . . .*)

Inspector (*chuckling*): Mike, remember when you and Velie were second-grade detectives and I was captain of that dumpy little West Side precinct?
Velie: An' Mike, will y'ever forget that case — the blonde babe who complained her husband was bringing suspicious characters to sleep over in the house —
Callahan (*laughing*): And it turned out they were all relatives of his —
Inspector (*laughing*): Because wifey had a habit of attacking hubby in her sleep with a nail-file, and the poor dope was scared to death to be alone with her? (*All laugh heartily*)
Ellery (*chuckling*): They'll bring out old snapshots next.

154

Nikki: Aren't you a policeman anymore, Mr. Callahan?

Callahan (*dryly*): Some say yes, some say no.

Velie: Mike's the ace investigator of the World-Wide Insurance Company now. An' look at me —

Inspector: What for? Ellery, you'll like Mike Callahan's style. He goes in for fancy deductions, the way you do —

Velie: Yes, sir. An' Mike always gets his man, too!

Nikki: That's more than I can say.

Ellery (*laughing*): Nikki . . . By the way, Callahan, what's the occasion for this visit? Purely social?

Callahan: No, Queen, I'm working under cover for World-Wide on a case involving the C.D. Black Company —

Nikki (*startled*): Ellery! Isn't that the firm which —

Ellery: Peace, my child.

Inspector: Black's? Oldest rare-book dealers in the city. What's up?

Callahan: The usual. Vanishing assets. But cleverly done. Anyway, you can do me a favor, Queen.

Ellery: Glad to, Callahan. Although I don't see —

Callahan: I was nosing around the Black store this morning when I overheard one of the employees telephoning. He made an appointment with you for this afternoon.

Nikki: A detective, all right! A snoop — like you, Mr. Queen.

Ellery (*chuckling*): That's right, Callahan — some old man named Burbage. Said he's the bookkeeper of the Black Company. But what's the point?

Callahan: None of the people down at Black's know who I am. I'd like to hear what this old fellow Burbage has on his mind, but I'd rather he didn't know I'm an insurance-company detective. Would you introduce me as your associate and let me sit in? (*Doorbell rings off*) That must be Burbage now. What d'ye say, Queen?

Velie: Say yes, Mr. Queen. Mike Callahan's an old buddy of ours. (*Doorbell rings again*)

Inspector: It's all right, Ellery. You can trust Mike. Answer the door, Nikki.

Nikki (*fading*): Enter trouble — I just know it . . .

Ellery: Of course you may sit in, Callahan! (*Door opens off; murmurs*)

Inspector (*low*): Velie, let's you and me duck into the other room. We don't want to scare this old bird with too many people.

Velie (*fading*): You'd scare a South American buzzard . . . (*Open, close other door as Nikki and Burbage ad libs fade on. Burbage gentle old voice. Very nice*)

Nikki (*fading on*): In here, Mr. Burbage.

Burbage (*same — nervous*): Thank you, thank you, Miss. Mr. Queen?

Ellery: I'm Queen. You're the gentleman who called me? (*Agreement*) This is Mr. Callahan, my assistant. (*Ad libs*) Sit down, Mr. Burbage. You seem upset.

Burbage: Thank you, sir. Oh, I am. Most dreadful situation . . . ! Mr. Queen, as I told you, I work for the oldest firm of rare-book dealers in the United States, the C. D. Black Company, Cooper Square . . .

Ellery: Notes, Nikki.

Nikki (*sighing*): Yes, Mr. Queen.

Callahan: You're the bookkeeper there, Mr. Burbage?

Burbage: Yes, Mr. Callahan. (*Proudly*) Oldest living employee of Black's. I'm sixty-nine, gentlemen. Started working for old Mr. Cyrus Black, the founder, in 1886 —

Nikki: Fifty-three years with one firm? That's wonderful.

Burbage: Yes, Miss, I was a boy of fifteen when I started. I've worked for three generations of Blacks — Cyrus, Darien — they're both dead — and now Darien's son, young Edmund Black. (*Sighs*) It's not like the old days . . .

Ellery: It rarely is, Mr. Burbage. May I ask what's troubling you?

Burbage: Well, sir . . . young Mr. Black, he doesn't know much about the rare-book business, and — well, the firm is in bad shape, and — well, some time ago Mr. Black was forced to take in a partner, Mr. Watson, Mr. Abner Watson —

Callahan: Abner Watson's one of the leading rare-book experts in the country, Queen. You've heard of him.

Ellery: Indeed I have. I assume, Mr. Burbage, that young Edmund Black brought Watson into the firm to supply the expert knowledge he himself lacks?

Burbage: Yes, Mr. Queen, the knowledge and also new capital. Well, for a time the firm prospered, chiefly because Mr. Watson developed a new type of business — he printed special editions of classics, limited to single copies. For wealthy collectors, of course —

Nikki: Editions of one copy! That's *really* hoity-toity!

Burbage: Beautiful books, Miss. Mr. Watson does all the work himself, by hand — he's an expert craftsman and has a private press and bindery in his Westchester home.

Ellery: I should say acquiring Mr. Watson as a partner was a stroke of awfully good luck for Mr. Black!

Burbage: Oh, it was for a time, sir. But then the Depression — the demand for expensive books fell off — and finally . . .

Callahan (*sharply*): Yes, Mr. Burbage?

Burbage: Well . . . when it seemed things couldn't get worse, they did. Valuable old books began to disappear — the choicest first-editions in stock. Mr. Black tried everything — but the thefts just keep taking place. It's driving him mad.

Ellery: Doesn't the Black Company carry burglary insurance?

Burbage: Oh, yes, Mr. Queen — the World-Wide Insurance Company.

Biggest in the field. They claim they're investigating, but they haven't turned up anything yet.

Callahan (*calmly*): Who's the present insurance investigator, Mr. Burbage? Any idea?

Burbage: I really don't know, Mr. Callahan. The last detective they had on the case was recalled and Mr. Black's been expecting a new one . . . Mr. Queen, I'm an old man — my whole life's been devoted to Black's — I'm as proud of the firm's reputation as I am of my own . . . Find the thief!

Ellery: Hmmm. Any idea how these thefts are being pulled off?

Burbage: No, sir. But . . . (*Nervous*) I *have* made a certain discovery . . .

Callahan (*sharply*): You have? What, Burbage?

Burbage (*agitated*): I can't tell you, though — I mustn't! Not yet, anyway . . . not yet . . . It's a secret. (*Slowly*) I've stumbled on a tremendous, a terrible, *secret.*

Nikki: A secret? That sounds exciting, Ellery!

Ellery (*dryly*): Most secrets do — until they're solved. So you feel you can't tell us what this secret is, Mr. Burbage?

Burbage (*agitated*): Oh, I can't! It would ruin not only the reputation of Black's but — but perhaps of the entire rare-book business! Oh, I know I'm sounding stupidly mysterious, gentlemen. But —

Callahan (*grimly*): If this secret is so tremendous, Burbage, you're not doing your firm a favor by keeping it to yourself!

Burbage: You don't understand, Mr. Callahan — how could you? Oh, this is the most impossible situation! But I can't tell you — I simply mustn't — not now. Mr. Queen, find out who the thief is — then I'll help all I can — Please!

Ellery: Does either of your employers — Black or Watson — know you've come to me for help, Mr. Burbage?

Burbage: No, sir. Mr. Watson — he isn't a man to ask anyone for help; and young Mr. Black — I love him as if he were my own son, but he's a scatterbrain — loves to amuse himself — he's always having parties, and practicing magic —

Nikki: Practicing magic! (*Giggles*) I'm sorry, Mr. Burbage.

Burbage (*bitterly*): I used to laugh myself. But he's like a child — eternally making up magic tricks — playing practical jokes —

Ellery (*suddenly*): Mr. Burbage, I'll look into your case.

Burbage (*gratefully*): Oh, thank you, Mr. Queen! Please believe me — if I could tell you more at this time —

Ellery: See Mr. Burbage out, Nikki. Good day, sir. You'll hear from us.

Nikki (*fading*): This way, Mr. Burbage. (*Ad libs of Burbage's adieux fading off — open, close door off under following*)

Ellery: Well, Callahan, know any more than old Burbage just told us? (*Open other door off*)

Callahan (*chuckling*): If I told you that, you'd know as much as I do.
Inspector (*fading on*): Velie and I heard the whole thing. What is that old fella — a nut? Secrets! Magic!
Velie (*fading on*): He ought to be in a home! Did you understand what the ol' geezer was drivin' at, Mr. Queen?
Ellery: Of course not, Sergeant. Mysterious hints — colossal secret . . . Ah, Nikki. How'd you like our visitor?
Nikki (*fading on*): Wasn't he the sweetest old man?
Callahan (*briskly*): Your sweet old man gave me a swell idea, Miss Porter. Thanks a million, Queen — I've got to run. (*Fading*) 'Bye, you two muggs — I've got a job of work to do!
Inspector (*as door opens off — chuckling*): Same old Mike!
Velie (*as door closes off*): Looks like Mike's got a head start on you, Mr. Queen. (*Laughs*)
Ellery (*grimly*): Think so, Sergeant? Nikki, is that new manuscript of mine ready for my publisher?
Nikki: I finished retyping it this morning, Ellery.
Ellery: Then stuff it into my black bag, and let's go.
Nikki: Go? Go where?
Ellery: To my publisher's, of course.
Velie (*chuckling*): On the way you wouldn't be stoppin' in at the C.D. Black Company, would you, Mr. Queen?
Inspector (*chuckling*): Looks as if Mike Callahan sort of got your monkey up, son.
Ellery: If your Mike Callahan wants a contest, he'll get it! Come on, Nikki!

(*Music up . . . and into ad lib murmur of many . . .*)

Rydell (*fading on*): Say, what was the battle going on in the office? I was fixing up stock —
Woman: *I* don't know, Mr. Rydell. I did hear Mr. Watson about something at Mr. Black. Anybody know what's the matter?
Man: All I know is, old Watson and young Black have been at it in Watson's private office for an hour. Haven't they, Miss Flanders?
Miss Flanders: They certainly have! But why did they ask all of us to meet here in the rear of the store?
(*Ad lib negatives*)
Rydell: Careful! Here comes the old crank. (*Door opens off*)
Watson (*fading on — crotchety raspy old voice*): Black! Are you coming out here with me, or aren't you?
Black (*fading on — young; coldly*): I'm coming, Watson.
Watson: Well, then, come on! (*Pause . . . murmurs up*) Silence, please!
Black (*quietly*): Let Mr. Watson speak, people. (*Murmurs down*)

Watson: Mr. Black's been called to Philadelphia on business —
Black (*curtly*): Make your announcement and get it over with, Watson.
Watson: Very well! As you all know, for the past six months the C.D.
Black Company's been victimized by a series of thefts. (*Murmurs up and down*) Most of the stolen books were rare, unadvertised items out of our private stock of first editions, which we've been holding back for a rising market. (*Viciously*) Well, I'm convinced those thefts are an inside job! (*Angry murmur low*) One of you is the thief! (*Up*)
Black: Wait — please! (*Murmur down*) I want you to know that Mr. Watson and I are in complete disagreement about this. I believe every one of you is incapable of dishonesty!
Watson (*coldly*): That's a matter of personal opinion. Anyway, the insurance company's failed to make any progress, and I've decided on a drastic step! (*Murmurs up*)
Flanders (*low*): Casper . . . I don't like the sound of that.
Rydell (*low*): The old — witch! He's blue in the face, Mae! I hope he chokes!
Miss Flanders (*low*): And poor Mr. Black looks so droopy . . .
Watson: Silence! (*Murmurs down*) Owing to insufficient insurance, these thefts have seriously undermined our financial position. If the thefts continue, we face bankruptcy. Well, the entire staff — every one of you — as of closing time tonight, is discharged!
(*Pause. Gasps*)
Black (*strained*): Sorry, people. But there's nothing I can do. Mr. Watson now owns fifty-one percent of the stock and has full power to dictate company policy.
(*Murmurs up*)
Rydell (*crying out*): But even if one of us *is* a crook, why make the rest of us suffer? (*Cries: "It's not fair!" etc.*)
Black (*low*): My hands are tied, Rydell. Mr. Watson's arranging to have two new clerks report tomorrow, and a new secretary-stenographer. We're shortening staff. Where's old Burbage?
Miss Flanders: He went out a while ago, Mr. Black, on some errand.
Black: I'm . . . glad he isn't here. (*Chokes up. Then harshly*) Anyway, I'll handle Burbage's bookkeeping myself for the time being. One of you — Miss Flanders — tell Burbage, will you? I . . . can't.
Miss Flanders (*tearfully*): Y-yes, Mr. Black. As soon as he gets back . . .
Watson (*harshly*): I may as well tell you that Mr. Black's persuaded me to make one promise — sentimental nonsense, but no one's going to accuse Abner Watson of being unjust. (*Bitter ad libs: "Oh, no." "Angel of mercy . . ." etc.*) So, if and when the mystery of these thefts is cleared up, all the old employees will be re-hired. That's all! Go back to your work! (*Fading murmurs*) Black! Where are you running off to?

Black (*shouting*): Philadelphia. (*Fading*) And I wish to heaven it were Antarctica!

(*Music up . . . and into street noises . . .*)

Nikki (*reading*): "C.D. Black Company, Old and Rare Books . . ."
Ellery: This is it. Now remember, Nikki, we're just shopping. (*Door opens. Tinkly bell*) A bell and everything . . .
Nikki: It's like the Old Curiosity Shop! (*Door closes . . . cut off noise*)
Ellery: Except that it's a dozen times larger. Lovely old book-smell, eh, Nikki? (*Low*) See Burbage anywhere?
Nikki (*low*): There he is — see him at the back of the store?
Ellery (*low*): Mmmmmm. Must have just got back from our place . . .
Nikki (*low*): Watch it! Here comes a clerk.
Rydell (*fading on*): Yes, sir? May I help you?
Ellery: Why — uh — yes. My — ah — fiancée and I are looking for something special in first-edition English poets. (*Fatuous*) You know — an engagement gift —
Nikki (*giggling — low*): If we *were* engaged, I'll bet you *would* pick something like a book to give me!
Rydell: English poets . . . Something special. Hmmm . . . I'd better get Mr. Watson to wait on you, sir.
Ellery (*quickly*): Isn't Mr. Black here?
Rydell: No, sir, Mr. Black's just gone to Philadelphia. If you'll be kind enough to wait . . .
Ellery: Certainly. What's your name, by the way?
Rydell: Rydell, sir, Casper Rydell. (*Fading*) I'll have Mr. Watson here in a moment . . .
Ellery (*low*): Nikki . . . be careful, now, but have a squint at that man at the next counter . . . the one scanning those books —
Nikki (*pause*): The funny-looking one all wrapped up in his coat — the man with the long bushy beard and black glasses?
Ellery (*low*): Yes . . . *Don't* be so obvious about it, Nikki. I don't like that gentleman's looks.
Nikki: I can't say I could go for him myself, but what of it?
Ellery: That beard isn't real, Nikki. He's disguised.
Nikki: Oh, you. You're always looking for *something* . . . Uh-uh. This must be Mr. Watson. What a mean-looking old man.
Watson (*fading on*): Is this the gentleman, Rydell?
Rydell: Yes, Mr. Watson.
Watson: Good day, sir. Mr. Rydell tells me you're looking for something special in an English first. Any particular poet?
Ellery: Well . . . I think John Keats ought be nice, don't you, sweetheart?

Nikki (*slyly*): Keats would be just *lovely*, ducky . . .

Watson: Keats? You're very fortunate. Rydell! That Keats up there — yes, yes, that's the one. Hand it to me, Rydell.

Rydell (*fading on*): Here you are, Mr. Watson.

Watson: Now here, sir, is a superb and exceptional book. A Keats first in the original boards, with paper label.

Ellery: Mmmmm . . . What do you think, love? (*Slight riffling*)

Nikki (*maliciously*): Isn't it the *sweetest* booky-wooky!

Ellery (*hastily*): Uh — very nice. Very nice. What's the price?

Watson: A much inferior copy sold at auction recently for nine hundred dollars. Of course, I needn't point out the freshness of this copy . . . Eleven hundred.

Nikki (*quickly*): Oh honeybunch . . . that's too much . . . don't you think — we still have to get the furniture, you know — for the . . . (*Shyly*) the baby's room . . . I mean, when we're married.

Ellery (*hastily*): Of course, my love! Well, sir, I don't know. It seems a lot . . . We'll think it over. (*Fading*) Come along, precious — we've still got to —

Watson (*viciously*): That's what the rare-book business has degenerated into! Every ignorant fool wants a first — Well, well, what are you frowning about, Rydell?

Rydell (*nervous*): That man with the black bag, Mr. Watson . . . I don't know why, but . . . he looked suspicious to me.

Watson: Suspicious? Nonsense, Rydell. Go back to your work . . . (*Pause . . . shouting, a little off*) Wait! It's gone.

Rydell (*stammering*): W — what's gone, Mr. Watson?

Watson (*yelling*): The Keats! The Keats first! Rydell, run after that man with the black bag and catch him!

Rydell (*fading*): Y — yes, sir! (*Running steps . . . Jerk open door with tinkly bell . . . up on street noises*) You! You there! Stop! (*Running on pavement*)

Ellery (*off*): Are you calling us, Rydell?

Rydell (*on . . . panting*): You've got to come back into the store, please! Immediately!

Nikki (*fading on*): For heaven's sake! Why?

Rydell: Please — come with me — (*Steps on pavement*) Mr. Watson will explain — (*Steps on store floor, close door with bell*) Here he is, Mr. Watson — here's the gentleman — the lady —

Watson (*rage*): Rydell! You're an idiot! You've brought back the *wrong man*!

Rydell (*gasping*): The wrong — But Mr. Watson, this is the gentleman who was handling the Keats — and he's carrying a black bag — you said the man with the black bag —

Watson (*same*): I meant the *other* man, the man with the beard and black glasses — *he* was carrying a black bag, too!

Rydell (*wailing*): Oh, my —

Ellery: What seems to be the trouble, Mr. Watson?

Watson: The Keats is gone! The Keats I was showing you. What did you do with it, sir?

Ellery: Why, I laid it down on the counter there —

Nikki: Then we all moved away . . . (*Spiritedly*) See here! Are you suggesting we're thieves?

Ellery (*smoothly*): Now, precious, let's be fair. You can't blame this gentleman . . . Mr. Watson, I insist on being searched.

Nikki (*outraged*): Ellery! You'll insist on no such thing!

Watson (*testily*): Search 'em, Rydell . . . Well! Go on!

Rydell (*embarrassed*): But Mr. Watson . . . Please, sir, if you'll —

Nikki (*grimly*): You try to search *me*, Mr. Casper Milquetoast Rydell, and you'll find out what it means to be punched in the nose by a lady.

Ellery (*cheerfully*): Well searched, Sir Casper. Now I suggest you examine my bag.

Watson: His black bag! Of course! (*Opening bag*)

Ellery: I assure you all you'll find inside my bag is the manuscript of my latest detective story — a poor thing, gentlemen, but mine own . . .

Rydell (*amazed*): A *detective*-story writer? (*Giggles*)

Watson (*panting*): All I'll find in this black bag is a miserable detective story, eh! Well, you're caught red-handed, you — you thieves. *Look* at this bag — crammed to the top with stolen books.

Nikki (*dazed*): Ellery . . . it *is*. Did you — I mean —

Ellery (*slowly*): Well, I'll be a ring-tailed baboon . . .

Rydell (*gasping*): Appelgate's *Napoleonic Wars* — the full set of six volumes! That's *ours*, sir!

Watson: And here's the Keats. Rydell, call the police.

Rydell (*fading*): Yes, sir. Watch yourself, sir — they're probably dangerous characters . . .

Watson (*shouting*): Marcus! Jones! Bellamy! Come here — we've caught two thieves . . . (*Murmurs fading on*)

Ellery: Whoa, gentlemen . . . May I ask what you're intending to do, Mr. Watson?

Watson: The *nerve* of him! Intending to do? Have you arrested, of course.

Ellery (*gasping*): Arrest me? (*Ad libs and Nikki laughs loud and long*)

(*Music up . . . and into Nikki's laughter*)

Ellery (*raving*): You can laugh if you want to — I want to get out of here. You there — officer — where's my father? Where's Sergeant Velie? I sent for 'em an hour ago.

Officer (*bored*): Keep your shirt on, brother. If you're who you say you are, (*Fading*) you'll get outa here fast enough . . .

Nikki (*giggling*): What's the matter, Mr. Queen, can't you take it? You've been dishing it out long enough.

Ellery: Locked up in the detention room of a station-house. I'll never hear the end of this from Mike Callahan. (*Door opens off — laughter*)

Nikki: Something tells me we're saved. (*Steps fading on*)

Ellery: Dad! Velie! Get Nikki and me out of here! (*Velie and Inspector fade on laughing*)

Velie: Hail, convicts! Well, well, don't they look pretty, Inspector? Mr. Queen, shame on you — stealin'!

Inspector (*chuckling*): So John Law's caught up with you at last, son. It's about time. (*Curtly*) All right, Officer, I've identified these two.

Officer (*fading*): (*Steps off*) Yes, sir. Sure, Inspector Queen.

Nikki: And look who's here, that bad old man who had Mr. Ellery Queen put in the coop. Hello, Mr. Watson.

Watson: Mr. Queen — dreadfully sorry — stupid mistake on my part.

Ellery: Next time you yell for the police, Mr. Watson, be sure first you've got the right man.

Nikki: You must admit we were caught with the goods, Ellery.

Watson (*nervous*): Please forgive me. Naturally, appearances . . .

Inspector: Mr. Watson's been thinking it over, and he realizes now the thief must have been that suspicious-looking man with the beard and the black glasses.

Velie: Yeah, he was the one musta swiped that set o' Napoleon an' the, now, Keats book — say, who *is* Keats? — an' slipped 'em into his *own* black bag . . .

Watson: You remember, Mr. Queen, you set *your* black bag down . . .

Inspector: So this bird in disguise picked up your bag by mistake, Ellery, and took the air, leaving his bag with the stolen books in it behind.

Nikki: Ellery, I'll bet that's just what happened!

Ellery (*glumly*): Most likely. Anyway, whoever that book-pilfering rascal is, he now has my bag with my new manuscript in it — and, Keats or no Keats, I want my manuscript back!

Nikki: It won't ever become a rare book, Mr. Watson, but you know these authors — they don't like losing their novels.

Velie: They'd just as soon lose their right eye. (*Chuckles*)

Inspector: Why not go after that bearded fella yourself, Ellery? He may come back to the Black store . . .

Watson (*nervously*): Splendid idea. I understand you're a detective, Mr. Queen. We've just discharged all our clerks, because of the recent thefts — we need new clerks anyway . . .

Nikki: You mean we should become clerks in your store? Oh, Ellery — let's!

Ellery (*shortly*): Absurd.

Velie: Do somethin' useful for a change, Mr. Queen —

Ellery (*same*): Childish idea.

Inspector: It *would* put you on the scene in case that thief came back, Ellery!

Ellery: Nonsense, dad. (*Fading as all begin to urge him ad lib*) No, no, it's no use, I tell you — won't hear of it . . .

(*Gabble-gabble music up . . . into chink of dishes . . . similar ad libs as at tail of preceding scene . . .*)

Inspector: More coffee, Nikki. Come on, son, don't be stubborn.

Nikki: Coming up! (*Pour liquid*) Don't be a kill-joy, Ellery. It ought to be fun!

Velie: Besides, you'd be stealin' a march on Mike Callahan. I thought you wanted to beat Mike to it!

Ellery (*irritable*): Gabble, gabble all afternoon, all through dinner . . .! I'd feel silly, I tell you! (*Doorbell off*)

Nikki (*fading*): Now who, for heaven's sake?

Inspector (*chuckling*): Probably someone with a warrant for *my* arrest! (*Door opens off, murmurs off, door closes off*)

Velie: This son o' yours gets mixed up in more cockeyed cases . . .

Ellery: Who's this? Mr. Casper Rydell, as I live and breathe!

Nikki (*fading on*): Ellery, here's Mr. Rydell to see you, and he's brought along another clerk from the Black store, Miss Flanders.

Rydell (*embarrassed*): We heard who you were, Mr. Queen, and I wanted to apologize about — searching you today . . .

Ellery: Nonsense, Rydell! I'm a confirmed criminal. Sergeant Velie, Inspector Queen . . . (*Ad lib greetings*)

Inspector: I understand you people lost your jobs today.

Velie: Sure, Watson was sayin' he'd fired the whole bunch.

Nikki: I'm so sorry. It isn't fair!

Miss Flanders: That's how we feel about it. You see, Casper and I — we — (*Begins to cry*) Oh, it's awful!

Rydell: Mae darling — please — (*Angrily*) I could wring that old buzzard's skinny neck!

Miss Flanders (*sniffling*): I'm sorry. But Casper and I — we were expecting to be married this Christmas —

Velie: Say, that's a mean trick, at that.

Nikki (*indignant*): He must think he's Old Scrooge!

Ellery: Too bad, Rydell. But why have you come to me?

Rydell (*helpless*): We didn't know where to turn. And hearing you're a detective . . .

Miss Flanders: All the employees of the store held a meeting right after closing today, Mr. Queen — this was our last day . . .

Rydell: With Christmas coming, things the way they are . . . it's bad.

Inspector: Watson fired that old bookkeeper, Burbage, too?

Miss Flanders: Yes, wasn't that mean? After fifty-three years with the Black store! What chance has Mr. Burbage to get a new job at his age?

Rydell: And Mr. Marcus, who used to be secretary to Mr. Edmund — his baby's in the hospital, and he's up to his ears in debt!

Miss Flanders: And Miss Peters, she's supporting an old mother —

Velie: Why don't this Edmund Black do somethin'? I thought he owned that store!

Rydell: Mr. Black's a gentleman, but Watson owns the controlling interest in the business, so what could Mr. Black do?

Miss Flanders: Mr. Queen, please, help us! Mr. Black made Watson promise we'd all get our jobs back if the thief is caught . . . We need our jobs, Mr. Queen. Please . . .

Rydell: It would be the most wonderful Christmas present . . .

Nikki (*quietly*): Well, Mr. Queen? Do we become book-clerks at the C. D. Black Company, or don't we?

Ellery (*grimly*): We do, Miss Porter. Sergeant, get Watson on the 'phone and inform him he'll have two new clerks tomorrow morning!

(*Music up . . . and into*)

Ellery (*acting as clerk*): Yes, sir, thank you, sir. If there's anything else Black's can do for you —

Customer (*nasty*): Don't try to sell me what I don't want! Give me that book, and let me get out of here!

Ellery (*humbly*): Yes, sir . . . here you are, sir . . . your change . . .

Customer (*fading . . . same*): Fools . . . ass . . . talk a man's ear off . . .

Ellery (*sore*): Why, you ill-tempered, opinionated, spavined . . .

Nikki (*fading on*): Uh-uh, Mr. Queen . . . mustn't say the naughty word . . . remember, the customer's always right.

Ellery: Nikki . . . thank heaven . . . now I *know* I shouldn't have let myself in for this . . . (*Lower*) Has young Black returned from Philadelphia yet?

Nikki (*low*): No . . . have you seen Mr. Watson this morning?

Ellery (*low*): Watson 'phoned to say he wasn't feeling well . . . he'll be down later. (*Tinkly bell off*) Nikki . . . look.

Nikki: Mike Callahan . . . does he know that we . . .

Ellery: Morning, Mr. Callahan . . . something in a first edition?

Callahan (*fading on . . . amused*): Well, well . . . your father told me you'd decided to work for a living, Queen . . . but I frankly didn't believe him . . . morning, Miss Porter. (*Nikki greets him*) Know who I am?

Nikki: Now what sort of question is *that*? You sound like Ellery.

Ellery: Callahan, don't tell me *you've* got a job at Black's, too.

Callahan (*low*): Not so loud, Queen. I'm the new secretary-stenographer to Edmund Black. Hadn't you heard? But you couldn't have . . . not even my new boss knows it yet . . . (*Laughs*)

Nikki: Such versatility . . . can you type and take shorthand?

Callahan: Oh, sure . . . I've used this secretary-stenographer dodge dozens of times in my business.

Ellery: But won't Black know you're the latest investigator of the insurance company, Callahan?

Callahan: Not a chance . . . I wangled the job last night through a business connection of Watson's who thinks I'm what I'm pretending to be . . . so far I haven't even got a name . . . your father arranged the whole thing.

Ellery: The traitor . . . then Watson doesn't know who you are, either?

Callahan: He does not . . . I haven't even met Watson yet . . . (*Chuckles*)

Nikki: Mr. Callahan . . . that chuckle is mean . . . you know something we don't.

Callahan (*chuckling*): I know what old Burbage was driving at.

Ellery: You mean that earth-shaking secret Burbage claimed to have discovered . . . the secret he said would ruin Black's?

Callahan: Yes, *sir* — and believe me, it's all Burbage said it was . . .

Ellery: When'd *you* find out, Callahan? And how?

Callahan: Last night . . . I came down here, let myself in, and scouted around. How? Observation . . . inference from facts.

Nikki: You just looked around right here . . . in the store?

Callahan (*laughing*): That's right, Miss Porter.

Ellery (*despair*): I don't believe it.

Nikki: Ellery Queen . . . you're actually blushing. You've snooped around here for an hour this morning . . . and you haven't seen a thing . . . unless Mr. Callahan swiped it.

Callahan: No . . . it's still here. (*Chuckles*)

Ellery (*grimly*): Callahan . . . either you're pulling my leg, or you're a better man than I am . . . which I'm loathe to admit.

Callahan: All right, Queen, I'll tell you the secret . . . it's —

Ellery (*quickly*): Uh-uh-uh nothing doing . . . if there's something to be nosed out here, I want to nose it out myself . . . maybe I can catch up with you before this case is over, Callahan.

Callahan: Not a chance . . . this rare-book racket just isn't down your alley, Queen.

Ellery (*chuckling*): We'll see about that.
Nikki (*briskly*): Score one for Mr. Mike Callahan.

(*Music up . . . into door opening . . . closing with tinkly bell*)

Nikki (*whisper*): Ellery, he's here . . . Mr. Callahan . . . there's the thief . . .
    he just walked into the store.
Ellery (*same, excited*): The man with the black bag, beard, and dark
    glasses . . . Nikki, act nonchalant; Callahan, walk over to him —
    pretend you're a clerk.
Callahan (*low*): Right, Queen . . . (*Steps*) . . . Uh — good afternoon, sir . . .
    May I help you? Something in a first edition, perhaps?
Bearded man (*disguised voice . . . husky*): Just browsing.
Callahan: Oh, certainly, sir . . . (*Steps . . . low*) Browsing he says . . .
    browsing for loot . . . (*All ensuing dialogue whispery*)
Ellery: Keep fussing with these books here, Nikki. Recognize the fellow,
    Callahan?
Callahan: No . . . all bundled up to the eyes, and that beard and those
    glasses . . . if he falls for our plant and tries to steal, we'll grab him.
Nikki: How about his voice, Mr. Callahan?
Callahan: A phony, like the beard . . . disguised it . . . here, I'll turn my
    back to him — you two face his way . . . tell me what he's doing —
    pretend we're just chewing the fat —
Ellery: He's just gone over to the counter on which the Keats is lying —
    the book we planted.
Nikki: There . . . he's putting the black bag down on the counter.
Callahan: Don't take your eyes off his hands for a second.
Ellery: He's removing his gloves . . . putting them into his coat pocket
    with his right hand —
Nikki: His left hand's resting on the bag . . . in plain sight —
Callahan: Has he touched the book? Has he?
Ellery: No . . . now he's in front of the book, hiding it . . . but his left
    hand's still on the bag and his right in his pocket . . .
Nikki: He's picking up his bag — walking away . . . shucks.
Callahan: Is the Keats we planted still on the counter?
Nikki: Yes, it is . . . He didn't touch it . . . not once.
Ellery: Got jittery, I suppose . . . not enough people around . . . there,
    he's walking out of the store. (*Open . . . close door . . . off . . . bell*)
Callahan: Too bad . . . (*Quick steps . . . stop*) Leaving the Keats behind . . . it
    must have broken his heart . . . (*Alarm*) . . . We've been bounced . . .
    (*Fading with running steps off*) You — come back here.
Nikki: Ellery, what's the matter?
Ellery: He tricked us, Nikki. (*Door opens with bells off*) Substituted a

dummy the same size and color as the Keats. (*Running steps . . . ad libs on mike, street sounds up . . . Callahan shouting ad lib outside*) Callahan, do you see him?

Callahan (*fading on*): Got away, hang it . . . had a cab waiting . . . (*Steps of three on pavement*) Got to hand it to him, that was neat, Queen. (*Door closes*)

Ellery: Too blasted neat to suit *me*.

Nikki: Two fine detectives you are.

Ellery: Don't rub it in, Nikki . . . Question is . . . how'd he *do* it . . . I'd swear his hands never touched that Keats.

Nikki: And his bag was never open . . . at any time.

Callahan (*beginning to laugh*): It wasn't? By George, I've been dumb . . . (*Laughs heartily*) Why didn't I think of it before?

Nikki: Think of what, Mr. Callahan?

Callahan: The identical stunt was pulled at Barbour's, the big book store, in 'Frisco . . . June of '29.

Ellery (*amazed*): You mean you know how he did it, Callahan?

Callahan: Yes, you see, this bearded phony has a —

Ellery (*quickly*): No, you don't. Callahan . . . I'll get to the bottom of this without your help, or perish in the attempt.

Nikki (*laughing*): Score two for Mr. Callahan.

(*Music up . . . and into opening and slamming of door*)

Ellery (*fading on . . . excited*): I've got it . . . I've got it.

Inspector: Got what, son?

Nikki: A high temperature . . . from the look of him, Inspector.

Ellery (*gleefully*): So Mike Callahan beat me to it, did he? We'll see . . . we'll see . . .

Nikki: Ellery Queen, stop babbling and explain why you packed me off to the apartment after closing time, and then stayed behind in the store?

Ellery: I merely remembered I'd been an idiot, Nikki . . . I hadn't examined the black bag which the bearded man had left behind him yesterday . . . (*Dumps heavy bag*) And this is it . . . it's been in Watson's office at the store since he had us arrested by mistake.

Inspector: Mmmm. I haven't examined it, myself. So this is the bag the thief mistook for yours, eh? The bag with the stolen books in it?

Ellery: Yes . . . and I've even brought the books with me . . . (*Opens bag, dump books on table*)

Nikki: That's right . . . there's the six-volume set of Applegate's *Napoleonic Wars*, and — Ellery, why did you bring the dummy of the Keats book the thief left behind today?

Ellery: For the obvious reason that he's got the Keats. Now let me give you good folks a little demonstration. I place this dummy volume in the *bottom* of the bag . . . like this . . . (*slight bump of book in bag*) See?

Inspector: I see, but it doesn't mean anything to me.

Ellery: It will . . . now I take the six volumes of Applegate . . . like this . . . (*Other bumps of books*) . . . and place *them* in the bag on top of the Keats dummy . . . and what do you see?

Nikki: Seven books in a bag . . . what are we supposed to see?

Ellery: Come, come, Nikki. How did the black bag look yesterday when Watson opened it at my invitation and found these same books inside — the same books, seven of 'em.

Nikki (*slowly*): How did the bag look . . . why . . . Ellery . . . *full*.

Ellery: Yes, crammed to the top . . . overflowing with books.

Inspector: But there's lots of room in the bag now . . . room to spare.

Ellery: Exactly dad . . . conclusion . . . this *can't* be the bag the thief left behind . . . it's a substitute bag . . . the thief managed to steal into Watson's office between yesterday and this evening and left this ordinary black bag, taking away the one he'd been foolish enough to leave behind.

Inspector (*slowly*): If he did that, then the original bag . . . the one he'd left behind, must have something about it which would give him away.

Ellery: Yes, and I know what. *This* bag's the same size as the thief's, yet its interior holds many more books. So the interior of the thief's bag was smaller . . . which means — it had a false bottom.

Nikki: A false bottom? But what good would that be to him?

Ellery (*grimly*): It enabled him to steal books, that's what.

Inspector (*thoughtfully*): False-bottom bag, huh . . . that's the kind of bag these stage magicians use, isn't it?

Ellery: Yes, it's used in conjuring stunts. Well, our thieving bearded man conjured books with it. The bottom of the bag is equipped with a so-called "spring-grip" device. You set the bag squarely on the top of the thing you want to steal, and the spring-grip mechanism, operating like the mouth of a trap, snaps *into* the bottom of the bag whatever the bag's resting on.

Nikki: So that's how he managed to steal the Keats today.

Ellery: Yes . . . I suppose he slipped the dummy onto the counter through a slash-pocket of his coat while he was putting away his gloves.

Inspector: I'll have to remember that dodge. Well, I've got to be getting downtown to Headquarters. (*Doorbell off*) I'll answer the door, Nikki, on my way out. (*Fading*) Night.

Nikki: Night, Inspector. (*Door opens off — ad libs*) Now who, for heaven's sake?

Ellery: Sounds like Sergeant Velie and — yes, old Burbage!

Velie (*fading on — calling*): Yeah, you'll find the report on the McCoy case on your desk, Inspector! (*Inspector's ad lib, door slam off*) Ah, good evening! I was just comin' up here and ran into this gent. He had the same idea.

Nikki: Hello, Mr. Burbage. Sit down. You look tired.

Burbage (*fading on*): Thank you, Miss, thank you. (*Ellery greets him*) Mr. Queen, I . . . couldn't resist stopping in — I'm so restless since we were all discharged yesterday — Have you made any progress? Any at all?

Ellery: Considerable, Mr. Burbage. In fact, I was just demonstrating how Black's stock has been disappearing.

Burbage: Really? How the books are being stolen? Remarkable, sir!

Velie: I see I've got some catchin' up to do.

Ellery: And what's more, I know who the thief is — the real identity of the bearded man!

Nikki: Ellery, you didn't say a word about *that*! Who is it?

Ellery: Don't ask me now. I'm saving *something* for Mr. Callahan!

Burbage: Well! I'm delighted, of course. But — after all — I mean, the thefts are incidental —

Velie: You better not say that around Headquarters, Burbage!

Burbage (*flustered*): I mean — have you found out the *secret*? That's the important thing!

Ellery: The secret you mentioned the other day? No, Mr. Burbage. You've been so close-mouthed about it, I don't even know what to look for.

Nikki: Mr. Burbage, why don't you tell us what that secret is?

Velie: Yeah, you're a citizen, ain't you? A citizen's got his dooties, too, ain't he? You better spill, Burbage.

Burbage (*nervous*): Yes . . . it's bound to come out sooner or later, anyway . . . But I don't feel right about revealing it without at least telling the owners of the company first — and Mr. Black is still in Philadelphia —

Ellery: But Watson's at the store right now. He told me he was going to work there all evening, Mr. Burbage.

Burbage: He's at the store? . . . In that case . . . Mr. Queen, if you'll come with me, I'll tell you and Mr. Watson together!

(*Music up . . . and into car pulling up at curb . . .*)

Velie: Here's the store. (*Emergency brake, shut off motor*)

Nikki (*as to old man*): Let me open the car door for you, Mr. Burbage . . . (*Opens car door. Burbage's thanks*)

Ellery (*sharply*): There's someone at the front door of the shop!

Burbage: At this time of night? I can't imagine who —

Velie: He's monkeyin' with the door! Hey, you!

Burbage: It's Mr. Edmund Black! (*Calling*) Mr. Black! (*Close car door and steps across pavement*)

Black (*fading on*): Burbage! (*Awkwardly*) Hello, Burbage. What are you doing here? And who are these people?

Burbage: I'm so glad you're back, sir! Oh. Miss Porter, Mr. Queen, and this gentleman — I don't know his name —

Velie: Sergeant Velie, an' thanks for the compliment. (*Ad libs*)

Ellery: We're down here with Mr. Burbage on a rather serious matter, Mr. Black. Some secret . . .

Black: Secret? What secret? Well, let's go into the store. Can't talk out here. (*Key in lock. Open door, bell, close*)

Nikki: It's so dark in here — (*Bump*) Ooop! (*Steps*)

Ellery: Let me take your arm, Nikki. Of course, Mr. Black, we thought you were still in Philadelphia. We came down to see Mr. Watson.

Black: What on earth for? Burbage, what is this business about a secret?

Burbage (*nervous*): It's — pretty dreadful, Mr. Black . . .

Black: More trouble, eh? Yes, Watson's here. There's a light showing through the transom of his office. (*Calling*) Watson! (*Pause*) Watson!

Nikki: He's rather old, isn't he? Perhaps his hearing — (*Stop steps*)

Black: Watson! (*Pause. Rattles doorknob*) Fell asleep, probably. (*Opens door*) Watson — (*Gasps. Nikki Groans. Other reactions*)

Ellery (*sharply — fading*): Get Nikki out of here, Sergeant!

Velie: Sure, Mr. Queen. Out you go, Miss Porter — come on, now —

Nikki (*fading*): I'll go — gladly.

Burbage (*on mike whisper*): Look at Mr. Watson — look at Mr. Watson —

Black (*hoarsely*): Queen! Is he — he's so still — is Watson —

Ellery (*slightly off*): Murdered!

(*Music up . . . into ad lib background murmur . . .*)

Ellery: It's murder, all right — Watson was shot in the chest — near the heart. No sign of the gun — murderer must have taken it with him. What do you think, Sergeant?

Velie: Well, Watson's sittin' behind his desk here, but he wasn't shot at the desk. He got it on the other side of the room, near that end-table — and this trail of blood-spots, shaky an' staggerin' — like, musta come from the old gink's wound.

Ellery: Mmmm. Blood-trail starts at the end-table and ends behind the desk at which we found his seated dead body . . .

Velie: Big clue, though, is this sheet o' paper with writin' on it. On the desk, in front of where Watson's sittin'.

Ellery (*thoughtfully*): No question but that Watson staggered across the room and had begun to write something. The paper is spotted with his blood, and the desk-pen with which he was writing is still clutched in his right hand.

Velie: What's that he wrote down? Kind of shaky, isn't it? Can hardly make it out. (*Slowly*) B-L-A-C-K apost'ophe S, then the word — let's see — "secret." "Black's secret." Say! Old Watson knew the secret Burbage's been yappin' about, too!

Ellery: Which reminds me. (*Calling*) Mr. Black!

Black (*fading on — hoarse, low*): Mr. Queen — can't you — can't you at least cover the body —

Ellery: Cover it, Sergeant. (*Ad lib from Velie*) Mr. Black, your partner before he died wrote down the two words: "Black's secret." Mr. Burbage has also been hinting vigorously about a big secret connected with your firm. What about it?

Black: "Black's secret . . ." And yes, Burbage did say, just a few minutes ago . . . It's beyond me, Mr. Queen. *I* don't know of any secret. All I know is — the choicest books in our stock have been disappearing. (*Calling*) Burbage!

Burbage (*fading on — unnerved*): Y-yes, Mr. Black. What a calamity! The thefts, Mr. Watson m-murdered . . .

Black: Burbage, what is this secret you've been hinting about?

Ellery: Come, come, Burbage — out with it!

Burbage (*wailing*): Mr. Black, I didn't know what to do — it was so . . . *terrible*, such an awful thing . . .

Black: For heaven's sake, Burbage — talk!

Burbage (*whispering*): Yes . . . Come with me, please. (*Steps*)

Velie (*fading*): An' I gotta stay here keepin' company with a stiff! Where's the Inspector, anyway?

Burbage (*over steps*): Gentlemen, I've devoted more than fifty years of my life to the study of rare books — as a hobby, you understand. It was the environment . . . Mr. Black, you know it's true — your father, your grandfather used to teach me . . . they liked me.

Black (*gently*): I know, Burbage. I remember.

Burbage: Stop here, please. (*Steps stop*) This is one section of the rare-book department, Mr. Queen. (*Panting as if lifting books*) Let me — show you . . . what I mean. Here are four valuable books . . .

Ellery: Mmmm. Browning first — Tennyson — Kelmscott edition of Chaucer — fourth-edition Shakespeare, London, 1685 . . . Beautiful specimens!

Burbage (*bitterly*): That's what *you* think!

Black (*alarm*): Burbage! Burbage! What are you driving at?

Burbage: They're all forgeries! (*Ad libs*) Yes, forgeries! They'd fool the finest collectors! Not more than six men in the United States besides myself could detect them — but I tell you they're forgeries, the cleverest I ever saw!

Ellery (*slowly*): Simply incredible. These specimens not genuine?

Black (*dazed*): But Burbage, even if these four *are* fakes —

Burbage (*wailing*): You don't understand, Mr. Black! It's not only these four — *it's practically every rare book in your stock! There's hardly an authentic old or rare book left on your shelves!*

Ellery (*whistling*): That *was* a secret to keep, Burbage! If it got out that the oldest rare-book firm in the country had been flooding the market with forgeries . . .

Black (*bewildered*): But this is — I can't believe . . . Burbage, you mean we've been buying forgeries without knowing it?

Burbage: No, sir. Not long ago some of these books were genuine. Now they're fakes. I know it. They're fakes! And we've been selling them!

Ellery: So someone's been slowly substituting clever forgeries for originals . . . And at the same time someone *else* has been stealing the forgeries, believing them to be genuine! (*Ad libs fading on*) Dad! So you've finally got here. Ah, Mr. Callahan. Greetings. (*Ad libs*)

Inspector: Mike and I just drove up together from Headquarters. Flint — Hagstrom — Piggott! Take over from Velie in that office! (*Ad libs fading*) Where's Nikki, Ellery?

Ellery: Poor kid's had a shock. Here she is now. Come here, Nikki —

Black (*fading*): Burbage, come back to my office. I want to go into this — this amazing forgery thing more thoroughly.

Burbage (*fading*): Yes, Mr. Black — yes sir.

Nikki (*fading on — weary*): Hello, I've been sitting out of the way — sort of — pulling myself together.

Callahan: Dead men are no sight for a young woman. Get out of this business. Well, Queen? I gather you've been busy tonight.

Ellery (*mocking*): Well . . . yes and no, Callahan. Of course, I've solved the case . . . (*Ad libs*)

Nikki: Ellery! *Already?* It gets faster every time!

Inspector (*chuckling*): What d'ye think of that, Mike Callahan?

Callahan (*same*): Interesting . . . if true.

Ellery: Oh, it's true, Callahan. (*Laughs*) Please forgive the crowing. You stole two marches on me, and I didn't enjoy the feeling.

Nikki: You see? He's even *laughing* last!

Ellery (*laughs*): This case comprises what might be called a crime triangle — it has three corners: forgery, theft, and murder. I suppose you're aware, Callahan, that most of the stock of the Black Company are forgeries?

Callahan: Yes, Queen. That's what I wanted to tell you, but you wouldn't let me.

Ellery: Well, the interesting part of this case is that *one* person forged the books, *another* person stole them, and still a *third* person murdered Watson. Three different crimes — three different criminals! (*Inspector chuckles*)

Nikki (*gasping*): Why, that's fantastic!

Ellery: Not at all, Nikki. Callahan, you solved the forgery secret before I did — and the secret of the black bag . . . score two for you. But how about the murder? Do you also know who killed Watson tonight?

Callahan: Of course I do. Only a half-hour ago I walked into your father's office at Headquarters and told him who did it. Right, Inspector?

Inspector: That's right, Mike.

Ellery: Well, I'll be . . . But maybe you've got the wrong answer, Callahan! Here, I'll tell you what we'll do! You write out the murderer's name on a slip of paper and hand it to Nikki. I'll do the same. She'll compare 'em!

Callahan: You're on, young fella. (*Pause, scribbling*) Here's mine, Miss Porter.

Ellery: And mine, Nikki.

Inspector (*chuckling*): Let's read those two names together, Nikki.

Nikki (*gasping after pause*): Well, I — *You've both put down the same name!* But —

Inspector (*laughing*): Looks like a draw to me, son.

Ellery (*astonished*): Dad, Callahan wrote the same name I did? Nikki? You're sure? (*Ad libs*) I can't believe it!

Callahan (*chuckling*): You're a stubborn cuss, aren't you, Queen? Don't you know when you've met your match? (*Pause*)

Ellery (*laughing*): Callahan, I salute you! You're a man after my own heart. It's a draw all right. Shake!

(*Music up . . . and into Jury spot*)

Challenge to the Listener

In his challenge, Ellery told the studio jury and the listeners at home that they had to answer three questions: who forged the rare books; who stole the rare books; and who murdered Watson.

(*Music up . . . into dinner-party atmosphere as in big hotel dining-room, string ensemble background . . . ad libs fading on with chink of china, glassware, etc.*)

Velie (*bellowing*): Garson, more wine!

Waiter (*fading on*): Yes, sir. (*Liquid poured*)

Velie: Swell feed, all right. Atmosphere an' everything!

Nikki: It's like a celebration.

Ellery: It *is* a celebration.

Velie: But what are we celebratin'?

Inspector (*chuckling*): The fact that my son's met his match. Mike, I've got to hand it to you. You've done what I've been trying to do — and haven't been able to — for years!

Callahan (*laughing*): Maybe you don't know how to go about it, Inspector. Kidding aside, though, the laurels really go to you, Queen. I got through on specialized knowledge.

Ellery: Oh, I don't know, Callahan. The method isn't important. The fact is, we fought a draw.

Nikki: Mutual Admiration Society!

Velie: They'll be holdin' hands next.

Ellery: Don't you think we owe these good people an explanation, Callahan?

Callahan (*chuckling*): I don't owe them anything. But you go ahead. I kind of like to listen to you talk.

Inspector: Velie, shut that door, will you? This palaver needs a little privacy.

Velie (*fading*): So that's why you ordered a private dinin'-room. (*Door closes off. Shut off all dining room noise, and orchestra. Velie fading on*) Shoot, Mr. Queen. I'm all ears.

Nikki: That's obvious, Sergeant. Ellery, *I'm* confused. Someone forges valuable books — someone else steals the forgeries — and someone *else* murders one of the owners . . .

Velie: And the two guys who know what it's all about go out an' celebrate!

Inspector (*chuckling*): Not to mention a certain Inspector of police who's helping them do it!

Nikki: It's all 'way over *my* head. What's the answer, Ellery?

Ellery: As I told you earlier tonight, Nikki, there are really three answers. Because there are three questions.

Callahan: The first being: who forged the rare books? That was easy.

Ellery: Very. Because you'll remember old Burbage said the forgeries were extremely clever — so good that only six men in America beside himself could have detected them.

Inspector: And Mike here's one of the six. Well, he ought to be. He's been in the insurance end of the book racket long enough!

Ellery: The big point is: Who was the forger? Obviously a man able to manufacture such remarkable forgeries that only a handful of experts could see through them, would have to be outstanding in the field of rare books. Did we have such a man in the case? Yes. A man who possessed the requisite knowledge — actually you yourself, Callahan, called him one of the leading rare-book experts of the country.

Callahan: That's right, I did.

Ellery: So he had the knowledge. But in order to manufacture the forgery he must also have the *craftsmanship*. And this man had it, because we knew that the one-book editions of great literary classics which he published, he made *with his own hands*! Burbage told us that.

Velie: I remember. But who was he talkin' about, again?

Ellery: Third, he must also possess the *equipment*, the *machinery*, to manufacture the forgeries. And this same man had those, too! Because Burbage also told us the man had a *press* and *bindery* in his Westchester home!

Nikki: *Abner Watson!*

Inspector: Yes Nikki. Watson was the forger, no doubt about it.

Velie: But . . . Watson *owned* the books. Why should he have forged his own books? That's screwy.

Callahan: He didn't own the books, Velie. He only *shared* in the ownership. Remember he owned only fifty-one percent of the stock of the Black Company.

Ellery: That's quite true. So it's obvious that old Watson was double-crossing his young partner, Edmund Black, by stealing the genuine books for himself and substituting clever but worthless forgeries for the company.

Inspector: The firm's been shaky anyhow, and I suppose this Watson was laying up a nest-egg for the expected bankruptcy.

Ellery: Well, that disposes of the forger. The second question is: Who was *stealing* the forgeries? (*Pause*) Well, what qualifications does the thief have to possess?

Nikki: He'd have to be someone pretty well-known to the people in the store, otherwise he wouldn't have disguised himself so *completely* — muffled to the ears in that coat, black glasses, that bushy false beard . . .

Callahan: Good for you, Miss Porter.

Ellery: Excellent, Nikki. But there are two other points of much greater importance. One, it had to be someone who was familiar with *stage magic* . . .

Velie: Sure — he used a magician's bag to swipe the books with!

Ellery: Yes — and secondly, and most important of all, *the only person connected with the store* who was NOT present IN the store on the occasion of the *attempted* theft of the Keats — the *first* attempt, Nikki, the one we witnessed the day Watson mistook us for the thieves . . .

Nikki: We saw all the employees, Mr. Burbage, Mr. Watson . . . it was Mr. Black . . . Black!

Inspector: Yes, young Black himself, with his "Philadelphia" gag.

Callahan: And Burbage told us Edmund Black was an amateur magician.

Velie: Black? The other partner? Watson was forgin' the company's stock and Black was stealin' it? But why?

Ellery: Obviously, Sergeant, for the identical reason — to double-cross his partner in the face of threatened bankruptcy. Of course, young Black didn't know the books he was stealing were forgeries. Burbage told us Black didn't know much about the rare-book business. Black's in for an unpleasant surprise, I'm afraid.

Inspector (*grimly*): More than one.

Nikki: But what about Mr. Watson's murder, Ellery? How did you know who did that? I still can't believe the whole thing.

Velie: It beats me. Inspector, you sure you ain't made —

Inspector (*satiric*): Velie, I'm sure I "ain't" made. Now be quiet and listen. Maybe you'll learn something.

Callahan: Yes, explain, Queen. Of course I know how *I* knew, but I still don't understand how *you* figured it out.

Ellery: It was childishly simple, Callahan. It all arose out of the two words Watson wrote down before he died. Let's reconstruct the scene. Watson was shot at one end of the room, near the end-table. The murderer then left, believing Watson to be dead. But Watson wasn't dead, because a trail of blood-spots led from the place where he was shot across the room, to the desk, where he sat down and began to write a message. Now there are only two plausible reasons why a victim should stagger with his dying strength across a room to write a message. The first is: to confess a crime of his own — that is, realizing he is dying, he wants to clear his conscience . . .

Nikki: But Ellery, isn't that what Watson started to do?

Velie: Sure, he wrote down "Black's secret" —

Inspector: I don't get this, Ellery. Black's secret was that practically all of their rare-book stock was forged, and Watson was the forger. So that explains what Watson was starting to write — a confession that he'd been the forger.

Ellery: Ah! But whose secret was it that Watson was the forger?

Callahan (*slowly*): What do you mean by that, Queen?

Ellery: Wasn't it *Watson's* secret?

Velie: Well, cert'nly, but . . .

Ellery: Then why should Watson have written "*Black's*" secret? It doesn't make sense! The fact is, had Watson been intending to confess, he would have sought a short-cut. Dying men don't write round-about, polished sentences. Watson was so weak he could only get out about twelve characters before he died. No, if he'd intended to confess he was a forger, in his dying condition I'm afraid he would have tried to write: "I forged books in store — Abner Watson," or something equally simple. He certainly wouldn't have started a sentence with "Black's secret," which would have forced him to continue in some such vein as: "Black's secret is that I, Abner Watson, have been forging . . ." and so on and so on. So I saw at once that the whole forgery-confession theory was improbable! He couldn't have meant Black's *secret*.

Inspector (*intently*): But if Watson didn't mean to confess, Ellery, what *did* he mean by writing those two words?

Callahan: To tell you the truth, Queen, I'm as puzzled on that point as your father is.

Nikki: There, Mr. Queen! Doesn't that restore your self-respect?

Ellery (*chuckling*): It helps, Nikki, it helps.

Velie: What's the second reason why a dying man would go to all that trouble to write, Mr. Queen?

Ellery: The second reason, Sergeant — the alternative — is . . . *to leave a clue to his murderer's identity*. Watson was dying in a shut-up store, at night, he hadn't the strength to call for help loudly enough to get it . . . Yes, Mr. Watson was trying to name his murderer.

Inspector: But Ellery, for pete's sake, that doesn't make sense, either! A man trying to name his murderer names him — he writes down the *name*. But Watson didn't write down the name — he wrote down "Black's secret!"

Callahan: That's right. If what you say is true, Queen, why didn't Watson write down his murderer's name?

Ellery: Fair question, Callahan. Answer: Because obviously he didn't *know* his murderer's name!

Nikki: Didn't know his murderer's name? But —

Inspector: Oh, *I* get it. Sure — that's right, Mike!

Callahan (*admiringly*): It is, at that. I never thought of that.

Velie (*howling*): *What's* right, for cryin' out loud?

Ellery: There was only one person involved whose name we *know* Watson was ignorant of, Sergeant. And that was . . . (*Pause*) Mr. Mike Callahan. (*Gasp from Nikki and Velie*) Mike Callahan himself told us that Watson and he hadn't even met — that "so far, I haven't even got a name," as he put it!

Velie: *You* — Mike? *You* bumped off the old guy? But —

Ellery: Oh, you aren't aware of the situation, Sergeant — I forgot. But let me finish. Watson was killed by Callahan. Watson didn't know Callahan's name. But he *did* know Callahan's supposed position — that of Edmund Black's new secretary! Because that's the dodge Callahan told us he was using — to become an employee of the store. Black's *secretary*. (*Pause*) Black's . . . secret . . . ary . . .

Nikki: Black's *secret*! You mean he was intending to write "Black's *secretary*" and never got past s-e-c-r-e-t, Ellery?

Ellery: Exactly. He died before he could finish the word. And that was my confirmation that Callahan was the murderer. Watson couldn't have meant Black's *former* secretary — a chap named Marcus, I

believe — because surely Watson knew the name of an old employee.
So he must have meant the new secretary — friend Callahan.

Velie: It's . . . But . . . you're all sittin' here as if nothin' happened!
Inspector, you can't let Mike — I mean . . .

Inspector (*soberly*): You don't understand, Velie. Tell him, Mike.

Callahan (*same*): It was a nasty business, Velie. In all my twenty years as
a cop and a private detective, I never found myself in a spot like that.
I was snooping in the store tonight, and surprised the old bird in his
office. I told him I was Black's new secretary, but he accused me of
being a spy — and I told him right out that I was looking for proof
he was the forger. He got mad and started to yell at me to get out. I
told him he didn't frighten me — that I was sure it was him and that
I was going to nail him if it was the last thing I did. Then he lost his
head and pulled a gun out of his drawer — I made a grab for it. He
was a wiry old bird and fighting mad too, and we had quite a scuffle.
I found myself fighting for my life. Finally I got the gun away from
him, but he made a lunge at me and the gun went off. Next thing I
knew, I was standing there with the gun in my hand, and he was
lying on the floor dead or I thought he was.

Inspector: Plain case of self-defense. Mike marched himself straight downtown
to my office at Police Headquarters and gave himself up. Told me the
whole story. Turned in Watson's gun, too. Technically, of course, he's
under arrest. But I don't think we'll have any trouble, eh, Mike?

Callahan (*chuckling*): I hope not. I want to spend Christmas with my family.

Velie: Well, it beats me!

Ellery: It beat me, too, Sergeant. When Mike wrote down his own name
on that scrap of paper he handed Nikki, I was flabbergasted. Imagine
a murderer confessing that way! Well, I'm glad it's turned out as it
has. The world hasn't lost much in seeing the last of Mr. Abner Watson.
A forger, a mean scoundrel, and a would-be murderer.

Nikki: Uh . . . Mr. Queen.

Ellery: Yes, Nikki.

Nikki: I hate to inject a note of pessimism into this gay *soiree*, but — in
all the excitement, haven't you forgotten something?

Ellery: I thought I'd covered everything. Forgotten something, Nikki?

Nikki (*laughing*): You've forgotten to get the manuscript of your detective
story back from Edmund Black! Don't you remember? He took your
bag with the novel in it by mistake?

Ellery: My manuscript! Why . . . the — the thief! (*Fading*) Goodbye!
(*Laughter of all up*)

(*Music up*)

Originally broadcast on January 7, 1940, "The Adventure of the Dying Scarecrow" is one of the best-known of all the Ellery Queen radio scripts, especially in its later incarnation as "The Adventure of the Scarecrow and the Snowman," when the show was shortened from an hour to thirty minutes. Its appeal is related to the bizarre image of a bleeding scarecrow, and also to the fact that (unlike some E.Q. programs) the main clue is simple enough that the studio jury figured it out.

The Adventure of the Dying Scarecrow

The Characters

Ellery Queen	The detective
Nikki Porter	His secretary
Inspector Queen	Of the New York Police
Sergeant Velie	Of the New York Police
Paw Mathew	Farmer
Maw Mathew	His wife
Jonathan Mathew	Their son, off stage
Jed Bigelow	Hired hand
Homer Clay	Farmer
Julie Clay	His wife
Dr. Harkness	Physician
Nurse, Waitress	

Setting: The Midwest, 1939

Ellery: This is the story of the Mathew family, Americans, who lived on the land.

The Mathews dwelt in the solitude of a lonely farm, where, by night, when the prairie winds swept over their sleeping fields, you could see their barn and sheds and pens and farmhouse as quiet little roots under the spreading orchard of the black sky.

We first saw their farm, however, in a smiling mood. It was on a summer's morning — early last July. We were driving back East from California — Nikki Porter, my father Inspector Queen, Sergeant Velie, and myself.

I remember now with pleasure what a lovely morning it was as we drove through that serene mid-western country. The sun ran

180

splashing over the country-side. The distant Mathew barn was red. The clapboard and shingled roof of the farmhouse were stained with the leafy shadows of old elms — pure white-and-green pastel. Beyond the road a herd of bossies, all red and brown and black, munched grass placidly. The swell and glow of the green and yellow fields, the gleaming fruit in the nearby orchards, caught my eye and enchanted them. (*Begin to fade voice as fade on purr of auto motor*)

And so, spying that quiet, peaceful farm, I shouted to Sergeant Velie, who was driving . . . (*Voice up*) Sergeant! Stop!

Velie: What for, Mr. Queen? We're in the middle of no place.

Nikki: We're in the middle of heaven!

(*Car stopping, cows, lowing off, birds, etc.*)

Inspector (*chuckling*): He wants to chase a butterfly.

(*Car stops, shut off motor*)

Ellery: Go on — sneer. Nikki understands my soul, don't you, Nikki?

(*Cows low off*)

Nikki: I certainly do; gentlemen, Mr. Queen is about to take color-movies of this perfectly glorious farm. Aren't you, Mr. Queen?

Ellery: Miss Porter, I am. (*Whirr of 16-mm. movie camera. Keep going till indicated*) Don't shake the car, dad. I'm trying — a — slow — panoramic shot.

Inspector: Must be the California influence.

Velie (*dreamily*): Inspector, you ain't got no poetry. Now take me. When I get out in God's country, an' I see birds an' farms an' cows an' stuff, I get a certain feeling —

Inspector: — that you'd like to be back on Centre Street in Charlie's, dipping your schnozz in a seidel of beer.

Nikki: Ellery! Get a shot of that scarecrow — over there — in the cornfield.

Velie: Say. Is *that* a scarecrow? I never seen one before.

Inspector (*chuckling*): And *he* gets a feeling.

Ellery (*over whirr*): Lonely beggar, isn't he?

Velie: Who — me?

Ellery: No, Sergeant, the scarecrow . . . ve-e-ery nice.

Inspector (*impatiently*): Oh, come on, son. What d'ye expect that scarecrow to do for you — come to life?

Nikki: Ellery, get that farmer, or hired hand, or whatever he is — in the picture. See him?

Velie: Yeah . . . walkin' t'ords the scarecrow, crost the field.

Ellery: Ye-e-es . . . very nice.

Inspector (*sharply*): Nice my foot. There's something wrong.

Ellery (*same*): He's frightened. (*Stop camera*)

Nikki: He's yelling something at us — can you hear what he's saying?
  (*Pause, faint shouting*)
Velie: Sounds like he's yellin' for help.
Inspector: Here he comes running towards this road.
Ellery: Come on.
  (*Open car doors, jump on road, run*)
Nikki (*panting*): Why — he's white as death.
Velie (*same*): Nice-lookin' young guy in those overhalls.
Inspector (*shouting*): What's the matter, youngster?
  (*Running in cornfield, trampling cornstalks*)
Ellery (*shouting*): What's wrong?
Bigelow (*fading in . . . terrified*): It's bleeding! It's *bleeding!*
  (*Steps stop . . . Bigelow pants, young, no dialect, but trace of mid-west intonation*)
Ellery: *What's* bleeding.
Inspector: What are you talking about?
Bigelow (*scared*): The scarecrow?
Nikki: The — *scarecrow!*
Velie: *Bleedin'?*
Ellery: Come on.
  (*Running steps through field*)
Bigelow (*panting*): I was — cutting across — to the orchard — when I
  happened to — look at — the scarecrow . . .
Inspector: I know. We saw you. (*Steps stop*)
Nikki (*awed*): It — *is* bleeding!
Velie: But how could a scarecrow bleed —
Inspector: Because this isn't a scarecrow, you cluck — it's a man dressed
  up like one. You — whoever you are —
Bigelow (*nervous*): Bigelow. Jed Bigelow. I'm the hired man on the
  Mathew place. This is the Mathew farm —
Ellery: Help us get this chap off the stake. (*They do so*)
Nikki (*sick*): He's been tied to the stake — by his belt —
Ellery (*panting*): These rags he's wearing — the straw hat —
Inspector (*same*): No wonder we — took him for a — scarecrow. Easy
  now, he's still alive.
Velie: You people always play jokes like this, Big'low!
Bigelow: I tell you I had no idea. There's always been a *scarecrow* on
  this cornfield stake —
Ellery: Please. Man's badly wounded, isn't he, dad?
Inspector: Unconscious . . . slight pulse-beat — very faint . . .
  (*Running steps off*)
Nikki: There's someone else coming.
Bigelow (*calling*): Homer! Look what we just found.
Clay (*fading on . . . panting*): Jed, whut the all-fired devil's goin' on here,

anyway? (*Medium age — mid-west dialect*) Who are these folks? Tramplin' my corn! What — (*Abrupt stop. Gasp*) Who —

Ellery: Who are you?

Clay (*dazed*): I'm Homer Clay — I run this farm fer ol' man Mathew — Jed, that's a — man, ain't it?

Inspector: Stop gassing. Where's the nearest hospital?

Bigelow: In the village.

Nikki: Hogsburg? That's six miles away, Inspector.

Ellery: Where's the nearest doctor — Clay, is it? Mr. Clay.

Clay: 'Most as far, Mister. What happened here, anyway?

Bigelow: We could 'phone the doctor from the house . . .

Inspector: Can't wait for the doctor — we'll have to rush this man to the hospital ourselves! Velie! You there — the hired man — Bigelow! Lend a hand!

Ellery (*grimly*): This is going to be a race with Old Man Death. Hurry, men!

(*Music up . . . and into ad lib murmur . . .*)

Inspector: Pretty nice little hospital for a small town.

Nikki: That doctor's taking his time in there! Oh, Sergeant, do you suppose that poor man will die?

Velie (*grimly*): If he don't he's made of iron . . . the way he's carved up!

Ellery: Tell me, Mr. Clay — who is the wounded man?

Clay: I dunno, Mr. Queen. Ain't never seed him afore. You, Jed?

Bigelow: You've got me, Homer.

Clay: An' Jed an' me, we been farmin' this country for a long time.

Inspector: Not a single identifying mark on him!

Nikki: How could there be? Didn't you say he's wearing your scarecrow's clothes, Mr. Clay?

Clay: Yep. Beats me.

Velie: An' how he got into that cornfield — an' who strapped him to that scarecrow pole . . . There's a mystery for you, Mr. Queen!

Ellery (*thoughtfully*): Yes, Sergeant . . . quite a mystery. Mr. Clay, who else lives on the Mathew farm — I mean, besides you and Jed Bigelow here?

Clay: Well, now, le's see. There's me — I'm married to the Mathew gal, Julie — goin' on seven year now, ain't it, Jed?

Bigelow (*low*): I suppose it is, Homer. You ought to know.

Clay: So there's my wife Julie, an' o' course there's Julie's paw, ol' man Mathew — ol' man Mathew really owns the place, though I run it. An' there's my maw-in-law, Mrs. Mathew, the ol' man's wife —

Bigelow: Ma Mathew runs the house, Mr. Queen — cooking, housekeeping, canning, feeds the stock, even helps out on the land. Wonderful woman.

Inspector: Old pioneer stock, eh?

Bigelow: Yes, Inspector. Strong as a plow-mare. Ma Mathew's been like a mother to me . . . I'm an — orphan.

Nikki: She sounds simply grand.

Clay: Yeah, she's all right, Maw is. An' young Jed here, he's like one o' the fam'ly. (*Chuckles*) Nice comp'ny fer my Julie, Jed is, come after sundown an' we set aroun' listenin' to the radio. Jed's a collidge man, he is!

Ellery: Really, Mr. Bigelow? Then how is it —

Bigelow (*low*): Oh, I spent a few years at the State Agricultural College, Mr. Queen. Bad mistake. (*Bitterly*) These days a poor man's better off without an education. Keeps him in his place!

Inspector: I wouldn't say that, son. You'll get your break.

Clay (*heartily*): Sure he will! That's what my Julie's allus tellin' him. (*Sadly*) Julie — she ain't well. Ain't well a-tall. She's took purty bad.

Velie: Your wife? Say, that's a shame, fella.

Clay (*sighing*): Yep, Julie she's been sort of ailin' since our baby was born dead — stays a-bed most times — ain't got the stren'th to git downstairs more'n once a week or so . . .

Nikki: Isn't that too bad, Mr. Clay . . . (*Door opens off*) Here's the doctor! (*Door closes off*)

Velie: How's your patient, Doc?

Inspector: Will he pull through?

Ellery: Has he a chance, Dr. Harkness?

Harkness (*fading on*): I'd say so, Mr. Queen. Fellow amazes me. With that chest-wound another man would have been dead long ago.

Ellery (*eagerly*): May we talk to him?

Harkness: He's still unconscious. Will be for some time. By the way, Homer — who is he, do you know?

Clay: *I* dunno, Doc. I was jest sayin' —

Harkness: Queer . . . I thought I knew everyone in the County.

Velie: Well, let's get movin', folks. Glad to hear the poor guy's not gonna kick off. What d'ye say?

Ellery: Wait, Sergeant. I'm — rather interested in this case.

Nikki: I knew it! I just *knew* it.

Ellery: Dr. Harkness, in view of the fact that the man's a stranger, identity unknown . . . I'd like your permission to photograph him. (*Ad libs*)

Harkness: Hmmm . . . True it can't do any harm — but the local police will have to . . .

Velie: Yeah, what about the locals? Ain't nobody even notified 'em there's been an assault?

Clay: Sa-ay, Jed, we oughta drop by an' sorta tell Jeff Whitaker what we found, fer a fac' . . .

Inspector (*sighing*): I might have known . . . Dr. Harkness, I'm Inspector Queen of the New York City police. (*Ad libs*) I don't think your local authorities will mind if I get things started . . .

Harkness: Of course, Inspector Queen. That's different —

Inspector (*sharply*): Ellery, take your photo. Doctor, no one is to see or talk to that man until we can question him. Notify us when he regains consciousness. (*Fading*) Velie, look up this Jeff Whitaker — sheriff, I s'pose — and tell him . . .

(*Music up . . . into car driving along country road . . .*)

Clay: Right friendly o' you folks to drive Jed an' me back to the farm . . . Mighty smart auto, huh, Jed?

Bigelow (*quietly*): What? Oh. Sure, Homer. It sure is.

Nikki: There's the farmhouse now.

Velie: Man, this sun is gettin' hot. (*Ad libs background*)

Inspector (*low, over them*): What are we going to do, Ellery? You still want to follow this thing up?

Ellery (*same*): Well, I've got the fellow's photograph —

Inspector: That drugstore in Hogsburg sure made a quick job of developing that film. Must have thought you were cuckoo. (*Dryly*) Might have been right, at that.

Ellery: I'm curious about these people at the Mathew farm, dad. Keep your eyes and ears open. (*Car slowing*)

Nikki: Here we are. Isn't it *peaceful*? (*Chickens off*)

Velie: I could sure use a cold drink . . . (*Car stops*)

Clay: Now you folks jest hop out an' I'll git Maw Mathew to fix you the coolest drink o' sweet cider y'ever sunk yer lip in . . . (*Car stops. Doors opening*) Jed, run on into the house an' tell Maw.

Bigelow: Right, Homer . . . Uh-uh. The old man.

Mathew (*old — cracked — off*): (*Yelling*) Stop where ye be!

Nikki (*startled*): Oh! Who's *that* just ran out of the house? He looks —

Velie: An' that's one wicked-lookin' shotgun he's wavin' over his head . . . Come 'ere, Miss Porter, quick!

Clay: Don't git a-scared, now. That's jest my paw-in-law, ol' man Mathew. (*Off a bit*) Hey, paw . . .!

Ellery: What's the matter with him?

Inspector: Pretty wild-looking old geezer, isn't he?

Mathew (*off a bit — yelling*): Don't ye come a step nigher!

Nikki (*gasping*): He's — threatening us with that shotgun!

Clay (*soothing*): Now, paw, it's all right — I know these folks . . . Git on back into the house.

Ellery: Mr. Mathew! If you'll put that shotgun down . . .

Mathew (*frenzy — screaming*): That' you, Jonathan — I knowed ye the minute I set eyes on ye!

Bigelow: Homer! Better get him inside. He's all upset.

Clay: Now, paw, be reas'n'ble.

Mathew (*screaming*): Leave me be, Homer. You — Jonathan. I warned ye never to come back to my house. Make tracks, or I'll shoot ye down dead.

Velie (*alarmed*): Hey. I don't like this . . . that gun . . .

Inspector (*sharply*): Take that shotgun away from the old fool, Clay. (*Clay arguing with Mathew off*)

Ellery: What's the trouble, Mr. Bigelow? Does the old man think I'm somebody he knows?

Nikki: Ellery, keep back. Who's this Jonathan he keeps raving about, Mr. Bigelow?

Bigelow: Should have warned you folks. Jonathan is old man Mathew's son. He's been gone a long time —

Mathew: Git, I tell ye. All right, ye got it comin', Jonathan. I'm a-tellin' ye, ye got it comin'!

Nikki (*screaming*): Look out . . . he's going to shoot.

Inspector (*shouting*): Duck behind the car.

(*Shotgun discharge*)

Velie: Back here, Miss Porter.

(*Another shot*)

Ellery: Nikki — keep down. Bigelow, for heaven's sake.

Bigelow (*calm*): It's all right, Mr. Queen. Homer Clay knows how to handle the old man.

Velie: Yeah. He sure does. The old lunatic's reloading.

Clay (*coaxing, off*): Now, paw, you gimme that shot gun.

(*Another shot*)

Mathew (*off*): Git outa my way, Homer. You — Jonathan — come out from behind that auto.

(*Another shot*)

Nikki (*calling*): Mr. Clay, you'll be hurt. Oh, look, he's walking right up to that crazy old man.

Clay (*off*): That's it, paw. Now gimme the gun . . . that's it . . . (*Fading*) Now we'll jest go on into the house, an' you'll be . . . (*Porch door slamming off*)

Velie: Whew! I just dropped ten years.

Bigelow (*wearily*): There's no danger. That shotgun is loaded with blank cartridges.

Inspector: Blanks. Fine time to tell us.

Ellery (*chuckling*): No wonder old Duesey didn't get punched full of holes . . . what's the matter with Mathew?

Bigelow: Why, the old man's son, Jonathan, ran away from home a dozen years ago — got into a nasty mix-up of some kind; old man Mathew swore he'd kill Jonathan if he ever showed his face again around the farm.

Nikki: Oh, his mind?

Bigelow: Yes, Miss Porter. He's strong as a bull, for all his age, but . . . really, he's quiet most of the time. It's only when he sees strangers that he gets worked up and starts shooting . . . everybody in Hogsburg knows about it — so nobody sells him real bullets.

Inspector: Be a lot kinder to put the old fellow away.

Bigelow: Well . . . Ma Mathew, she won't hear of it. Homer and me — we watch him. He keeps that shotgun with him all the time . . . sleeps and eats with it beside him . . . (*Porch door slamming*) Here's Homer now.

Ellery (*calling*): How's your father-in-law, Mr. Clay?

Clay (*off*): Fine, fine. Come on, folks. (*Steps up on porch, on mike*) I jest put him in his room up in the attic. Sleeps alone up there . . . (*Opens screen door*) Come on in. (*Door closes*)

Nikki: Isn't it cool in here.

Velie (*nervous*): You sure the ol' maniac — man's in his cage?

Clay: Aw, don't fret 'bout *him* . . . (*Calling*) . . . Maw. Hey, maw. (*Lower*) Right in the parlor here, folks. (*Calling*) Maw. We got company.

Mrs. Mathew (*old — vigorous . . . perhaps deep voice*): (*Fading on*) Lan' sakes, Homer, whut ye yellin' yer fool head off? Oh! . . . Comp'ny. An' me up to my elbows in cracker meal. Come in folks — set. I'll git ye some cold cider . . . (*Ad libs of thanks*)

Clay: Hold yer hosses, Ma. This is Mizz Porter, Mr. Queen, Inspector Queen, Sergeant Velie. (*Ad libs*)

Mrs. Mathew: Right nice meetin' ye. Now you folks set right down an' take a load off yer feet . . . (*Creaky sofa and chairs*) . . . It's mighty hot out, an' cider goes down real nice on a hot day . . . (*Fading*) . . . Jed, you interdooce these folks to Julie . . .

Bigelow: Julie! (*Slowly*) I didn't even see you sitting here, Julie —

Clay (*heartily*): Why, Julie, ye're downstairs. Whut ye settin' here in a corner of the parlor fer? Folks, this is my wife, Julie Mathew Clay . . . (*Ad libs*) . . . Jed, you pull up those new shades. Settin' in the dark like a mouse . . . (*Laughs, shades up off*)

Julie (*weak dull voice . . . medium age . . . eerie quality . . . no dialect*): I'm so glad. I'm so glad. It's so nice having you . . . it's so very nice having you . . . (*Ad libs*)

Bigelow: Here, Julie, let me put this pillow behind your head.

Julie (*dreamy*): Thanks, Jed. You're so very nice —

Clay: Talks purty, don't she? Went right through two years o' collidge, my Julie did.

Julie (*dreamy*): Miss Porter, you're so beautiful. Are you married?

Nikki (*startled*): Why . . . thank you . . . no, Mrs. Clay —

Julie (*dreamy*): I had a baby once. It died. It was the sweetest baby. They let me see it. Blue eyes, it had, and silky blonde hair.

Nikki (*pained*): Oh, Ellery! She's —

Clay (*hastily*): Now, Julie. Ye know, we don't talk 'bout the baby. Maw, where's that cider?

Mrs. Mathew (*fading on*): It's a-comin'. (*Tray down, glasses*) Now why's ever'body so still? Julie, you been talkin' 'bout the baby again. (*Gently*) You jest keep shut, Julie . . .

Julie (*dreamy*): It was a girl . . . the sweetest little girl . . .

Velie (*low*): Say, this house gives me the jeepers. That old nut in the attic . . . this woman here . . . (*Pour cider*)

Inspector (*low*): Ellery, show 'em that photo and let's get out of here. I'm beginning to feel funny myself.

Mrs. Mathew (*cheerfully*): You put *this* inside o' ye, folks.

(*Ad libs while handing out cider*)

Ellery: Thank you, Mrs. Mathew . . . uh, by the way, do you recognize the face of the man in this photo?

Clay: Yeah, Maw, durnedest thing happened. Ye know that ol' scarecrow in the south cornfield.

Inspector: Never mind that, Clay; know this man, Mrs. Mathew?

Mrs. Mathew: Why, he's sleepin', ain' he; cur'ous kind o' photo. No, sir, cain't say I do. More cider, Mizz Porter?

Nikki (*nervous*): No — no, thank you, Mrs. Mathew.

Julie (*dreamy*): I was going to name her Mary-Ann —

Velie (*low*): Let's scram outa here, for cryin' out loud.

Clay (*fading on*): Talkin' o' photos, now here's an ol' photo o' Jonathan . . . Julie's brother . . . in this here fam'ly album . . .

Mrs. Mathew: Homer, whut would these folks be wantin' with — put that album away, Homer.

Ellery: Please. May I see that photograph of Jonathan, Mr. Clay? (*Pause, low*) No, dad, it's not the same man.

Inspector (*low*): No resemblance, whatever. Well, one thing's sure, Ellery. Someone tried to murder our friend the scarecrow man, and I'm beginning to think we *ought* to hang around Hogsburg until we can talk to him. Uh, thanks, Mrs. Mathew. Best cider I ever tasted.

Mrs. Mathew: Thank ye! I ain't one to sing my own praises, but I will say I make the best cider in the County. Ye know, we been farmin' this land ever since the ol' Injun days — I mean the Mathew folks an' my own folks . . . (*Fading*) . . . (*Sneak music*) . . . sorta growed up on the land . . . and know every inch of it.

(*Music up . . . and into car stopping at curb*)

Harkness: Here's the Hogsburg Hospital . . . (*Car doors, steps on sidewalk, etc . . . under dialogue*) Let me help you, Miss Porter.
Nikki: Thank you, Dr. Harkness.
Inspector: Decent of you to come over to our hotel yourself, Dr. Harkness.
Harkness: You asked me to notify you. (*Open front door . . . close . . . steps under dialogue*)
Velie: Three days in this one-horse town. An' that so-called hotel. Oh, say, doc, I kinda forgot you're a native of these parts.
Harkness (*laughing*): It's all right, Sergeant. Hogsburg hardly ever arouses the enthusiasm of visitors.
Ellery: You say the man regained consciousness yesterday, Dr. Harkness?
Harkness: Yes, and he's so much better this morning, I felt it quite safe to let you question him . . . down this corridor, please . . . morning, nurse.
Nurse (*passing*): Good morning, Dr. Harkness.
Nikki: Has he spoken yet? Told his name, or what happened to him?
Harkness: No, he wouldn't talk and I didn't press him. Maybe you people will have better luck. Queer sort of chap . . . here we are . . . (*Steps stop*)
Ellery (*eagerly*): I'm very anxious to speak to him . . .
Harkness: I want to warn you — he's a stubborn customer. Like that Missoura mule old man Mathew once had . . . well, that's another story. Don't go easy on him — he's made a remarkable recovery.
Inspector (*grimly*): Open the door, Doctor.
Harkness: Yes, Inspector.
(*Open door*) (*Pause, gasps*)
Nikki: The bed's — empty.
Velie: And the window's open.
Inspector: I'll be darned . . . flew the coop.
Ellery (*groaning*): No — it's not fair . . . three days, waiting, and now —
Harkness (*sneak music*): (*Fading, shouting*) Nurse. *Nurse!* . . . how on earth did you permit the patient to get out — leaving him by himself —

(*Music up . . . and into same recitatif theme as in beginning . . . played softly under Inspector's monologue*)

Inspector (*recitatif . . . over theme*): Well, that was the start of the strangest case I can remember, and I've seen some strange ones in my time.
 We notified the local authorities, searched high and low, but we couldn't find our vanished scarecrow man. And no one in or around

Hogsburg recognized the fellow from the photo Ellery'd taken in the hospital when we brought him in.

Well, we finally had to give up and drive back to New York — a pretty gloomy crew. Seemed as if the case of the scarecrow man was finished . . . an unsolved mystery. Wasn't our business, anyway.

But then five months later — early December it was, about a month ago — Ellery got a letter from Hogsburg. From a man named Small — Sam Small. Small was a justice of the peace in Hogsburg — we'd talked to him in July when we were there looking for the man who'd skipped from the hospital.

Well, this Sam Small wrote that when we pumped questions at him in Hogsburg five months before, he'd lied to us. Said he *did* know who the scarecrow man was — knew all along. 'S I remember it, his exact words in the letter were: — "Me and the Hogsburg Town Clerk were the only outsiders in town knew who this feller was, and the Hogsburg Town Clerk, he's been dead these three years." And Small said that if we'd come out to see him, he'd tell us the whole story. Seems he was pretty sick and couldn't get about.

Well, sir, we hit that trail westward pronto — couldn't have kept us away with a Supreme Court order. And what d'ye think happened? We got out to this Sam Small's place in Hogsburg, and we found that Small had died a few days before! Yes, sir, he'd passed on, and his widow didn't know a thing about the story her husband'd written us he wanted to get off his chest.

So, while we were in the neighborhood, we decided to drive over to the Mathew place. I s'pose it was because we all felt in our bones that the stranger who'd been stabbed and strapped up to that scarecrow pole in the Mathew cornfield was some way involved with the Mathew family.

The Mathew farm didn't look so pretty in winter. Matter of fact, it was snowing hard when we drove up, whipping up to a blizzard . . . and there was something about the whole place — the stripped fields, the bony farm buildings, the wind going at a great rate . . . that gave us the shivers. (*Fading*) And then, just as we drove into the yard in front of the Mathew farmhouse with the snow almost a solid sheet and the wind howling . . . (*Into car with chains stopping. Wind howling — suppressed blizzard*)

Nikki: Any port in a storm! Even this port! (*Open car doors, wind up*)

Velie: Look out, Miss Porter! There's the old nut again! (*House door banged open off*)

Mathew (*shrieking*): I spy ye, Jonathan! I'm a-goin' to kill ye dead! (*Two shots from shotgun*)

Inspector: Maybe those are blanks, but — duck, Ellery!

Nikki: He thinks you're his son, again, Ellery!

Clay (*fading on*): Paw! Paw Mathew! Put that fool gun up!

Mrs. Mathew (*fading on*): Shootin' at strangers, paw! Shame on you . . . Why, it's Mr. Queen an' — My land! Come in outa this blizzard!

Mathew (*fading off — screaming*): I'll kill the young skunk! Homer Clay, you leave off a-shovin' me . . . !

(*Running steps up to porch*)

Ellery: Hullo, Mrs. Mathew! May we come in out of the storm?

Mrs. Mathew: May we — I never heard such a thing in my born days! Inside, all of ye! (*Door opens. Closes. Cut storm*) Git yer things off. Jed! Oh, Je-e-d! Here's them nice folks from Noo Yawk!

Bigelow (*fading on*): Why, it's the Queens! And Miss Porter — Sergeant — (*Ad libs while removing coats*)

Velie: Mmmm. Somethin' smells good.

Mrs. Mathew: That's my corn-bread bakin'. Ho-mer! How's Paw?

Clay (*fading on*): I quietened him down, Maw. Put 'im back up in the attic. Sorry, folks. Well, well! Nice su-prise, ain't it, Jed? Come on in the parlor . . .

Inspector: How's your wife, Mr. Clay?

Clay: Poorly, Inspector. Julie's in her room upstairs —

Mrs. Mathew: Weak's a new-born calf. Here we are — now, set! I'll rustle up somethin' hot —

Ellery: Thanks, Mrs. Mathew, but we can't stay. We just dropped by while passing through Hogsburg —

Bigelow: Wherever you're bound for, Mr. Queen, you won't make it today. Road's piled up in high drifts already.

Nikki: Oh, dear! What will we do?

Mrs. Mathew: Ye'll stay here, that's whut ye'll do! We got acres o' room upstairs — I declare, I don't know whut Paw went an' built such a big house for . . . (*Protests ad lib*)

Clay: But Maw's right! Why, we got so much room they's a sep'rate room fer Maw, an' fer me, an' fer Julie, an' fer Jed, and o' course Paw, he's up the attic . . .

Mrs. Mathew: You put Mizz Porter in that northeast bedroom, Homer, an' — le's see, now . . .

Clay: There's that big upstairs parlor we made a bedroom, Maw — with the big bed an' the single bed —

Inspector: That'll be fine for us three men, Mr. Clay.

Velie: Darn' nice o' you people to put us up this way.

Nikki: It certainly is. Seems like taking advantage, somehow —

Mrs. Mathew: Now I won't hear 'nother word! Ye're stayin'. (*Sneak music. Fading*) You jest warm yer bones by this fire, an' I'll go fix a nice hot lunch . . .

(*Music up . . . and into opening door — outdoors . . .*)

Nikki: Still snowing, Ellery. Oh, isn't it glorious?

Ellery: Mmm! Two feet deep already, not counting the drifts. Though Jed Bigelow says it will probably stop snowing late tonight and they'll have this road cleared to the main highway by tomorrow morning . . . (*Steps across porch*)

Nikki: Who cares? Oh, there's Mr. Clay! What's he doing? Oh, Mr. Cla-a-ay!

Clay (*off*): Howdy! C'm on over an' watch this. (*Off porch*)

Nikki: Ellery, let's! (*Sloshes through snow. Blows on stake, off*)

Ellery: Careful of that drift, Nikki! What are you doing with that stake, Mr. Clay? (*Stop sloshing*)

Clay (*fading on — chuckle*): Fixin' to make a snow-man. (*Blows up*) There she is! (*Stop*) Nice an' steady.

Nikki: Snow-man! That's *wonderful.* I haven't built a snow-man since I was a little girl!

Clay (*chuckling*): Seein's how that's how 'tis, Mizz Porter, you pitch right in an' he'p me. (*Sounds of snow packed*)

Ellery: Think I'll try *my* hand at it, by George. (*All laugh. Continue packing under dialogue*) Seeing this stake, Mr. Clay, stuck in the ground this way, reminds me —

Clay: O' that feller we found in the cornfield las' summer? Does, at that.

Nikki: Ever hear anything more about him, after he disappeared from the Hogsburg Hospital? Oh, let me make the head!

Clay (*cheerfully*): Nope . . . There! He's comin' 'long fine.

Ellery: Making this snow-man for your own amusement, Clay?

Clay (*chuckling*): Lordy, no. Look up at the winder there.

Nikki: It's Julie! She's watching from her room!

Clay: Yep. Julie sure loves a snow-man. Cain't go outdoors, so I make it for her in the front yard, where she kin look out an' see it . . . I'll finish it now, folks.

Ellery: There's something about this snow — (*Laughs. Plop of snow clod*) Duck, you innocent!

Nikki (*spluttering, laughing*): Ellery Queen, you shoved that snow right in my mouth! *All* right, Mr. Queen —

Ellery (*laughing*): I was only fooling, Nikki! (*Snowball*) Ooop!

Nikki: Want to play some more, Mr. Queen?

Ellery (*spluttering*): No — I — give up! That's — *cold!*

Clay: There! Ain't he a humdinger? Hi, Julie! Like it? Ju-lie! (*Window opens off*) Like it, Julie?

Julie (*off*): Oh, Homer, he's beautiful!

Nikki: Hi there, Julie! (*Ellery ad lib ditto*)

Clay: Wait a secon', Julie, he ain't finished! . . . There!
Nikki: Of *course*. A straw bonnet!
Clay: Now eyes an' nose an' mouth an' buttons . . .
Ellery (*chuckling*): That's a mortal waste of coal, Mr. Clay!
Julie (*clapping her hands off*): A pipe, Homer! Stick a pipe in his mouth!
    Oh, how the baby'd have loved it!
Clay (*low — hurried*): Don't pay no mind, folks . . . Sure, Julie!
Nikki: Of course. Who ever heard of a snow-man without a pipe!
Ellery (*cheerfully*): A corn-cob, Mr. Clay.
Clay: Yep. Gotta have a corn-cob . . . Blame it! I went an' left my corn-
    cob up in my room — an' we better not bother Paw Mathew — he
    keeps *his* corn-cobs up in the attic, an' he's up there now — like as
    not start shootin' . . . (*Door opens off*) Hi, Jed! Come 'ere.
Velie (*off*): What goes on?
Nikki: Sergeant! Inspector! See what we've made for Julie!
Inspector (*fading on — chuckling*): Say, that's some snow-man!
Bigelow (*fading on*): Hey, Julie!
Julie (*off*): Oh, Jed, isn't he *beautiful?* The baby would —
Clay (*quickly*): Gimme one o' them two corn-cobs o' yourn, Jed. Gotta fix
    up a proper smokin' snow-man.
Bigelow: Here you are, Homer. This one's gone sour on me, anyhow.
Clay: Thank ye, Jed . . . There! *Now* how's he look, Julie?
Julie (*clapping hands off*): Beautiful, Homer!
Velie (*laughing*): Whatta man!
Inspector: Ellery! Take a look — Say, where'd Ellery go?
Nikki: That man! He was here a minute ago . . . Ellery! (*Door slams*)
Ellery (*off*): Here I am!
Velie (*groaning*): He an' his movie-camera!
Ellery (*fading on*): Well, our friend here's such a fine figure of a snow-
    man, we've just got to take his picture! (*All laugh over whirr of 16-mm.
    movie camera. Fade into . . .*)

(*Music up . . . suggest winter night, howling dog, etc . . . into Velie snoring
off . . . sustain . . . turn over in bed on mike . . .*)

Ellery (*low*): Dad? Did I wake you?
Inspector (*same*): Aren't you sleeping either, Ellery? Lord, I've been
    shivering all night. Hardly closed my eyes.
Ellery: Sub-Arctic in this bedroom. I wasn't cut out for the pioneer
    existence, I guess. Beginning to get light out . . .
Inspector: Colder'n old Scrooge's heart in this bed. Listen to Velie snore!
    He'd sleep on a grave. (*Pause*)
Ellery: It isn't just the cold, dad. It's . . . this house.

Inspector (*quietly*): Yes . . . there's a shadow over the place . . .

Ellery: The shadow of that cornfield scarecrow . . . (*Pause*) What time is it, anyway?

Inspector: Wait till I stick my arm out . . . Wow, it's like ice! Devil with it! Brrr . . . (*As if huddling in bed*)

Ellery: I wonder how Nikki's making out . . . Come on, dad. Let's try to get some sleep. (*Turns over*)

Inspector: All right, let's. Who's stopping you? Ellery, don't hog the comforter! (*Turns over. Sleepily*) 'F only Vesuvius over there would stop erupting . . . (*Snores . . . Pause*)

Ellery (*sharp whisper*): Dad! (*Quickly turns over — bedspring squeaks*)

Inspector: Hunnnnh'. What — Ellery, for the love of Mike!

Ellery (*same*): There's someone outside our door, dad!

Inspector (*alertly*): Yeah? (*Pause. Then sudden guarded knock on door*) (*Slowly*) Now who in time would that be? (*Knock again — guarded. Snore off stops with snort*)

Velie (*off — sleepy*): Hey, who's doin' that? G'on — beat it — let a guy sleep! (*Knock again faster*)

Ellery: Persistent cuss, whoever it is. Feel like braving the Antarctic rigors of this floor, dad?

Inspector: You asking me? Answer is no . . . Velie!

Velie (*with a start*): Hunnnh? Hey, what is this! Whadda ya want, Inspector? I ain't hardly closed my eyes . . .

Inspector: If you'd close your snoring mouth, you big cluck, you'd do *me* a favor! Answer the door. (*Knocks again. Very loud*)

Velie: Not me, brother. (*Calling angrily*) Go away! (*Mutters off*) Answer the door! Don't even let a guy sleep . . .

Ellery: *All* right. *I'll* go! (*Getting out of bed*) Ow! Floor's like an iceberg! Hand me my robe, dad!

Inspector: Here you are, son. Put your slippers on. (*Knocks again*)

Ellery: Such solicitude! (*Shuffles across floor. Opens door*) Yes?

Nikki (*frantic*): Ellery! I thought you'd never answer!

Ellery (*alertly*): Nikki! Come in. (*Close door*) Nikki, you'll freeze in that thin wrapper —

Nikki (*sobbing*): Oh, Ellery — I just saw it —

Ellery: Saw what, Nikki? Why are you crying?

Inspector (*fading on*): Nikki honey! What's the matter?

Nikki (*sobbing*): I . . . couldn't sleep. I got up and — and looked out my window at the snow-man, and . . . (*Ad libs*)

Velie (*fading on*): Miss Porter! What happened? (*Nikki crying*)

Inspector: Now control yourself, Nikki. Stop it!

Ellery: You got up and saw the snow-man, Nikki. And?

Nikki (*sobbing*): He's . . . he's *bleeding!*

(Dramatic music up . . . into cautious steps . . . open front door . . . wind up)

Inspector: Less noise, Velie! We don't want to wake the others!
Velie: All right, all right . . . He *is* bleedin! *(Close door)*
Nikki *(crying)*: I told you — that red-brown stain all over the chest of
the snow-man . . . *(Whirr of movie camera)*
Inspector *(slowly)*: Like the stain on the scarecrow last summer . . . Ellery!
What in thunder are *you* doing?
Ellery *(intently)*: Photographing the snow-man, that's what! There. That's
enough footage . . . *(Stop whirr)* Well, let's look at that stain. *(Steps off
porch through snow)*
Inspector: Knock the thing down, Velie. *(Demolishing snow-man)*
Velie *(low)*: If this aint blood — real blood — I'll hand in my badge.
Nikki *(sniffling)*: I never was so shocked . . . I know I'm being very silly
to carry on this way about a joke . . .
Ellery *(gently)*: Nikki. Get back in the house.
Nikki: But Ellery —
Inspector *(sharp)*: Nikki — go back. *(Nikki frightened ad lib fade)* *(With
footsteps off)* Joke, huh? Some joke.
Velie *(slowly)*: It's a — dead man under this snow, Mr. Queen.
Ellery *(grave)*: Of course, Sergeant . . . Strapped to the pole by his belt!
That's reminiscent! Dead — you're sure?
Inspector *(grimly)*: Deader'n a cold-storage mackerel. Two stab-wounds
in his chest. See — here —
Velie: Lemme brush this snow off from around his head . . . *(Brushing
sounds. Gasps from all)* I'll be . . .
Inspector: It's the same man! The man who —
Ellery *(dazed)*: The man who escaped from the Hogsburg Hospital! *The
scarecrow man!*

(Music up . . . short . . . into)

Inspector: We'll catch pneumonia in this snow! *(Stamps feet)*
Ellery: Where's Velie, for heaven's sake? Here — ease this poor fellow
down, dad . . .
Inspector *(over grunting)*: Send — Velie — to scout around and — freeze
to death while you wait! Okay.
Ellery: Death in the snow . . . If he could only talk!
Inspector: He'll never talk again in *this* world, son.
Ellery *(helplessly)*: A corpse, and we don't even know who he is! Dad,
how long do you figure he's been dead?
Inspector: Hard to say. Packed in snow this way . . . At a guess, I'd say
late last night, around the time it stopped snowing.

Ellery: And we slept through the whole thing!

Inspector: Wonder just where the crime was committed. The snow around the snow-man was all trampled when we got here a few minutes ago, but that single set of tracks leading from here around the house seems to suggest —

Ellery: We'll know — I hope — when Velie gets back. Wherever the crime was committed, the murderer then carried his victim to this spot, demolished the snow-man Homer Clay built yesterday, slung the dead man on the stake with the victim's own belt, and rebuilt a snow-man around the corpse. Man-sized job, the whole business.

Inspector: Why'd he rebuild the snow-man, though?

Ellery (*grimly*): Rather obvious, dad. If the blood from the man's wounds hadn't seeped through the snow-covering, how would we have known there was a corpse inside the snow-man?

Inspector: Mmmm . . . but the killer couldn't hope to conceal his crime forever, Ellery. Sooner or later the snow-man would be knocked down or broken up . . .

Ellery: Yes, but by that time *we'd be gone*. The murderer did it to keep us from discovering the crime! (*Steps in snow fading on*) Ah, here's the Sergeant!

Inspector: You took your sweet time! My feet are numb! What did you find out, Velie?

Velie (*fading on*): Whadda ya think *my* feet are made of — mahogany? I swear I got two toes frost-bit!

Ellery: Sergeant, where does this single set of tracks lead?

Velie: To the barn. There's some blood in there, and signs of a slight struggle, so that's where this guy got it.

Inspector: No other clue?

Velie: Not a blame thing.

Ellery: These tracks don't tell us anything. Whoever made them was wearing huge galoshes — could have been anyone.

Inspector: Find the tracks of the dead man, Velie? — I mean, where he came from? Where he entered the Mathew property?

Velie: There ain't no other tracks, Inspector. Anywheres around the house or barn or leadin' to or from the road.

Ellery: So the victim must have got to the barn to hide himself before the snow stopped last night. Mmmm . . .

Inspector: No other tracks also means that *the killer came from this house!* Killer's tracks were wiped out by the snowstorm, but by the time he'd killed this man in the barn, the snow had stopped, and the tracks he made lugging the body from the barn to the snow-man remained.

Ellery (*slowly*): Yes, dad . . . it would appear that way . . .

Inspector (*sharply*): We'll have to wake 'em all up in the house and start questioning again! (*Grimly*) Cover this poor guy up, Velie. Ellery, let's get to work!

(*Music up . . . into same recitatif theme played softly under Nikki's monologue . . .*)

Nikki (*Recitatif — over theme*): There was — I don't know exactly how to describe it — something about that house, that farm, those people, that — well, frightened you. You felt it the minute you stepped into the Mathew farmhouse — you felt it right through Ma Mathew's hearty welcome and the delicious smell of her corn-bread. It was in every corner of those big countrified rooms. It sat on every piece of mail-order furniture. Maybe it was because of that poor woman Julie sitting quietly in a rocker talking about her dead baby in that sweet, dreamy, unearthly voice. Or because of old Mr. Mathew, with his wild white hair and powerful shoulders, raving his poor head off in his attic room about his runaway son Jonathan and how he'd shoot the boy dead if the rascal ever showed his face around the farm again.

Whatever it was, it was there. And it grew worse after that terrible discovery of the dead man covered with a shell of snow . . . The Mathews shut up tight. They wouldn't talk at all. The Inspector and Ellery questioned and argued and talked themselves hoarse, but it was no use — they all claimed they'd slept right through the cold night and had heard nothing. And no one on or off the Mathew farm could identify the dead man — for the second time.

Finally we packed up and left the case to the local police. Ellery was more irritable than I've ever seen him before. He felt that somehow it was his fault, which was absurd, as we all told him. But he wouldn't be consoled. Weeks passed, and Ellery refused to forget the unsolved case. He'd haul out his reels of sixteen-millimetre movie film that he'd taken on our two trips, and he'd run the little movies off, over and over, looking for I don't know what. I don't think he did, either.

Well, one night, only a short time ago, Ellery was running the same movies off again. First he showed the pictures he'd taken of the snow-man built by Homer Clay . . . (*Begin to fade off voice and fade on 16-mm. projector*) . . . then the shot of the blood-stained snow-man he'd taken the following morning . . . (*Up with projector*)

Ellery (*excited*): Wait! (*Pause*) Oh, I've been blind! (*Shuts off projector*) Nikki, snap the lights on!

Nikki: Why, of course, Ellery . . .

Inspector: What's the matter, son?

Velie: Why all the excitement, Mr. Queen?

Ellery (*babbling*): Why didn't I see it before?

Nikki: What are you talking about, Ellery?

Ellery: About the murder of that man — the scarecrow man, the snow-man! I know who killed him! (*Ad libs*)

Inspector: Now? After all these weeks?

Velie: You mean to say you know who that dead guy was?

Ellery: Who he was? Oh, that. I've never been puzzled by that, Sergeant. I don't know his name — probably never will but I've known for some time just how he fits into the scheme of things . . . (*Ad libs*) Of course. The identity of the victim didn't bother me . . . It's the identity of the *killer* that held me up!

Nikki: But how in the world —

Ellery: You mean to say you didn't see what *I* just saw on that screen?

Inspector: What d'ye mean — just saw? Two snow-men, that's all!

Ellery: Yes, but didn't you notice the *difference* between the snow-man Clay built that afternoon for Julie, and the snow-man we found next morning with the dead man inside?

Nikki: Difference? Well, they weren't exactly the same size or shape, of course . . . What kind of difference, Ellery?

Ellery: The difference was not *in* the snow-men, but in the snow around the snow-men — at their feet! (*Ad libs*) You can run the film over if you don't believe me . . .

Velie (*hastily*): We believe you, we believe you!

Inspector: What was this difference in the snow around their feet?

Ellery: Well, in the first pictures — of the snow-man Clay built, the real snow-man — the snow was *trampled* around its feet.

Nikki: Well, of course! We were all milling about there.

Ellery: But in the case of the second snow-man, the one that bled, the surrounding snow showed signs of having been *shoveled up*! I just noticed it. After looking at that film a dozen times, I just noticed it!

Velie: Shoveled up, Mr. Queen? I don't get it.

Ellery: Don't you see? After hiding the body in the made-over snow-man, *the murderer then began shoveling all around the thing*!

Inspector: Killer'd dropped something in the snow and couldn't find it again!

Nikki: He'd lost something and was *looking* for it?

Ellery: Yes, Nikki. And what had the murderer lost? An object that was *missing* in our shot of the *second* snow-man! Didn't you notice? An object that was *present* in the pictures of the snow-man Homer Clay had built — the first one!

Velie: Missin'? I didn't see nothin' missin', Mr. Queen.

Ellery: The corn-cob pipe, Sergeant!

Inspector (*slowly*): He's right at that. The first snow-man had Jed

Bigelow's corn-cob in its mouth. Now I remember the second snow-man, the one with the body in it, *didn't* have a corn-cob.

Nikki: You mean that while the murderer was building the second snow-man, the pipe got lost in the deep snow around his feet, Ellery?

Ellery: Yes! And the murderer dug around there looking for it and never did find the corn-cob, because if he had, he'd have stuck the pipe back in the snow-man's mouth!

Velie: But why the dickens would he want that sour old corn-cob?

Inspector: To stick in the mouth of the snow-man, Velie — so we wouldn't notice any difference between the one Clay built and the one with the body in it! To delay discovery of the crime!

Nikki: But Ellery, you said you knew who killed that poor man. What's the missing corn-cob got to do with it?

Ellery (*chuckling*): The missing corn-cob, my child, told me who the killer was! Start packing, folks — we're going back to the Mathew farm!

(*Music up . . . and into jury spot*)

Challenge to the Listener

Ellery: Well, Ladies and Gentlemen, at that time I had a theory, based on logical deduction, as to who killed the scarecrow man — or, if you prefer, the snow-man . . . who was the dead man? Who tried to kill him twice? What is your theory to explain the tragedy at the Mathew Farm?

(*Music up . . . into car, chains on snowy road . . .*)

Inspector: There it is.

Nikki: It's awfully desolate-looking. Fields covered with snow — trees like skeletons — those icy-looking buildings . . .

Velie: I'm beginnin' to feel like a commuter. This is our third trip out here, ain't it?

Ellery (*grimly*): And our last, Sergeant. Here we are. (*Car stops. Car doors open — out into snow*)

Nikki (*slowly*): Ellery . . . there's something wrong.

Ellery (*same*): Yes, Nikki, apparently there is . . . (*Steps in snow*)

Inspector: House is boarded up! (*Steps on porch*)

Velie: Don't look like a dead dog lives here.

Nikki: And there's the barn with its doors sagging . . . I don't see their livestock, either, do you?

Inspector: Gone. Cleared out!

Velie: Hey, here's a sign says "Farm For Sale"!

Ellery (*groaning*): That long trip — for nothing!

Nikki: Then you didn't expect to find the Mathews gone?

Ellery: Of course not! I can't imagine — unless — (*Pause*)

Nikki (*as if shivering*): I'm . . . cold. And it isn't just the temperature. Ellery . . . let's clear out of here.

Inspector: Amen to that. Place always did give me the willies. (*Steps across porch*)

Ellery: I've *got* to find out what's happened! (*Steps through snow*) Question is — whom to ask? With the Mathews gone —

Velie: How about that Mrs. Small — you know, the wife of the Justice o' the Peace who died 'fore we could find out what he knew about the scarecrow guy?

Ellery (*mumbling*): Yes. Mrs. Small — (*Steps stop*) Get in, Nikki. (*Car doors closing*)

Nikki: Or better still — Dr. Harkness, in Hogsburg! *He* ought to know what's happened to the Mathews.

Inspector: Nikki's right. (*Start motor*)

Ellery: Hogsburg Hospital, Sergeant! (*Drive off. Fade*)

(*Music up . . . and into ad libs . . .*)

Harkness: Of course I know what's happened to the Mathews. I'm surprised you people don't. It was in all the papers.

Inspector: Local papers, most likely, Dr. Harkness.

Nikki (*eagerly*): What happened, Doctor?

Harkness (*sighing*): Sad business, sad business. There's a curse on that Mathew place. (*Laughs*) I suppose that sounds funny coming from a medical man.

Velie: After spendin' a couple o'nights there, Doc — I dunno what's funny about it!

Ellery (*impatiently*): Let's have the story, Dr. Harkness.

Harkness: Well, you remember the old fellow — old man Mathew . . . (*Ad lib agreement*) Of course, he was a psychopathic case. I warned them time and again. Well, one day old Mathew got hold of some real bullets for that shotgun of his —

Nikki: Oh!

Ellery (*slowly*): Old man Mathew loaded his shotgun, Doctor? . . . He tried to kill somebody?

Harkness: He *did* kill somebody. (*Gasps. Pause*) He got the notion in his crazy head that Jed Bigelow, their hired man, was really his long lost son Jonathan, and he went for Jed with his shotgun.

Velie: He killed that nice young fella?

Harkness: No, Sergeant. Jed was lucky. The old lady, Mrs. Mathew, saw what was happening, tried to grab the gun to prevent her husband's shooting Jed, the gun went off and — well, she got it instead . . . Ma Mathew is — dead.

Nikki: How — awful. (*Ad libs low-voiced*)

Inspector: And what happened to the old man, Dr. Harkness?

Harkness (*gravely*): When old Mathew realized what he'd done, he ran into the barn and, before Jed or Homer Clay could stop him, he killed himself. (*Sighs*) Great tragedy, great tragedy. It was an unlucky family.

Ellery: Yes, Dr. Harkness. Unlucky is the — exact word. (*Pause*)

Inspector: Tough, all right. What's become of Clay, and his wife Julie, and young Jed Bigelow?

Harkness: Julie saw the whole thing from her window . . . (*Harshly*) I made it plain to Homer that if he didn't take his wife at once to a different environment, I wouldn't be responsible . . . Jed just disappeared.

Nikki: So they're gone . . . We saw the "For Sale" sign.

Harkness: Yes, the place is in the hands of an agent. Did you want to talk to them, gentlemen? Perhaps I can find out for you where they are . . .

Ellery (*slowly*): No, Dr. Harkness. Let them alone. They've had enough trouble for one lifetime. Come on, you three. We're going back to New York.

Harkness: But what did you want to see them about, Mr. Queen?

Ellery (*quietly*): It doesn't matter.

(*Music up . . . into dishes, etc.*)

Nikki: Golly, it feels good to get inside a warm place again!

Inspector: That *fire* feels good.

Velie: Not a bad joint. Maybe we oughta stop here overnight . . . More coffee, beautiful.

Waitress: Yes s'r. (*Pours liquid*)

Nikki: Well, Ellery?

Inspector: You promised you'd clear this business up on our first stopover, son . . .

Velie: Yeah. Satisfy my curiosity, Mr. Queen.

Ellery (*sighing*): I suppose I must. This case has pretty well depressed me . . . (*More briskly*) Well, the secret of the scarecrow man's identity lay in the letter which that Justice of the Peace, Sam Small, sent me —

Velie: You mean when he wrote askin' us to come out to Hogsburg — he'd tell us who the stranger was?

Ellery: Yes, Sergeant. Remember Small said in his letter that "only two outsiders" in Hogsburg knew who the stranger was — himself, and the Hogsburg Town Clerk?

Nikki: Yes, but what of it? Was that a clue, Ellery?

Ellery: Yes, Nikki — a vital clue to the identity of the stranger! Why should Small say that he and the Town Clerk were the only *outsiders* who knew the secret of the stranger's identity? If he phrased it that way, it was because there must have been a group of *insiders* who knew — and who would those insiders be but the Mathews, on whose property both crimes were committed? Now what was Small, the man who wrote us that letter?

Inspector: Small was Hogsburg Justice of the Peace.

Ellery: Yes, and the other outsider who knew, according to Small, was the *Town Clerk*. Now, what could a Justice of the Peace and a Town Clerk know that *other* outsiders of a rural community might not know? (*Pause*) Well, what do we associate with the office of a Justice of the Peace?

Velie: Marriages!

Ellery: Yes, Sergeant — and do marriages involve a Town Clerk? They certainly do in a rural center like Hogsburg. The Town Clerk probably issues the marriage license — certainly records the marriage in the town rolls.

Inspector: So you figured the Town Clerk and Small knew who the stranger was because one had issued his marriage license or recorded the marriage, and the other had married him?

Ellery: Precisely. And to whom had the stranger been married? Well, what woman at the Mathew place was of marriageable age? Only one, Julie.

Nikki: But Julie's married to Homer Clay, Ellery!

Ellery: Then quite obviously Julie and this stranger had been married *before* Julie's marriage to Homer Clay.

Velie: Go on, go on, Mr. Queen!

Ellery: We also know that the stranger was murdered by someone *from* the Mathew house during the night we stayed over. The lack of escaping footprints in the snow, around the house and leading to the road, proved that. Well, why should someone in the Mathew house want to kill that stranger? What do we know about him now? That he'd once been secretly married to Julie — secretly, because if it had been an open marriage the man's photograph would certainly have been recognized by other citizens of Hogsburg than the Justice of the Peace. So there's a motive ready-made: Someone in the Mathew house killed that man *to keep the fact of his secret prior marriage to Julie from becoming known!*

Inspector: Mmmm. Stacks up. Julie and this stranger are married secretly, her father learns about it, and either drives the man away or buys him off. Must have been something pretty raw about the man and the marriage. And then, if the Mathew family never bothered to get Julie a divorce — believing the stranger'd never turn up again —

Nikki: Then, while Julie married Homer Clay, she'd be committing bigamy!

Velie: And man, *that* would be a secret they'd *have* to keep!

Ellery: I imagine it went something like that. At any rate, the husband did turn up again — last July. This time, perhaps, he couldn't be frightened away or bought off with peanuts. With Julie a bigamist, his position was — well, pretty strong. He'd probably make huge and insolent demands . . . Whatever he did demand, one of the Mathews decided that Julie had had enough trouble. It was easier to kill the fellow. So the murderer stabbed him early that summer morning and, because it was broad daylight and the body couldn't be disposed of more permanently until nightfall, the murderer hid the body in the scarecrow's clothes, intending to get rid of it that night. But the bloodstain Jed Bigelow saw on the scarecrow's breast spoiled the plan.

Inspector: All right, then the husband, who didn't die, beat it from the Hogsburg Hospital. But why'd he come back in December?

Ellery: Desire for revenge — more demands — we'll never know. Anyway, he hid in the barn, was surprised by the same murderer, was attacked again, and this time the murderer hid the body within the snow-man so that we wouldn't discover the crime before our departure — and we wouldn't have, either, but for that second bloodstain.

Nikki: But *who* killed him, Ellery! That's what I want to know!

Velie: Double ditto!

Ellery: The missing corn-cob told me who killed him.

Inspector: How, Ellery?

Ellery: Waitress! Another cup of coffee, please.

Waitress: Comin' up. (*Pour coffee*)

Nikki: Ellery, don't be exasperating!

Ellery (*gravely*): I knew the murderer wanted a corn-cob and hadn't located the one which had dropped into the deep snow, because if he'd found that missing corn-cob it would have been stuck back into the snow-man's mouth — and it wasn't. But suppose the murderer had been Homer Clay, or Jed Bigelow, or old man Mathew? (*Pause*)

Inspector: Suppose it had? Could have been any one of 'em, far as *I* can see. Except maybe Bigelow.

Ellery: Oh, no, dad! Because we know *each of the three men could easily have got another corn-cob to stick into the second snow-man's mouth!*

Velie: How d'ye figure that, for cryin' tears?

Ellery: Didn't Homer Clay tell us only the previous afternoon, during
the building of the first snow-man, that *his* corn-cob was in his
bedroom? Didn't he also say that his father-in-law, old man Mathew,
kept *his* corn-cobs in his attic room? And didn't Clay ask Jed Bigelow
for *one* of Jed's *two* corn-cobs — meaning that Jed had one left? So
the murderer couldn't have been any of those three men, because
each of them had at least *one* corn-cob which he could have procured
safely, without trouble, and in a few minutes, from his own room!
And don't forget — each one occupied a *separate* room — Clay told
us that, too — so that there was no danger of awakening anyone on
the trip into the house to get the corn-cob for the snow-man's mouth
. . . If not the three men, then who was left?

Nikki (*slowly*): Ellery Queen, if you're going to say . . . That leaves only
the two women of the household . . .

Ellery (*quietly*): Yes, Nikki, the two women. Could the murderer have
been Homer's wife, Julie? No. It was a man-sized job to drag the
dead body to the front of the house, demolish the first snow-man,
place the dead body on the stake, and then build a new snow-man.
Julie was an invalid — "weak as a new-born calf" — sick, constantly
ailing, no strength. No, Julie couldn't have done it.

(*Pause*)

Velie (*shocked*): The old lady!

Nikki: Mrs. Mathew!

Inspector: Ma Mathew?

Ellery (*quietly*): Yes, Julie's mother, the only possibility left — Ma Mathew.
Did Ma Mathew have the strength required to commit both crimes
and the rest of it? Oh, yes. Jed Bigelow told us she was as "strong as
a plow-mare." That she did all her own housework, cooking, fed the
stock, even helped with the work on the farm! A farmer's wife of the
old stock . . . Yes, Ma Mathew would have the strength — not only of
body but of grim purpose, too.

Nikki (*whispering*): Ma Mathew killed that man to protect her daughter's
reputation and save what was left of the poor thing's life?

Ellery (*gently*): Yes, Nikki. *Ave atque vale* . . . Waitress! The check!

(*Music up*)

A family curse. A ghostly woman in a summerhouse. Ellery Queen loved mysteries which seemed to admit only a supernatural solution — and "The Adventure of the Woman in Black," broadcast on January 14, 1940, is one of his most effective uses of fictional creepiness.

The Adventure of the Woman in Black

The Characters

Philip Jurney	A British novelist
Norma Jurney	His wife
Dr. Lansing	His physician
Ogilvie	Friend of the family
Tebbetts	A Cockney
John Keith	Jurney's half-brother
Clemence Hull	Jurney's sister
Ellery Queen	The detective
Nikki Porter	His secretary
Inspector Queen	Of the New York Police
Sergeant Velie	Of the New York Police

Setting: A country estate, near New York City, 1940

(*Music up . . . into car on gravel, slowly . . .*)

Jurney (*medium age, pronounced British accent*): (*Jittery*) Decent of you to drive me home, Doctor.

Lansing (*medium age, American*): (*Chuckling*) It isn't every night I get a chance to chauffeur a major British novelist, Jurney.

Jurney (*bitterly*): I'm afraid your major British novelist isn't long for this world, Dr. Lansing.

Lansing: Nonsense! (*Stops car*) Before you go into the house, Jurney, take that Death-where-is-thy-sting look off your face. You'll frighten your wife to death.

Jurney: Yes, Norma's worried enough as it is. Well, thanks, Dr. Lansing . . . (*Opens car door*)

Lansing: Before you go, Jurney! . . . I want to warn you again. Slow down.

Jurney: Now? When I'm almost finished with my novel?

Lansing: Now look here. I found a few things wrong with you tonight, Jurney, but nothing that can't be cured by rest, fresh air, relaxation. Your trouble is nervous fatigue. Overwork. Jurney, you're headed for a serious crack-up unless . . .

Jurney (*very tired*): Well, writing sixteen hours a day for months can't be expected to tone up a man —

Lansing: You can abuse your nervous system just so long, my dear man, then it rebels. Of course, if your novel's more important to you than your — (*Hesitates*) — your health . . .

Jurney (*laugh*): You almost said "your sanity," didn't you?

Lansing (*hastily*): No, no, Jurney!

Jurney (*tensely*): It's my magnum opus, Dr. Lansing. I can't stop now. (*Oddly*) Perhaps I've been hurrying it along so because I have a premonition of . . . (*Stops. Getting out of car*) Well, thanks again, Doctor. Brilliant moon tonight, eh?

Lansing: What? Oh. Yes. Jurney, perhaps I'd better walk you across the garden to the house —

Jurney (*off a little*): I'm perfectly all right, Doctor.

Lansing: Hmm! Very well. Get a sound night's sleep, and give me a ring in the morning.

Jurney (*off a little*): You've been terribly kind. (*Slams car door — off further*) Good night, Dr. Lansing.

Lansing (*slowly*): Night, Jurney . . . (*Steps on gravel fading. Doctor sighs on mike. Starts car. Begins to reverse*)

Jurney (*far off — terrified*): Doctor! Dr. Lansing! (*Stops car*)

Lansing (*calling*): What? What's the matter, Jurney!

Jurney (*nearer — same*): Wait! Stop your car! (*Open car door*)

Lansing: For heaven's sake, Jurney! What's wrong? You're trembling!

Jurney (*fading on — panting*): You carry a revolver in your car, don't you, Dr. Lansing? You told me —

Lansing: Why, yes. These outlying roads at night . . . Why?

Jurney: Let me have it!

Lansing: Now just a moment, Jurney. You're upset —

Jurney (*hysterical*): Let me have it, I say! At once!

Lansing (*soothing*): Of course, old man. Just a moment. (*Opens car locker*) Now tell me —

Jurney: Give me that revolver, Dr. Lansing!

Lansing (*smoothly*): In a moment, in a moment, Jurney. But first tell me what's upset you so.

Jurney (*panting*): Come along! (*Quick steps on gravel*) After I left you — I walked up the gravel path — and just as I got abreast of the summerhouse — you know, the little white summerhouse — in the garden here —

Lansing: Yes? Yes, Jurney?

Jurney: I saw . . . Here! Stop! (*Steps stop*) Do you see it? The summerhouse? You must see it — the moon's shining directly into it — it's almost light as day inside —

Lansing: Of course I see into the summerhouse, Jurney. But what —

Jurney (*desperately*): Don't you see that — *woman?*

Lansing (*amazed*): Woman? (*Slowly*) *What* woman, Jurney? Where?

Jurney: That woman — in the summerhouse — wearing a black veil . . . Good lord, man, don't you see a woman in black sitting behind that white table in there?

Lansing (*soothing*): Uh . . . Jurney. Let me take you into the house.

Jurney: No! Dr. Lansing, do you see a woman in black inside that summerhouse, or don't you?

Lansing: Now, Jurney. Let me take your arm —

Jurney: But — I see her so . . . so . . . Lansing! For the love of heaven! Don't you see what she's doing? She just rose from the table — she's pushed it aside — now she's coming round the table to the summerhouse doorway — she's standing just in the doorway, looking at us . . . in black, all in black!

Lansing (*gently*): Jurney, listen to me. You're overworked. Your nerves are raw. There's no one standing in the doorway of the summerhouse. We'll go inside and I'll give you a sedative —

Jurney (*hysterical*): If you don't see that — that creature, then she's come! The Woman in Black — she's come!

Lansing: Jurney. Don't be difficult, now —

Jurney (*raving*): The Woman in Black! She did for my father, for my father's father . . . She's followed me from England! Ogilvie knows all about her. Ogilvie knows —

Lansing: You mean that Scotsman friend of your family's? You pay too much attention to his ghost-stories, Jurney . . . Come along, now —

Jurney: No — wait! If it's the Woman in Black, then she's a ghost — and if she's a ghost . . . (*More quietly*) Doctor, hand me your revolver.

Lansing: Why do you want my revolver, Jurney?

Jurney: Hand it to me, I say! (*Slight scuffle*)

Lansing (*alarmed*): Mr. Jurney! Now please —

Jurney (*tensely*): Don't be alarmed, Dr. Lansing. I know what I'm doing! You say there's no one in that summerhouse doorway? You can't see her?

Lansing: Jurney, there's no one in this garden but you and me. Be careful with that gun, please — give it back to me — it's loaded —

Jurney (*grimly*): Not until I've put a bullet through her, Doctor. The Woman in Black is my family ghost, and ghosts are immune to bullets, aren't they? So let's see if — (*Click as if hammer on empty chamber*) Empty chamber, hang it all! (*Revolver shot*) That's better! (*Pause. Wildly*) She's *still standing there*! I sent that bullet directly through her heart — *and she's still standing there*! (*Sobs*)

Lansing (*gently*): Of course, Jurney. I told you no one's here. Let me have the revolver . . . That's it. Now come into the house . . . (*Steps on gravel*)

Jurney (*brokenly*): She's come . . . the Woman in Black . . .

Lansing: It's an hallucination, Jurney. You don't believe this twaddle about family ghosts, do you? A man of your intelligence . . . (*Steps stop*) Jurney, why are you stopping? *Don't* look back!

Jurney (*feverishly*): I've got to see if . . . Dr. Lansing, she's gone! She's not there any more! (*Steps again*)

Lansing (*to himself*): Thank heaven! (*Cheerfully*) There? You see? Now we'll put you to bed, Jurney, give you something to make you sleep . . . (*Steps stop*)

Jurney (*muttering*): Yes . . . sleep . . . (*Bell rings*)

Lansing: And you'll feel worlds better in the morning. (*Door opens*) Ah, Tebbetts.

Tebbetts (*Cockney, oldish*): H'Ev'ning, Dr. Lansing. H'Ev'ning sir. (*Alarmed*) Doctor, what's the matter with —

Lansing (*over closing door*): Sit down here in the foyer a moment, Jurney . . . (*Low*) Mr. Jurney is a little ill, Tebbetts. Is Mrs. Jurney at home?

Tebbetts: Yes, sir! But Mr. Jurney, sir — 'e gave me a fair start, 'e did, sir — pale as a ghost —

Lansing: Yes, yes, Tebbetts! Fetch Mrs. Jurney! Right away!

Tebbetts (*fading*): H'I shall, sir! Right aw'y, sir!

Lansing (*gently*): Now Jurney, if you'll try to brace up for your wife's sake — here, let me help you off with your coat — (*Jurney begins to laugh hysterically . . . fade off*)

(*Music up . . . and fade into ad libs . . .*)

Ellery (*thoughtfully*): Remarkable experience, Mr. Jurney. Remarkable.

Nikki: I'm all one big goose-pimple!

Inspector: A man in your profession ought to watch himself better, Mr. Jurney. Overwork, Dr. Lansing?

Lansing: Yes. Common phenomenon with these fellows, Inspector. This hallucination of Jurney's —

Ogilvie (*oldish — Scotch brogue*): 'Twas *not* hallucination, Dr. Lansing. 'Twas the Woman in Black . . .

Ellery: Oh, come, Mr. Ogilvie. By the way, you're the friend Mr. Jurney mentioned? I've read some of your books on the supernatural.

Ogilvie (*dryly*): Verra good of you, Mr. Queen. I see you don't believe.

Well, Philip Jurney here did not believe, either. And do you disbelieve now, Jurney?

Jurney (*desperately*): I don't know what to believe *or* disbelieve, Ogilvie. I saw that black-clad . . . *thing* with my own eyes. I saw her move — float, almost, in that bright moonlight . . .

Ellery: Mmm. As I understand it, Mr. Jurney, you've been living in America only a few months?

Jurney (*wearily*): Yes. British, of course. But my half-brother John Keith and the rest of my family have been here for many years.

Inspector: Your brother is in business here?

Jurney: He owns a string of cinemas — has his own projection room at the house, in fact. I . . . well, since my father's death I've been at . . . loose ends. I thought I'd write my new novel in America, and Mrs. Jurney and I have been living at my brother John's home.

Nikki: That's where you gentlemen had this experience?

Lansing: Yes, last night, Miss Porter, in the garden at John Keith's house. I'd driven Jurney back from my office.

Ellery: Is your wife English, too, Mr. Jurney?

Jurney: No, Mr. Queen. Daughter of one of your American diplomats. We met in London.

Inspector: Who else lives in the Keith house with you?

Jurney: Our sister Clemence — Clemence Jurney Hull.

Ogilvie: Mrs. Hull's a widow — her husband died in a motor accident a few weeks ago. Verra sad.

Nikki: How awful! Are you staying at Mr. Jurney's brother's house, too, Mr. Ogilvie?

Ogilvie: Yes, lass — as Philip Jurney's guest.

Ellery: Just why have you come to me, Mr. Jurney?

Jurney: Because — either I'm going mad, or . . .

Lansing (*wearily*): You're not going mad, Jurney. There's a distinction between madness and hallucination induced by nervous exhaustion and . . .

Ogilvie (*sharply*): Dr. Lansing, 'twas the Woman in Black!

Jurney (*desperately*): Mr. Queen, if Ogilvie's right — I'm going to die! (*Ad libs*) Ogilvie knows all about the Woman in Black. Tell them, old chap.

Ogilvie (*deliberately*): The Woman in Black, gentlemen, is the ghost of the Jurney clan. (*Ad libs*) Verra well — scoff! But I was the friend of Jurney's father, and of Jurney's grandfather, and I tell ye *they* believed in that ghost, too!

Inspector: Maybe they did, Mr. Ogilvie — but what's this talk of dying, Mr. Jurney?

Jurney (*wearily*): My father died in an airplane crash over the Channel. My grandfather before him died in a fox-hunting accident.

Ogilvie (*excited*): And to each Jurney, a little before he died, appeared the Woman in Black! (*Pause*)

Lansing: Forgive my saying — Drivel!

Ellery: No, no, Dr. Lansing. Let's not take the narrow view. This Woman in Black — a ghost — appears only to some member of the Jurney family?

Jurney: Yes, Mr. Queen. Three times. The family legend has it that after the third visitation the Jurney thus honored — (*Bitter laugh*) — dies.

Ogilvie (*grimly*): 'Tis been that way for many generations.

Nikki (*quickly*): Is last night the first time you've seen this — well, ghost, Mr. Jurney?

Jurney (*faintly*): Yes . . . the first time . . . (*Forced laugh*) Twice more, eh, Ogilvie? Then —

Ellery: Mr. Jurney, how good a marksman are you with a revolver?

Jurney (*wearily*): Oh, excellent.

Inspector: You say you shot right *through* that apparition?

Jurney: Yes, she was standing in the summerhouse doorway and I put a bullet through her heart. No question about my aim. There was a full moon, and Dr. Lansing and I weren't ten yards from the summerhouse when I fired.

Ogilvie (*sadly*): Ye can't shoot a ghost, laddie.

Ellery: I wonder if I might examine that revolver, gentlemen. Do you happen to have it with you?

Lansing: It's here in my medical bag. (*Open bag*) There you are, Mr. Queen.

Ellery: Thanks, Doctor. (*Breaks opens gun. Spins chamber*) Hmmm. Holds six cartridges when fully loaded. Dr. Lansing, has this revolver been out of your possession since Mr. Jurney fired it last night?

Lansing: No. It's just as it was when Jurney handed it back to me. (*Close gun*)

Ellery: Then I think we'll dedicate the next few moments to the Ghost of Science. Nikki — out of that sofa!

Nikki: Ellery! Don't aim that — that thing at me!

Inspector: What are you doing, son?

Ellery (*cheerfully*): Taking the first step in a check-up of the authenticity of Mr. Jurney's family ghost. Keep back, please. (*One revolver shot. Exclamations*)

Ogilvie: Mon's stark daft!

Inspector: Ellery, you fired right *into* our sofa!

Nikki: Ho-hum. You need a new sofa anyway, Inspector.

Ellery: Now let's see if we can find the bullet . . . (*Cushions moved*) Ah! Here's the little beauty. Very nice. Dad, hang on to this slug, will you?

Inspector: What do you want with the slug?

Ellery: Comparison. Ballistics check-up. I have an idea . . . (*Breaks open gun. Spins chamber*) Ah, four bullets left in the cylinder. (*Snaps gun*) I'll keep this weapon, if you don't mind . . . (*Jurney groans*) What's the matter, Mr. Jurney?

Nikki: He's ill!

Inspector: Of all the fool stunts — (*Jurney groans again*)

Lansing (*sharply*): Jurney! Here, put him on the sofa, please. (*Ad libs as they do so*) Jurney! What's wrong?

Ogilvie (*anxiously*): So pale! — Laddie, speak up!

Jurney (*gasping*): My — heart . . . it hurts . . .

Lansing (*sharply*): Brandy. Quickly!

Nikki (*off*): Oh, where's the brandy?

Ellery: There, Nikki — the decanter on the table!

Nikki (*off*): Oh, yes . . . (*Bottle, glass, pour liquid. Fade on*) Here, Doctor . . . !

Lansing: Thank you. Jurney — drink this. Drink it!

Jurney (*gasps*): I feel so — odd . . . (*Drinks*)

Lansing: Lie still, now, Jurney. My bag, please . . . stethoscope . . .

Inspector: Here you are, Doctor! (*Open bag. Pause*)

Lansing: Mmm . . . Mmm . . . All right, now, Jurney. Just lie quietly . . .

Jurney (*whispering*): Yes . . . Dr. Lansing . . .

Ellery (*low*): What's the matter with him, Doctor?

Ogilvie (*anxious*): Is he — is it his —

Lansing (*low*): Heart-attack. We'll have to get him home to his brother's house immediately. I detected a cardiac condition last night, when I examined him at my office, but it didn't seem serious. All the excitement, however —

Nikki (*low*): He doesn't know?

Lansing (*same*): I didn't tell him. I shan't tell him, either, for some time. The way his nerves are . . . (*Fading*) Ogilvie, help me get him into his coat, will you?

Ogilvie (*fading*): Yes, Doctor.

Ellery (*grimly*): Nikki, get your coat, too.

Nikki: Why — where are *we* going, Ellery?

Ellery: We're going back to Keith's house with Philip Jurney, Mr. Ogilvie, and Dr. Lansing!

Inspector (*low*): You're not taking that yarn about a ghost seriously, are you, Ellery?

Ellery (*grimly*): Seriously enough to try and save Jurney's life!

(*Music up . . . and into*)

Lansing (*cheerfully*): There now! Feeling better, Jurney?

Jurney (*weakly*): Yes, Dr. Lansing. Norma, my dear . . .

Norma (*American, young — trying to control herself*): Oh, Philip! Don't talk — don't move — just try to go to sleep, darling . . .

Jurney (*sleepily*): Yes, Norma . . . Don't worry, my — dear. (*Trailing off*) I'll be . . . all . . . right . . . (*Pause*)

Norma (*crying softly*): He's so white, so weak-looking! Dr. Lansing, is it — serious?

Lansing (*low*): No, Mrs. Jurney. He'll be all right if he takes care of himself.

Ellery: Will he sleep through the night, Doctor?

Lansing: Oh, yes. I've given him a sedative. Now Mrs. Jurney, you've got to do your part, too. If you carry on this way —

Norma (*tearfully*): I'm sorry. It's that novel of Philip's. Day and night, without a let-up —

Ellery: It's undoubtedly your husband's nerves, Mrs. Jurney. Overwork can play the devil with a man.

Lansing: He'll have to take it easy. Just have to. A good long rest will make a new man of him.

Norma: But he won't, Dr. Lansing. Philip's so stubborn, so — so *set* when he's writing. I don't know what we'll do. He won't give up his novel — I know he won't.

Lansing (*grimly*): Then I can't be responsible for his life, Mrs. Jurney. It's up to you. Well, that's all we can do tonight. I'll drop in tomorrow morning. Coming, Queen?

Ellery: Yes, Doctor. (*Opens door*)

Norma: I'll stay here with Philip. If he should wake up . . . Night, Doctor, Mr. Queen. You've been so kind —

Ellery: Please, Mrs. Jurney. Glad to help. Good night. (*Ad lib goodnights. Closes door. Steps on stairs*) Dr. Lansing, tell me. You're absolutely certain there was no one in that summerhouse last night?

Lansing (*wearily*): Queen, I'm telling you I stood as close to Jurney as I'm standing to you, and there was simply no one there.

Ellery: What do you think of this family-ghost yarn?

Lansing (*snorts*): That old wives' tale? You'd think a man as civilized as Philip Jurney — Of course, it's his nerves. (*Opens door. Ad libs up*)

Nikki: How is Mr. Jurney, Ellery? (*Closes door*)

Ogilvie: Mortal shape, eh?

Keith (*slight British accent*): Well, gentlemen? How is my brother?

Lansing: Sleeping, Keith. He'll be fine if you see to it he takes it easy.

Keith: Poor Philip. It's going to be a job —

Nikki: Ellery, this is Mr. John Keith, Mr. Jurney's half-brother. (*Ad lib greetings*)

Lansing (*tired*): Well, I'll be going.

Tebbetts (*fading on*): Your 'at and coat, sir.

Lansing: Thank you, Tebbetts.

Tebbetts (*anxiously*): Mr. Jurney's h'all right, sir?

Lansing: For the time being — yes, Tebbetts. (*Fading*) Good night. (*Ad libs*)

Tebbetts (*fading*): This w'y, Doctor . . .

Ogilvie: That Tebbetts! Old washer-lady, bless his heart. Been in the Jurney family service all his life. Well, I believe I'll turn in m'self. (*Ad lib goodnights, Ogilvie fading*)

Ellery: Mr. Keith, before I go I should like to examine that summerhouse.

Keith: Certainly, Mr. Queen. (*Steps. Dialogue over steps, opening front door, steps on gravel*) Rum show, eh?

Ellery: Then you know just what happened last night?

Keith: Yes. I couldn't sleep, worrying about Philip.

Nikki: What do *you* think about that Woman in Black, Mr. Keith?

Keith (*wearily*): Rubbish. Lansing's utterly right. Poor Philip's seeing things. Runs in the family. We had a milit'ry uncle once who used to see the shade of a Borneo head-hunter.

Ellery: No doubt but that your brother's in bad shape.

Keith: Writes himself ragged. Always was that way.

Nikki: Is your sister, Mrs. Hull, a writer, too?

Keith: Clemence? Lord, no. And even if she were, poor Clemence wouldn't be fit for anything with the tragedy she's just gone through. You haven't met Clemence, have you? (*Ad libs*) Wanders around in her widow's weeds like a lost soul. She *is* a lost soul . . . Here we are, Mr. Queen.

Ellery: Mmm. Nice bright moon tonight, too. I imagine Jurney and Dr. Lansing stood just about here when Jurney fired that shot.

Nikki: Even I couldn't miss at this distance!

Keith: Poor Philip. Shooting through an empty doorway!

Ellery: Let's see what he hit. (*Steps on grass*)

Nikki: The bullet! You want the *bullet*, Ellery?

Ellery: You're psychic, Miss Porter. (*Steps on wood*) Is there a light in here, Mr. Keith?

Keith: Yes. I'll snap the switch. (*Click of light-switch*)

Ellery: That's better! Now let's see . . . directly through the doorway . . . then the bullet should be imbedded in the rear wall about . . . *here!*

Nikki: Ellery! *There's* the bullet-hole! (*Prying sounds*)

Ellery: *And* the bullet, unless I'm — very — much — mistaken. Ah! Yes, Mr. Jurney's bullet sped right through a ghost. I don't see any blood in that doorway, do you?

Keith: Of course not.

Nikki: If that Woman in Black had been flesh-and-blood, standing in the doorway in Mr. Jurney's line of fire — why, she'd have been shot in the heart!

Ellery: Right, Nikki. Bullet struck the rear wall about chest-high. Well, I'll keep this slug as a souvenir. (*Steps on wood*) Thanks, Mr. Keith.

Keith: Not much of a case for you, I'm afraid. (*On grass*)

Ellery: On the contrary, Mr. Keith. It's a good deal of a case. By the way. Would you mind identifying those upper windows of the house which face that little summerhouse?

Keith: The upper windows? My sister Clemence's bedroom, my projection-room, Philip's library, Philip's bedroom — that's where the night light's burning — and Norma's bedroom.

Ellery: Thank you, Mr. Keith. (*Steps on gravel*) Well, here's my car.

Nikki: We'll be saying good night, Mr. Keith.

Ellery: *I'll* be saying good night, Nikki. I've a job for you, if Mr. Keith's agreeable.

Keith: I? Of course, anything I can do to be of service —

Nikki: A job for *me*, Ellery?

Ellery: Yes, Nikki. I take it, Mr. Keith, that restraining your brother Philip Jurney from finishing his novel is going to be difficult. Now, Miss Porter is a trained literary secretary —

Nikki: Oh. I *see*. (*Low*) How sweet of you, Mr. Queen!

Keith: I say, that's a splendid notion! Miss Porter could relieve Philip of a lot of work, couldn't she? Taking notes, typing, and what-not?

Ellery: I think so. What do you say, Nikki?

Nikki: But Ellery, I've no change of clothing —

Ellery: I'll send you a complete wardrobe in the morning.

Nikki (*low*): Thoughtful! (*Louder*) *Very* well, Mr. Queen. Maybe I'll like Mr. Jurney so well I won't come back to you. After all, you're only a detective-story writer, and he — he's a major novelist!

Ellery (*chuckling*): It would serve me right at that . . . Well, then, that's settled — (*Nikki screams*)

Nikki (*screaming*): *Look!* Oh — *look!* (*Sneak music*)

Keith (*alarmed*): What's the matter, Miss Porter?

Ellery: Look where, Nikki?

Nikki: The summerhouse — that woman . . . in black! (*Pause*)

Ellery: There *is* a woman in the doorway — and she *is* dressed in black! You there —!

Keith (*quickly*): Wait, Mr. Queen. Don't frighten her. That's my sister Clemence — she's in mourning, you know . . . a little melancholy . . .

Nikki (*relieved*): Oh . . . ! My heart almost stopped!

Ellery: Mrs. Hull, eh? There, she's leaving. Must have slipped into the summerhouse while we were standing here on the drive, talking.

Keith: If you'd like to speak to her . . . Clem —!

Ellery (*quickly*): Never mind, Mr. Keith. Let's not upset the poor woman.

Keith: I'd better see she gets into the house. When you're ready,

Miss Porter — I'll tell Tebbetts to fix up a room for you . . . (*Fading*) Night, Mr. Queen . . .

Ellery: Good night, Keith! (*Pause*)

Nikki (*low*): Ellery, I . . . don't like this . . . job you just gave me. Big-hearted!

Ellery (*low*): Please, Nikki. It's vitally important.

Nikki: But *why?*

Ellery: Because I want someone on these premises whose eyesight I can trust!

Nikki: You mean . . . about that . . . g-ghost?

Ellery (*grimly*): Yes, Nikki. Keep your eyes open, and the moment you see a female ghost dressed in black — *not* Mrs. Hull — make tracks for the nearest phone!

(*Music up . . . and into*)

Nikki (*filtered throughout*): Thanks for the valise!

Ellery: Least I could do, Nikki. Sleep well last night?

Nikki: What do you mean "sleep"? I was seeing ghosts all night!

Ellery (*chuckling*): How's Philip Jurney today?

Nikki: So much better he insisted on getting right to work on his novel again. Dr. Lansing and Mrs. Jurney and the others — they're frantic.

Ellery: Has the celebrated novelist accepted his new secretary without protest?

Nikki: I like that! He practically kissed me. (*Door opens off*) Not that I'd have minded — he *is* handsome . . .

Ellery: *Very* obvious, Miss Porter. (*Ad libs on*) Oh, dad. Sergeant Velie . . . Nikki, keep your eyes open for that ghost!

Nikki (*grimly*): Don't worry, I shall. And if I see her — watch my dust!

Ellery (*laughing*): 'Bye.

Nikki: *Goodbye!* (*Hangs up phone*)

Ellery (*eagerly*): Well, dad? What did you find out?

Inspector (*fading on*): Plenty. Sit down, Velie. Take a load off those Number Twelves.

Velie: Thirteen. 'Lo, Mr. Queen. How's your ghost?

Ellery: Gone into hiding, Sergeant. Well, dad?

Inspector: Velie and I, we've checked the whole thing.

Velie: An' it checks. Nothin' phony about any o' those people. They're all what they claim to be.

Inspector: And as far as Jurney's will is concerned —

Ellery: Ah! You checked that, too, eh? Fast work, dad! Who gains by Jurney's death?

Velie: Who'd you think? Always lookin' for somethin' complicated!

Inspector: Norma Jurney — Jurney's wife.

Velie: Sole bene — bene — She's the only one who collects.

Ellery: Is it a big estate?

Velie: Puh-lenty. Say, why'n't you write somethin' like this *Royal Row-gue* that Jurney wrote —

Inspector: *Royal Rogue*, you cluck!

Velie: Whatever it is. All the dough he's made outa royalties, movies, serials . . .

Ellery: There's only one Philip Jurney, I'm afraid, Sergeant. No one else benefits under Jurney's will?

Inspector: Not a living soul. Not even the sister.

Ellery: Hmmm. How about that ballistics report, Sergeant?

Velie: You mean on those two slugs — the bullet you dug outa the summerhouse woodwork an' the bullet you fired into the sofa? Well, the comparison tests check okay. The lab says both those slugs came outa Dr. Lansing's gun. No question about it.

Inspector (*thoughtfully*): So there was no trick involved and Jurney *did* fire a bullet through that summerhouse doorway, thinking he was plugging a ghost.

Velie: If y'ask me, which you ain't — that guy's slap-happy from writin' too much, an' that's all there is to this case. You mark my words, Mr. Queen, one o' these days you're gonna get that way, too! It's no life for a man, writin'. (*Ellery and Inspector laugh*) I always say — Git out in the open. Breathe deep. Use your muscles. I always say —

Inspector: You always say too blamed much, Velie! (*Fading*) I hope Nikki's all right in that house, Ellery. I don't like the idea much of that kid sleeping in a place where . . .

(*Music up . . . and into typewriter —*)

Jurney (*dictating over typewriter — tense, ragged*): ". . . in darkest silence." Period. New paragraph, Miss Porter. (*Pause. Slowly*) "Fraunton crushed the tender gorse beneath his hunting boots, grinding his heel in the face of that ancient enemy . . ." (*Pause*) "Ancient enemy . . ." (*Typewriter stops*) Wait — wait —

Nikki: You're tired, Mr. Jurney. Don't you think you've dictated enough for tonight?

Jurney (*tensely*): No! I've got to finish! "Ancient enemy . . ."

Nikki: But there's so much time — the rest of your life —

Jurney (*hoarsely*): Time! No, Miss Porter. There's so *little* time . . . (*Pacing*) And if I should die —

Nikki (*quickly*): Now you *are* going to stop, Mr. Jurney! Mrs. Jurney will be furious with me. I promised her I'd let you work only until . . .

Mr. Jurney! I *asked* you not to keep pacing up and down before the library window. You know what Dr. Lansing said about keeping out of drafts —
Jurney (*tensely*): Please. Please. I must go on. (*Steps stop*) Where was I? Oh, yes. "Ancient enemy —" (*Gasps*)
Nikki (*alarmed*): Mr. Jurney! What —
Jurney (*screaming*): Look! Look!
Nikki: What — where —
Jurney (*same*): The Woman in Black! — there she is again! — standing in the doorway of the summerhouse down there! — with the moonlight . . . moonlight . . . (*Sigh. Falling body*)
Nikki (*shouting*): Mr. Jurney! Oh, he — he fell! Help! Somebody — help, help! (*Open door quickly off*) Thank heaven — Tebbetts — look —
Tebbetts: What's the commotion, Miss? H'It's Mr. Jurney! (*Nikki crying*) Mr. Jurney, sir — h'it's Tebbetts —
Nikki: Is he — is he —
Tebbetts (*distressed*): F'inted, Miss! H'I'll call Dr. Lansing — h'at once!

(*Music up . . . and into ad libs*)

Norma (*frantically*): We've got to get Philip away from here. Oh, why doesn't Dr. Lansing come out of Philip's room?
Nikki: Mrs. Jurney — please. You must control yourself.
Keith: Yes, Norma. If Philip hears you carrying on, it's bound to fret him —
Ogilvie: Where's that widow sister of yours, Keith? It's verra strange she isn't here, at a time like this.
Keith: Clemence shrinks from — things like this, Ogilvie. You can scarcely blame her, after her tragedy —
Norma: Let poor Clemence stay in her room. It's this house! John Keith, I know it's awful of me to say it — it's your house — but we *must* get Philip away to some quiet, restful place — in the South, perhaps — or maybe going back to England would . . .
Nikki: Just keep calm, Mrs. Jurney. You're right to want to take your husband away, but you've got to wait until he's strong enough —
Norma: I'll tear up that novel of his! I'll burn it!
Ogilvie (*glumly*): It's the ghost — the Woman in Black —
Keith (*sharply*): Shut that dour Scots mouth of yours, Ogilvie! Woman in Black! You'll have us all seeing things!
Ogilvie (*stiffly*): If an Ogilvie isn't welcome in this house, John Keith . . .
Keith: Forgive me, old boy. My own nerves are — (*Door opens off*) Here's Lansing! Doctor —
Norma: How is my husband, Dr. Lansing?
Ogilvie: Is the poor lad taken bad, Doctor?

Nikki: What is it, Dr. Lansing? What happened to him?

Lansing (*fading on — grave*): Another heart attack. (*Gasps. Norma cries*) You say, Miss Porter, that Jurney cried out something about a ghost, then fainted?

Nikki: Yes. The Woman in Black — in the summerhouse —

Ogilvie (*muttering*): 'Tis the second visitation . . . one, two . . . and when she appears the third time . . .

Keith (*shrilly*): Oh, *stop* it, Ogilvie!

Lansing: You'll all have to stop it. Jurney needs a cheerful atmosphere more than anything else in the world. And I absolutely forbid his getting out of bed.

Norma: Can't I take Philip away from here, Doctor?

Lansing: Not until I give the word, Mrs. Jurney. Then — yes — I agree. This is a bad place for him . . .

Tebbetts (*fading on*): H'It's Mr. Queen and H'Inspector Queen and a large gentleman . . .

Nikki: Oh, they've finally come!

Keith: Show them in, Tebbetts!

Tebbetts: Very good, sir. (*Off*) H'If ye'll come this w'y, gentlemen . . . (*Ad libs fading on*)

Ellery (*fading on*): We got here as fast as we could after your call, Nikki. Hullo! (*Ad lib greetings*)

Velie: Where's this female boogey-man?

Inspector: How is Mr. Jurney, Dr. Lansing?

Dr. Lansing (*fading*): Another heart-attack, Inspector . . . (*Ad libs in background*)

Ellery: Nikki, may I talk to you a moment? (*Over ad libs*)

Nikki: Oh, Ellery, it was hideous! He turned green, I swear and his eyes — they simply popped —

Ellery (*low*): After Jurney cried out and fainted, Nikki — did you run over and look out that window?

Nikki: Yes — while I was shouting for help —

Ellery: And did *you* see a Woman in Black in the summerhouse?

Nikki: No, Ellery. There was no one in the garden. Poor Mr. Jurney! He's convinced, I know, that he's going to die. He's been so *depressed.* If he should "see" that ghost once more —

Ellery (*gloomily*): Yes, he'd probably pass out from sheer fright. Amazing. Simply amazing case . . .

Jurney (*off — feeble*): Norma . . . ! Dr. Lansing . . . !

Norma: Wait! That's Philip! Oh, Doctor . . . (*Fading*) I'm coming, Philip — I'm coming, darling . . .

Lansing (*fading*): Have to get him quiet . . .

Ellery (*low*): Dad. Velie. Come here.

Inspector (*fading on — low*): There's something — creepy about this, Ellery. And yet . . . I don't like it.

Velie: English ghost! Why'n't she go back where she came from? Y'know what? This case smells!

Nikki: Ellery . . . I'm afraid.

Ellery: I should never have placed you in this position, Nikki. But I didn't realize the danger —

Nikki: Danger! You think — (*Norma Jurney and doctor fading on*)

Inspector: Watch it! Here they come.

Norma (*fading on*): Philip wants to read — he insists on reading his favorite book of short stories —

Lansing (*fading on*): I'd rather he didn't, Mrs. Jurney —

Keith: You'd better not cross Philip, Dr. Lansing.

Ogilvie: Yes, the lad gets verra excited —

Ellery: What *is* Mr. Jurney's favorite book of short stories, Mrs. Jurney?

Norma: *The Short Stories of Oscar Wilde*. Miss Porter, would you mind — that fourth shelf —

Nikki (*fade a bit*): Fourth shelf, Mrs. Jurney? (*Off*) *Short Stories of Oscar Wilde* . . . Oh, there it is. (*Pause. On mike*) Here you are, Mrs. Jurney.

Norma: Thank you. Dr. Lansing, is it all right —?

Lansing: I suppose so. But see he doesn't read too long.

Keith: Let me have the book, Norma. (*Fading*) I'll give it to Philip . . .

Ogilvie (*fading*): Wait, Keith! I'll go with ye. Perhaps a fine rousin' laugh will cheer the poor mon up . . . (*Norma, doctor ad libs fading too*)

Inspector: Well?

Velie: What danger, Mr. Queen?

Nikki: You were saying something about it's being dangerous for me to stay here . . .

Ellery (*grimly*): Unguarded. Let's say I'm being careful, Nikki. Sergeant, if you'll be good enough —

Inspector: What d'ye want Velie to do, son?

Ellery (*grimly*): I want him to hang around this house tonight. And Sergeant — keep your eyes wide open!

Velie: Protect Miss Porter, huh? Now that's a job I can put me heart an' soul in. (*Grimly*) An' if I see that ghost — lady or no lady! — I'll bust her right in the nose!

(*Music up . . . and into opening door, closing*)

Inspector: Well, that's that. Tough day. I'm dog tired.

Ellery (*fretfully*): I hope Jurney gets a good night's sleep tonight. If anything should happen —

Inspector (*yawning*): Oh, you're as jittery as he is. Poor fella's seeing things. I don't think this is a criminal case at all. Well, I guess I'll hit the hay — (*Phone rings*) I'll take it. (*Picks up phone*) Yes?

Jurney (*filtered throughout — low, excited*): Mr. Queen? I wish to speak to Ellery Queen!

Inspector: Who is this?

Jurney: Philip Jurney! Hurry, please!

Inspector: Hold the wire . . . Ellery, it's Jurney!

Ellery: Jurney! (*Pause*) Hello! Hello! Jurney? This is Queen. Where are you?

Jurney: At home. In my bedroom. Queen, the most frightfully important thing's occurred —

Ellery: Now Mr. Jurney, you're all excited again, and you know you're not supposed to —

Jurney: Bother that! *Queen, there's a plot against my life!*

Inspector (*low*): Batty. Batty as a bat. Now he's got delusions of persecution!

Ellery: Hold it, dad . . . Yes, Mr. Jurney? What do you mean?

Jurney: It isn't the family legend that's been haunting me, Queen — it isn't that at all! And it *wasn't* a ghost I saw twice in the garden!

Ellery: Of course it wasn't, Mr. Jurney. It was just your imagination —

Jurney: You think so? You think so? I tell you, Queen, I've just seen through the whole thing! (*Laughs hysterically*) Good old Oscar — to the rescue!

Ellery: I beg your pardon?

Inspector: Batty. Plain batty.

Jurney: Oscar Wilde! I've been reading in the *Short Stories of Oscar Wilde*, and something I've read — it came over me like a flash — Queen, this is a plot to take advantage of my overworked, nervous condition! It's a plot to frighten me to death — to drive me insane —

Ellery: Calm down, Mr. Jurney. Please.

Jurney (*muttering*): Yes. Yes. It's a plot —

Ellery: Who's behind this plot? Whom do you suspect?

Jurney (*tense*): Queen, I'm positive that it's — (*Scream, muffled. Thud over wire. Click of phone filtered*)

Inspector: What is it, Ellery? What's happened?

Ellery: I don't know, dad! He screamed, then there was a thud . . . (*Jiggles hook*) Jurney! Jurney! The phone's dead, blast it!

Inspector (*urgently*): If he was phoning from his bedroom, that's an extension. Try the main Keith number!

Ellery: Yes! (*Click. Rapid dialing*)

Tebbetts (*filtered*): H'Are you there? I mean — 'ello!

Ellery: Tebbetts? This is Ellery Queen!

Tebbetts: What — ag'ine? Beg pardon, sir!

Ellery: Never mind that! Is Mr. Jurney all right?

Tebbetts: Mr. Jurney? H'Of course, sir!

Ellery: Oh, bother! Put Sergeant Velie on the wire.

Tebbetts: Sergeant Velie? 'E's gone h'out for a breather in the garden with Dr. Lansing, sir —

Ellery: Then Miss Porter! Quickly, Tebbetts!

Tebbetts: Yes, sir. 'Old the line, sir. H'I'll 'ave Miss Porter take h'it h'upstairs on 'er h'extension. She's h'in 'er room, sir . . .

Ellery: Yes, yes, hurry, Tebbetts . . . Blast that Cockney!

Inspector: Well?

Ellery: Apparently no one at the house knows anything's wrong. Velie's out strolling with Dr. Lansing — Nikki's in her room . . . Hello! Nikki?

Nikki (*filtered*): Ellery? What's the matter?

Ellery: Don't *you* know?

Nikki: Ellery Queen, are you in your right mind?

Ellery: Nikki, listen to me. Is anything wrong at the Keith house?

Nikki: Wrong? Of course not.

Ellery: Who is with Philip Jurney?

Nikki: No one. He calmed down beautifully, and Dr. Lansing said he could read a little longer. He's in his room — either reading or asleep. Mrs. Jurney's gone to bed.

Ellery: Nikki. I want you to go to Jurney's bedroom at once and look in. Or — no. Find Velie and have *him* do it.

Nikki: But why, Ellery? I don't see —

Ellery: Do as I say, Nikki! Now! I'll hold on.

Nikki (*scared*): All right, Ellery . . .

Inspector: Well? Well, Ellery?

Ellery: We'll know in a moment, dad. I don't understand it myself. Mrs. Jurney sleeps in an adjoining bedroom. Unless — (*Pause*)

Inspector (*significantly*): Unless Mrs. Jurney —

Ellery: Well, we'll know in a moment. I wish they'd hurry up!

Inspector: Maybe Jurney saw that ghost again, and had another heart attack —

Ellery: I don't think so, dad. He said something about having read a short story in that volume of Oscar Wilde which convinced him the ghost thing was an illusion. Said he knew now there was a real plot against his life —

Inspector: If that's the case —

Nikki (*filtered — shrill — tense*): Ellery! Ellery!

Ellery: Here's Nikki! . . . Yes, Nikki? How is he? How is Jurney?

Nikki (*same*): Sergeant Velie says — (*Sobs*)

Ellery: Yes, Nikki? Nikki, for heaven's sake!

Nikki (*same — sobbing*): Oh, Ellery . . . Philip Jurney's — dead!

(*Music up . . . and into ad lib murmurs off . . .*)

Inspector: Velie, you ought to be . . . Aaaah!

Velie (*very aggrieved*): But gosh, Inspector, how was I to know? There's the guy in his bedroom, an' he's okay — I was right there with Dr. Lansing when the Doc give him a last once-over, an' Jurney was fine — an' then the Doc an' me, we went downstairs an' had a smoke outside —

Ellery: That was unintelligent, Sergeant! I thought I told you —

Velie: Say, that makes me sore! You jumpin' me, too, Mr. Queen? I ain't no sightseer! This guy's seein' ghosts, ain't he? So I figgers — s'pose it's a plot. S'pose that ghost is real — I mean, a real phony, not just somethin' Jurney thought he saw. So I says: I'm gonna watch that summerhouse. That's why I went outside with the Doc. I didn't wanna take no chances on that ghost showin' up an' Jurney seein' her from his bedroom winda. How'd I know someone was gonna pop him on the skull with that bronze water-bottle from the night-stand next to his bed?

Inspector: All right,*all* right, Velie. I suppose it was unavoidable. Where's Nikki, Ellery?

Ellery: Helping the doctor work over Mrs. Jurney.

Velie: Yeah, an' talkin' about boners — how about that better half o' Jurney's? She was asleep — *she* says — in the next room to his. But why didn't she hear him scream, huh? Y'know what *I* think? *I* think Mrs. Jurney —

Inspector: Don't strain yourself, Velie! Mrs. Jurney says she slept right through it. Matter of fact, she took a sleeping tablet —

Velie (*glumly*): *She* says.

Inspector: Yes,*she* says! (*Fading*) Flint! Aren't you men through mugging this room yet, for the love o' pete?

Ellery (*quietly*): Where is it, Sergeant?

Velie (*blankly*): Where is what, Mr. Queen?

Ellery: That volume of Oscar Wilde short stories Jurney told me he was reading. Just before he was murdered. I don't see it in this room.

Velie: Say, that's a fact. (*Calling*) You guys! Anybody find a book aroun' here — Oscar Wilde? (*Ad libs of men's negatives*)

Inspector (*fading on*): What's this about Oscar Wilde?

Velie: Ain't you heard, Inspector? Oscar's missin'.

Ellery (*thoughtfully*): Yes, Oscar's missing, dad . . . and I think we've got our whole case.

Velie: Huh?

Inspector: We've got —? Little Caesar!

Ellery: I think I know what story Philip Jurney was reading — the Oscar Wilde story that opened his eyes and told him the truth. The secret of the case lies in that Wilde story! That's why the murderer took it from the scene of the crime.

Inspector: I've got a headache.

Velie: He gets speedier every case! Guy gets knocked off — he takes one look around — whammo! He knows who done it! He an' Oscar Wilde!

Ellery: I know the story behind this case, Sergeant, *without* the help of Oscar Wilde! And you can take my word for it — it's one of the most ingenious crimes in the lexicon of murder!

(*Music up . . . and into jury spot*)

Challenge to the Listener

Ellery's challenge does not survive, so the publisher takes the opportunity to admit that he thought he had worked out the solution — and was wrong!

(*Music up . . . and into steps in gravel . . . ad libs . . .*)

Velie: Come on, folks, come on. They're waitin'.

Nikki: Take it easy, Mrs. Jurney. Please —

Norma (*dead voice*): Philip's dead. He's dead. Philip. He's dead . . .

Lansing (*sharply*): Pull yourself together, Mrs. Jurney. Here, Miss Porter. Let me have her . . .

Nikki: She looks so — so *stony* . . .

Ogilvie: I tell ye, John Keith, that Philip Jurney saw that apparition a third time before a human hand bearing a water-bottle struck at his head!

Keith (*stridently*): Ogilvie, I swear — if you don't stop — I'll — (*Ellery, Inspector ad libs fading on*)

Inspector (*fading on*): Here they come, Ellery. All right, people, stop right here! (*Steps stop*)

Ellery: Is everyone here?

Velie: Whole kit an' caboodle of 'em, Mr. Queen.

Nikki: Except Mrs. Hull — Mr. Jurney's sister.

Inspector: Where's the Cockney? Tebbetts!

Tebbetts (*fading on — breathless*): 'Ere H'I h'am, sir . . .!

Inspector: Quiet, please! We've asked you all to come out here in the garden, facing the summerhouse, because my son says this is the spot where the crime took place . . . (*Ad libs*)

Ellery: Yes! Because while Philip Jurney was murdered in his bedroom tonight — the original crime, the *prepared* crime, took place here —

at this very spot — several nights ago, when Jurney first "saw" the ghost of the Woman in Black. (*Norma cries. Lansing, Nikki ad lib soothing her*)

Ogilvie: There! Did I not say 'twas the ghost?

Keith: Ghost! Ogilvie —

Velie: Quiet, you bow-legged ol' grave-robber!

Inspector: Quiet! (*Ad libs down*)

Ellery: Who murdered Philip Jurney? (*Pause*) I admit frankly we can't answer that question on the basis of any *direct* evidence. There are no clues on the scene of the crime. Anyone in the household could theoretically have slipped into Jurney's bedroom tonight and murdered him — anyone but Dr. Lansing, of course, who was in Sergeant Velie's company continuously from a period when Jurney was visibly alive until the time Jurney was found visibly dead.

Lansing (*fervently*): Thank heaven for that! That's all I'd need to ruin my practice — a charge of murder.

Nikki: But Ellery, if there were no clues, then how can you know who . . . attacked Mr. Jurney?

Ellery: The identity of Jurney's killer, Nikki, is deducible from *other* facts.

Keith: Which other facts, Mr. Queen?

Ellery: The facts, Mr. Keith, surrounding the riddle of the Jurney family ghost — the so-called Woman in Black. Look. Ask yourselves the question: Who, or what, was the Woman in Black? A little thought will educe four possible answers. First: That, as Mr. Ogilvie has stubbornly insisted throughout, the Woman in Black *was* a ghost.

Ogilvie: 'Twas what she was, and is, Mr. Queen.

Velie: Oh, for the love of little green apples!

Inspector: Ellery! You can't mean that you believe —

Ellery: Whether I believe in ghosts or not, dad, whether there *are* ghosts or not, the fact remains that the Woman in Black was *not* a ghost, and I can prove it!

Ogilvie: Ye prove that, Mr. Queen, and ye're a better mon than many who've tried!

Ellery (*softly*): But it's provable, Mr. Ogilvie. When Jurney and Dr. Lansing told me in our first talk what had happened in this garden, precisely what were the facts? Jurney said the Woman in Black was sitting *behind a table* inside the summerhouse, that she rose, *pushed the table aside*, and *walked around* the table to stand in the doorway. Now I ask you: Did you ever hear of a ghost who pushed a table aside, Mr. Ogilvie? Or who walked *around* things? Ghosts walk *through* things — they're not stopped by the solid materials of our three-dimensional universe! No, if that Woman in Black had been an apparition, Mr. Ogilvie, she'd have floated through that table as if it didn't exist.

Ogilvie (*muttering*): I didn't know that. Jurney didn't say . . .

Ellery: Now. If the Woman in Black wasn't a ghost, what *could* she have been?

Lansing: Oh, come, Mr. Queen. She was the non-existent product of poor Jurney's shattered nervous system.

Ellery: Yes, Dr. Lansing, hallucination was a second possibility. Well, was she an hallucination? Let's see. Within a day from the first time Jurney saw her, he suffered a heart-attack. Then he saw her a second time, and suffered a second heart-attack . . .

Inspector: But Ellery, so far it *could* have been an hallucination —

Ellery: Yes, dad, but what happened then? Jurney earlier this evening read something in an Oscar Wilde story which gave him a flash of inspiration. He told me over the phone that he knew now he was the victim of a plot *to frighten him to death*, and he was about to accuse the person he suspected when he was attacked and murdered. The mere fact that Jurney *was* murdered under these circumstances proves there *was* a plot to kill him through working on his shattered nerves. And if Jurney *was* meant originally to be frightened to death, then arranging to have him see the family ghost, the Woman in Black, was obviously the *keystone* of the plot. Therefore the Woman in Black was *not* an hallucination, but *a prepared element of the crime*.

Velie: So Jurney didn't see a ghost, an' he didn't get the heeby-jeebies. Then what, Mr. Queen?

Ellery: Then, Sergeant, there was the possibility that what Jurney had seen was the *image* of a woman — not the woman herself, but a *picture* of her.

Nikki: Oh! The motion-picture projector — the projection room upstairs facing this garden! (*Ad libs*)

Inspector (*incredulously*): A *movie*, Ellery?

Ellery: Yes, dad, it was conceivable that someone had used the white summerhouse as a *screen* — projecting a film of a woman dressed in black from the upper window of Mr. Keith's projection-room *into* the summerhouse.

Keith: But Mr. Queen, I didn't —

Ellery: The theory didn't hold water. Because to get a clear motion picture on a screen outdoors — and Jurney said he saw the woman *clearly* — you need *darkness* . . . absence of light. But we know it was very *bright* out here that night — Jurney had said the moon was "brilliant," and that it was shining directly into the summerhouse! Under those conditions, if a motion-picture image *had* been thrown on the summerhouse, the image would have been very faint . . . not clear at all. (*Ad libs*) There was another reason, too. A motion picture image doesn't push aside a solid table any more than a ghost does. (*Pause*)

Nikki: Then what's left, Ellery?

Ellery: The only tenable possibility, Nikki — that the Woman in Black was a real, flesh-and-blood woman! (*Ad libs*)

Inspector: But Ellery, she *couldn't* have been flesh-and-blood! Jurney shot a bullet right through her without hurting her!

Ellery (*calmly*): Then obviously Jurney only *thought* he shot a bullet through her. Obviously no bullet *did* go through her.

Velie: But Mr. Queen, we got the solid slug from his bullet you dug outa the summerhouse back wall!

Ellery: We've got *a* slug from *somebody's* bullet, Sergeant, not from Jurney's. We've proved the woman *was* a real woman. Therefore no bullet went through her. Therefore the gun from which the bullet in the wall was fired — the gun Dr. Lansing gave me — was *not* the gun Jurney used that night. How do I know? Because Jurney pulled the trigger of *his* revolver *twice*!

Inspector: How does that tell you anything, Ellery?

Ellery: Let's see. According to Jurney's story, the first time he pulled the trigger there was only a click — he even remarked that it must be an "empty chamber." The second time he pulled the trigger there was actually the sound of a shot. So that accounted for *two* cartridge-chambers in the cylinder of the revolver — one for the click, one for the shot. Now what is the cartridge-capacity of the revolver Lansing gave me?

Nikki: It has six chambers. You said so yourself.

Ellery: Yes, that revolver has six chambers. Here it is. (*Spins cylinder of revolver*) And then, in our own apartment, I fired *another* shot into our sofa, to get a bullet-slug for ballistics comparison purposes. So after I fired *my* shot from this revolver, how many bullets could possibly be left if it was the same revolver Jurney had used?

Velie: One click . . . one shot by Jurney . . . one shot by you . . . three from six — There shoulda been *three* bullets at the most left in the gun, Mr. Queen.

Ellery: Ah, Sergeant! But after I'd fired my shot, how many bullets did I remark *were* left in the revolver Dr. Lansing gave me? *Four. Four* bullets left, not three. So the revolver Lansing gave me couldn't possibly have been the one Jurney used, and Lansing was deliberately lying! (*Murmur — bustle — fast*) Who could have *switched* revolvers? Only one person — the man who told me himself the gun hadn't been out of his possession or tampered with since Jurney had fired it — the criminal mind behind the whole amazing plot — the man who was trying literally to *frighten* poor Jurney to death — (*Scuffle off*) Dad — Velie — *stop Dr. Lansing!*

(*Music up . . . into ad libs, dishes . . . "Coffee?" etc.*)

Inspector: Ahhh, that's better. Well, son, clean up this business.

Velie: Yeah, there's still a lot I don't understand.

Nikki: You're not alone, Sergeant.

Ellery (*chuckling*): Well, the doctor was behind the plot on three counts. He had sole possession of the revolver and so was the only one who could have switched guns and given me a different one. Also, he was the only one who could have planted in the summerhouse wall, to be found by me later, a real bullet from the revolver he then turned over to me. And finally, Lansing was the only one with Jurney at the time Jurney first saw the Woman in Black — a real woman, mind you, whose very existence Lansing denied, almost sending poor Jurney into hysterics and certainly bringing on the next day's heart-attack.

Nikki: But Ellery, if Jurney didn't fire a shot from this revolver, what did happen?

Ellery: He must have fired a similar revolver loaded with *blank cartridges*, Nikki.

Velie: Blanks! Sure!

Ellery: Yes, Sergeant, Dr. Lansing had prepared a revolver filled with blanks just to cover the possibility that Jurney might want to take a shot at the "ghost" — he knew Jurney's reputation as a marksman and something of Jurney's doughty British character. Obviously the doctor wanted to protect the real-life Woman in Black from being killed or wounded by Jurney. Besides, the doctor knew that if Jurney saw a bullet apparently go through the woman it would help the illusion tremendously.

Inspector: But Ellery, Lansing couldn't possibly have murdered Jurney himself in the bedroom.

Velie: Sure, that sawbones was with me durin' the crime.

Ellery: Therefore this was the crime of *two* people, accomplices — the doctor and someone else. It had to be. Because Lansing was needed to work the ghost-trick from the revolver end, and a woman was needed to act the part of the ghost.

Nikki: So that's why you had that woman arrested —!

Ellery: Yes, Nikki. Since Jurney had to die, then he must have stood in the way of the doctor and the doctor's female accomplice. But who gained by Jurney's death? There was only one person in whose way Jurney stood — the only one who gained — Jurney's sole beneficiary under his will — his wife, Norma Jurney!

Inspector: So that's how you knew Mrs. Jurney's been the Woman in Black!

Velie: Love, huh? The doc and Jurney's wife . . . He figgered he'd marry her after Jurney was dead, and they'd live off Jurney's dough . . .

What some guys won't do to run their necks in the ol' marriage halter!

Nikki: And Mrs. Jurney, then, murdered her husband?

Ellery: Since Lansing couldn't physically have done it, yes, Nikki. And she was the obvious suspect for the actual murder, anyway. Occupied the very next room, therefore could easily have overheard Jurney talking to me on the phone . . . I don't think Lansing would have sanctioned murder as cold-blooded as that. His is a more subtle mind.

Inspector: According to her lights, she couldn't help it. She thought Jurney was going to spill her name, or Lansing's, and she just went for him with that water-bottle.

Nikki: Gosh! Ellery . . . what was that Oscar Wilde story Jurney was reading that gave him his inspiration?

Ellery: Oh, that. (*Chuckling*) Dad, please hand me *my* copy of *The Short Stories of Oscar Wilde* . . . Yes, on the top shelf. That's it.

Inspector: Here you are, son. (*Riffle pages*)

Ellery: Let me read you an excerpt from a short story by Wilde called "The Canterville Ghost," undoubtedly the story Jurney, obsessed with ghosts, was reading. The conversation is between Lord Canterville and Mr. Hiram B. Otis, the American Minister. Lord Canterville remarks: "It (meaning the Canterville Ghost) has been well-known for three centuries, since 1584, in fact, and *always makes its appearance before the death of any member of our family*." Mr. Otis replies dryly: "Well, *so does the family doctor*, for that matter!" (*Pause*)

Velie: Boy, I wish I'd 'a' said that!

Nikki: You will, Sergeant — you will! (*All laugh*)

(*Music up*)

*Manfred B. Lee and Frederic Dannay sympathized with the homeless and others
on the margins of society. As far as Ellery Queen was concerned, no one, no
matter how down-and-out should be "forgotten." "The Adventure of the Forgotten Men" was broadcast on April 7, 1940.*

The Adventure of the Forgotten Men

The Characters

Manhattan	One of the Homeless
Kansas	One of the Homeless
California	One of the Homeless
Dixie	One of the Homeless
Yank	One of the Homeless
Ellery Queen	The detective
Nikki Porter	His secretary
Inspector Queen	Of the News York Police
Sergeant Velie	Of the New York Police
Thaddeus V. Titus	Blustery plutocrat
Mac	Watchman

Setting: New York City, 1940

(*Music up . . . into crackling of wood fire . . . faint background of normal city
traffic . . . outdoors . . .*)

Manhattan (*New York intonation, but educated, young*): How are you making
   out with that fire, Kansas?
Kansas (*midwest farm accent*): Could use more wood, Manhattan.
Manhattan: Where's Dixie and California? I detailed them to find more
   wood!
Kansas: Here's ol' California now. What's that he's luggin'?
   (*Footsteps fading on*)
California (*fading on — old man*): Look what I found! (*Barrel on ground*)
   Say, this fire feels good. (*Rubs hands*) Mighty nippy fer April. Yes, sir,
   good an' nippy.
Kansas: A sugar-barrel! Give it here, California — we'll have a real fire
   in no time a-tall!
Manhattan (*sharp*): Kansas. Wait. This looks like a good strong barrel.

229

(*Thumps on barrel*) Yes, *good* and strong. You need a new table in your shack, California!

California (*chuckling*): Well, sir, it's a fac' that ol' fruit-crate I'm a -usin', she's on her last legs.

Manhattan: Take the sugar-barrel for a new table. And bring Kansas the old fruit-box to feed our supper-fire.

California (*fading with footsteps*): You're the boss man, Manhattan!

Kansas: Good ol' California . . . What that ol' berry-picker needs is some o' that hot corn bread an' fried ham my maw used to stuff down my craw back in Kansas. (*Softly*) On my farm . . . (*Harshly*) What's fer supper tonight, Manhattan?

Manhattan: Five mackerel-heads, soup-greens, four potatoes, and a loaf of bread must be about a week-old. Could be worse, Kansas.

Kansas (*passionately*): You mean if we wuz dead? Manhattan, when you die, they bury ye, an' yer troubles are over. But this livin' on a vacant lot, sleepin' worse'n hound-dogs in shacks built outa packin' cases an' mud, eatin' like pigs what decent folk throw away —

Manhattan (*low*): Stop it, Kansas.

Kansas: We ain't even dyin' quick! We're jest *teasin'* ourselves to death!

Manhattan (*low*): You know our rule, Kansas — no looking back. We've got to keep looking *ahead*, Kansas. When you look back you go to pieces . . .

Kansas (*heavily*): Yeah. Yeah, Manhattan. (*Steps fading on*) Atta boy, California. Give that fruit-crate here. (*Thud of box. Begins to break flimsy box up*)

California: Sorta sorry to see the ol' table go. Got so I was mighty fond o' that fruit-box. Yes, sir. (*Briskly*) What's on the menu, Manhattan? Meat, mebbe? I could go fer some nice, juicy meat. (*Fire up*)

Manhattan: Fish-stew, California.

California: Fish-stew? Well, now! Sounds interestin'. Where's the fish? (*Clunk of can hopelessly*) Oh . . . Yeah. Fer a minute there I thought . . . mebbe . . . a *whole* fish . . . (*Pail set down*)

Kansas: Dang it, we need more wood! This crate won't last no time! Where's that Dixie? (*Stirring of can*)

California: Here he comes. (*Calling*) Dixie! Shake a leg with that there firewood!

Manhattan (*sharply*): Is that the friendly cop with Dixie? No, it's a stranger! Watch yourselves, men. (*Sounds stop except for fire crackle*)

Dixie (*fading on steps of two — broad southern accent*): Hallelujah, boys! Ah located a gold-mine over on Secon' Avenoo. Real white man is bossin' a buildin' job there. Said ah could take all the wood Ah wanted. (*Dumps wood*) How's 'is?

Manhattan (*quietly*): Who's your friend, Dixie?

Dixie: Down-an'-outuh. He needs a flop real bad.

Kansas: Come closer to the fire, brother. (*Step or two in*)

Yank (*New England twang*): Thank ye kindly! (*Coughs*)

Manhattan (*sharply*): You'd like to come into our camp?

Yank: I'd take it real friendly o' you boys. My name is —

Manhattan: Never mind your name. Only people with a decent place to sleep, and decent food to eat, and decent work to work at, have a right to names! From now on you're Yank. Understand? *Yank.*

Yank: Yes, sir, I'm Yank. (*Coughs*) Anythin' ye say.

Manhattan: Yank, this isn't a camp of bums. We're four self-respecting Americans who've hit bottom. We won't panhandle. We won't take charity. We want work, and we *look* for work. We live here on this filthy vacant lot, beholden to no one, because when our luck changes we want to feel like free men. Understand?

Yank: No. I mean — yeah, sure, I jest want a flop.

Manhattan: We have a community of our own here, and laws to live by, and anyone who joins us has to abide by them. California, what's our motto?

California: All fer one, one fer all.

Manhattan: How do we live, Kansas?

Kansas: We share our food, our money, hard luck — everythin'!

Manhattan: What do we expect of one another, Dixie?

Dixie: A square deal an' trust every man to do the right thing.

Manhattan: Got all that, Yank?

Yank: I'd be proud if ye'd take me in. (*Coughs hard*)

Manhattan: Good! Meet Kansas — (*Ad libs*) California — (*Ad libs*) you know Dixie already, and I'm Manhattan . . . (*Bitter laugh*) the remains of a once promising architect. Got anything to contribute to the general fund, Yank?

Yank: All I got's the clo'es I'm wearin' an' thutty-seven cents cash. (*Chink of coins*)

Manhattan: Give the thirty-seven cents to Kansas — he's our treasurer. (*Yank coughs*) What's the matter — aren't you feeling well?

Yank (*coughing*): Bad cold. Seems like I cain't git rid of it.

Manhattan: Then you'll occupy my shack — that two-room "suite" over there — till you're better. It's the least draughty one on the lot.

Yank: Cain't rightly find words to thank you boys . . .

Manhattan: Forget it. Kansas! Take ten cents out of the treasury and buy some vegetables to add to the stew! (*Ad lib*) California! Add some water to that stew — it's burning down. (*Ad lib*) Dixie, don't waste that firewood! (*Ad lib*) Yank, you come with me, and I'll do something for your cold. This camp isn't Park Avenue, but it's made up of real men, and that's why it's got a future!

(*Music up . . . and into*)

Dixie (*whisper*): Manhattan!

Manhattan (*low*): What are you whispering about, Dixie?

Dixie: Manhattan, Ah made a bad mistake bringin' that Yank aroun' last night. He's a chiseler!

Manhattan (*sharply*): What d'ye mean, Dixie?

Dixie: Middle o' last night Ah hadda git up fer somethin', an' passed your shack where Yank slept. Manhattan, Ah saw that Yank countin' a roll o' bills! (*Pause*)

Manhattan (*grimly calling*): Kansas! California!

Kansas (*little off*): What's the matter, men?

Dixie: Yank. He's a yella dawg!

California (*fading on*): Yank's holdin' out on the camp?

Kansas (*fading on*): Why the ornery polecat.

Manhattan (*grimly*): Let's go! (*Determined steps on. They stop. Open door of shack*) Yank! Come on out of my shack! (*Cough fading on with wooden steps*)

Yank: Mornin', boys. (*Alarmed*) What's the matter? (*Steps of all on*) Where ye takin' me, so quiet?

Manhattan: To the council-fire. We're going to have a trial!

Yank: A trial? Ye mean ye have trials in this camp? Who . . . who's on trial? (*Fire crackling on*)

Manhattan: You are. (*Steps stop*) Yank, sit down on that rock.

Yank (*scared*): But . . . but I ain't done nothin'. I . . .

Kansas (*growling*): Siddown, chiseler! Go ahead, Manhattan.

Manhattan (*coldly*): Yank, last night you heard our laws. You were told that one law is — we share the little we've got. We asked you what you had, and you said only your clothes and thirty-seven cents. Right?

Yank: Yeah, an' I gave the thutty-seven cents to Kansas, like ye tol' me, Manhattan!

Dixie: Yella dawg, Ah seen you with m'own eyes durin' las' night countin' a roll o' bills in Manhattan's shack!

Yank (*yelling*): It's a lie! Dixie's lyin'!

Manhattan (*softly*): Have you any money on you now, Yank?

Yank: No! I give ye all I had!

Manhattan: Search him, men. (*Slight scuffle. Panting*)

California: No money, hey? Manhattan, here's four dollars in his pants pocket! (*Ad libs: "Four dollars!" "That coulda fed us meat fer a week!"*)

Yank (*whimpering*): Ye got no right manhandlin' me!

Manhattan: Boys, what's your verdict? Kansas? (*Kansas says: "Guilty."*) California? (*California Says: "Guilty."*) Dixie? (*Dixie says: "Guilty."*) Yank, you've been tried and found guilty of holding out on the camp!

Kansas (*grimly*): Pass the sentence, Manhattan!

Manhattan: As president of this court, Yank, I sentence you to banishment from our camp. (*Yank whimpering*) Kansas, give him back his four dollars, and his thirty-seven cents, too!

Kansas: Here's yer dirty dough. Now beat it.

Yank (*beginning to fade footsteps*): All right! But before I go . . . I got to get —

Dixie (*over quick steps on*): Hol' on there! Where yuh think yo're goin'?

Yank (*fading*): (*On mike*) To the shack! To the shack! (*Slight scuffle*) Leggo o' me! (*Steps out*)

California: Ye heard the sentence! Git outa our camp, chis'ler!

Yank: Please, fellers — I gotta go back to the shack — jest fer a couple o' minutes —

Manhattan: There's nothing in that shack that belongs to you. You came here with the clothes on your back. You'll leave the same way.

Kansas (*menacing*): Get goin'!

Yank (*fading over steps yelling*): I'll have the law on ye! I'll clean you sewer-rats out! I'll squeal to the cops! I'll . . .

California: Dirty skunk.

Dixie: Yella houn'-dawg.

Kansas: Ain't fit to associate with men.

Manhattan (*quietly*): Just the same — why did he want to go back to my shack? Men, something tells me we're going to have trouble with Mr. Chiseler Yank!

(*Music up into cab stopping at curb. Open car door . . .*)

Ellery: Here you are, driver. (*Coins. Close door. Drive off*) Come on, Nikki.

Nikki: Come on where? This is just an empty lot with some horrible little shacks on it, Ellery!

Ellery (*grimly*): Believe it or not, four decent Americans have been *living* in these shacks for some time!

Nikki: No wonder there's been a murder here! Which one of them was murdered, Ellery?

Ellery: Dad told me over the phone that the victim was a transient, a man they nicknamed Yank. He slept here just one night, about a week ago, and they kicked him out the next day for breaking one of their rules. And here, a whole week later, his body pops up in the same shack he occupied! (*Ad libs faintly on*)

Nikki: Look at that crowd! Who's that policeman waving to us? Ellery! It's Sergeant Velie — in a patrolman's uniform! Hi, Sergeant!

Velie (*fading on*): Shhh! Don't call me Sergeant, Miss Porter! I'm on a special job, masqueradin' as the cop on the beat.

Ellery: Really, Sergeant? Anything to do with this murder?

Velie: We dunno, Mr. Queen. A week or so ago the rich guy that owns that big office buildin' across the street from this lot — a Mr. Titus — had a valuable diamond ring hooked outa his pocket. Titus had just had it fixed or somethin' an' was takin' it back to his wife. There's been other pickpocket jobs reported from this neighborhood, so the Inspector detailed me to climb into a uniform an' scout aroun' on the beat.

Ellery: I'd like to see Dad.

Velie: O.K. This way. (*Steps on*)

Velie (*crowd ad libs fading up*): Come on, Folks — move on! This ain't Bank Night! (*Ad libs down in background*)

Inspector (*off*): Wait there, Manhattan! I want some more chin-chin with you! (*Steps stop with fade on*) Ah, Ellery, Nikki. (*Ad libs*) Velie! Why didn't you report that four men were camping on this lot? They're squatting on private property!

Velie (*embarrassed*): Well, Inspector . . . they're good guys . . . on'y down on their luck. They don't panhandle or hook stuff or nothin'. They're tryin' to hang on to their self-respect. I was just givin' 'em a break.

Nikki (*laughing*): Sergeant! You're a sentimentalist! (*Soberly*) But it was swell of you, just the same.

Inspector (*low*): You big lug . . . I'd have done the same myself. Well, long as you're here, son, you may as well look the body over. (*Steps on*) It's in the second "room" of the two holes in this shack — a bare cubbyhole — nothing in it at all! Come in. (*Opens shack door. Closes door — cutting ad libs and traffic*) There's Mr. Yank over there on the dirt floor — nice and dead.

Nikki (*faintly*): Oh! His head . . .

Ellery: Skull beaten in by some blunt instrument. (*Fading*) Let's have a look at the unfortunate Mr. Yank . . . (*Door opens — ad libs back off*)

Inspector: Manhattan, will you and the boys come in here. (*Steps fading on over threshold — door closes*)

Manhattan: I didn't sleep here last night, Inspector Queen. I got a job for the night driving a truck on a special run over to Jersey. I don't know how this man Yank happens to be found dead in my shack. We kicked him out a week ago and hasn't seen him since. (*Others agree*)

Inspector: I know, I know. Which one of you found his body?

California: I did. Californy, they call me. Yes, sir, I come 'long this mornin', peek in, an' there's this yella dawg layin' . . .

Inspector: None of you heard anything from this shack during the night? (*Ad libs: "No." "Not a blame thing."*)

Ellery (*off*): Dad!

Nikki: Ellery's found something, I think!

Inspector: What is it, Ellery?

Ellery (*fading on*): Look at the dead man's hands! (*Pause*)

Velie: Well . . . we're lookin'.

Nikki: They just look like awfully clean hands to *me*.

Inspector: What's the point, son?

Ellery: Index finger of right hand as long and well-developed as the middle finger!

Velie: A dip!

Inspector (*softly*): Yes, sir. That *is* a pickpocket's forefinger! (*Low*) Velie, now maybe we can identify the corpse. These men don't know who he was.

Nikki (*low — excited*): I'll bet this dead man was the pickpocket you've been searching for, Sergeant!

Velie: If he was, that plootocrat Titus who had his wife's di'mond ring swiped'll be happy! He's been raisin' cain.

Inspector: Check through the petty-thief files at the Rogues' Gallery, Velie. He's probably on file!

Velie (*fading, steps — wood*): I'm on my way. (*Opens shack door off, ad libs off*) Say, here's Mr. Titus an' Mac, the watchman of his office-buildin' across the street. Hi, Mac. Step right in, Mr. Titus. Inspector's inside . . . (*Fading*) I'm goin'!

Titus (*blustery plutocrat business man*): I'll step right in! I'll step on someone's neck! (*Close door*) As for you, Mac — you're fired! Understand? Fired!

Mac (*broad Irish brogue*): Aw, say, Mr. Titus — these bhoys wasn't doin' no harm — it's just an empty lot —

Inspector: Hold on! I'm Inspector Queen. Do you realize a man's lying dead here, Mr. Titus — murdered?

Titus: I realize that I own this lot, and that my watchman here has been permitting a gang of worthless bums to erect these filthy shacks, deface my property . . . !

Kansas (*growling*): Bums, are we? Why, you —

Dixie (*softly*): Hush yo' mouth, Kansas.

Manhattan: Mac, we're sorry. We didn't think you'd get into trouble. Mr. Titus, you mustn't discharge Mac. He needs his job —

Mac (*low*): 'Tain't your fault, Manhattan. 'Tis me usual Oirish luck . . .

California: 'Tis so our fault, Mac! Listen, Mister, we'll get off your property. Jest let Mac keep his job.

Dixie: 'Tain't fair takin' a job away from a hard-workin' man, Mistuh Titus.

Titus (*harshly*): You're trespassers! A lot of dirty, ragged, no-good, worthless . . . (*They all growl at him*)

Nikki (*indignantly*): Don't you dare talk to these poor men that way! Can't you see they're just down on their luck? They'd be clean and decent-looking if men like you would give them the honest work they're pleading for!

Ellery (*gently*): Nikki . . . Mr. Titus, I'm sure when you calm down you'll realize that these men deserve the encouragement and practical help of those of us in the community who are more fortunate. All they want is a chance to earn their living, and they're trying desperately to find jobs. Can't you —

Titus (*angrily*): They're on my property and they've got to get off! I'm a banker, not an employment agent. You there — you're an officer — arrest these men on a charge of vagrancy, trespassing, and defacing property!

Nikki: Don't you do it, Inspector.

Inspector (*coldly*): Nikki! Sorry, Mr. Titus. This is a murder-case, and these men are material witnesses. They stay until they're cleared.

Ellery: If I may suggest, Mr. Titus, you really shouldn't fire your watchman for risking his job to help out a few down-and-outers! It wouldn't look well in the newspapers, would it?

Titus (*cough*): Uh . . . yes, yes. I hadn't thought of that. I mean — perhaps I *have* been hasty . . . (*Brusquely*) Mac, go back to your job!

Mac (*eagerly*): Yes, sor! (*Steps of both fading*) And thank ye, sor . . . (*Door opens off*)

Titus (*off*): And — ah — Inspector. My wife's diamond ring. See that you get it back. Good day! (*Door closes off*)

Nikki: Good *riddance*!

Dixie: My, oh my — how Ah dislike that man.

Kansas: Well, I don't know but what I'd be pretty sore if I'd lost a di'mond ring.

California: What we gonna do when we gotta leave here?

Manhattan: Don't know where we'll be able to stay now.

Inspector: Ellery, come outside.

Ellery: Yes, dad. (*Steps of two on*)

Nikki (*fading*): You're Manhattan, aren't you? Perhaps Mr. Queen and I (*Door opens on*) can get some work for you and these other men. (*Door closes on*)

Inspector (*low*): Ellery, there's something peculiar about this case. This man Manhattan told me that all last week — after they kicked Yank out and Manhattan took back his shack — there's been a prowler!

Ellery: Prowler? In this shack? At night?

Inspector: Yep. Manhattan sleeps in the bigger of those two cubbyholes — adjoining that bare one where we found Yank's body — and every night last week someone kept sneaking into the little cubbyhole through the open window. Manhattan's a light sleeper, he says —

Ellery: He'd wake up and scare the prowler off?

Inspector: Yes, each time. Manhattan said that when they kicked Yank out of camp, the fellow wanted to go back into Manhattan's shack for a few minutes, but they wouldn't let him. Know what I think, Ellery? Yank *hid* something in this shack!

Ellery: Probably the diamond ring he stole from Titus. I'm convinced Yank was the pickpocket who's been operating in this neighborhood.

Inspector: So it was Yank who stole in here every night last week — trying to get back the diamond he'd had to leave!

Ellery: Not Yank, dad. A sneak-thief like Yank wouldn't risk it — not with Manhattan *in* the shack. I think Yank sent an emissary all week — a messenger!

Inspector: Messenger! What d'ye mean — messenger?

Ellery: I have an idea . . . but it would sound fantastic. Dad, if I'm right, that prowler will return, murder or no murder. So let's be here tonight to catch him!

(*Music up . . . into low ad libs . . .*)

Nikki (*whisper*): Crowded in this hovel this way . . . Ellery, nobody in his right mind would try to sneak in now!

Inspector (*low*): Nikki's right, son. It's a bum steer.

Ellery (*low*): Perhaps. But I think not — (*Low whistle off*)

Nikki: There's Sergeant Velie's signal from outside!

Ellery: Someone *is* coming! Quiet! (*Pause. Stealthy sounds as if animal crawling through window*) Now! Dad! Nikki! Turn those flashlights on him!

Inspector: Velie! Block that window from outside! You there — halt! (*Clicks. Pause, police dog growls savagely*)

Nikki (*screaming*): It's a *dog* — a *police dog*!

Inspector: Ellery! Look out! (*Dog barks angrily*)

Ellery: I thought so! Easy now, old chap . . . no one wants to hurt you . . . (*Dog growls and barks*)

Velie (*off*): No one wants to hurt *him*? That's a hot one! Wait till I climb through this window . . . (*Feet landing on floor*) Nice doggie . . . (*Furious bark*) Uh-uh . . . (*Ad libs trying to quiet dog. Door opens. Ad libs of four outcasts and Mac on: "Where'd the police dog come from?" "Watch it — he looks dangerous!" Etc.*)

Inspector: You men — keep away!

Ellery: Nikki — get back!

Nikki: I'm back as far as this wall will let me, Mr. Queen!

Manhattan: Outside, boys. Mac, you'd better get back on your watchman job across the street. If old man Titus finds out you've been here again . . .

Mac: But Oi heard all that barkin' . . . where's the dawg come from? (*Barks stop. But continue low growls*)

Inspector: He just wants us to keep our distance. So this is the prowler who's been paying you a visit every night, Manhattan! (*Chuckles*) Ever see him before?

Manhattan: No, Inspector. (*Others chime in*)

Ellery: Quiet, old boy, quiet. I can barely make out from here three initials on his collar. S . . . J . . . B . . .

Velie: S.J.B.? Say, that fits . . . We identified Yank at the Gallery tonight . . . His real name was Samuel J. Bullock! S.J.B. !

Inspector: This was Yank's dog, all right! I see it all now. Yank got suspicious that the heat was on, and felt he ought to hide out for a while. That's why he maneuvered to get into this camp — and he ditched his dog as too dangerous an identification!

Ellery: Yes, but Mr. Dog was faithful, and hung around, and when Yank was evicted from the camp the dog rejoined his master. Then all week Yank, lacking the nerve to come back himself for what he'd left in the shack, sent the dog — police-dog breed, highly intelligent, trained by a thieving master to retrieve loot . . . Here, boy. We don't mean any harm . . . (*Growl, snap of jaws*)

Nikki: Ellery! He almost bit your hand off! Look out!

Ellery: Easy, boy . . . (*More growls, another snap*)

Velie: Mr. Queen, watch yourself! Don't try to pet him!

Nikki: He's trying to bite your hand, Ellery!

Ellery: Got to get this fellow's confidence, Nikki! Yank kept sending the dog for the diamond ring, so the dog must know where it's hidden!

Inspector: Ellery, at least put a glove on — he's got sharp fangs!

Manhattan: Mac, give Mr. Queen those gloves you're wearing! (*Steps fade in — dog growls*)

Mac: Easy boy. Here y'are, sor.

Ellery: Thanks, Mac. (*As if putting gloves on*) There! Now, old fellow . . . what say you and I get a little closer, eh?

Nikki: Ellery — not *too* close!

Ellery: Have to chance it, Nikki . . . Can't we be friends? I've always had a soft spot for dogs, old boy. (*Whimper*)

Velie (*awed*): He's lettin' Mr. Queen pat his head!

Ellery: Good dog! What's your name, eh? (*Low friendly bark*) May be on your collar. Let's see . . . Ah! Buck, all right Buck, live up to your bread. Where's that diamond ring hidden? Look for it, Buck. Find it! (*Low*) Keep back, you people . . . Find it, Buck!

Inspector: Well, I'll be —! He's obeying orders!

Ellery: Where is it, Buck? Here — *in* the floor? Of course! Dig, Buck! (*Dog scraping up dirt*)

Nikki: He *is* digging — at that spot in the dirt floor that's all loose and soft!

Inspector: Looks as if that one spot was recently dug up.

Ellery: That's the boy, Buck! Look! He's dug up a small box!

Nikki: He wants to carry it out of the shack!

Ellery: No, you don't, Buck. Let's have it. (*Growl*) Now, now, let's — have — it . . . Good dog! Let's see Mr. Titus' diamond ring. (*Snap of case*)

Nikki: Empty! The ring's not in the case!

Inspector: Aaaah. Might have known. That turned-up earth. Velie, get Moneybags Titus down here right away!

Velie: It'll be a pleasure to give him the bad news!

(*Music up . . . into door of shack closing . . .*)

Titus (*fading on*): (*Over steps*) Well? Well? What is it now?

Inspector: Mr. Titus, can you identify the case your diamond ring came in? Is this it?

Titus: Yes! (*Snap of case*) But it's empty! Where's my ring? That ring was worth five thousand dollars! What sort of policemen are you? Finding the *box*! What good's the box? Find the ring!

Ellery (*softly*): You'd like to have your ring back, Mr. Titus?

Titus: Like to have it back! What are you, an imbecile? Of course I'd like to have it back! It's a family heirloom — money couldn't buy it! I'll give a liberal reward —

Ellery (*soft*): Ah. You'd give a liberal reward. Well, Mr. Titus, I'll get your ring back for you if you'll reward me by helping these four men — and others like them — to get on their feet again!

Titus: What's that? What do you mean, sir?

Nikki: I know what he means! You've got an empty lot here, Mr. Titus — it's no good to you or anybody else — why don't you do something with it?

Ellery (*chuckling*): Exactly my thought, Nikki.

Titus: Preposterous! I suppose *you* can tell me what to do with it.

Ellery: If you'll permit me, Mr. Titus, I can. This lot would make an ideal site for a poor people's park, or a children's playground. The gentleman who calls himself Manhattan was, I understand, an architect. Let Manhattan design your civic project. The other men are only too eager to work. They'll help Manhattan. There are hundreds of other unfortunates just as anxious to earn an honest living. Is it a trade?

Titus (*harrrumphing*): Hmmmm! Yes . . . constructive suggestion. Most constructive. Playground, eh? "The Thaddeus V. Titus Playground." Yes . . . not a bad thought. (*Steps fading — door opens off*) You men! You want jobs, eh? (*Ad libs eagerly off*) Willing to work, are you?

Kansas (*off*): Mister, you *show* us some work! ·

California: I'd even go back to pickin' berries!

Dixie: Berries, cotton, or anythin', suh.

Manhattan (*quietly*): Try us, sir.

Titus: Well, here's the thought I had. (*Fading*) You see, I was thinking
    I'd put up a playground . . . (*Closes door*)

Nikki: *He* was thinking!

Velie: Not so loud, Miss Porter! He's bein' a good citizen now, but maybe
    it didn't altogether take yet!

Inspector: Wait-a-minute! Ellery, you promised Titus if he'd employ
    these men, you'd get his diamond ring back! How?

Velie: Say . . . if you know who has the diamond ring, Mr. Queen, then
    you know who swiped it from Yank —

Nikki: And if you know who stole the ring from Yank, you know who
    murdered Yank!

Ellery (*chuckling*): Yes, children, I know who murdered Yank!

(*Music up . . .*)

Challenge to the Listener

"And there," Ellery Queen told the jury and the radio audience, "you
have the mystery. What is your solution?"

(*Music up . . .*)

Ellery: Dad, reconstruct what happened in Manhattan's shack on the
    night Yank was murdered.

Inspector: Well, the empty box the dog dug up, and the recently-turned
    earth at that spot, tell the story. Yank sent his trained dog Buck here,
    night after night, to retrieve the box he'd buried in the dirt floor.
    Each time Buck came back without the box — Manhattan scared
    him off. So last night, while Manhattan was out on a job, Yank came
    here himself, dug up the box, took the diamond ring, threw the empty
    box back in the hole, and put the earth back again, but carelessly. It
    must have been Yank, because he was the thief, and only the thief
    would know where he'd buried his loot.

Ellery: Exactly. But Yank was murdered in this very room, and the
    diamond is gone. Conclusion: When Yank dug up the diamond,
    someone was watching him through the window! That person came
    in here and murdered Yank for the diamond!

Velie: But we know all that, Mr. Queen. Question is: Who?

Ellery: Nikki, remember you remarked when I examined Yank's body
    that his hands were "awfully clean"?

Nikki: Well, they were. What of it?

Ellery: The floor of the shack is earth. We've deduced that Yank *dug* in that earth to retrieve the hidden diamond. *How* had he dug? With his bare hands? No, then we'd have found a corpse with *dirty* hands, not clean. With some tool? Possibly, but as dad remarked at the time, the room where the diamond was buried is absolutely bare. One of two possibilities, then: Either Yank dug in the earth floor with some tool which the murderer took away with him after his crime, or else Yank dug with his hands protected by gloves, and the *gloves* were taken away by the murderer. In either case, to account for Yank's clean hands when we know he dug in dirt, the murderer took away either a digging tool *or* a pair of gloves belonging to Yank.

Velie: Gloves! Say —

Inspector: Wait a minute, Velie! Go on, son.

Ellery: Now. Remember what happened when I first approached the dog? Buck made two successive attempts *to bite my hand*. But when I tried a third time — *with my hands covered by gloves* — the dog immediately grew friendly! What was the sudden change in me that won his trust? Only the fact that I'd put on a pair of gloves. Then it was the *gloves* that won Buck's confidence. Why? Obviously, *because the dog knew those gloves and trusted them*. Conclusion: Buck, a police dog, a one-man breed, *smelled his master's scent in those gloves!* Those gloves had belonged to Buck's master!

Nikki: And Buck's master had been Yank!

Ellery: Yes, Yank. So we now know Yank owned a pair of gloves. Therefore, we also know what it was the murderer took from Yank's body besides the stolen diamond ring — it wasn't a digging tool he took, but Yank's gloves!

Nikki: But why did he take the dead man's gloves at all?

Inspector: That's easy, Nikki. If the gloves were found on the dead man's hands, filthy with earth, the police would know Yank had been digging for something before he was murdered. And the killer was afraid that if the police identified Yank as the thief who stole Titus' diamond ring, we'd guess Yank had been killed *for* the ring.

Ellery: Yes, by taking the gloves away, the murderer was trying to conceal his motive — his motive and the fact that he now had Titus' ring. So it's a simple case. Whoever had possession of Yank's gloves was Yank's murderer. Who stupidly kept possession of Yank's gloves? — the gloves Buck had confidence in? — From whom did I *borrow* those gloves in order to pet Buck?

Velie: *The watchman of Titus' buildin' across the street!*

Nikki: *That man they call Mac! You borrowed the gloves from Mac!*

Ellery: Yes, my love. So dad, if you'll search Mac's person and rooms and effects, you'll find the diamond ring he murdered Yank for. Then we can return the ring to Mr. Titus, and Mr. Titus will have to keep his end of the bargain we made — to put those four forgotten men back on the road to work and faith in the future!

(*Music up*)

Ellery Queen's case broadcast on May 5, 1940, was another impossible crime. The announcer (Bert Parks) told the audience that "Ellery Queen again gives you a chance to match wits with him, as he relates a new story of a crime he alone unraveled."

The Adventure of the Man Who Could Double the Size of Diamonds

The Characters

Professor Lazarus	Explorer into hidden secrets
Mr. Kenyon	American investor
Mynheer Van Hooten	Dutch investor
Mr. Bryce	British investor
Monsieur Masset	French investor
Wolfe	Kenyon's servant
Ellery Queen	The detective
Nikki Porter	His secretary
Inspector Queen	Of the New York Police
Sergeant Velie	Of the New York Police
Dr. Cook	A physician

Setting: New York City, 1940

(*Music up and fade*)

Lazarus: It may seem fantastic to you, but I can double the size of diamonds. (*Pause*)

Kenyon (*roars with laughter*)

Lazarus: Why are you laughing, Mr. Kenyon?

Kenyon (*stops . . . coughs*): Hrrm! You're an inventor, you say, Professor Lazarus?

Lazarus: Inventor, chemist, physicist, explorer into the hidden secrets of Nature. Mr. Kenyon, I'm told you're one of the leading diamond experts on Maiden Lane.

Kenyon (*gravely*): Thank you, Professor. And you — uh — say you can *manufacture* diamonds? (*Suppresses a laugh*)

Lazarus (*excited*): Yes, Mr. Kenyon. My new process will revolutionize

243

the diamond industry — change the financial structure of the world!

Kenyon: Financial structure of the wor —? (*Laughing, then as if wiping tears away*) Sorry, Professor Lazarus . . . I . . . I've got a tickle.

Lazarus (*offended*): They laughed at Leeuwenhoek and Pasteur and Galileo. Well, laugh! Let 'em all laugh! (*Mutters*) They always laugh at a genius . . .

Kenyon (*sharply*): See here, man. You expect me to believe you've discovered a process by which you can manufacture diamonds at a cost that's not prohibitive? Fairy tales!

Lazarus: Mr. Kenyon, give me a perfect diamond, and in seven days I'll return it to you *twice as large*!

Kenyon: The man who could double the size of diamonds! (*Laughs*)

Lazarus (*excited*): *Don't* laugh at me! I've done it, I tell you!

Kenyon (*mock gravity*): Sort of scientific miracle, eh?

Lazarus: Scientific fact! I can double the size and weight of any natural diamond! I've found a way to make diamonds *grow*.

Kenyon (*amazed*): I believe you're really serious.

Lazarus: Serious! I've devoted my whole life to it! (*Earnestly*) Mr. Kenyon, my life's savings have gone into perfecting the formula and developing the apparatus. I need financial backing and perfect diamonds to work with.

Kenyon (*thoughtfully*): Perhaps I've been hasty, Professor, but — no, it's too ridiculous.

Lazarus: I don't blame you for being skeptical, Mr. Kenyon. You're a business man. So I don't expect you to take me on faith.

Kenyon (*surprised*): You mean you're actually prepared to demonstrate your process, Professor?

Lazarus: Of course, Mr. Kenyon!

Kenyon: *Under any conditions I may impose on you?*

Lazarus: Absolutely any conditions!

Kenyon (*very serious — abrupt*): Professor Lazarus, be back here tomorrow!

(*Music up . . . into ad libs of slight argument . . .*)

Van Hooten (*Dutch accent*): And I say it is all poppycock!

Kenyon: It won't hurt to look, will it, Van Hooten?

Bryce (*British accent*): Kenyon's right, Van Hooten. You've been stuck away in that Amsterdam diamond-exchange of yours so long you've grown barnacles. Take a chance, old boy!

Van Hooten: All right, I take a chance, Mr. Bryce. Doubling the size of diamonds! (*Short laugh*) I don't know whether it is to laugh, or to cry.

Kenyon: Fine! Then you're with us, too, Bryce?

Bryce (*chuckling*): Hard to convince, but open to proof. The true British spirit, Kenyon. Yes, I'm with you and Van Hooten. How about you, Monsieur Masset?

Masset (*French accent*): I am thinking.

Van Hooten (*snort*): Masset is thinking! Do not breathe.

Kenyon: We really need you in this little syndicate we're forming, Masset. As a lapidary you've no equal. You're better qualified than any of us to detect a possible fraud.

Masset: Monsieur Kenyon, that is a bouquet I cannot resist smelling! Gentlemen, I, Masset enters the syndicate! (*All laugh a little*)

Van Hooten: But to double the size of diamonds! This professor is a fraud. He must be.

Bryce: I know it sounds like a fantastic idea . . .

Masset (*thoughtfully*): *Qui sait?* In the eighteenth century le comte Saint-Germain proved to King Louis the Fifteen that not only could he remove flaws from diamonds but actually increase the size of pearls!

Van Hooten (*scoffing*): A legend, Masset! Folklore!

Bryce: Well, we'll soon see. Personally, I think the man's a quack, Kenyon.

Kenyon: Judge for yourselves. Now we're all agreed on our conditions, gentlemen? (*Ad libs of assent interrupted by door opening off*) Yes, Wolfe? He's here?

Wolfe (*off*): Yes, Mr. Kenyon. It's Professor Lazarus.

Kenyon: Send him in. And remember, Wolfe — no interruptions!

Wolfe (*off*): Yes, Mr. Kenyon. This way, Professor Lazarus.

Lazarus (*off*): Thank you, thank you! (*Door closes*)

Kenyon: Come in, Professor! I want you to meet some business friends of mine. We've decided to form a little syndicate . . . just in case. Mynheer Van Hooten, the Amsterdam diamond merchant — Mr. Bryce, the London diamond-dealer — Monsieur Masset, the famous lapidary.

Lazarus: A syndicate, eh? Excellent, excellent. Delighted!

Van Hooten: Don't be too delighted, Professor Lazarus. We are a court of examination — no more!

Bryce: Frankly, Professor, we don't know whether you're the genius you claim to be, or a lunatic.

Masset: You will find us hard, Professor Lazarus. We do not believe you. But on the million-to-one chance that you have really stumbled on a new scientific principle . . .

Kenyon: In a word, we're willing to be shown.

Van Hooten: Providing, of course, that the conditions under which the experiment is conducted protect the syndicate against any possibility of loss, Mynheer!

Lazarus: Naturally, naturally, Mr. Van Hooten. You would be fools not to protect yourselves!

Kenyon: All right, then. Professor, do you see the steel safe-door in that wall of my office?

Lazarus: Yes, Mr. Kenyon?

Bryce: That safe-door leads into Mr. Kenyon's strong-room. The strong-room is completely lined with steel and has only one means of entrance and exit — the burglar-proof safe-door you see there.

Masset: In that strong-room, *mon professeur*, you will *try* to double the size of diamonds!

Lazarus: I understand. But air — I'll need air to breathe —

Kenyon: My strong-room is air-conditioned. Incidentally, I'm having the door-combination changed. And only Van Hooten, Bryce, Masset and I will know the new combination!

Van Hooten: You comprehend, Professor? Not you! You will be admitted by one of us into the strong-room each morning, and released each night!

Lazarus: Very fair, very fair, gentlemen. But may I make one condition? No one must disturb my work. I refuse to allow anyone to enter that strong-room the entire week of my experiment — either while I'm working there during the day, or while it's locked up for the night!

Van Hooten (*suspiciously*): Ah! And why is that, Professor?

Lazarus: Obviously I must protect *myself*. I can't afford to let anyone learn the secret of my process! (*Ad libs: "That's fair," "of course," etc.*)

Masset: Agreed, then. But we warn you, *monsieur le professeur*! That room will be guarded as if it were the Bank of France!

Bryce: We should have experienced searchers to see that — (*Coughs*) — the Professor doesn't carry off our diamonds some night after his day's work.

Kenyon: How about four detectives from Police Headquarters? Two to stand guard outside the strong-room all day, two all night.

Van Hooten: And each night when you leave the strong-room, Lazarus, you will be searched from head to foot!

Bryce (*smoothly*): And to leave utterly nothing to chance, gentlemen — I suggest we have a trustworthy physician in attendance to — ah — complete the nightly search. (*Enthusiastic agreement from others*)

Kenyon (*dryly*): You see, Professor, we're taking no chances. Since we're each lending you a valuable diamond to experiment on, take my word for it — you won't get the slightest opportunity to steal them!

Lazarus: Steal! I'm a scientist, not a thief! Very well, we start tomorrow when I bring my apparatus in. But remember: Absolute secrecy! If the world learned of what we can do, the value of diamonds would be ruined forever! (*Ad libs*) Tomorrow each of you have a perfect diamond for me, in Mr. Kenyon's office, and I promise you — in one week four diamonds will have grown to twice their present size! (*Laughs*) Like the Count of Monte Cristo — in one week you'll be able to cry: The world is mine!

(*Music up . . . into Kenyon's ending story . . .*)

Kenyon: . . . and then, Mr. Queen, Professor Lazarus went to work in my strong-room at the office.

Ellery (*thoughtfully*): Amazing. Amazing story, Mr. Kenyon.

Inspector: So that's why you asked for the services of four of my detectives a week ago, Mr. Kenyon! (*Chuckles*) Weren't you gentlemen a little inebriated when Lazarus turned on his highfalutin' talk?

Nikki: Why, it's fantastic! An Arabian Nights' story!

Ellery: Why did you bring your friend Dr. Cook with you, Mr. Kenyon? No offense, Doctor; just curiosity.

Kenyon: Dr. Cook is the physician who's been examining Lazarus every night when he quits the strong-room.

Dr. Cook (*straight — curt, clipped*): Would have refused anyone but Kenyon, Mr. Queen. Old friends. But of all the nonsense! Wait till you hear the end of this!

Kenyon: In the week that's passed since the Professor began his mysterious work in my strong-room, we've taken every precaution against fraud, Mr. Queen. Well, this afternoon at five we let the professor out, as usual. Seventh day — his time was up. "Well?" we demanded. "Show us our diamonds, twice as large!" The Professor was nervous . . .

Inspector: Doubling the size of diamonds! (*Chuckling*)

Nikki: Of course he failed, Mr. Kenyon?

Ellery: And asked for more time? That would be the natural development.

Kenyon: Exactly what happened! Well, the detectives and we five men — we searched him — Dr. Cook here examined him with special care — and then, satisfied the diamonds weren't on him, we let him go for the night.

Dr. Cook: And the syndicate went into a huddle. (*Chuckles*)

Kenyon: After an argument, we decided to extend the Professor's time a few days. The others left, I went out for dinner . . . and started to worry. Suppose something *was* wrong! I'd got the other three into this; they'd contributed valuable diamonds as well as I . . . Well, I ran back to my office. The two detectives on night-duty let me in — I unlocked the safe-door of the strong-room and went in . . .

Inspector (*sharply*): Don't tell me . . .

Nikki: The four diamonds you gave Lazarus to work on —

Ellery: They were gone from the strong-room, Mr. Kenyon?

Kenyon (*despairing*): Vanished! Not a sign of them! I turned that strong-room upside down! Tore his apparatus to pieces! Then I called the detectives in. They thought I was crazy, till they saw for themselves.

Ellery: Seems simple enough, Mr. Kenyon. Professor Lazarus managed to smuggle the diamonds out with him during the past week, perhaps taking one diamond at a time, and your nightly searches just didn't turn up his hiding-place.

Kenyon: Impossible, Mr. Queen! We didn't overlook even the most far-fetched hiding-place! That's why I stopped to pick up Dr. Cook on my way to see you tonight, after I left messages for Van Hooten, Bryce, and Masset that the diamonds were gone.

Dr. Cook: I give you my word, Mr. Queen — I can't imagine where the fellow could have been hiding those diamonds when he took them out.

Ellery: How about his clothing?

Kenyon: We examined every stitch on his body every night — not only we four, but the detectives, too!

Inspector: The men I put on this job, Ellery, wouldn't slip up on a body-search. They're perfectly reliable.

Nikki: I know! Lazarus must have a hump on his back — a false hump! Or else he's got a hollow wooden leg, or something!

Dr. Cook: No hump, false limb, finger . . . nothing like that.

Ellery: How about his hair, Doctor? Has he a beard?

Cook: No beard, and the man's as bald as an eagle.

Ellery: His mouth, Doctor. Did you examine him there?

Cook: Lazarus has no teeth of his own. He uses dental plates, which I examined carefully every night. No cavities of any kind. Nor could he have taken the diamonds out in his ears or nasal openings.

Nikki: A glass eye! I'll bet that's it!

Dr. Cook: No, Miss Porter. He has two very sound eyes.

Ellery: Possibly he carried some *object* out of the strong-room in which a diamond might have been concealed. A watch — cigaret case —

Inspector: Wallet? Tobacco pouch? A finger ring?

Kenyon: No, Inspector — Those were examined.

Nikki: Maybe a cane! A walking-stick that's hollow!

Kenyon (*sighing*): The Professor has no stick. I tell you we examined everything. Even his pen and pencil.

Ellery: Mr. Kenyon, is there a drain or water-tap in the strong-room?

Kenyon: No opening of any kind except the air-conditioning vent and intake — and they were thoroughly searched.

Nikki: Then couldn't he have hidden the diamonds *inside* of him, Dr. Cook?

Ellery (*chuckling*): Excellent question, Nikki! Could he?

Dr. Cook: I performed every conceivable test that would be conclusive, Mr. Queen — gastroscope, otoscope, nasal speculum, and so on. If X-Ray or fluoroscope would have helped, I'd have used those, too, because Mr. Kenyon and his associates told me to leave absolutely nothing to chance. I give you my word as a medical man, Mr. Queen — Professor Lazarus did *not* hide those four diamonds anywhere *in* his body!

Ellery: It appears we're dealing with the most ingenious thief of modern times. We'll have to see your Professor Lazarus . . . (*Phone rings*)

Nikki: I'll answer it, Inspector.

Inspector: No, I'll take it, Nikki. Probably Headquarters, with my men's report of the theft . . .

Ellery (*fade*): Fascinating problem, gentlemen! (*Pick up phone, on*)

Inspector: Hello! Who?

Velie (*filtered*): This is Velie, Inspector!

Inspector: Yes, Velie?

Velie (*filtered*): I'm calling from downtown.

Inspector: Why aren't you home with your wife?

Velie (*filtered*): I'm married to my job, ain't I? Inspector, you'll have to buzz down here. A murder.

Inspector: Why do they always pick out a man's bedtime! Well, well, Velie. Where is it?

Velie (*filtered*): Some crummy hotel — the Jolly, or Jelly, or somepin', on East Twenty-fourth. Guy was found dead in his room by a chambermaid. Somebody's conked him.

Inspector: I'll be right down. Identify the corpse yet, Velie?

Velie (*filtered*): Oh, sure. Some nut inventor, from the papers in his room . . .

Inspector: Nut invent —! (*Hoarsely*) Velie! What was his name?

Velie (*filtered*): Aw, you wouldn't know him, Inspector. A phony professor. Let's see, now. Yeah . . . Lazarus — Professor Lazarus!

(*Music up . . . siren-chase theme . . . into hubbub . . .*)

Velie (*over hubbub*): Say, Whitey! Inspector's yellin' for that fingerprint report! (*Ad lib*) What? That's nice! The old man'll love that! . . . Joe! Ain't you through with the corpse? Get pictures of the struggle — bloody lamp, overturned chairs, torn clo'es . . . man, what a brawl this musta been!

Inspector (*calling*): Velie! Where's Prouty? . . . Quiet, men!

Velie (*bellowing*): Qui-et, you hyenas! (*Hubbub down*) Doc Prouty's gone already, Inspector. Nothin' sensational, he says. Guy just died from those blows on the head while he was fightin' with his killer. Happened tonight.

Inspector: That's *very* helpful! Ellery, did you see this?

Ellery (*absently*): What, dad? Oh, sorry.

Nikki: Ellery Queen! You don't seem the least bit interested! What is it, Inspector?

Inspector: Look.

Nikki: Oh, what a *beautiful* diamond.

Velie: My old woman'd give her right eye for a sparkler like that. Where'd you find it, Inspector?

Inspector: In Lazarus' right hand. Mr. Kenyon!

Velie: Kenyon! Over here, Mr. Kenyon!

Kenyon (*fading on — very upset*): Oh! This is simply awful. I hope you won't keep me any longer than you have to.

Ellery (*low*): Let's see the diamond, dad . . . Hmm . . .

Inspector: Kenyon, do you recognize this diamond? (*Pause*)

Kenyon: It's Bryce's! The diamond Bryce contributed to the syndicate for the Professor's experiment!

Inspector: That settles it. Only Van Hooten, Bryce, Masset, and Kenyon knew about Lazarus' experiment — even the detectives on day and night duty didn't know what was going on!

Velie: So it musta been one of the syndicate that bumped off the dead con man.

Kenyon: One of *us*? Don't be —! (*Thoughtfully*) One of *us*?

Inspector: One of you four men came to the professor's hotel room tonight, caught him with the stolen diamonds, and tried to take them away. Lazarus fought back and was beaten to death with this heavy metal table lamp. Murderer grabbed the diamonds and beat it.

Nikki: But in the excitement he overlooked one of the diamonds — the one in the dead man's hand —

Velie: Or maybe he thought he'd taken all four and didn't find out it was only three till he got away — then he was scared to come back.

Nikki: But the big question is: Which of the four members of the syndicate killed Professor Lazarus?

Inspector: What d'ye think, Ellery?

Ellery (*thoughtfully*): Three secrets may have died with Lazarus. First, the secret of his diamond-doubling process — whose authenticity I doubt. Second, the secret of his murderer's identity — in this well-lighted room, after a considerable struggle, Lazarus must certainly have recognized his assailant. And third, the secret of how Lazarus managed to spirit those diamonds out of Kenyon's strong-room — past the suspicious eyes and searching hands of the four owners of the diamonds, two experienced detectives, and a medical doctor!

Nikki: It's enough to make you dizzy. I can't *imagine*!

Ellery: At the moment, neither can I, Nikki. I confess — I'd rather know how Lazarus accomplished the thefts than who murdered him!
Velie: You would.
Inspector: Velie!
Velie (*hastily*): Yeah, Inspector?
Inspector: Round up Van Hooten, Bryce, and that French lap — lap — whatever he is! — Masset. Get 'em down here on the double and we'll go over 'em — lightly!
Velie (*fading*): Lemme slap on the hot towel . . .!
Inspector: Ellery, *you* can play around with the mystery of how Professor Lazarus stole those diamonds — *I* want to know who beat him to death!

(*Music up . . . into grilling ad libs . . . Bryce saying: "Yes, that is my diamond, Inspector." Others demanding to get their property back . . . Masset — "yes and where is mine?"*)

Inspector: Murderer's got 'em! I want to know where you men were tonight. Bryce?
Bryce (*nervous*): I was out strolling . . . returned to my hotel, found Kenyon's message that the diamonds had been stolen . . . thought it was a — a joke . . .
Inspector: Mynheer Van Hooten? You were in the Park writing poetry, I suppose?
Van Hooten (*yelling*): I go back to my New York office! Later I go back to my hotel — find Kenyon's message —
Inspector (*softly*): So you've no alibi, either. How about you, Monsieur Masset?
Masset: I, too, *Monsieur l'inspecteur* — I return to my office on Maiden Lane. And I, too — I later find Monsieur Kenyon's message about the theft of the diamonds . . .
Velie: For a bunch of business men, these guys were sure push-overs for that con-man Lazarus!
Nikki: Yes, Sergeant, and the Professor would have got away with it, too, if one of them hadn't gone to his hotel, killed him — and stolen the diamonds himself!
Ellery (*gently*): Hush, Nikki. Let dad handle this.
Nikki (*indignant*): I know, Ellery, but such *deceit*, such — such bloodthirstiness! They're all trying to look so innocent!
Van Hooten: I want back my diamond! Get it back, I say!
Masset (*bitterly*): Mine, too. Bryce, you are fortunate. Your diamond was left behind. But mine —
Bryce: But how did he *do* it? I can't understand it!

Inspector: There's a lot of things I can't understand! Hold it, you four. Ellery, come here a minute. (*Pause*)

Ellery (*low — absent*): Yes, dad?

Inspector: Any ideas?

Ellery: Dad, I'm baffled. Completely! It's an impossible crime!

Inspector: What's impossible about it? No tricks to *this* murder. All we have to do is find the murderer —

Ellery: I don't mean the murder, dad — I mean Lazarus' theft of the diamonds from Kenyon's strong-room! I shan't sleep till I find out how he smuggled them past seven searchers!

Inspector: Hang it, son! This is a murder-case, not a puzzle!

Ellery: This time *you* handle the murder, dad — I'll take the puzzle. (*Thoughtfully*) I've *got* to figure out how the Professor did it!

(*Music up . . .*)

Velie: Blank wall, that's what it is, Inspector.

Inspector: And your check of the alibis, Velie?

Velie: Whaddaya mean alibis? Van Hooten an' Masset claimin' they were workin' in Maiden Lane . . . but no one *saw* them! Bryce takin' a walk all by his lonely . . . (*Door opens off*) Oh — good mornin', Miss Porter. (*Door closes*)

Inspector (*glumly*): Morning, Nikki.

Nikki (*fading on*): *Good* morning! My, such gloomy faces. No luck on the murder, Inspector Queen?

Inspector (*glumly*): I guess luck will be our only hope of solving it at that, Nikki. Ellery's no help.

Nikki: He *has* been acting remote. Where is he this morning?

Velie: Aw, the Master-Mind's in his bedroom poundin' the floor like an expectant papa.

Inspector: Ellery didn't sleep a wink all night, Nikki.

Velie: If y'ask me, for once in his life the Maestro's stumped. (*Door opens off*) Aha! He enters!

Ellery (*off — brisk*): Morning, everybody!

Inspector: Come on, son — have some breakfast. You must be all tuckered out after last night.

Velie: Forget it, Mr. Queen. You can't hit the jackpot every time. (*Ellery chuckles*)

Nikki: Ellery Queen! You're grinning! Inspector, Sergeant — he *knows* something! (*Ad libs*)

Ellery (*on mike*): Certainly I know something. I've spent ten sleepless hours figuring it out!

Nikki: And just what is it you've been puzzling over, Mr. Queen?

Ellery: How Lazarus managed to smuggle those diamonds past seven searchers. (*Inspector, Velie groan — Nikki expectant*) I've thought of every conceivable way in which he could have stolen the diamonds. Dad — I've solved the puzzle of the theft!

Inspector (*sarcastically*): Fine! Now you can start solving the puzzle of the murder.

Ellery (*as if to himself*): Yes, I'm sure I'm right — it's the only possible answer. *I know how those diamonds got out of the strong-room!*

Velie: Okay, Mr. Queen, so you win the puzzle champeenship of the world. But for cryin' out loud —

Inspector: How about the murder? Ellery, we've got to know who murdered Lazarus!

Ellery (*absently*): Oh, that? Yes, dad, I know that, too.

(*Music up . . . into jury spot*)

Challenge to the Listener

While the members of the jury were composing themselves to give their answers to the mystery, the announcer, Bert Parks, told the audience that "Gulf No-Nox Gasoline ends motor knocks under all normal driving conditions, and makes your car feel so frisky you'll think you have two extra cylinders under the hood."

(*Music up . . .*)

Inspector: We're losing time, Ellery! Tell me who murdered Lazarus.

Ellery: To do that, dad, I'll have to begin with the theft of the diamonds . . .

Velie (*groaning*): There he goes again.

Nikki: The man with the one-track mind!

Ellery (*gently*): But it's the heart of this case, children. How did Professor Lazarus get those diamonds past seven searchers — the four owners, the two detectives, and the doctor? I saw no light until I asked myself one tremendously simple, one gigantically obvious, question: *Was it really Professor Lazarus who took those diamonds out of the strong-room?* (*Pause. Ad libs*)

Nikki: Oh, dear. Oh, *dear!* That's the answer!

Ellery: Yes, Nikki! A score of facts proved that not only *didn't* Lazarus take those diamonds out, he *couldn't*. It was *impossible* for Lazarus to have smuggled them past the seven men — and you can't find the answer to an impossibility. Therefore *Lazarus* wasn't the thief — someone *else* must have been!

Inspector: But Ellery, only Professor Lazarus entered that strong-room all week — a condition he'd laid down himself before he began working there!

Ellery: Yes, but is it *true* no one else entered that strong-room? It is *not* true. Because one other person *did* go in there before the diamonds were reported gone — and by his own admission was in there *alone!* And what's more, when he left the office, he knew he wouldn't be searched — because all four men were protecting themselves against *Lazarus.* Therefore I knew that the only other person known to have been in the strong-room alone *must* be the thief! And who was that person?

Nikki: Kenyon! It was Mr. Kenyon!

Inspector: Sure! Kenyon himself told us he returned to his office last night, "worried" that something was wrong — that the detectives on guard let him in — that he went into the strong-room *alone*, and the detectives didn't rush in there until he yelled the diamonds were gone!

Velie: Boy, that's masterful. Kenyon goes in, swipes the ice himself, then comes out, hollers he's been robbed, beats it over to the Professor's hotel room, kills the ol' guy, scrams, hides the di'monds, then picks up Dr. Cook an' brings him to you, Mr. Queen, to back up his story about how hard they searched Lazarus!

Ellery: Yes, and in giving us that story, he brilliantly distracted our attention from himself and directed it towards Lazarus as the thief. Quite a psychologist, Kenyon! One of the cleverest rogues in my experience. He devised a theft of such colossal simplicity that I was nearly taken in by the complicated props!

Nikki: Then Professor Lazarus wasn't a confidence man at all! *Could* he double the size of diamonds, Ellery?

Ellery: Well, he didn't, Nikki, so I imagine the poor fellow was just an earnest crank who thought he'd solved one of the riddles of the universe.

Nikki: Wasn't it foolish of Kenyon to overlook the diamond in the Professor's dead hand — Bryce's diamond?

Ellery: Overlook it! Nikki, Kenyon left that diamond there *purposely.* For the same reason he *killed* Lazarus . . . to clinch the illusion that it was Professor Lazarus who'd stolen the diamonds in the first place.

Inspector: Wait a minute, Ellery. Granting Kenyon was the only one who could have taken the diamonds out of the strong-room, how does that prove he also killed Lazarus?

Velie: Yeah, why couldn't it 'a' been one o' the other guys who bumped off the professor?

Ellery (*laughing*): Kenyon's magic spell is still on you. Don't you see? The murderer planted one of the four diamonds in the victim's hand.

To *leave* a diamond in the victim's hand meant that the murderer had to *have* the diamond. Who had the diamonds? The thief. Therefore the thief must have been the murderer. And who is the only possible thief? Kenyon. Conclusion: Kenyon is the murderer!

Nikki: Q.-E.-D.!

Velie (*awed*): Gosh! Inspector, why can't *we* figger 'em out so nice an' clean?

Inspector (*sadly*): Velie, I've been trying to answer that question ever since I became a father!

(*Music up*)

This is one of the publisher's favorites of the early Ellery Queen radio shows, not only because it has a dying message but also because it is one of the very few cases which the publisher was able to solve. He hopes that you won't. It was broadcast on June 23, 1940.

The Adventure of the Dark Cloud

The Characters

Ellery Queen	The detective
Nikki Porter	His secretary
Margaret Valentine	A socialite
Percy Valentine	Her brother
Mr. Valentine	A "1929 millionaire"
Alfred Crockett	His brother-in-law
Captain Bye	Skipper of the "Dark Cloud"
Inspector Queen	Of the New York Police
Sergeant Velie	Of the New York Police

Setting: Long Island Sound, 1940

(*Gay nautical music . . . (sailor's hornpipe) . . . up . . . into whistles and put-puts of passing pleasure-craft as if heard from yacht anchored in Long Island Sound . . . no fog horns . . . set sound then cut everything but faint slap of water . . . splash of diving body . . . off*)

Nikki (*on*): (*Gaily*) Ellery, come here to the rail quick!
Ellery (*fading on*): What's all the excitement, Nikki?
Nikki: Margaret Valentine and her brother Percy are diving off the yacht . . . (*Calling*) . . . Hi, Margaret. That was a *dandy* dive.
Margaret (*off . . . spluttering . . . in water . . . young deb*): It was terrible! Percy Valentine, you stop that! . . . (*Splashing off*)
Percy (*off . . . laughing . . . young society . . . spluttering*): . . . Hey! I was only fooling. (*Glug glug as if ducked; Ellery, Nikki laugh*)
Nikki (*happily*): Golden sun — blue water — colored sails — and a week-end on a millionaire's yacht . . . how did you ever manage it, Ellery?
Ellery: *I* didn't — it was dad's work.
Nikki: Does the Inspector know the Valentines? Don't tell me your father's cultivating the Social Register. (*Yells from Percy and Margaret*)

256

Ellery (*chuckling*): Hardly. Dad's tie-up with the gold-and-plush Valentine family is through that gabby old South African uncle of theirs, Alfred Crockett. The old man is Mr. Valentine's brother-in-law. He asked us out this weekend for what I think is a very special reason. (*Pause*) . . . There's the Valentine launch now, Nikki. See it?

Nikki: Oh, yes. Putting out from the dock. Isn't that the Inspector and Sergeant Velie in it?

Ellery: Yes, Mr. Valentine ran the launch over himself to pick them up . . . (*Another yell: "Percy, stop it!"*)

Nikki: He's *such* a nice man.

Percy: Come on in, beautiful, I'll teach you how to swim.

Nikki (*calling, laughing*): I've been taught how to swim, thank you. (*Steps on deck fading on*) 'Lo, Mr. Crockett!

Crockett (*fading on . . . old, British accent, growly voice*): Enjoying yourselves?

Ellery: Immensely, sir. When do we put out to sea?

Crockett: Soon as the launch gets back, I imagine. Like a bit of a sail m'self, y' know. Deep-water man!

Margaret (*off*): Hi, Uncle Baas. You all right?

Percy (*off*): Got everything you want, Uncle Baas?

Crockett (*calling*): Perfectly all right, thank you . . . (*Dryly*) . . . Quite solicitous, my niece and nephew.

Ellery: Yes, they seem very fond of you, Mr. Crockett.

Crockett (*dryly*): Millionaire uncles who retire in South Africa and come to America to live out their lives with their only kin are *usually* well-received, Mr. Queen.

Nikki (*low*): Uh-uh! (*Loud*) Mr. Crockett, why do Margaret and Percy call you "Uncle Baas?"

Crockett: Eh? Oh! Baas is the Boer word for "master," or "boss." Spent all my life in South Africa, y'know. Diamond mining. Jewels . . . (*Enthusiastic*) . . . Something special about jewels, y'know. Get into a man's blood! When I retired, I converted my entire fortune into jewels . . . Isn't that Inspector Queen in the launch?

Nikki: Ellery, they're almost to the yacht! See, they're waving.

(*Put-put of motor well off, fading in slowly behind next scene*)

Crockett: Wonderful man, your father, Mr. Queen.

Ellery: I think so, sir. Known my dad long?

Crockett: A few weeks. We met by accident. I'm interested in police, y'know. Sort of hobby. Feel safer with police about. Man never knows in a strange country.

(*Percy, Margaret ad libs fading on*)

Nikki: Here're Margaret and Percy. Enjoy your swim, you two?

Margaret (*fading on*): Swellegant! Uncle Baas! There's a breeze, and you aren't wearing your tippet.

Crockett (*testily*): Now Margaret, I'm quite all right.

Percy (*fading on*): You'll catch cold, Uncle Baas.

Margaret: Uncle Baas is *so* careless, Mr. Queen. Uncle, I'm *so* glad you decided to come live with daddy and us. Now you've got a family to take care of you.

Crockett (*dryly*): Rather possessive family, Margaret. *Babying* me! Mustn't do this, that, mustn't spend a shilling.

Percy (*laughing*): And make believe you don't like it, you old fraud. See you later, Nikki. Come on, Marge.

Margaret: It *is* whipping up. Brr! We'd better change.

Crockett (*quietly*): *Very* solicitous, Mr. Queen. (*Brightly*) And here they are! Inspector Queen! Glad to see you, sir. And Sergeant Velie! Come aboard! Come aboard. (*Put-put dies, as motor shut off*) (*Wash and bump of launch*) — Captain Bye, help these gentlemen aboard!

Bye (*fading on*): Aye, Mr. Crockett — make that launch fast, Tom.

Inspector (*little off*): Lo, kids! Enjoy yourselves? (*Ad libs response*)

Velie (*little off*): Man, what a boat!

Valentine (*off . . . hearty . . . society business type*): Hullo, there. Here, let me help you up, Inspector Queen.

(*Steps off up metal gangway*)

Inspector (*off*): Thanks, Mr. Valentine, but I can still navigate under my own steam. Sorry if the Sergeant and I held you up, Mr. Crockett.

Crockett (*cordially*): Not at all, not at all.

Velie (*fading on*): Boy oh boy, what a boat. What air. What water. Mr. Crockett, you're aces. And so're you, Mr. Valentine. Darn nice o' you to ask us.

Valentine (*cordially*): We're happy to entertain any friends of my brother-in-law, Sergeant . . . Captain Bye!

Bye (*off . . . salty Yank, oldish, twang*): Aye, Mr. Valentine?

Valentine: Put her out to sea, Captain.

Bye (*off*): Aye, sir . . . (*Fading*) . . . Cast off . . . Tom. Bill, get that gangway up . . . (*Other ad libs of command in back*) (*Put-put of launch off*)

Valentine: If you gentlemen will join me in the lounge, I think the steward might be able to fix a drink or two, eh?

(*All fade laughing, and talking over steps on deck except Ellery and Nikki. Captain. Bye's orders still under faintly. Engines start well off and throb faintly.*)

Nikki (*deep breath*): What a *glorious* idea this was — *whoever* thought of it, Ellery? I'm going to love this week-end.

Ellery (*thoughtfully*): I wonder.

Nikki: You wonder what?

Ellery: I wonder if the name of Mr. Valentine's yacht isn't significant.

Nikki: *The name of the yacht?* What is it? I didn't notice.

Ellery (*grimly*): "The Dark Cloud."

Nikki (*startled*): "The Dark Cloud" . . . (*Laughing*) . . . Oh, Ellery. Stop being such a gloom and come on. We're going to have *fun!*

(*Music up . . . into slight throb of engines . . . faint sound of waves . . . ad lib general murmur . . . clink of glasses, on*)

Nikki (*uncertainly*): It's getting a little rocky, isn't it?

Ellery: Moon's clouding over, too . . . thank you, steward.

Inspector: What's your professional opinion, Captain Bye?

Bye: We're in for a spell o' weather, Inspector. Nothin' to be consarned about.

Velie: Maybe *you* ain't consarned, Cap'n, but . . . (*Heave of wave off*) whoop! (*General laughter at his distress . . .*)

Valentine: You'll get used to it, Sergeant.

Inspector: Mr. Crockett, may I see you for a moment.

Crockett (*low*): Of course, Inspector.

Inspector (*low*): Mr. Crockett, I think it's time you told us the real reason why you've invited us to spend a week-end on your brother-in law's yacht. Eh, Mr. Crockett?

Crockett (*low*): Well — I'd rather explain that later. Right now, I just want you to keep your eyes open and let me know what you think . . .

Inspector: Well don't you want —

Crockett: And now, if you'll all excuse me —

Margaret (*concern*): Uncle Baas! Is anything the matter?

Percy: You feeling sick, Uncle?

Valentine: Nothing wrong, I hope, Alfred?

Crockett (*testily*): No, no. Just thought of something I must do; Captain Bye, didn't you say you had a thingumbob, a whatchacallit — a dictatin' machine in your cabin? Want to dictate some — letters.

Bye: Ye're welcome to use it, Mr. Crockett.

Crockett: Thank you, Captain . . . Good night . . .

Nikki: Now what on earth would the skipper of a yacht be needing with a dictaphone, Captain Bye?

Captain Bye (*chuckling*): I'm by way o' bein' a writer, Miss Porter. Adventure stuff, you know, French Foreign Legion stories, Alaska, gold-rush, Wild West, pirates —

Ellery: Really, Captain? Do you publish?

Valentine: Publish! Why, Mr. Queen, Captain Bye writes under a dozen different names — don't you, Captain?

Bye (*modestly*): It's a prime fact. Pulps. Two cents a word. Keeps an old man busy . . . (*Pause*) (*Drinks glasses, etc.*)

Nikki (*yawning*): Ooooooh . . . sorry. What *do* people do on yachts at night? Day times you can swim and sun yourself, but —

Percy (*archily*): If you'll stroll around to the stern with me, Nikki, maybe I can convince you night-time at sea can be interesting too!

Margaret: Don't you do it, Nikki. Percy's a regular wolf. Let's play a game.

Valentine: Bully idea. Captain Bye, you're usually the life of the party. Anything to suggest?

Bye: Mr. Valentine, I have . . .

Inspector (*chuckling*): What's the game, Captain Bye?

Bye: Kind of charades, ye might call it. Where ye act out somethin'? In my game ye act out the title of a book by a famous author. But ye . . . gotta pick a book by some author who's got the *same first name* as yer own.

Nikki: I don't quite get that, Captain.

Bye: Well, look. My first name's Jack. So I'm a-goin' to pick a book by an author whose first name is Jack. All right. Now I'll act the book-title out. (*Bye howls in ludicrous imitation of a wolf, general laughter . . . Percy: "Sounds like a sick banshee."*)

Ellery (*laughing*): What in heaven's name is *that* hideous sound supposed to convey, Captain?

Bye (*disappointed*): Don't ye git it?

Velie: I do! It's the howl of a wolf.

Inspector: That's it, Velie. *Call of the Wild*, by Jack London. (*General laughter . . . Ellery: "Very good, Sergeant." Nikki: "Sergeant Velie, you're marvelous." Valentine: "I only hope I can do as well."*)

Margaret: I've got one. I've got one!

Percy (*jealously*): You would, Marge.

Nikki: Go ahead, Margaret.

Valentine: Act it out, Margaret.

Velie: I hope it isn't too hard.

Margaret (*giggling*): Here goes. (*Makes wind noises . . . Velie: "Sounds like a hurricane or sompin'!"*) Get it?

Bye: That's a mighty hard one. Try it again, Miss Margaret.

Margaret (*laughs*): If you can stand it, Captain . . . (*More wind noises*)

Nikki: I know. *Gone With the Wind* . . . by *Margaret* Mitchell. (*Laughter and ad libs . . . Ellery: "Brilliant, Nikki." Velie: "Gosh, I shoulda got that one."*)

Margaret: You're too smart, Nikki. Daddy, you try one.

Valentine: I? Mmmm. (*Chuckles*) . . . All right, see what you can do with this one?

Percy: Whoa, dad . . . what's the idea of sticking your finger straight up in the air and then lowering it slowly . . .

Valentine (*little irritation*): I'm not finished, Percy. (*Makes bubbly sound as if underwater, laughter of all*)

Ellery: I know what *that* one is, Mr. Valentine. The finger slowly sinking is supposed to represent the periscope of a submerging submarine . . .
Velie: A what? (*Surprised laughter*)
Nikki: Submarine. Bubbly sounds, the sea . . . Submarine — result — *Twenty Thousand Leagues Under the Sea.*
(*Well off mike . . . heave of ship into wave*)
Margaret: By *Jules Verne.* Oh, that's right, Mr. Queen, isn't it, daddy?
Valentine (*chuckling*): Certainly is . . . (*Nikki: "Mr. Queen solves another." Inspector: "Good work son." Bye: "Clever lad you've got there, Inspector Queen."*) Percy, why don't you illustrate your intelligence?
Percy: What intelligence? Okay . . . watch this . . .
Velie (*low*): Psst. Mr. Queen, what do *I* do when it's my turn? Who's an author named Tom?
Ellery: No problem with a name like Tom, but "Ellery" — that's a puzzler.
Nikki: You can always pick one of your books, Ellery. (*Inspector: "Wait a minute, I've got it. Beau Geste by Percival Wren."*) But how about me? I have the stickler — Nikki. Was there ever an author named Nikki Something? (*Ellery laughs*)
Percy (*background up*): Right, Inspector.
(*A wave off, over the bow*)
Nikki: Whoo! I felt that one.
Velie: A boat ain't no place for a flatfoot.
Ellery: It *is* getting rough, isn't it, Captain Bye?
Bye (*abruptly*): Ye'll have to excuse me, ladies and gentlemen . . . (*Fading*) . . . Gotta be gittin' back to the bridge . . . (*Pause . . . wind and waves up stronger*)
Velie (*groaning*): Oooohh . . . I'm gettin' . . . dizzy.
Valentine: That's too bad, Sergeant . . . (*Ad libs: Percy: "Come on, Marge. Let's go on deck and look at it." Marge: "All right." Velie: "Do you do this for pleasure, Mr. Valentine?"*)
Nikki (*on mike*): Storm *is* getting worse, Ellery. Looks as if we might be in for trouble.
Ellery (*quietly*): Yes, Nikki, I think we are.
Nikki: Ellery!
Ellery: I think we're in for trouble, Nikki . . . but not from the Atlantic Ocean.

(*Music up . . . faint background of storm . . . open cabin door on mike . . .*)

Ellery (*fading on . . . concerned*): Nikki! What's the idea sitting out here in the lounge all by yourself in the middle of the night?
Nikki (*sickish*): Oh, Ellery, I tried to get to sleep, but . . . the yacht's pitching so . . . I don't feel very — comfortable inside.

Ellery (*tender amusement*): You poor kid. Bad sailor, eh?

Inspector (*fading on*): Anything wrong, Nikki? Why, your cheeks are clay-white.

Nikki: Feels more like . . . poison green . . . to me . . .

Ellery: Let's walk Nikki around the deck a bit, dad. (*Steps*)

Inspector: To tell the truth, I'm none too happy myself . . .

Nikki (*groaning*): Fresh air. Week-end at sea. Roll on! I guess I'm just a poor stenographer at heart.

Inspector: Why the gloom, son? You under the weather, too?

Ellery (*absently*): Eh? Oh, I was just thinking about that South African millionaire friend of yours, dad, and his fortune in jewels.

Inspector (*chuckling*): Yes, Uncle Baas Crockett's quite a character — he and his jewels! Here's the storm door.

(*Open door . . . up on storm, but not too much . . . mostly high wind . . . steps on deck*)

Nikki: I hope Mr. Crockett hasn't got his jewels on the yacht. That's all I'd need right now — the excitement of a jewel robbery. (*Faint yell off of Captain Bye*) What's that?

Inspector (*sharply*): Somebody's yelling for help. (*Yell again*)

Ellery: Up forward. That's Captain Bye's voice, dad.

Inspector: Something wrong — come on! But watch your step! (*Running steps . . . yelling fades on*)

Nikki (*panting over steps*): I knew it! I just *knew* it!

Inspector: There's Captain Bye — standing in front of his cabin. Why the bellow, Cap'n?

Bye (*stop steps under*): . . . (*Fading on . . . very nervous*) Inspector Queen. Mr. Queen! Thank the stars ye've got here.

Ellery (*sharply*): What's the trouble, Captain?

Bye: I jest got here to my cabin from the bridge. I thought Mr. Crockett had finished dictatin' on my dictatin' machine, an' left, long ago . . . but I found him . . . still here. (*Opens cabin door*) Look at him. (*Pause*)

Nikki (*whisper*): Dead. Mr. Crockett's . . . *dead*.

Inspector: Come in. Shut the door, Captain. (*Closes door . . . shut out storm*) Well, Ellery.

Ellery (*grim*): Dead, all right. Murdered a few minutes ago!

Nikki (*shocked*): He was still dictating into the machine when he was shot to death. Look! His hand is still clutching the mouthpiece of the machine.

Bye (*brokenly*): Poor Mr. Crockett . . . (*Whir of machine*)

Ellery: What are you doing, dad?

Inspector: Playing the cylinder back to hear what Crockett was dictating when he died . . . (*Pause . . . whir up*) Well, I'll be — (*More whir*) Hallelujah! (*Stop whirring*)

Ellery (*excited*): What was Crockett dictating, dad?
Inspector: A new will. (*Nikki exclaims* . . . "*A will*") And what's more, we're in luck, son. The wax cylinder caught the whole crime — just as it happened.
Ellery: Let me listen to that record, dad?
Nikki: I want to hear it, too!
Inspector: Nikki, run below deck and haul Velie out of his bunk. Velie's a whale of a mechanic, and I think he can rig this machine up to the amplifier of the radio so that the Valentines can hear the sound-record of the murder.
Nikki: Why?
Inspector (*grimly*): I want to watch the faces of the Valentines when they hear what the late Mr. Crockett had to say about them.

(*Music up . . . into Margaret crying . . . Valentine and Percy soothing her in background . . . Open, close cabin door*)

Nikki: Well, Inspector?
Inspector (*fading on*): Checked the crew. They all have perfect alibis. It's one of this Valentine bunch.
Ellery: How are you coming with that rig-up, Sergeant . . . ?
Velie (*panting*): Just about got it, Mr. Queen. I dunno how good the amplification's gonna be, but it's the best I can do . . . All set.
Inspector: Quiet, please. Mr. Valentine, Margaret and Percy Valentine — we're going to let you hear what dear Uncle Baas Crockett was saying just before one of you shot him to death. (*Gasps*) Get that cylinder going, Velie.
Velie: Right, Inspector. (*Slight scratch sound . . . a slight filter on what follows . . . voice and sounds*)
Crockett (*filtered*): Last will and testament of Alfred Crockett. I, Alfred Crockett, being of sound mind and having the intention of making final disposition of all my worldly goods . . . (*Scratches up somewhere in middle*)
Ellery: Fix that, Sergeant, can you?
Velie: Just a minute. Told you it mightn't be good . . .
Margaret (*sobbing*): It's Uncle Baas' voice. His *voice*!
(*Ad libs Percy and Valentine soothing her*)
Nikki (*shocked*): A dead man's . . . voice!
Velie: Okay, now! (*Record on as before*)
Crockett (*rather clearly, still slightly filtered*): . . . and I declare invalid and of no force the will I made out two months ago which left my entire fortune in jewels to my dead sister's family, the Valentines. I have asked Inspector Queen and his son to spend the week-end with me

because I now have good reason to believe that the Valentine family are deceitful frauds, and I want the Queens to expose them for the cheats, false-faces, and fortune-hunters that they are. They've lost their former great wealth and are putting on a show on borrowed funds to impress and coddle me, all for the sake of inheriting my jewels. (*Gasps from Valentines*) My jewels are in a safe-deposit vault at my bank in New York City. I therefore bequeath to the Red Cross my entire fortune in (*Bang of revolver shot . . . Crockett cries out in pain . . . door slams off. Crockett's dying pant*) Jewels! Jewels! . . . (*Dying groan . . . thud of body . . . followed by slight scratches of record and whirring . . . turn off machine*)

Nikki (*whisper*): We actually heard . . . Mr. Crockett die and his murderer escape . . . (*Margaret bursts into new sobbing*)

Ellery: Remarkable. The shot, Crockett's cry of pain, the running steps of the murderer fleeing the cabin in the belief that Crockett was dead, the slam of the cabin door, Crockett's dying words, the thud of his body . . . remarkable.

Inspector (*grimly*): Velie, d'ye find the revolver yet?

Velie: It ain't on *this* hooker, Inspector — Cap'n Bye says —

Bye (*soberly*): It musta been *my* shootin' iron, Inspector. I kept one in that locker near the cabin door, an' it ain't there now. Everybody on "The Dark Cloud" *knew* I kept it there, too. (*Darkly*) An' I mean *everybody*!

Ellery: By this time the revolver's at the bottom of the sea.

Inspector: One of these "frauds," as Crockett called 'em, shot the old man. Come on! Which one?

Valentine (*gasping*): You're insane.

Inspector: Am I, Mr. Valentine? You people were fakers, broke. You were sweet to your rich relative from South Africa — showed him a good time, put on an act for him! — just so he'd make you his heirs and recoup your fortunes!

Margaret (*coldly*): Daddy, do we have to sit here and listen to this *policeman* insult us —

Inspector: You do, Miss Valentine! One of you sneaked into the Captain's cabin, overheard Mr. Crockett dictating the new will cutting you out, and killed him *to keep his old will in force!* Because the will on this cylinder is not a legal will, having no signature or witnesses, and being unfinished and not in written form!

Ellery: Undoubtedly Crockett intended to have the cylinder's contents typed and witnessed legally as soon as "The Dark Cloud" made port Monday morning!

Percy (*coldly*): This is ridiculous. Uncle Baas was senile. We're not broke —

Bye (*indignantly*): Oh, ain't ye, Mr. Percy Valentine! Inspector, I'm a

man who minds his own business, but Mr. Crockett was real nice,
an' I ain't holdin' my jaw a mite longer! They're so broke, these
fancy Valentines, they don't even own this yacht no more!
   (*Nikki, Inspector, Velie exclaim*)
Valentine (*menacing*): Bye, you hold your tongue, or —
Ellery (*evenly*): You'd better take your own advice, Mr. Valentine. "The
   Dark Cloud" is *not* the Valentines' yacht? Then whose is it, Captain?
Bye: It's mine. Oh, it used to be their'n, but when they lost everythin' I
   bought it from 'em dirt cheap an' I been hirin' it out to 1929
   millionaires ever since!
Inspector: My, my! It *is* coming out!
Bye: The Valentines comes to me a few months back — to hire "The
   Dark Cloud." Wanted to fool the ol' man, an' part o' the deal was I
   should make out like it was still the Valentines' yacht! An' don't ye
   call me a liar, Mr. Valentine! I kin prove it!
Valentine (*sullenly*): We have nothing to say just — now.
Inspector (*grimly*): Go back to your quarters and stay there. Velie, stand
   guard in Captain Bye's cabin here. Captain Bye, turn this death-ship
   around and head back for New York!

   (*Music up . . . into peaceful running of engines, no storm . . . but faint swish
   of water . . . slow footsteps on deck . . .*)

Nikki (*moaning*): I'm *stiff*! All night in a deck-chair! Thank goodness
   the storm's over, anyhow. Are we almost in, Ellery?
Ellery: It won't be long now, Nikki. (*Thoughtfully*) Curious case . . .
Inspector (*dreamily*): He was a nice old fella, Crockett. (*Abruptly*) Well,
   there's the sun.
Ellery: I wonder how Velie is. It's awfully quiet.
Nikki: The Sergeant? But he's in Captain Bye's cabin watching the scene
   of the crime, Ellery!
Ellery (*uneasily*): I know. But I have the strangest feeling . . . Here's the
   cabin. (*Steps stop. Calling*) Sergeant?
Inspector (*calling*): Velie! (*Pause*) Must be snoozing. Try the door, Ellery.
   (*Rattle knob*)

   (*Play fast*)

Nikki: Locked!
Inspector: Locked! Maybe he — (*Rattle furiously*) Velie!
Ellery: Sergeant Velie! Open this door!
Nikki: Ellery! Look through this window! The Sergeant — lying on the
   floor — (*Begins to weep bitterly*) Sergeant Velie's been m-murdered!

Ellery (*shouting*): Velie *is* on the floor!

Inspector: *Tom Velie?* (*Roaring*) Break 'er down! (*Smash against door with ad libs*) Again, son! (*Door gives*) Tom!

Nikki: Poor Sergeant Velie.

Ellery (*gravely*): Struck on the head, dad.

Inspector (*brokenly*): Poor old Tom. (*Hard*) When I get my hands on the murdering devil who did this —

Ellery: Dad! (*Velie groans*) He's alive!

Nikki: Alive! — Sergeant! Wake up! Open your eyes! How's your head?

Velie (*groaning*): Is it . . . still there? Oooh!

Inspector (*anxiously*): Are you all right, Tom? Feel all right?

Ellery: Let me explore that bump on your skull, Sergeant.

Velie: Ouch! That hurts! I musta dozed off. All of a sudden I sorta wake up, 'cause it seems to me I'm hearing footsteps. But before I can see what's happenin' — zingo! (*Groans*) My head . . . (*Nikki's soothing ad lib*)

Ellery (*sharply*): Murderer came back. *He came back to the scene of his crime.* Why? Must have had an overpowering reason. Took a desperate chance . . . Ah!

Nikki: Ellery! Those little jagged bits of black wax on the floor near the dictating machine!

Velie: The record of old man Crockett's voice!

Inspector (*blowing up*): Pesky killer came back and smashed the record to a thousand pieces!

Ellery: No, dad. He only *thought* he did.

Nikki: Why, Ellery — here are the pieces — and the cylinder's gone from the machine!

Ellery: Luckily I removed the real cylinder last night and slipped in an old one of Captain Bye's. The Crockett cylinder is safe! — and the murderer's made a serious mistake! (*Exclamations*)

Velie: Don't tell me just because this ornery yacht-prowlin' pirate clunks me on the head an' tries to break up the Crockett cylinder, you know who he is, Mr. Queen!

Ellery (*grimly*): Sergeant, that desperate act of our murderer is all I needed to make my case complete!

(*Music up . . . and into jury spot*)

Challenge to the Listener

Ellery told the studio jury that they had to identify the murderer and specify the clues. Bert Parks interrupted by betting Ellery a tank of Gulf No-Nox that he could solve the mystery. He lost.

(*Music up* . . .)

Inspector: Ellery, talk!
Ellery: The murderer returned during the night to destroy the wax cylinder which recorded the death-scene. He took a desperate chance. Why?
Inspector: To destroy the cylinder as evidence.
Ellery: But why? What was there on that cylinder which was so dangerous to him? Aside from Crockett's voice, there was merely the shot, and the slam of a door. Nothing incriminating to any individual in those, is there? So the thing the murderer was afraid of, the thing he risked exposure to destroy, *must lie in something Crockett said on the record!*
Nikki: Something the dead man said that the murderer was afraid would give his identity away!
Velie: But Mr. Queen, we all heard the record — I didn't hear nothin' that was a giveaway . . .
Ellery: Well, let's see. The spoken clue Crockett left could not have been *before* he was shot, because if you'll recall his words before the shot he gave no indication he even *suspected* anyone would attempt to murder him. Therefore the clue must lie in what Crockett said *after* the shot. But what did he say after the shot? Just one word! So the clue to his murderer's identity must lie in that word! Let me play back to you what we heard, beginning right before the shot. I've marked the place on the cylinder. (*Repeat sound of whirring, scratchiness, cut in suddenly on* . . .)
Crockett (*same filtering*): — jewels are in a safe-deposit vault at my bank in New York City. I therefore bequeath to the Red Cross my entire fortune in — (*Bang of revolver shot. Crockett cries out in pain, door slam off. Crockett's dying pant*) Jewels! Jewels . . . (*Dying groan. Thud of body — cut off record fast. Note: replay exactly as in original scene!!!!*)
Velie: Jools! He said jools, an' kicked off!
Nikki (*bewildered*): Jewels . . . But I don't see —
Inspector: Crockett was simply finishing the sentence he'd begun — he said he was leaving to the Red Cross his entire fortune in . . . bang! . . . "jewels." His entire fortune in jewels!
Velie: So how's that a clue to his killer, Mr. Queen?
Ellery: A man dying — in fact, he did die within a second after uttering that last word — and all he was trying to do was *finish a sentence?* (*Laughs*) Dad . . .
Nikki: Then what *was* Crockett trying to do?
Ellery: Nikki, in uttering the word "jewels" the dying man thought he was leaving a clue to his murderer's identity! — he and his murderer thought Crockett *did* name him, or he wouldn't have come back to destroy this cylinder!

Inspector: A murderer named (*Spelling*) J-E-W-E-L-S?

Ellery: Not J-E-W-E-L-S but J-U-L-E-S! Jules, a man's first name! The two words sound the same and, dying, Crockett didn't realize the word would be misunderstood!

Nikki: Jules!

Inspector: Of course! Crockett was murdered by his brother-in-law, Margaret and Percy's father . . . the only person on the yacht without an alibi who *is* named Jules . . . Mr. *Valentine*!

(*Music up* . . .)

Ellery: And that, ladies and gentlemen, is how I knew Alfred Crockett was murdered by Mr. Jules Valentine —

Parks (*breaking in*): *Wait* a minute, Ellery. Not so fast! It's all right for *you* people to know Mr. Valentine's first name was Jules — but how are we in the audience supposed to know? *We* never heard Mr. Valentine called Jules!

Ellery (*laughing*): No? Bert, don't you recall that game of charades on the evening of the crime?

Parks (*blankly*): Why, yes, Ellery, but —

Ellery: Remember the idea was that each player had to choose a book written by an author *whose first name was the same as the player's first name*?

Parks (*doubtfully*): Well, yes. I remember Captain *Jack* Bye chose a book by *Jack* London, *Margaret* Valentine chose one by *Margaret* Mitchell . . .

Ellery: And which book did *Mr.* Valentine choose, Bert?

Parks: *Twenty Thousand Leagues Under the Sea*, by Jules Verne. (*Surprised*) *Jules* Verne!

Ellery (*laughs gently*): So you see, Bert, you *did* know Mr. Valentine's first name was Jules!

Parks (*ruefully*): Mr. Queen, I drain the cup of mortification. You win!

Frederic Dannay and Manfred B. Lee were fans of Sherlock Holmes — Dannay said that "Sherlockophilly" was "an incurable malady," and he was active in the Baker Street Irregulars — Lee, who was less of a joiner, attended only once. It was natural that the cousins would give Ellery a case that Holmes had failed to solve. Dr. Watson wrote: "A problem without a solution may interest the student, but can hardly fail to annoy the casual reader. Among these unfinished tales is that of Mr. James Phillimore, who, stepping back into his own house to get his umbrella, was never more seen in this world." Here is Ellery's solution, broadcast on January 14, 1943.

The Adventure of Mr. Short and Mr. Long

The Characters

Ellery Queen	The detective
Nikki Porter	His secretary
Inspector Queen	Of the New York Police
Sergeant Velie	Of the New York Police
Napoleon Short	The Twenty Per Cent King
Jonathan Long	Mr. Short's man
Telegraph messenger	
Coal man	

Setting: New York City, 1943

(*Music up . . . into Ellery coughing*)

Nikki: Now come on, Ellery — Drink the rest of your orange juice.
Ellery: But Nikki, I don't *want* orange juice. I want to get out of bed. (*Another coughing spell*)
Nikki: With that cough? Drink it! (*Ellery gulps*)
Ellery: Nikki, it's just a cold — and we've got a lot of work to do on my novel — (*A few coughs*)
Nikki: You're staying in bed, Mr. Queen, until you stop coughing. You can dictate from bed.
Ellery (*grumpily*): All right. Get your notebook.
Nikki: Well, that's better. Never knew a man yet who didn't act like a puppy with a sore nose when he was sick. (*Door opens off*) Inspector?
Inspector (*off*): Yes, Nikki! (*Fading on*) How's the sick man? (*Ellery coughs*) Say, that's a bad cough, son —

269

Nikki: And he wants to get out of bed, Inspector!

Inspector (*grimly*): Oh, he does? Well, he's not going to, and that's final. (*Chuckles*) It's a shame, too.

Ellery (*grumpily*): What's a shame? What are you looking so delirious about, dad?

Inspector: It's a great day, son. Yes, sir! I've got a rendezvous with Velie to close the book on the career of a guy who should have been in jail years ago.

Ellery (*alertly*): Who's that, dad?

Inspector: Little Napoleon.

Ellery: "Little Nap!"

Nikki: *Who* is Little Napoleon, Inspector?

Inspector: Napoleon Short, Nikki — The Twenty Per Cent King.

Ellery: And I have to be laid up! I'm getting out of —

Inspector: You're staying right where you are. (*Chuckles*) We were tipped off that Little Nap made a reservation on this morning's plane to South America. So I threw a squad around his house last night and we'll grab Mr. Nap when he leaves with that satchel full of John Q. Public's dough.

Nikki: What's his racket, Inspector?

Inspector: He "invests" your money for you. Guarantees twenty per cent interest.

Nikki: But how can he keep paying twenty per cent?

Ellery (*with a cough*): It's very simple, Nikki. Little Nap takes your hundred dollars, pays out twenty — that leaves him eighty.

Nikki: But Ellery, he can't do that indefinitely!

Inspector: There's always a fresh crop of suckers, Nikki. The new money keeps paying off the old interest.

Nikki: But eventually a lot of people must want all their money back!

Ellery: When that unhappy moment comes, Nikki, Little Nap packs up the remaining assets and departs hastily for cooler climes. Same old story, dad. Remember that William F. Miller and his "Franklin Syndicate" in eighteen ninety nine?

Inspector: Yep. Well, this time Little Nap waited too long. So we're going to recover the sucker money and wrap up Napoleon for immediate delivery to the D.A. (*Fading*) Nikki, take care of Ellery!

Nikki: I will, Inspector!

Ellery: Blast it . . . Dad! Let me know how you make out!

(*Music up . . . into exterior. Occasional traffic off*)

Velie (*guardedly*): Hi, Inspector.

Inspector (*fading on*): Morning, Velie. How goes it?

Velie: Smooth as a baby's neck, Inspector. Not a soul's left the house since we checked Little Nap in last night. I've been watchin' from the front gate here. Huh . . . Here comes Little Nap now!

Inspector (*grim humor*): Marching out of his front door with his black bag. Down, Velie! Let him walk right into the arms of the law.

Velie: What a runt.

Inspector: Five foot one of pure cussedness. Wait a minute — why's he stopped? What's he looking up at the sky for?

Velie (*intently*): Says to himself: "Looks like rain. So I'll turn around and go back into the house for an umbrella —" *and there he goes, Inspector*!

Inspector: Where, Velie? I've lost him under that portico in front of the door! Let's get closer — I want to make sure he doesn't pull a sneak. (*Steps on gravel*)

Velie: That little twerp is li'ble to pull anything — There he is, Inspector! (*Steps stop*) See him now?

Inspector: Yeah. Yeah. Back into the house. (*Front door slams off*) We'll wait right here, Velie, till he comes out again. Got to nab him with that bag on him.

Velie: Inspector, if Little Nap gets outa this house without us or the boys spotting him, he ain't a fraud artist — he's a magician!

(*Music up . . . time interval theme . . . into*)

Inspector: Well, Velie? What do the men say?

Velie (*fading on a bit breathless*): They say nobody's left the house, Inspector. So he's still inside.

Inspector: Fifteen minutes to get an umbrella? Use your head, Velie! Little Nap spotted us — he's up to something. I'm not waiting any longer! (*Running steps up onto porch over Velie's ad lib*) Ring that bell!

Velie: I tell ya, Inspector — (*Faint ring off*) — it's okay. (*Door opens on*) Uh, uh. Who's *this* beanpole?

Long (*fading on*): Yes, sir?

Inspector: Where's Little Nap?

Long (*blankly*): Beg your pardon, sir?

Inspector: Napoleon Short! Where is he?

Long: Oh. Mr. Short is not here, sir.

Velie: Now, listen, Daddy Longlegs, Little Nap came outa here fifteen minutes ago, ducked right back in — and he ain't been out since.

Inspector: I'm Inspector Queen of Police Headquarters. Quit stalling! Where's Short?

Long: But you must be mistaken, sir. Mr. Short did leave fifteen minutes ago, but I didn't see him return —

Inspector: Well, we did. Velie, search the house. I'll wait here in the foyer with this man.

Velie (*fading*): Short's last stand, huh? Playin' hard to get —

Inspector: So you're covering up for him. Who are you?

Long: Mr. Short's man, sir, Jonathan Long, sir.

Inspector (*chuckling*): Quite a team, aren't you? A five-footer named *Short*, and you're six-foot four, Mr. *Long*, if you're an inch.

Long: Yes, sir. Mr. Short wouldn't engage anyone but a very tall person. (*Confidential*) The Napoleonic complex, I think, sir.

Inspector: That is why Mr. Short insists upon wearing a beard. Makes him feel more masterful. Well, he'll get a quick trim in Sing Sing. (*Calling*) Velie! Find our friend yet?

Velie (*off*): Not yet, Inspector! Nap must *like* to play peekaboo!

Inspector: Long, why's it so cold in this house? Run out of oil-ration coupons?

Long: Oh, no, sir. We burn coal.

Inspector: Then why don't you burn some? The temperature here would discourage an Eskimo.

Long: I was about to go down to the cellar, sir, when you arrived. We're expecting a coal delivery this morning — I was going to put the last few shovelsful in the furnace . . .

Inspector: Well, don't let me keep you. But come right back. Brr. (*Calling*) Velie, how long does it take to find one man in one house?

Velie (*off*): You tell me, Inspector! I'm still lookin'!

(*Music up . . . short . . . into . . .*)

Inspector: What's the matter, Velie? Where's Little Nap?

Velie (*fading on*): Inspector, I'm baffled.

Long: I told you, sir — Mr. Short isn't here.

Inspector: Then you didn't cover everything, Velie.

Velie: Izzat so? I looked my eyes out! Every room. He ain't here.

Inspector: Aaaa. Did you look in the basement? The attic? All the closets?

Velie: I tell ya I looked every place, Inspector.

Inspector: But —! Velie, you stay here in the house. I'll send a few of the boys in to help you make another search. Meanwhile, you — Long — don't leave this house. Is that clear?

Long (*politely*): Perfectly, sir.

Inspector: Velie, keep your eye on this long drink of water. He's too smooth to suit *me*. Another thing. I'm giving strict orders to the men on duty outside that no one leaves this house except you and me, Velie, unless he's got one of my cards as a pass — and signed by me, to boot!

Velie: But Inspector, I tell you little Nap ain't here.

Inspector (*snarling*): He *must* be here! Long, get out of my way. (*Opens door*) I'm going home and talk to Ellery! (*Slams door*)

(*Music up . . .*)

Ellery (*coughing*): You've got it all down, Nikki?

Nikki: Yes, Ellery. Full description of Mr. Short's house and all the rooms.

Ellery: Now dad. You and Velie saw Little Nap come out through the front door. You saw him pause, look up at the sky, and . . . you *unquestionably* saw him go back inside?

Inspector: How many times do I have to tell you? He went back in!

Ellery: Then that's a fact. You know, dad, there's something amusingly weird about this case.

Inspector: I'm not amused.

Ellery: No, I mean about Little Nap going back into his house as if to fetch an umbrella. Nikki, would you hand me that omnibus volume of Sherlock Holmes?

Nikki (*puzzled*): Sherlock Holmes? Just a moment. Here, Ellery. (*Turns pages*)

Ellery: Ah, dad, let's see . . . ah, here we are, let me read you a sentence from the Holmes tale called. "The Problem of Thor Bridge."

Inspector: Ellery, for Pete's sake —

Ellery: No, listen, this is Dr. Watson writing about one of Holmes' unrecorded cases. I quote: "Among these unfinished tales is that of Mr. James Phillimore, who, stepping back into his own house to get his umbrella, was never more seen in this world."

Nikki: Well, isn't that a peculiar coincidence?

Ellery: Sherlock Holmes failed to solve that case, it's been said. (*Chuckles*) Perhaps we'll have better luck.

Inspector: Who cares about Mr. James Phillimore? I want to find Mr. Little Nap and a flock of sucker money!

Ellery: Mmm. After Nap went back into the house, no one left it, you say?

Inspector: My men had every possible exit covered, son.

Ellery: Obviously, then, Little Nap is still in there.

Nikki: But Ellery, Sergeant Velie and the other detectives searched every nook and cranny!

Ellery: That's what makes this such an interesting problem, Nikki. Dad, let's start at the bottom of the house and work up. How about the cellar?

Inspector: Solid concrete. Floor, ceiling, walls all tapped.

Ellery: Any packing cases in the cellar? Old trunks?

Inspector: No. All we found down there are two coal bins. One empty, the other with a couple of shovelsful of coal in it. The basement's out, Ellery.

Ellery: The ground floor —

Nikki: Three rooms — living room, study, kitchen.

Ellery: Living room first. Dad, how about the fireplace?

Inspector: Thoroughly investigated. Also all the walls, floor, ceiling — not only in that room but in every room in the house, Ellery.

Ellery: Does the living room have a grand piano?

Inspector: By Jove, yes! I wonder if Velie looked in there.

Ellery: Note, Nikki: Search interior of piano. Now — the kitchen. Closets? Pantry?

Inspector: All covered.

Ellery: Refrigerator? Remember, Little Nap's very tiny — only five foot one and skinny as a spindle.

Inspector: I'd better check with Velie on that, son.

Nikki (*as if noting*): Check . . . refrigerator . . .

Ellery: The study. Is there a safe?

Inspector: Yes. Nap's man, Long, opened it for us. Nothing in the safe but unimportant papers.

Ellery: What about the foyer, dad?

Inspector: Suit of armor.

Nikki: I'll bet that's it!

Inspector: You'd lose, Nikki. We looked inside.

Nikki: Oh sure! I suppose all the closets were searched, too?

Inspector: Every one in the house, upstairs and down. *And* the bathrooms. And the attic and roof — and garage —

Ellery: That's the whole house, then. Nikki, go back to Short's house with dad. When dad's checked the piano and refrigerator, you phone me the results.

Nikki: I can see it coming, though — Napoleon Short isn't hiding in any of those places, Ellery!

Ellery: I'm inclined to agree, Nikki. (*Coughs*) Toughest case all winter, and I have to investigate it on my back!

(*Music up . . . into*)

Velie: What did Ellery say, Miss Porter?

Nikki: Quoted Sherlock Holmes, Sergeant.

Velie: The English dick? (*Doorbell rings*)

Inspector: Long. What's that bell?

Long: This back door, Inspector.

Inspector: Velie, unlock it and slide the bolt.

Velie: Uh-huh. (*Unlocks . . . slides bolt. Opens door*) Yeah?

Coal man (*fading on*): Coal company. Got two tons to deliver.

Nikki: It's about time. It was warm here for a while, but now it's getting cold.

Coal man: Well, if . . .
Velie: Now, now. Don't step inside, fella.
Inspector: Velie, go outside with this man. Let him run his coal chute into the cellar window to the bin, but he's not to set foot in any part of the house.
Velie: Yes, sir. Anybody with you, my anthracite friend?
Coal man: I got a helper.
Inspector: Stick with both of 'em every second, Velie. (*Closes door. Slides bolt*) Now, Nikki, let's you and me search those places Ellery mentioned!

(*Short music bridge to . . . rings back door bell. Slides bolt. Unlocks door. Opens it . . .*)

Inspector: Oh, Velie. Well? What about the coal?
Velie (*fading on*): It's in, Inspector.
Coal man (*fading on*): Hey, this big guy says I gotta have a pass to let me and my helper out. What goes here, anyway?
Inspector: Here's your pass. Velie, go out with 'em — and better examine that truck, just to make sure. (*Closes door. Slides bolt*) (*Calling*) Nikki! Where are you?
Nikki (*off*): In the study alcove off the foyer, Inspector!
Inspector (*over steps*): Who are you talking to on the 'phone, Nikki?
Nikki (*fading on*): Ellery, Inspector. He's furious.
Ellery (*filtered throughout*): Nothing in the piano, Nikki?
Nikki: Strings and sounding board, Ellery.
Ellery: Don't be cute! Refrigerator?
Nikki: Filled with goodies. Which reminds me. I'm starved.
Ellery (*groaning*): A man vanishes like the Cheshire Cat and she's hungry! What about the car in the garage?
Nikki: He's not in it, Ellery. Now what shall I tell the Inspector to do?
Ellery: Blessed if I know. Anything new happen?
Nikki: A coal truck just delivered two tons of coal.
Ellery: What! (*Excitedly*) Let me talk to dad.
Nikki: Inspector, your celebrated son wishes a word with you.
Inspector (*grunts*): Now Ellery, keep your shirt on. I kept the two coal men from entering the house and Velie was with 'em every minute. So Little Nap can't have sneaked out through the cellar window.
Ellery: I realize that, dad. But don't you see that he may be playing hide-and-go-seek with you?
Inspector: Come again?
Ellery: While you were searching one part of the house, Nap may have been hiding in another part. When you came to *his* part, he slipped

off to still another place! How do you know he wasn't in the coal bin when the coal started sliding down the chute? How do you know he isn't buried under the coal *at this moment?*

Inspector: I'm ready to believe anything.

Ellery: You'd better check, dad. And call me back.

Inspector: All right. (*Hangs up*)

Nikki: What's Ellery say, Inspector?

Inspector (*groaning*): As soon as Velie gets back into the house, Nikki — we start shoveling coal!

Nikki: And for goodness sake, Inspector, while you're at it, put some in that furnace.

(*Short bridge to . . .*)

Inspector: Well, Velie?

Nikki (*giggling*): Sergeant, you look like an end man in a minstrel show.

Velie (*fading on*): Shovel coal! Keep the furnace going. What else do you gotta do on this job? Look at me! My wife'll have a fit.

Inspector: Never mind your wife. Did you transfer all that coal to the other bin?

Velie: Yeah! (*Cunningly*) And guess what we found under that coal, Inspector.

Inspector (*biting eagerly*): What Velie?

Velie (*bellowing*): Coal dust! (*Phone rings; pick up*)

Nikki: I'll get it. Hello? (*Ellery, filtered burble*) Just a minute, Ellery! Inspector, it's Ellery and he's all agog!

Inspector: Thanks, Nikki. Hello, son.

Ellery (*filtered throughout*): Dad! Was Little Nap under the coal?

Inspector: He was not! Any more bright ideas, Mr. Queen?

Ellery: Mmm. Well, the coal was a long shot. But we had to eliminate it. Dad, I know where Little Nap is!

Inspector (*belligerently*): Where?

Ellery: In the only place left for him to hide in.

Inspector: I'm still listening.

Ellery: You said Nap's study is off the foyer. You listed all the study furniture. But dad, you left out one thing.

Inspector: You're lying there in bed halfway across town and you're telling me I left out something? What?

Ellery: A study usually has a desk. You didn't mention one?

Inspector: I didn't? Well, it's a fact there *is* a desk here . . . By thunder, Ellery, you're right! And it's one of those old-fashioned roll-top desks at that! Hold on. Velie! Ellery's solved it.

Nikki: He has, Inspector?

Velie: Where's he say Little Nap's hidin'? If he says the flour barrel, I quit!

Inspector: In that roll-top desk, Velie. Search it!

Velie (*fading a bit*): Say, we did miss that before. (*Grim*) Nap, come on outa there. (*Slides roll-top off*) Huh?

Nikki: It's empty.

Inspector: Solved it! Ellery! (*Ellery ad lib*) You were wrong, my son. The desk is empty . . .

Ellery: But it can't be — (*Doorbell rings off*)

Inspector: Hang on a minute. Velie, answer the front door bell.

Long (*fading on*): But I'll answer it, sir.

Inspector: Long, you'll stay where you are! (*Door opens off*) Velie, who is it?

Velie (*off*): Telegraph boy, Inspector, with a wire for Long.

Long (*eagerly*): I'll take that, thank you, sir —

Inspector: You will not. Don't move! Velie, grab that wire.

Ellery (*filtered*): Dad, who's that wire from?

Inspector: Wait, this phone has a long cord — I'll take it out into the foyer. (*Quick steps*) Hold on, son. Nikki, take the phone. Velie, give me that wire.

Velie: Here you are, Inspector. Long, stand still.

Long: But it's my wire, sir . . . (*Ripping of envelope*)

Nikki: The Inspector's opening the telegram, Ellery.

Ellery: For pity's sake, *what's it say*, Nikki? (*Coughs*) Hang this cough!

Inspector (*spluttering*): But — but it *can't* be! It's impossible!

Messenger: Can I please have a pass or somethin' to get outa here? The guy at the gate says I gotta have a pass. I got telegrams to deliver, you know.

Inspector: Here, Velie. Give him this pass.

Velie: Now scram, squirt. (*Messenger ad lib fading. Close door*) What's the wire say, Inspector?

Inspector: Nikki, hand me that phone. (*Nikki ad lib*) Ellery, listen to this! (*To himself*) I can't believe it —

Ellery (*shouting*): Dad, will you *please* —?

Inspector: It's from Napoleon Short! Yes! It's addressed to his man, Long, and it says: "Got out of house as planned. Bring clothes and papers to meeting place agreed on. Signed — Napoleon Short."

Long (*snarling*): Out of my way!

Inspector: Velie, grab Long. Don't let him get away.

Velie: Oh, no, you don't, flunkey — (*Struggle off*)

Nikki: Sergeant — look out —

Velie: Oh, yeah? (*More struggle off*)

Ellery: Dad, for heaven's sake, what's going on there?

Inspector: Long tried to beat it. Velie's wrestling with him — trying to get him down on the floor, but he can't. (*Sarcastic*) What's the matter, Velie — didn't you have your vitamins today?

Velie (*panting*): I can't get this guy off his feet. Okay, brother, I'll cut you down to size! (*Sock. Thud*)

Nikki: What a fall was there, my countrymen. (*Long groans*)

Inspector: Velie's got him, son. But how did Little Nap get out of the house? I'll swear nobody left here!

Ellery: Yes . . . (*Chuckles*) . . . Yes, of course!

Inspector: Yes-of-course *what*, Ellery?

Ellery (*laughs*): Of course I know where Napoleon Short is!

Inspector: Zatso? You thought you knew once before, Ellery, and you were wrong.

Ellery: No, dad. (*Chuckles*) I've solved Sherlock Holmes' problem of the man who went into his house for an umbrella and was never more seen in this world! This time I'm sure.

(*Music up . . . into jury spot*)

Challenge to the Listener

When this show was broadcast, the United States was at war — hence the reference to the sneakiness of "Japs" in the solution. Before the jury came on, the announcer (now Ernest Chappell) read an announcement asking women to train to be Army and Navy nurses.

(*Music up . . . into*)

Inspector: You've *solved* it, son? But what — where — how?

Ellery (*filtered throughout*): Never mind, now, dad. Did you ask the telegraph messenger the obvious question?

Inspector: What obvious question?

Ellery: Oh, lord. Dad, maybe it's still not too late. Where's the boy now?

Inspector: He just left. Wait a minute — I still see him through the foyer window. Piggott just passed him through the front gate.

Ellery: Good. Get that boy back, dad, and bring him to me here. I'll ask him that question myself!

(*Short music bridge to . . .*)

Velie: Okay, so we've got the messenger boy outside your bedroom, Maestro. Now what?

Ellery: Fine, Sergeant. Keep the boy there for a moment.

Inspector: What I want to know, son, is — where's Little Nap?

Nikki: Yes, Ellery — how did he get out of the house with a dozen detectives watching every possible exit?

Ellery: Elementary, Nikki. Dad, just answer my questions. Is Little Nap in that house now?

Inspector: No, son. I'll stake my shield on it.

Ellery: If he isn't *in* the house, then he must be *outside* the house. Right?

Nikki: Naturally.

Ellery: How many people left the house during the day, dad? — not including yourselves or the detectives.

Inspector: I told you a dozen times, Ellery: *No*body left that house.

Ellery: Oh, but that's not so, dad. *Three* people left it.

Velie: Three? Inspector, he's delirious.

Ellery: Come, come, didn't the coal men come to the house and then leave it? That makes two —

Inspector: But they never stepped into the house, Ellery!

Velie: And I was with 'em every second while they sent the coal down the chute from outside the house, Maestro. I even examined the truck before they left.

Inspector: So Little Nap wasn't in the truck, and he wasn't one of the coal men, Ellery . . .

Ellery: Oh, you're quite right about that. So that eliminates two of the three persons who left the house. Therefore, by Sherlock Holmes' favorite process of elimination, the *third* person must be Little Nap.

Nikki (*excited*): I've got it! Ellery, you're wrong! Little Nap never left the house at all, Inspector!

Inspector: But Nikki, we searched it from top to bottom. If he was in the house all the time, *where* was he?

Nikki: He was in front of your eyes, Inspector. Little Nap . . . was . . . *Long, the servant!*

Velie: He played two parts? Say . . .

Inspector: Nap is five foot one, Nikki. Long is six foot four!

Nikki (*airily*): He faked the extra height, Inspector. Used stilts, or something.

Ellery: Stilts? No, Nikki. Velie actually wrestled with Long and couldn't even get Long *off his feet?* If Long were on stilts, no matter how strong he was, *you* could have pushed him over, Nikki. No — call in that telegraph boy, Sergeant, and I'll ask him the obvious question dad forgot. (*Open door*)

Inspector (*exasperated*): *What* obvious question, for pete's sake?

Velie (*fading on*): Here's the boy, Maestro.

Messenger (*fearfully*): What — what do you want, Mister?

Ellery: I want to ask you a question, sonny. (*Chuckles*) Here it is: *You're Napoleon Short, aren't you?* (*Gasps of all*)

Inspector (*spluttering*): He's Little Nap, Ellery? This boy?

Ellery: What makes him a boy, dad? His small size. His clean-shaven cheeks. His messenger's uniform. His high-pitched voice. No, no, he's not a boy — he's a man. Napoleon Short, in fact. He must be. He's the only other person who left the house.

Messenger (*snarling*): Think you're clever, don't you?

Velie (*chuckling*): He *knows* it, Nap. Stand — still —!

Inspector (*softly*): I get it.

Nikki: But Ellery, how did he leave the house in the first place in order to come back as the messenger?

Ellery: He didn't leave at all, Nikki.

Inspector: Now I see it! He prepared his escape in advance. He had this telegraph messenger's uniform ready. And a telegram, which he'd sent to himself some time ago. All he had to do today was change the date and reseal the envelope.

Ellery: Yes, dad, and when he spotted you this morning waiting for him outside the house, he quickly went back in, shaved off his beard, put on the uniform, told Long to play stupid, and then hid in the only place you did *not* search —

Inspector: The roll-top desk!

Ellery: Precisely. Just before I phoned about the desk, he saw that the coast was clear — nobody was in the study or foyer. So he jumped out of the desk, ran to the front door, opened it, went out and stood in the portico —

Velie: They why didn't Piggott at the front gate see him, Ellery?

Ellery: He couldn't, Sergeant. Remember when you and dad first saw Little Nap re-enter the house this morning, dad said you'd "lost" him — couldn't see him in the portico until you got closer to the front door? So then Nap rang the bell, delivered his "telegram," and calmly asked for a pass to get him off the premises!

Velie: Makin' this little devil sneakier than a Jap. Come along quietly, Napoleon, or I'll break you in little pieces.

Nikki: That was a mighty clever plot, Ellery.

Ellery (*chuckling*): Yes, Nikki. Or to put it in the immortal style of the Old Master: I especially call to your attention, my dear Nikki, the brilliant wording of Little Napoleon's spurious telegram. It convinced Inspector Queen that this daring criminal had escaped, when all the time he was *in* the house waiting for a pass from the Inspector himself to get him out!

(*Music up*)

"The Adventure of the Murdered Moths," broadcast on May 9, 1945, features a young man just returned from the war and a hoped-for wedding — and Nikki Porter would like it to be two weddings. Ellery, however, is more interested in the clue of the dead moths.

The Adventure of the Murdered Moths

The Characters

Ellery Queen	The detective
Nikki Porter	His secretary
Inspector Queen	Of the New York Police
Sergeant Velie	Of the New York Police
Seth Brown	Restaurant owner
Jess Pendleton	Potential bridegroom
Virginia Wender	Potential bride
Mr. Wender	Her father
Morton Pingle	Wholesale Ladies' Wear

Setting: En route to New York City, 1943

(*Music up . . . into car on road. Dialogue in car.*)

Inspector (*sarcastic*): D'ye know where we are, Ellery?
Ellery: Well, dad, we're somewhere . . . between . . .
Inspector (*snarling*): Between nowhere and no place!
Nikki: The great sleuth can't find the road home.
Velie: And I'm starvin'. Ain't that a roadhouse? Slow down, Maestro!
   (*Car slows*)
Ellery (*reading*): "Seth Brown's Overnight Cabins."
Velie: "Home Cooking. Steak Dinner, one dollar and fifty cents — Southern Fried Chicken, one dollar." Stop the car! (*Car stops. Brake*)
Nikki: Do you think we ought to chance it? (*Car door*)
Inspector: I doubt it, Nikki.
Velie: What d'ye mean? (*Slam car doors. Walking*) Now do I want steak, or do I want chicken? Steak, I guess. Mama mia! (*Opens door with tinkly bell*) Yep, and I'll top it off with blueberry pie.
Inspector (*sourly*): It's a dump. (*Closes door with bell*)
Nikki: At least people *eat* here. That young couple over there.

281

Velie: Sure they do. (*Gallant*) Your chair, Miss P! (*Chair scrape and her laughing ad lib*) Sit, gentlemen! (*Chair. Bangs on table*) Service, Garson!

Inspector: Save your strength for that steak, Velie. (*Slap*) Look at these moths! (*Swinging door with loud squeak opens and swings back off*)

Nikki: Not so loud, Inspector. Here comes the Prop.

Brown (*fading on*): Evenin', folks. What'll it be?

Velie: I think I may safely say we'll all have a steak dinner, mine host.

Brown: Steak? No steak.

Velie: Oh. Had a rush on it, uh? Okay. We'll take the Southern Fried Chicken.

Brown: Chicken? No chicken. (*Pause*)

Inspector: Ask him about the blueberry pie, Velie.

Brown: No blueberry. Choice of tomato or veg'table soup, beans or spaghetti, rice puddin' or apple pie, milk or coffee. What's your pleasure?

Velie (*angry*): Then what's the idea o' that sign?

Brown: Told m'wife I oughta take it down. But she said it would draw business.

Ellery: It will also repel it, Mr. Brown. Nikki?

Nikki (*sighing*): Just coffee, Ellery.

Ellery: On two.

Inspector: On three. (*Softly*) And you, Velie?

Velie: Well, uh . . . (*Defiant*) Tomato soup — beans — rice puddin', and coff — and milk. (*Mutters*) I'd like to *meet* your wife, Mr. Brown.

Brown: Wife? No wife. She left me two weeks ago. Mad at me. Now she's spreadin' stories like to ruin my business. (*Fading*) Tomato soup — beans (*Swinging door off. Pause. Then Inspector, Ellery, Nikki burst into laughter*)

Velie (*hotly*): All right, laugh! You read the sign!

Jess (*fading on*): Excuse me — (*Laughs out*) We were sitting over there and —

Inspector: Yes? What is it, young man?

Jess: Uh . . . my name's Jess Pendleton. We uh . . . we have a sort of a problem, my girl and me, and . . . (*Calls*) Virginia, come on over. Come on.

Virginia (*shyly off*): But Jeff . . . (*Fade on*) do you think . . .?

Jess: Aw, sure, dear. These look like nice folks. I'd like you to meet . . .?

Inspector: I'm Inspector Queen — Nikki Porter, my son Ellery, Sergeant Velie.

Jess: This is my — this is Virginia Wender. (*Ad libs*)

Ellery (*kindly*): You say you have a problem?

Jess: Well uh . . . we want to get married tonight —

Nikki: I wish I had that problem.

Jess: But the Justice of Peace down the road says we've got to have witnesses.

Virginia (*anxiously*): We want to do it right, you know —

Nikki (*warmly*): Well, that's no problem!

Inspector: Wait, Nikki. You two kids look kind of young —

Virginia (*quickly*): Oh, I'm over eighteen, Inspector —

Jess: It's true I'm only twenty-two, Inspector — but I just got out of the Army. I was overseas eighteen months.

Virginia: Jess has the Purple Heart, and the —

Jess: Nix, Ginny! Anyway, I guess I've been through enough to know what I want.

Virginia (*breathlessly*): So would you be our witnesses? Please?

Nikki: Ginny, I'll be *two* witnesses.

Virginia: Thanks, Miss Porter!

Ellery: I'm in. But we've got to find some flowers —

Virginia: Oh, no, Mr. Queen. Don't bother —

Nikki: Nonsense, Ginny. What's a wedding without flowers? Besides, being the only other woman there, I'll be *sure* to catch the bridal bouquet. (*All laugh*)

Velie (*singing loudly*): Here cooooomes the bride . . . (*Swinging door off — always the double squeak*)

Brown (*off*): Ya call me?

Velie: Shake a leg, Brownie! We're goin' to a weddin'. Got some wine?

Brown: Wine? (*All: "No — wine."*) That's right. (*All laugh*) C'n give ya soda pop. (*Fading*) I got cream, sass, orange —

Nikki: Oh, make it orange, Mr. Brown! That's closest to orange blossoms!

Ellery: Yes — let's toast the bride.

Brown (*off*): Orange all round —

Virginia: Oh, Jess . . .!

Jess: Now, Ginny, if you cry — (*All laugh. Door with bell opens off fast*)

Wender (*off, roaring*): There you are, Virginia! Come in, Morton! (*Slams door off*) (*Laughs all cut off*)

Virginia (*faintly*): Daddy. (*Heavy steps fading on*)

Velie (*low over steps*): Uh-uh. The old man.

Nikki (*same*): Don't tell me that character with him is the disappointed suitor. (*Steps stop*)

Wender (*fading on*): Virginia, you've given Morton Pingle and me quite a chase. Morton, come here!

Pingle (*off*): Yes, Mr. Wender. (*Fading on*) Virginia — do you realize the position you put me in by running off with this — this fellow?

Nikki: I was right.

Ellery (*gently*): Just listen, Nikki.

Jess (*respectfully*): Now look, Mr. Wender —

Wender: Pendleton, you're an irresponsible rascal!

Jess: Don't talk to me that way, Mr. Wender —

Virginia: Jess. Please, Jess —

Pingle: I ought to — to bop you on the nose! Stealing my financée!

Jess (*thru his teeth*): Start bopping, Pingle —

Inspector (*mildly*): Just a minute, Jess. Mr. Wender, what's all the fuss about?

Wender (*coldly*): And who are *you*, sir?

Inspector: Inspector Richard Queen, New York Police.

Wender: Oh, is that so? Inspector, arrest this fellow!

Inspector: Young Jess? On what charge, Mr. Wender?

Wender: Of abducting my daughter Virginia!

Virginia (*hotly*): Inspector, Jess did no such thing! I went of my own free will! It was my idea!

Wender: Silence, Virginia! Inspector, there must be some charge. Isn't he violating the law in eloping with a seventeen year old girl in the State of New York?

Jess: Virginia's eighteen, Mr. Wender.

Wender: Are you telling me my own child's age? She won't be eighteen for six months! (*Pause*)

Jess (*choked*): Ginny. Is that true?

Virginia (*bursting into sobs*): Jess, I — I lied to you because I knew you wouldn't do it if —

Pingle: They've trumped that up!

Inspector: Wait a minute. Who are *you*?

Pingle: My name is Morton Pingle. I'm Mr. Wender's junior partner. Wender & Pingle, Wholesale Ladies' Wear. I'm engaged to marry Miss Wender.

Virginia: I never wanted to be! You made me, papa!

Wender: I know what's best for my own daughter.

Jess: Say, Mr. Wender, you're living in 1890, aren't you? (*All now talk hotly at once*)

Wender: You stay out of this, you fortune-hunter!

Jess: Oh, yeah? You're just an old creep!

Virginia (*crying*): Jess — papa —

Pingle: Virginia, you'd better be quiet —

Virginia: Don't you talk to me, Morton!

Inspector: Here, here! (*Argument out*) Mr. Wender, just what do you have against this boy Jess Pendleton?

Wender: Why, he hardly knows her. We hardly know him — his background, his connections — anything! He got back from overseas — he *says* — found out Virginia has a wealthy father, turned her silly little head — and away they go!

Jess (*quietly*): We love each other, Inspector. And I wouldn't take a nickel of his money if I were dying of hunger.

Virginia: Neither would I! (*Sobs*)

Wender (*storming*): I'll attend to you, young lady —!

Ellery. (*mildly*): Mr. Wender. (*Wender:* "*Huh?*") Boys and girls grow up pretty fast these days, you know. I think you're wrong about Jess. But Jess, if Virginia isn't eighteen, you're in an indefensible position.

Inspector: My son's right, Jess. You'd better wait until Virginia's eighteen.

Velie: It's only six months, kid — and the old squoonch can't *force* her to marry this *Pingle.*

Virginia: I don't want to wait six months! (*Crying*) I want to marry Jess now — tonight —

Wender: Well, you're not going to, Virginia. Tomorrow morning we'll leave right from here for a little vacation of five or six weeks. (*Virginia:* "*No!*") A change of scene away from this boy —

Pingle: And when you get back home, Virginia, I'm sure you'll feel differently about *me.*

Virginia: Oh, no, I won't, Morton!

Wender: That's enough, Virginia! Who runs this place?

Brown: I do.

Wender: We'll have to stay here overnight. What accommodations have you?

Brown: One de luxe cabin, where m'wife and me used to live before she run out on me and —

Wender: I'll take that one. How about my daughter and Mr. Pingle?

Brown: Single-room cabins. All got bathroom, stove, and fixin's. If you want somethin', you press the button next to your bed. Reg'lar hotel.

Wender: Put my daughter in the cabin next to mine. And I want the key to her cabin.

Virginia (*crying heartbrokenly*): I'll never forgive you, papa. Never! Never!

Jess: Darn it, I'm *not* going to stand for —

Inspector (*gently*): Let it ride for now, Jess.

Wender: Virginia, you're going to bed at once. I'll give you two of my sleeping pills to quiet you down. Show us to our cabins, Proprietor.

Brown: Huh? Brown's the name. (*Fading*) This way —

Pingle (*fading*): It's for your own good, Virginia —

Virginia (*fading*): You let me alone, Morton Pingle —! (*Door with bell opens off*)

Wender (*off*): What are your rates, Brown?

Brown (*off*): Dollar a night. Your cabin two dollars.

Wender (*off*): What! Two — (*Cut off by door slam. Pause*)

Jess: The old lard-head. I'd sure like to —

Inspector: Now listen, boy. Whatever you're thinkin' — stop.

Jess: I suppose. (*Fading*) Well . . .
Ellery: Where are you going, Jess?
Jess (*off, casual*): Nowhere. I'll stick around. (*Door with bell opens off*) Be
   seeing you —
Inspector: Jess —! (*Door closes off. Pause*)
Nikki: There goes our wedding. And Sergeant, you never did get your
   dinner.
Velie: I ain't hungry no more, Miss Porter. Inspector, what d'ye say?
   Let's be on our way.
Inspector (*uneasily*): Well, Velie, I . . . How do you feel about this, son? I
   don't like the looks of it.
Ellery (*slowly*): Neither do I, dad. I think we'd better stay overnight, too.

(*Music up . . .*)

Announcer: It is later that night. The Queen party are finishing an
   uninspired meal in Brown's roadhouse . . . (*Into clink of dishes, cutlery,
   no talk. Door with bell opens and closes off*)
Brown (*fading on*): Enjoy your vittles, folks?
Velie (*muttering*): D'ye serve stomach pumps with it?
Ellery: I'll take the check, Brown.
Brown: No rush, Mister. Settle up in the mornin'. I better clear these
   dishes away.
Nikki: Have you seen that boy around the cabins, Mr. Brown? Jess
   Pendleton?
Brown: Nope. Guess he's pulled freight. Lucky, that boy is. Marriage is
   trouble. If I hadn't married Mrs. Brown, she couldn't 'a' left me —
   now, could she? And if she couldn't 'a' left me, she couldn't be settin'
   up nights right now thinkin' o' ways to ruin my place o' business.
   Now could she?
Inspector: Huh? No, Brown. Well, it's still dark out there in those cabins —
   I guess everything's all right. And it's almost midnight. (*Yawns*) Our
   cabins ready, Brown?
Brown: Just fixed 'em for ya.
Velie: Guess I'll hit the hay, too, Inspector.
Inspector: Right, Velie. You kids turning in?
Nikki: I'm not a bit sleepy. (*Wistful*) Are you, Ellery?
Ellery: No. We'll stay up a while longer, dad.
Inspector: Night. Which cabin's mine, Brown?
Brown: Nine. The Sergeant in ten. (*Door with bell opens off and close*)
Brown (*over close*): You folks can come into my kitchen. Keep me company.
   I got to wash the dishes.
Ellery: Thanks, Brown. (*Swinging door opens*)

Nikki: But Ellery — it's so lovely *outside* . . .

Ellery (*chuckling*): Trust myself alone with you? (*Swinging door closes. Serious*) I don't know what's the matter with me tonight. I'm as jumpy as a cat.

Nikki: It's because you were so close to a wedding. They make you break out in a rash, don't they? (*Tray with dishes down with bang and rattle*)

Ellery: Maybe I'll surprise you some day, Nikki. (*Water tap on. Hold. Rattle of dishes under*)

Brown: Now don't be hasty, Mister. I was hitched to that woman fifteen years. Perfect marriage — I didn't pay no attention to her a-tall. Then one day two weeks ago she ups and throws that bread knife at me. Like to slice m'ear off. And she walks out. Then she wants support. Nothin' doin', I says! So now she's tryin' to ruin me. That's marriage for ya. Uh, uh. (*Shut off tap. Dishes out*) There's Number three cabin callin'. At midnight! Drat it.

Nikki: Where, Mr. Brown? How do you know?

Brown: That 'lectric signal box behind you, Miss.

Ellery: Oh, over our heads. Um-hm. Number three. That's old man Wender's cabin, isn't it?

Brown: Yep, the de luxe number. Salesman feller sold me that there gadget. Press a button in yer cabin and the number pops out up here. (*Fading*) 'Scuse me. (*Opens door without bell off*) Got to see what the old squint wants. (*Closes door off*)

Ellery: I hope there's no trouble . . .

Nikki (*indignant*): It's a darned shame. She's a dear little girl, and Jess is a nice boy.

Ellery: It won't hurt them to wait six months, Nikki.

Nikki: You *would* take her father's side! You talk about marriage like — like this Brown man! I'd like to hear *Mrs.* Brown's side of that story. I wonder what Mrs. Brown looks like.

Ellery (*absently*): Mrs. Brown? She has a hatchet-face, a chin like a tank, a brown wart on the end of her nose, and she wears gold-rimmed glasses.

Nikki: What???!! Piffle.

Ellery: You don't believe me.

Nikki: How could you *possibly* know —?

Ellery: I'll prove it to you as soon as Brown gets back — (*Door without bell opens off*) Oh, Mr. Brown!

Brown (*off, hotly*): Know what that feller Wender wanted? (*Door closes off. Fading on*) Says to me: "I can't sleep. So I turned my bedlight on and I wanted to take my sleepin' pills, but where's a *glass* for water, my good man?" I says to him: "Mister, this ain't the Ritz, but what's that look like at yer elbow? A can o' beans?" Water glass right on his night-table! Durn fool. (*Turn on tap, dishes again*)

Nikki: Go ahead, Ellery. Ask Mr. Brown.

Ellery: Mr. Brown, what's your wife look like?

Brown: M'wife? Skinny mean face — wears specs — got a chin would scare a layin' hen —

Nikki: What! (*Ellery chuckles*) But her *nose* . . .

Brown: Nose? Got a big wart on it. Why?

Nikki (*gasping*): Ellery Queen, you're a *magician*.

Ellery (*chuckling*): Not this time, Nikki — I was ribbing you. (*Serious*) I spied a female face at the kitchen window there a few minutes ago — before you went out, Brown. She was glaring at you so venomously I knew she was Mrs. Brown. (*Dish breaks*)

Brown (*scared*): She's *here*? She's after me! She'll do me in — said she would, when I wouldn't support her! You better stick with me — don't leave me!

Nikki: Oh, she won't try anything with people around, Mr. Brown.

Brown: You don't know my wife! (*Panic*) Where you goin'?

Ellery: Out for some air. How about it, Nikki?

Nikki: At last!

Brown: Here — wait. Wait for me!

(*Semi-humorous music up . . . into strolling outdoors*)

Nikki (*softly*): Beautiful night . . . isn't it, Ellery?

Brown (*nervous*): But it's clabberin' up to rain, Miss —

Nikki: You still here? (*Through her teeth*) Mr. Brown, we haven't seen a sign of your wife, and we've been walking around for an hour. Aren't you tired?

Brown (*nervous*): N-no, Miss. Not the least bit.

Ellery: Apparently old boy Wender isn't, either. There's his cabin light still on — been on since midnight. Isn't that Cabin three, Brown?

Brown: Yes, sir. Now as I was sayin' —

Nikki: *Don't*, Mr. Brown. (*Softly*) Ellery. Look up.

Ellery: Huh? Up where, Nikki?

Nikki (*soft*): Up in the sky. (*Steps stop*)

Brown: Don't see nothin' up there but the moon.

Nikki: Mr. Brown, if you don't —! (*Stops. Then softly*) Isn't that a *gorgeous* moon, Ellery?

Ellery: The gibbous phase. Between half and full.

Nikki (*desperately*): And *I'm* over eighteen, Ellery . . .

Brown (*puzzled*): What's that got to do with it?

Nikki (*very angry*): Mr. Brown, I'm going to ask you to — (*Sounds of fight and cries off*)

Ellery: Wait. (*Pause. Cries and fight up*) Something wrong. Near Wender's cabin! (*Run fast*)

Brown (*off a bit*): Wait — wait for me!

Nikki (*running*): Isn't that Jess Pendleton yelling . . .?

Jess (*off, fight near now*): I'll teach you, Pingle — (*Fading on with furious fight full*) — not to make any more trouble —!

Virginia (*screaming*): Jess! Don't! Be careful!

Pingle: Virginia, he'll . . . kill me . . . ! (*Smack. Groan, etc.*)

Ellery: Here! Jess, stop that. Stop it! (*Fight gradually out*)

Jess (*panting*): I *will* kill him, Mr. Queen. He's a rat and a sneak!

Pingle: I'll have you thrown into jail for this, Pendleton. I'll — (*Running fades on*)

Velie (*fading on*): Hey, what gives out here?

Inspector (*ditto*): You people are making enough noise to wake the dead! Virginia, what's the matter?

Virginia (*indignant*): Papa locked the door of my cabin, Inspector, but Jess managed to get in a few minutes ago, and we were talking things over, when we heard a noise outside, and Jess caught Morton Pingle snooping at the window —

Jess (*bitterly*): And Pingle said he'd snitch to Mr. Wender — as if we're a couple of nasty kids! — and he said a lot of other things — about Virginia —

Pingle: Inspector, he assaulted me! Virginia, your father's going to hear about this — right now!

Ellery (*quietly*): I should think, Pingle, he'd have heard about it already. Dad, doesn't it strike you as odd that Wender's slept through all this racket? It woke you and Velie up — and your cabins are much farther away. (*Pause*)

Inspector (*queerly*): Yes . . . and there's his light on.

Velie: His cabin was dark just before midnight, when the Inspector and me passed here on our way to bed.

Brown: He called me at midnight for a water glass, Sergeant. Took some sleepin' pills.

Nikki: Then that's what it is. He's fast asleep.

Ellery (*abruptly*): Let's have a look. (*A few steps*)

Velie: Shades are drawn — can't see in. (*Steps stop*) What's he got his windas all shut for?

Inspector (*calling*): Mr. Wender! (*Pause*) Mr. Wender?

Velie (*roaring*): Mr. *Wender!* (*Heavy knocks*) Hey, in there! (*Pause*)

Virginia (*with slight panic*): Papa! Wake up! (*Pause*)

Nikki: Virginia, don't look so worried. He took some sleeping pills — that's a drug —

Ellery (*sharp*): Wait. Breathe in — deeply. (*Various sniffs*)

Nikki: It's *gas!*

Inspector: Good lord. Hope that door's not locked. (*Tries door*) It's open! (*Opens cabin door. All choke*)

Ellery (*shouting*): Keep the women away! Room's full of it! (*Fading with coughs*) Dad — that gas stove —

Inspector (*fading ditto*): Right, son — (*Coughs off*) Velie, open all the windows!

Velie (*off . . . coughing*): Wow. (*Windows being opened as we hear all three coughing off*)

Virginia: But where is papa? (*Hysterical*) Is he in there?

Nikki: Virginia, stop that —

Jess: Ginny, no. You can't go in there!

Pingle: Virginia, don't be a fool!

Ellery (*fading on, choking*): Easy, dad. Easy with him . . . Lay him down here on the ground —

Virginia: Papa!

Inspector (*shouting*): Velie, snap that bedlight off in there! If there happened to be a short, we'd all be blown sky-high! And don't stay in there — we'll have to keep out till the gas clears!

Virginia (*scared*): Why doesn't he move? Papa, wake up!

Nikki: Behave yourself, Virginia.

Jess: I'll take care of her —

Inspector (*grave*): Too late, Ellery?

Velie (*fading on*): No use — huh, Maestro?

Ellery: He's dead. Past any possible help.

Pingle: G-goodness. Took some pills and fell asleep, and a gas leak in the stove overcame him. What an accident . . .!

Inspector (*dryly*): Mr. Wender was overcome by gas while under the influence of sleeping pills, Mr. Pingle — but not from a gas *leak*. Four gas cocks on that stove were wide open. That's no "accident," Mr. Pingle — that's *murder.*

(*Music up . . .*)

Inspector: How's the cabin now, Velie?

Velie (*fading on*): Pretty well aired out, Inspector.

Ellery: Then let's have a good look inside. You people stay out here! (*Footsteps*) Turn the bedlight on again, Sergeant.

Velie (*stumbling about*): Wait till I find it. Ah! (*Click off. Pause*)

Inspector (*grave*): Nikki, close the door. (*Cabin door closes*) Not much to see, son.

Ellery: His box of pills — open — glass of water — his clothing on the chair. Not much is right.

Velie: Accordin' to what happened, the dirty work was done after midnight. Where was everybody after midnight?

Inspector: You and I were in our cabins, asleep, Velie.

Ellery: Nikki, Brown, and I were strolling around —

Nikki: Trying to locate Mrs. Brown . . .

Velie: Pingle has no alihi, and neither have the two kids.

Nikki: Why, Sergeant, Virginia and Jess were together — in her cabin!

Inspector: By Virginia's own statement, Nikki, Jess didn't get there till a few minutes before we found the body. I'd say the boy's in a bad jam. Blast it!

Velie: He's got the motive.

Nikki: I don't believe it! Not Jess — No. He's too fine a boy.

Ellery: We're getting nowhere. (*Sharp*) Here. What's this?

Inspector: What's what, son?

Velie: Why are you starin' at the foot of the bed, Maestro?

Nikki: All *I* can see there are a couple of dead moths.

Ellery (*intent*): Yes, Nikki — two dead moths. Undoubtedly killed by the gas fumes.

Inspector (*dryly*): If you're looking for dead moths — here are two more in the middle of the room, Ellery.

Velie (*off*): And here's another moth corpse near this winda, Maestro. (*Guffaws*)

Ellery (*very serious*): Five dead moths. See any more, anywhere?

Inspector: Here are a few live ones that just flew in.

Velie: But no more dead ones, Maestro. You gonna make an arrest?

Ellery (*quietly*): Yes, Velie. (*All laugh*) But I'm serious. (*All stop laughing*)

Nikki: What's this, Ellery? Some more of your magical deductions? What do dead moths have to do with this?

Ellery: They tell me, Nikki, who murdered Mr. Wender.

(*Music up . . . into jury spot*)

Challenge to the Listener

Again the announcer — this time Don Hancock — took the time for a commercial: "Anacin is made like a doctor's prescription . . . There's nothing to fuss with, nothing to mix or fill." Meanwhile, the studio jury tried to figure out how dead moths identified a murderer.

(*Music up . . .*)

Velie: All right, get in there. (*Closes door with tinkly bell*) Sit down.

Inspector (*dryly*): Mr. Queen wants to make a speech. Go ahead, son.

Ellery: When we found Wender's dead body, the bedlight in his cabin was *on* — you, dad, told Velie to snap it off. Remember? And I myself remarked to Nikki during our stroll that Wender's light was still on and had *been* on *since midnight*. In other words, it looked as if around midnight, Wender, unable to fall asleep, had turned his bedlight on, taken his sleeping pills, sunk into a deep slumber — and then the murderer had sneaked in, turned on the gas, and left the sleeping man to be asphyxiated. It looked as if Wender had been murdered *after* midnight — during the period *when his bedlight was on*.

Inspector: Well, sure, son. What . . .?

Ellery: But the moths, dad! The five moths that were also asphyxiated! We found them in the wrong place!

Velie: Where would you expect to find them, Maestro — in Wender's wallet? (*Snorts*)

Ellery (*evenly*): Well, Velie, I would expect to find them *near the place where moths are normally found in a lighted room!*

Nikki (*startled*): Near the *light*. Moths always flutter around a light!

Ellery: Bedlights are always at the head of a bed — did we find any dead moths at the head of Wender's bed? No! We found two at the *foot* of the bed, two in the middle of the room, and one near a window! And that's all!

Inspector (*slowly*): It means that when those moths were overcome by the gas, the bedlight was *out*.

Ellery: Yes! Therefore the light was out when *Wender* was overcome, too! In other words, Wender died *not* in a lighted cabin, but in the *dark*! But when was Wender's cabin dark?

Inspector: I myself said just before midnight that all the cabins had been dark the whole evening.

Velie: And I said Wender's cabin was still dark when the Inspector and me passed it a couple minutes later on our way to bed.

Ellery: Conclusion: Wender was already dead by midnight — he died *before* his bedlight was turned on *at* midnight! Nikki, what did happen at midnight?

Nikki: Why, the electric call box in the kitchen showed a signal from Cabin three, so Mr. Brown went out to see what Mr. Wender wanted.

Ellery: And Brown returned to say *Wender had just asked him for a water glass*. Impossible! Wender couldn't have asked for *anything* after midnight — he was dead!

Inspector (*slowly*): Brown lied. You lied, Brown.

Brown: N-no. I didn't — I mean —

Ellery: Yes, Brown, you lied. Why? Why should you have told Miss Porter and me that Wender was alive — when he was already murdered? Well, what did your lie accomplish? It made it look as if Wender wasn't murdered till *after* you returned from Cabin three — it enabled you, by sticking close to us for an hour afterward — till the very discovery of the body — to establish an ironclad alibi! (*Steps running frantically*)

Inspector: Velie, stop him. (*Struggle off*)

Velie (*off*): No, you don't, Brown! (*Smack. Groan. Struggle*) (*Fading on*) Go ahead, Maestro. Mr. Brown is sorry he was so rude.

Ellery: The rest is simply reconstructed. Brown went to Wender's cabin some time before midnight — probably when he left ostensibly to fix our cabins up for the night. He found Wender already asleep, in a dark cabin, having taken his pills. So Brown searched Wender's clothes.

Nikki (*puzzled*): For what, Ellery?

Ellery: Obvious, Nikki. For money! Wender said he was wealthy, and he'd mentioned before all of us that he was going to take Virginia right off in the morning on a five or six week vacation — so Brown knew he must be carrying a lot of cash.

Inspector: And when Brown found the money, he decided to kill Wender — knowing Jess Pendleton would be the prime suspect, and figuring the missing money would be overlooked in the fuss about Jess!

Ellery: Yes. So Brown opened the gas cocks wide, shut the windows, and left Wender to die in his sleep of asphyxiation. But now Brown had to fix himself an alibi. So after you and Velie left for bed, dad, Brown invited Nikki and me into his kitchen — and suddenly called attention to the electric signal box, as if a call had just come in. He actually said: "There's Number three cabin calling." We didn't *see* the number three *flash* on the box — it was behind and over our heads. He'd undoubtedly fixed the "three" up there by hand some time before. Then Brown went back to Cabin three, dashed in and *turned Wender's bedlight on* — and came back to tell us Wender wanted a glass for his pills. And the illusion was complete. We could see Wender's light burning, Wender was apparently still alive, and when eventually we discovered the body, we could only think that he had been murdered *after* Brown's midnight visit to the cabin —

Nikki: Exonerating Brown, because he stuck to you and me like a leech after that to give him his alibi! You — worm!

Brown (*snarling*): A pack o' lies, that's what it is! Dead moths —!

Inspector: Phone the local police, Velie. (*Velie ad lib fade*) (*Kindly*) Well, Virginia? What are you going to do?

Virginia (*whisper*): We'll wait till I'm eighteen to marry, Inspector.

Jess: That's right, sir.

Ellery: Good! And I promise you kids we'll give you a bang-up wedding!
 Eh, Nikki?

Nikki: Could you make that *two* bang-up weddings, Mr. Queen?

Ellery: Uh . . . come on — we all need some sleep!

(*Music up*)

CRIPPEN & LANDRU, PUBLISHERS
P. O. Box 9315
Norfolk, VA 23505
E-mail: info@crippenlandru.com

Crippen & Landru publishes first editions of short-story collections by important detective and mystery writers.

☞This is the best edited, most attractively packaged line of mystery books introduced in this decade. The books are equally valuable to collectors and readers. [*Mystery Scene Magazine*]

☞The specialty publisher with the most star-studded list is Crippen & Landru, which has produced short story collections by some of the biggest names in contemporary crime fiction. [*Ellery Queen's Mystery Magazine*]

☞God Bless Crippen & Landru. [*The Strand Magazine*]

☞A monument in the making is appearing year by year from Crippen & Landru, a small press devoted exclusively to publishing the criminous short story. [*Alfred Hitchcock's Mystery Magazine*]

THE TRAGEDY OF ERRORS
by
Ellery Queen

"Ellery Queen *Is* the American Detective Story"

So wrote the great critic Anthony Boucher about the contributions of Ellery Queen to the mystery story. Queen appeared in novels and short stories, in the movies and on television, on the radio and even in comic books. His creators, Frederic Dannay and Manfred B. Lee dominated the mystery world through their work as novelists, critics, anthologists, and editors.

In honor of the seventieth anniversary of the first Ellery Queen novel, Crippen & Landru is proud to publish the first completely new Ellery Queen book in almost thirty years. "The Tragedy of Errors" is the lengthy and detailed plot outline for the final, but never published EQ novel, containing all the hallmarks of the greatest Queen novels—the dying message, the succession of false solutions before the astonishing truth is revealed, and scrupulous fairplay to the reader. And the theme is one that Queen had been developing for many years: the manipulation of events in a world going mad by people who aspire to the power of gods.

The Tragedy of Errors and Others also contains the six hitherto uncollected Ellery Queen short stories, and a section of essays, tributes, and reminiscences of Ellery Queen, written by family members, friends, and some of the finest current mystery writers.

Trade Softcover, $20.00

13 TO THE GALLOWS

by

John Dickson Carr and Val Gielgud

First Publication!

Never before published! Four plays written during the early 1940s, two by John Dickson Carr alone and two in collaboration with the BBC's Val Gielgud.

Inspector Silence Takes the Air is set during World War II at emergency studios in a provincial town. There, a murder takes place – and the weapon disappears.

In *Thirteen to the Gallows,* also set in a BBC studio, a woman falls to her death from a tower – it is murder, but no one is near her, and the only clue is a scattering of Arum Lilies.

Intruding Shadow is filled with mysteries within mysteries, as Carr expertly shifts the audience's expectations from one suspect to another.

She Slept Lightly features the ghostly appearances of a young woman during the Napoleonic Wars.

The book concludes with an alternate ending for one of the plays, cast lists, and contemporary reviews of the original productions. Edited by Carr expert, Tony Medawar.

Numbered, cloth edition, with Carr radio script in separate chapbook,
$43.00
Trade Softcover, $20.00

LOST CLASSICS

Crippen & Landru is proud to publish a series of *new* short-story collections by great authors of the past who specialized in traditional mysteries. Each book collects stories from crumbling pages of old pulp, digest, and slick magazines, and most of the stories have been "lost" since their first publication. The following books are in print:

Peter Godfrey, *The Newtonian Egg and Other Cases of Rolf le Roux*, introduction by Ronald Godfrey. 2002.

Craig Rice, *Murder, Mystery and Malone*, edited by Jeffrey A. Marks. 2002.

Charles B. Child, *The Sleuth of Baghdad: The Inspector Chafik Stories*. 2002.

Stuart Palmer, *Hildegarde Withers: Uncollected Riddles*, introduction by Mrs. Stuart Palmer. 2002.

Christianna Brand, *The Spotted Cat and Other Mysteries from Inspector Cockrill's Casebook*, edited by Tony Medawar. 2002.

William Campbell Gault, *Marksman and Other Stories*, edited by Bill Pronzini; afterword by Shelley Gault. 2003.

Gerald Kersh, *Karmesin: The World's Greatest Criminal — Or Most Outrageous Liar*, edited by Paul Duncan. 2003.

C. Daly King, *The Complete Curious Mr. Tarrant*, introduction by Edward D. Hoch. 2003.

Helen McCloy, *The Pleasant Assassin and Other Cases of Dr. Basil Willing*, introduction by B.A. Pike. 2003.

William L. DeAndrea, *Murder – All Kinds*, introduction by Jane Haddam. 2003.

Anthony Berkeley, *The Avenging Chance and Other Mysteries from Roger Sheringham's Casebook*, edited by Tony Medawar and Arthur Robinson. 2004.

Joseph Commings, *Banner Deadlines: The Impossible Files of Senator Brooks U. Banner*, edited by Robert Adey; memoir by Edward D. Hoch. 2004.

Erle Stanley Gardner, *The Danger Zone and Other Stories*, edited by Bill Pronzini. 2004.

T.S. Stribling, *Dr. Poggioli: Criminologist*, edited by Arthur Vidro. 2004.

Margaret Miller, *The Couple Next Door: Collected Short Mysteries*, edited by Tom Nolan. 2004.

Gladys Mitchell, *Sleuth's Alchemy: Cases of Mrs. Bradley and Others*, edited by Nicholas Fuller. 2005.

Philip S. Warne/Howard W. Macy, *Who Was Guilty? Two Dime Novels*, edited by Marlena E. Bremseth. 2005.

Dennis Lynds writing as Michael Collins, *Slot-Machine Kelly: The Collected Private Eye Cases of the One-Armed Bandit*, introduction by Robert J. Randisi. 2005.

Julian Symons, *The Detections of Francis Quarles*, edited by John Cooper; afterword by Kathleen Symons. 2006.

Rafael Sabatini, *The Evidence of the Sword and Other Mysteries*, edited by Jesse F. Knight. 2006.

Erle Stanley Gardner, *The Casebook of Sidney Zoom*, edited by Bill Pronzini. 2006.

Ellis Peters (Edith Pargeter), *The Trinity Cat and Other Mysteries*, edited by Martin Edwards and Sue Feder. 2006.

Lloyd Biggle, Jr., *The Grandfather Rastin Mysteries*, edited by Kenneth Lloyd Biggle and Donna Biggle Emerson. 2007.

Max Brand, *Masquerade: Ten Crime Stories*, edited by William F. Nolan. 2007.

Mignon G. Eberhart, *Dead Yesterday and Other Mysteries*, edited by Rick Cypert and Kirby McCauley. 2007.

Hugh Pentecost, *The Battles of Jericho*, introduction by S.T. Karnick.; afterword by Daniel Phillips. 2008.

Victor Canning, *The Minerva Club, The Department of Patters, and Others*. 2009.

SUBSCRIPTIONS

Crippen & Landru offers discounts to individuals and institutions who place Standing Order Subscriptions for its forthcoming publications, either all the Regular Series or all the Lost Classics or (preferably) both. Collectors can thereby guarantee receiving limited editions, and readers won't miss any favorite stories. Standing Order Subscribers receive a specially commissioned story in a deluxe edition as a gift at the end of the year. Please write or e-mail for more details.

WITHDRAWN
BY
WILLIAMSBURG REGIONAL LIBRARY

CPSIA information can be obtained at www.ICGtesting.com
Printed in the USA
BVOW00s1317211013

334112BV00001B/2/P

9 781932 009163